The Oligarchy and the Old Regime in Latin America, 1880–1970

The Oligarchy and the Old Regime in Latin America, 1880–1970

Dennis Gilbert

ROWMAN & LITTLEFIELD
Lanham • Boulder • New York • London

Published by Rowman & Littlefield
A wholly owned subsidiary of The Rowman & Littlefield Publishing Group, Inc.
4501 Forbes Boulevard, Suite 200, Lanham, Maryland 20706
www.rowman.com

Unit A, Whitacre Mews, 26–34 Stannary Street, London SE11 4AB, United Kingdom

British Library Cataloguing in Publication Information Available

Library of Congress Cataloging-in-Publication Data

Names: Gilbert, Dennis L., author.
Title: The oligarchy and the Old Regime in Latin America, 1880–1970 /
   Dennis Gilbert.
Description: Lanham : Rowman & Littlefield, 2017. | Includes
   bibliographical references and index.
Identifiers: LCCN 2016048953 (print) | LCCN 2017003921 (ebook) |
   ISBN 9781442270893 (cloth : alkaline paper) | ISBN 9781442270909
   (paper : alkaline paper) | ISBN 9781442270916 (electronic)
Subjects: LCSH: Latin America—History—1830– | Latin America—Politics
   and government—1830–1948. | Latin America—Politics and government—
   1948–1980. | Oligarchy—Latin America—History. | Aspíllaga family. | Prado
   family. | Miró Quesada family. | Oligarchy—Peru—History. | Peru—
   History—1829–1919. | Peru—History—1919–1968.
Classification: LCC F1413 .G55 2017 (print) | LCC F1413 (ebook) |
   DDC 980.03—dc23
LC record available at https://lccn.loc.gov/2016048953

∞™ The paper used in this publication meets the minimum requirements of American National Standard for Information Sciences—Permanence of Paper for Printed Library Materials, ANSI/NISO Z39.48–1992.

Printed in the United States of America

Contents

Boxes, Figures, Photos, and Tables

BOXES

FIGURES

PHOTOS

TABLES

Introduction

> In all societies . . . two classes of people appear: a class that rules and class that is ruled.
>
> —Gaetano Mosca (1895)

In the last decades of the nineteenth century and early years of the twentieth, a new class consolidated its wealth and political power in most Latin American countries. Busy ports, expanding rail networks, and cities striving to remake themselves in the image of fashionable Paris, with grand avenues and beaux arts opera houses—these were material evidence of the emergence of this class, which Latin Americans would call "the oligarchy." The unprecedented wealth of the oligarchs derived from flourishing export economies that supplied sugar, cotton, coffee, beef, copper, and other primary products to the industrializing countries of the North Atlantic.

This book analyzes the history of the Latin American oligarchy over nearly a century beginning in the 1870s and focusing on five countries: Mexico, Brazil, Argentina, Chile, and Peru. It explores the rise and ultimate demise of oligarchic power in these countries during the era I call the Old Regime. I divide the Old Regime into two periods, whose timing varies from country to country: the oligarchic republic and the contested republic. In the era of oligarchic republics, which straddled the turn of the century, the oligarchs ruled openly, directly, and more or less exclusively; presidents were commonly coffee barons or sugar planters; and the principal challenge to oligarchic rule was conflict among the oligarchs themselves. In the subsequent period of contested republics, the power of the oligarchs, though still formidable, was challenged by others and, to the degree possible, hidden from public view. At some point, determined by national circumstances, the oligarchy ceased to be a significant force in the affairs of each country, marking the end of the Old Regime.

I examine the oligarchy from two perspectives, on the assumption that much is to be gained by understanding both the forest and the trees, since each illuminates the other. Part I offers a comparative, macroscopic view of oligarchic power structures and their evolution in the face of growing resistance in each of the five countries. Part II presents a fine-grained portrait, focusing on one country, Peru, and on three powerful Peruvian families: the Aspíllagas, North Coast planters; the Prados, bankers and politicians; and the Miró Quesadas, publishers of the country's most influential daily newspaper. The rich material I gathered on these families offers a sense of the everyday exercise of oligarchic power. We see the oligarchs arranging the removal of an uncooperative local official, controlling labor through means subtle and brutal, extending car and home loans on easy terms to rising military officers, and contributing to a "bolsa" (purse) to finance the overthrow of an unfriendly government. We also see how divergent interests, idiosyncratic concerns, and personal ambitions sometimes divide the oligarchs, undermining their collective power. And we find that the oligarchs are both empowered and constrained by their shared participation in an intimate upper-class social world.

My central concerns here revolve around oligarchic power. What were the bases of oligarchic power? What were the challenges it faced? How did it evolve? Related concerns include the following. What were the social origins of the families of the oligarchy, and what were the sources of their fortunes? How were oligarchic clans led and organized? How were they connected to one another and to upper-class society? How did the oligarchs relate to other elites, especially the military and traditional provincial landowners? How did they respond to popular resistance to their rule? What developments, in each national case, produced the collapse of the oligarchic republic and, later, the eclipse of oligarchic power at the end of the Old Regime? Finally, why did oligarchic power endure longer in some countries than in others? And why, in particular, did the Old Regime survive for three quarters of a century in Peru—longer than in any of the other countries?

OLIGARCHY, ELITE COHESION, AND SOCIAL CHANGE

"[I]t is always an oligarchy that governs," asserted Vilfredo Pareto in his classic treatise on politics and society. Pareto's contemporary Gaetano Mosca similarly claimed that "in all societies—from [the most primitive] to the most advanced and powerful—two classes of people appear: a class that rules and class that is ruled." Mosca's explanation was disarmingly simple: "An organized minority" inevitably dominates "an unorganized majority." He argues that "a hundred men acting uniformly in concert, with a common understanding, will triumph over a thousand men who are not in accord and can therefore be dealt with one by one." Both Pareto and Mosca recognized that oligarchies rise and fall. Pareto is remembered for his observation, "History is a graveyard of aristocracies." He blamed the decline of ruling elites on the moral deterioration of their members. Mosca emphasized the effects of changes in the larger society. But both contended that a failing elite would inevitably be replaced by a new ruling minority.[1]

Two lines of criticism have been commonly leveled at Pareto, Mosca, and other ruling elite theorists.[2] We can think of them as aimed, respectively, at Mosca's organized minority and his *un*-organized majority. The first raises the question of elite cohesion. As political theorist Robert Dahl explained, it is not difficult to define a potential ruling elite which, by virtue of the offices or resources its members command, has a high "potential for control." But if the members are divided by, for example, conflicting interests, ideologies, or ambitions, they will have "low potential for unity" and, therefore, limited effective power (Dahl 1958).

The second might be described as the Marxist objection, though it does not depend on wholesale acceptance of Marxist theory. Marx described, most dramatically in *The Communist Manifesto*, the revolutionary transformation of European society set in motion by an entrepreneurial bourgeoisie. Among the results of this process, quite obvious in Pareto and Mosca's day was the emergence of a modern working class and the labor and political organizations defending its interests. The majority was not, in fact, "unorganized." It was increasingly organized and challenging the rulers of Europe. The outcome of this process was still uncertain. Perhaps it would take the form of broadly representative democracies or of systems of competing elites representing opposing class interests. If Marx was right, the working class would take power. Whatever happened, Pareto and Mosca were quite certain that a minority would rule, whether in the name of democracy or some class or classes made little difference.

In the late nineteenth and early twentieth centuries, when Pareto and Mosca were writing in Europe, oligarchic power in Latin American appeared invulnerable. But over a period of decades it would be challenged in ways that the critics of ruling elite theory could have anticipated: from within and from below—by weakened elite cohesion and by new political forces representing the working class and later the middle sectors of society. These developments, which account for the ultimate demise of oligarchic rule in Latin America, will be central to my account of the history of Old Regime.

WHY THESE COUNTRIES?

The countries chosen for this study, Mexico, Brazil, Argentina, Chile, and Peru, accounted for about three quarters of the Latin America's exports, land area, and population around 1910, when oligarchic power was at its zenith across the region. Although they had in common export-oriented economies and oligarchy-dominated polities, these five countries were, as will be shown in chapter 2, varied in demography and levels of economic and social development. None of them is wholly "representative" of the region, but together they are illustrative of the range of Latin American experiences.

These considerations aside, Mexico, Argentina, and Brazil were included in this study because they were and are Latin America's largest, most populous, and most influential countries. Chile was selected because the history of its national elite presents intriguing comparisons with the other four. And like the other countries, Chile is the subject of a substantial and relevant scholarly literature, without which a comparative study would have been impossible. I was originally drawn to Peru, the focus of part II, because it was famous as the country ruled by a rich and powerful few, sometimes referred to as "The Forty Families." In the broader Latin American context, Peruvian oligarchy could be considered what Max Weber called "an ideal type"—that is, an exemplar that brings together the defining characteristics of the species. In particular, the Peruvian oligarchy was (1) a small, predominantly planter-banker elite that (2) established a regime led by planters and (3) created a unifying upper-class world of intimate social ties and elite institutions centered in the national capital. The other national cases can be seen as variants on this basic model.

Wealthy elites are notoriously resistant to study. They like to control the narrative about themselves and are able to shield information about their lives and activities from scrutiny. In Lima, I gained access to upper-class informants with the help of mutual acquaintances. This tactic guaranteed a gracious reception, but it did not necessarily produce useful information. Fortunately, I landed in Peru in the mid-1970s, a propitious moment for researching the history of the oligarchy. In late 1968, a left-wing military government had come to power with an anti-oligarchic program and rhetoric to match. As happened in Russia at the fall of the Soviet Union, rich sources for the study of the Old Regime in Peru soon became available, including the archives of family-owned sugar plantations and comprehensive information on the wealth and incomes of the richest Peruvians. Moreover, the oligarchs, under attack, were anxious to defend the past and uncharacteristically willing to talk. I was able to interview members of the three families I studied and many other important figures of the Old Regime. Among them were men old enough to have been prominent in national affairs through much of the twentieth century—men in their seventies, eighties, and nineties. One of my respondents, Luís Miró Quesada, had been a member of the Peruvian Congress in 1902. At age ninety-four, he was still a lucid, imperious figure, very much in control of his oligarchic clan.

Nearly four decades after my conversation with Miró Quesada, I retrieved the boxes of archival and interview notes and other research materials collected in the 1970s (some of which had already attracted the critical interest of the rodents residing in the attic of a very old campus building). For this book, I have revisited this material, with the advantages of a rich body of subsequent scholarship, a comparative perspective, and, I hope, some scholarly maturity gained in the interim.

SOURCES AND CITATIONS

With rare exceptions, I promised anonymity to the people I interviewed, so that they might speak freely about powerful people and sensitive matters. Ironically, this guarantee was probably most important to members of oligarchic clans who answered questions about their own kin. In such cases, I name the family, but protect the identity of the individual. Given their national prominence it would have been impossible to disguise the families.

I have made extensive use of correspondence from the archive of the Aspíllagas' plantation, Cayaltí, then housed at the Centro de Documentación Agraria (CDA) in Lima. The letters are cited in the text by author and date. The authors usually members of the family, are identified by their initials, as follows:

AAB = Antero Aspíllaga Barrera
AG = Augusto Gildemeister
GAA= Gustavo Aspíllaga Anderson
IAA = Ismael Aspíllaga Anderson
JG = Juan Guildemeister
LAA = Luis Aspíllaga Anderson
NSS = N. Silva Salgado
PB = Pedro Beltrán
RAA = Ramon Aspíllaga Anderson
RAB = Ramon Aspíllaga Barrera
RN = Ricardo Neumann
RAF = Ramon Aspíllaga Ferrebú (from private archive)

For further information on documentary sources, see the Archival Sources section.
In order to reduce the weight of citations in the text, especially in part I, I have listed by country in the bibliography many helpful general sources I consulted but may not have cited.

GPS FOR READERS

This book covers nearly a century in the histories of five countries and several generations in the histories of three very prolific families. Readers new to the subject matter may feel that they are being asked to find their way through a dense jungle of events, dates, and personalities. I've tried to make the trek easier by eliminating unnecessary detail and providing summary guidance. At the conclusions of chapters 2 and 3, readers will find charts (tables 2.1 and 3.1) with essential information about the five countries in the eras of the oligarchic republics and the contested republics. At the beginning of part II, there is an abbreviated chronology of the Old Regime in Peru, with key events and personalities. And at the start of each of the family chapters, there are charts with short lists of major family figures organized by generation. These should relieve the confusion created by elite naming conventions. The Prados, for example, were led through four successive generations by men named

Mariano Ignacio Prado. They can be distinguished by the period of their prominence and by their full names, which, following Spanish custom, add the maternal surname after the paternal. Mariano Ignacio Prado Ugarteche (1870–1946), for example, was the son of General Mariano Ignacio Prado (1826–1901) and Magdalena Ugarteche.

ABOUT MONEY

Occasionally, the text refers to earnings or to amounts spent (or misspent) for various purposes. Were these figures given, as in the original source, in the local currency of the time, they would be meaningless to most readers. Unless otherwise noted, they have been converted into their equivalent at the time in U.S. dollars, a more stable currency, relevant to the international markets on which the oligarchy depended.

ACKNOWLEDGEMENTS

Making sense out of a century of oligarchy in five countries was harder than I naively anticipated. I have benefited from the candid assessments and thoughtful sugges-tions of friends and colleagues who read the manuscript at various stages of its development, including Peter Klaren, Tim Wickham-Crowley, Paula Alonso, Bill LeoGrande, Mike Gonzales, and Joel Horowitz. If this project had been a criminal matter, Peter would qualify, at very least, as an unindicted co-conspirator, since he urged me, for years, to return to the Peruvian material and generously abetted my efforts. I am especially grateful to my Hamilton College colleagues Dan Chambliss, Steve Ellingson, and Yvonne Zylan, who read the entire manuscript at a late stage and forced me to tighten my argument; they now know more about nineteenth- and twentieth-century Latin America than they ever hoped or wanted to. I am eternally grateful to our department secretary, the talented Robin Vanderwall, who helped me resolve a long series of practical and technical problems.

NOTES

1. Pareto 1935 [1916]: 1426, 1430 and Mosca 1939 [1896]: 50.
2. Bottomore (1966) provides an excellent account of elite theory and its critics.

I

THE OLIGARCHY AND
THE OLD REGIME

1

Origins and Organization

Prestige is the shadow of money and power.

—C. Wright Mills

SOCIAL ORIGINS

Juan Anchorena was among the beneficiaries of one of Argentina's great colonial fortunes. When he died in 1895, he left approximately 2.8 million acres of rural land, including 600,000 acres on the pampas, the fertile plain south and west of Buenos Aires, and half a million head of cattle. The Anchorena fortune originated in the commercial activities of a mid-eighteenth century Spanish immigrant. It was increasingly invested in land and, perhaps for that reason, had somehow survived the successive upheavals of postcolonial history (Hora 2001a: 601–602, 2001b, n.d.).

Anchorena's contemporary Agustín Edwards Ross could not claim deep colonial roots, but he was likely the wealthiest man in Chile when he died two years later. His estate included many valuable rural and urban properties, shares in the Banco Edwards, the newspaper *El Mercurio*, and a neo-classical mansion occupying an entire block in Santiago. He had served as senator and cabinet minister and had seen his children marry into prestigious upper-class families. Agustín's paternal grandfather was the twenty-seven-year-old surgeon on a British ship that called at the Chilean port of La Serena in 1807. He fell in love with the country and a young woman he met, married her, "changed his faith and nationality and stayed forever." By mid-century the doctor's son had accumulated a notable fortune in mining, finance, and speculation which his grandson would expand to colossal proportions (Bauer 1975: 193–194).

Among Peru's major sugar planters at this time were the Pardos and the Aspíllagas, families with contrasting histories. The Pardos were descended from a colonial official.

9

The enormous, neo-classical "Palacio Edwards" in Santiago, Chile, was built in 1888 and occupied by the Edwards family until 1913.

Source: Dir. Arquitectura, Min. Obras Publicas, Chile.

In the wake of the independence struggle, which ended in 1825, and the destructive civil wars that followed, the Pardos regained their financial footing with an advantageous marriage and participation in the lucrative, mid-nineteenth-century guano trade. In 1872, the family purchased Tumán, the north coast plantation which would sustain the Pardos over the next century.[1] Ramon Aspíllaga came to Peru as a child with his mother at the very end of the colonial era. He accumulated a modest fortune, which his sons, the Aspíllaga Barreras, expanded, as owners of the sugar plantation Cayaltí. The Aspíllaga brothers were educated in exclusive private schools and, by 1890, had been admitted to Lima's elite Club Nacional. Politically, they were among the most influential families of the Old Regime. (The Aspíllagas are the subject of chapter 6.)

The Anchorenas, Edwards, Pardos, and Aspíllagas illustrate the mixed social origins of the oligarchy. Historians of the era have remarked on the shallow roots of many oligarchic fortunes. Fairly commonly, oligarchs-to-be were immigrants of limited means or their sons and grandsons, like the Edwards and the Aspíllagas. By the end of the nineteenth century, many nouveaux riches families, of both immigrant and domestic origins, had won acceptance by elite society. "Blood and gold" marriages, joining parvenus and aristocrats, were a hallmark of this process. Of course, such unions provided a means of renewal for older families with diminished means. This process of consolidation provided a social basis for the elite cohesion that was politically crucial for the oligarchy.

Table 1.1 traces the social origins and economic bases of the families of the Peruvian oligarchy. The Peruvian families referred to in this book are, unless otherwise indicated, included in this list. As noted in the introduction, Peru was reputed to be ruled by a tiny elite, "the 40 families." I never found a list of the forty. My own list consists of the twenty-nine families in table 1.1. These Oligarchic 29, as I will call them, were selected by seven knowledgeable judges, among them two members of families listed, a lawyer with many upper-class clients, two prominent journalists (one closely associated with certain figures of the oligarchy and the other known for anti-oligarchy crusades), and one of the top leaders of the mass-based APRA party (American Popular Revolutionary Alliance).[2]

The judges were asked to list the families of the oligarchy based on their importance during the period 1930–1960. As the family profiles indicate, almost all the families selected had gained their position well before that period. They were typically of late-colonial or nineteenth-century origins. Many families of the colonial elite, battered by the upheavals that came with independence, did not survive the nineteenth century. More than half of the twenty-nine were descended from immigrants to Peru from other parts of Spanish America, Italy, or Germany. Both those with colonial roots (eight families) and those who came later rode the late nineteenth-century waves of export expansion to accumulate fortunes in coastal agriculture, mining, or related commercial and financial activities. Their progress can be gauged by the dates of first admission to the selective Club Nacional indicated in table 1.1. By 1900 over 60 percent and by 1920 all but four of these families were represented in the club, an achievement indicating both affluence and a degree of acceptance by elite society.

The origins of oligarchic fortunes in other Latin American countries suggest a broadly similar pattern. Early in its national history, Chile was dominated by a Basque-Castilian aristocracy of central valley landowners of late-colonial origin. But after 1850, this elite was increasingly penetrated by new families, like the Edwards, typically with fortunes originating in trade or mining. By the 1880s, the majority of the wealthiest Chileans were of postcolonial origin. Their success was soon reflected in club memberships, prestigious marriages, purchases of Central Valley estates, and access to oligarchic political circles (Bauer 1975: 17–18, 30–31; Pike 1963: 16).

For Argentina, Balmori et al. (1984) traced the social origins of most of the 198 founders of two key oligarchic institutions: the elite Jockey Club and the Rural Society, known as the representative of the major landowners of the pampas. All but a few were descended from late-colonial or early national immigrants to what is now Argentina. (Since the two founder lists were from 1882 and 1866, respectively, they would not include families that became important in the late nineteenth century.) Family fortunes were typically accumulated over three generations. The first-generation immigrants were small-scale retail merchants, whose sons began to accumulate land. The remarkable third generation, which rose to prominence in the booming half century after 1860, expanded family landholdings, invested in urban

Table 1.1. Origins of Peruvian Families: The Oligarchic 29

Family	Social Origins/Date Arrival	Origin of Fortune	Year of Entry into Club Nacional
Aspíllaga	Chilean immigrants, 1823	Late 19 C. sugar	1886
Ayulo	Merchant. Italian immigrant, 1785	19 C. commerce, guano; 20 C. banking	1883
Banchero	From middle-class provincial family of Italian origin	1950s and 1960s; fishmeal	—
Barreda	Colonial family, 1796	Late 19 C. guano, land	1869
Beltrán	Ecuadorian immigrant, mid-19 C.	Late 19 C. coastal agriculture	1872
Benavides	Colonial family	Early 20 C. military, politics, land, mining	1912
Bentín	Arrived with Simon Bolivar	Late 19 C. mining	1895
Berckemeyer	German immigrant, 1850. Family owned important commercial house in Hamburg	Late 19 C. commerce, later industry	1899
Brescia	Italian immigrant, c. 1890. Son married daughter of prestigious family	Early/mid-20 C. real estate and agriculture	1954
Carrillo de Albornoz	Titled colonial family, mid-17 C.	Coastal agriculture	1903
Chopitea	Basque immigrant, mid-19 C.	Late 19 C. sugar	1894
Fernandini	Provincial official, mid-19 C.	Late 19 C./early-20 C. mining	1912
Ferrand	French immigrant. Likely late 18 C.	Early 20 C. commerce, agriculture, industry	1925
Gildemeister	German immigrant from Bremen, mid-19 C.	Mid-19 C. commerce, mining, later sugar	1859
Graña	Galician immigrant, mid-19 C.; married into landed family	Late 19 C. cotton	1897
Lavalle	High colonial official	Early/mid-20 C. banking and other investments	1892
Larco	Italian immigrants; merchants, 1856	Late 19 C. sugar	1900
Málaga	Son of provincial official	Late 19 C. mining	1907
Miró Quesada	Panamanian immigrant, 1847; merchant	Late 19 C. newspaper publishers	1875

Table 1.1. (Continued)

Family	Social Origins/Date Arrival	Origin of Fortune	Year of Entry into Club Nacional
Mujíca	Colonial official, end 18 C.	Late 19 C. mining, coastal agriculture	1875
Olaechea	Colonial family. (Col. de Milicias), late 18 C.	Late 19 C. coastal agriculture, law	1895
Orbegoso	Colonial family; military officer, 1645	Major landowners since colonial times	1890
Pardo	Colonial official, 1794	Mid/late 19 C. guano, sugar	1881
Picasso	Italian immigrants, mid-19 C.	Late 19 C. commerce, coastal agriculture	1895
Piedra, de la	Ecuadorian immigrants, mid-19 C.	Early-20 C. provincial commerce and industry, later sugar	1918
Prado	Immigrant from France, 1770; provincial elite of Huanaco, late colonial period	Late 19 C. military, politics, banking	1890
Ramos	Chilean immigrant, late 1820s	Coastal landowners since 19 C.	1907
Rizo Patron	Immigrant from Argentina, 1826	Late 19 C. mining	1926
Wiese	German immigrant from Hamburg, 1869	Early-20 C. commerce and mining, later banking	1917

Sources: Much of the material for this table was gathered through interviews. Information on social origins/ arrival date for most families listed can be found in Lasarte Ferreyros (1938, 1993). Dates of entry into the Club Nacional are from the Club's *Memorias*, 1896–1960. The information on the social origins and fortunes of individual families in the table was drawn from interviews and the following published sources. **Aspíllaga**—see chapter 6; **Ayulo**—Quiroz 1988: 66; **Banchero**—Thorndike 1973; *El Correo,* December 11, 1972; **Beltrán**—*El Comercio* 1919; *Peruvian Times,* September 6, 1944; **Benavides**—Lasarte 1938; **Bentín**—Velez Picasso n.d.; Bollinger 1971: 172; Thorp and Bertram 1976: 73; **Berckemeyer**—Glade 1969: 607 n.65; *El Comercio,* June 22, 1974; Paz Soldan 1921: 56; **Brescia**—Basadre 1971: 633; **Chopitea**—Parker 1919: 435–437; Kenashiro and Rueda 1972: 27, 50–52; **Fernandini**—Basadre 1971: 633; Bertram 1974a: 105; Barreto and de la Fuente 1928: 126–128; **Ferrand**—Escuelas Americas 1943: 272; **Gildemeister**—Pacheco 1923: 104–108; *Boletin de la Sociedad Nacional Minera,* May 31, 1898; Basadre 1964: VII, 3202–3203; Klaren 1976; **Graña**—Paz Soldan 1921: 176; **Larco**—Klaren 1976; **Lavalle**—Mendiburu 1931: VI, 415–416; **Malaga**—Pacheco 1923: 125–128; **Miró Quesada**—see chapter 5; **Mujica**—Lasarte 1938; Paz Soldan 1921: 260–261; Rodriguez Pastor 1969; **Olaechea**—Lasarte 1938; Senado 1961: 45; *Revisita Historica* 1956–1957; **Orbegoso**—Moreno Mendiguren 1956: 379–380; Bravo Bresani in Bourricaud *et al.* 1972: 55; **Pardo**—Paz Soldan 1921: 287; Barreda y Laos 1954; Basadre 1971: 409–410; Martin 1948; **Picasso**—Paz Soldan 1921: 298; Sacchetti 1904: 198; *El Comercio* 1919: 952–953, 960; **Piedra**—Vda. De la Piedra, S.A., n.d.; **Prado**—see chapter 4; **Ramos**—Escobar y Bedoya 1887; **Rizo Patron**—Bertram 1974a: 82; Basadre 1971: 633; Bollinger 1971: 172; **Wiese**—Osma 1963: 75–76; Bertram 1974b: 281

enterprises such as banking, and, collectively, held most of the major national political offices.

For a later period, 1885 to 1925, Losada (2007) traced the family origins of Argentines who held key economic positions in Buenos Aires (including corporate executives and shareholders, bankers, major landowners, and directors of the powerful Rural Society and the Industrial Union). About 60 percent of the members of this economic elite were of postcolonial origins.

The available evidence on the social and economic origins of the Brazilian and Mexican oligarchies is less systematic but points in the same direction. Claims of deep colonial roots among planter elite of São Paulo, Brazil's wealthiest state, were "largely a myth," according to a study of the state under Brazil's oligarchic republic. Families of nineteenth-century origin were typical. For those with new fortunes, "marriage ties . . . provided a means for dressing up unadorned family trees" (Love 1980: 84).

In Mexico, Olegario Molina and Luís Terrazas, the leading figures of the Yucatán and Chihuahua oligarchies described in chapter 2, built colossal family fortunes in the late nineteenth century. Chihuahua and the Yucatan were economic backwaters, distant from the traditional centers of wealth and power, that came to life in the flourishing economy of that period, providing new opportunities for ambitious men like Molina and Terrazas. The Molinas were descended from eighteenth-century Spanish immigrants to Yucatan. The family had lost whatever wealth it had accumulated in the political upheavals of the mid-nineteenth century, but was able to provide Olegario (b. 1843) with an education that included degrees in law and engineering. In the 1880s, he became involved in the lucrative henequen trade (Wells 1982: 233–235). In Chihuahua, Luís Terrazas was about twenty years old when his father died in 1849, leaving Luís and five siblings a modest estate consisting of a grocery store, a soap factory, a slaughterhouse, a few head of cattle, and some urban properties. An adroit politician and gifted entrepreneur, Luís married well and built an empire on cattle, mining, and banking on both sides of the international boarder.

During the same period, the leading merchants of Monterrey, Mexico, expanded their fortunes by investing in manufacturing—initially dedicated to processing raw materials for export and later to serve domestic markets (Saragoza 1988: 36). In Mexico City, a group of well-educated technocrats were at the center of a metropolitan oligarchy. Known as the "cientificos," they were typically men of middle-class origins who had grown rich through their connections to dictator Porfirio Díaz, to the banking system they had designed for him, and to the foreign investors they served as intermediaries.[3]

In sum, whatever their social roots, most oligarchic families accumulated their fortunes during the late nineteenth century through enterprises associated in some way with the booming Atlantic economy. A remarkably high proportion of the oligarchs, at least in Spanish America, were descended from immigrants of the late-colonial period (e.g., the Pardos and Molinas) or nineteenth century (e.g., the Edwards). Under the Bourbon monarchs, the late eighteenth century was a period of economic and political renewal in the Spanish Empire, creating tempting opportunities for ambitious migrants. There is little evidence of significant family wealth maintained continuously from colonial times to the oligarchic era. But some clans with colonial roots appear to have recovered their positions by marshaling family prestige, social networks, superior education, and whatever material resources they had preserved to invest in the new economy.

The last decades of the nineteenth century and the first years of the twentieth presented a window of opportunity when great fortunes were assembled and new families were incorporated into oligarchic political circles and elite society. A growing world economy and the associated advances in transportation and communication opened the window, but the opportunities that materialized were finite. There was only so much land apt for export production on the Peruvian coast, São Paulo's rural frontier, or the Argentine pampas; and there were only so many promising mine properties to be discovered and developed in the Andes. The prices of these resources rose steeply, limiting prospects for newcomers. Bank credit was generally monopolized by established oligarchic clans. Over time, the growth of export production tended to outstrip demand, so that, by the 1920s, the "Golden Age of export-led growth" was waning (Thorp 1986: 67). For all these reasons, the window had closed.

By 1910, the consolidation of upper-class society, that had joined older families with newer wealth, was complete. Thereafter, the barriers of social exclusion surrounding the elite were higher. Some new fortunes appeared, a few new names were added to club rosters (note the dates of admission to the Club Nacional in table 1.1), and new blood and gold marriages were celebrated, but never so regularly as during the previous era.[4]

FAMILY ORGANIZATION: THE PRADOS AND MIRÓ QUESADAS IN PERU

The great oligarchic fortunes were dynastic fortunes—held together by kinship and passed from generation to generation. In the societies where they developed, formal institutions, such as governments, courts, and financial systems, were weak and undependable. The oligarchs, like the less fortunate in this uncertain world, were compelled to depend on their families. Oligarchic enterprises were family enterprises. Oligarchic careers were shaped by family needs. Oligarchic political strategies were family strategies, built around family interests. Those who dealt with the oligarchs in politics or business thought of them as representatives of their kin.

Contemporaries referred to the families of the oligarchy as "clans." Like the clans of simpler societies studied by anthropologists, they defined themselves as the descendants of a founding ancestor—typically a planter, miner, banker, or merchant who initiated the family fortune in the late nineteenth century. How oligarchic clans were organized, led, and sustained is suggested by the experience of the four families, examined in this section and the next. Here we look at two Peruvian families, who

are the subjects of separate chapters in part II: the Prados, masters of a financial
empire centered on Lima's Banco Popular, and the Miró Quesadas, publishers of *El
Comercio,* for decades the city's most influential daily (Gilbert 1981).

The members of these clans were bound to one another by a sense of common identity rooted in descent and by their participation in a shared estate. The
Miró Quesadas conceived of the clan as the surviving five "branches" of the family, descending from the children of publisher José Antonio (1845–1930) or "the
newspaper family." The Prados reckoned similarly with regard to the descendants
of General Mariano Ignacio Prado (1826–1901), a former president, and the Banco
Popular. (See family genealogies, figure 7.2 and figure 8.2.) These families made a
clear distinction between members of the clan and other relatives, even close kin they
might see regularly, who were not in the line of descent. Clan solidarity was periodically affirmed through participation in ritual events such as birthday celebrations of
important clan members, weddings, receptions, and funerals, gatherings which all
living descendants of José Antonio or the General were expected to attend.

For the Miró Quesadas, the Prados, and similar oligarchic families, the clan
encompassed both males and females lineally connected through any combination of
paternal or maternal links to the founder. This conception was rooted in the Iberian
legal traditions that regulate inheritance in Latin America, reflecting an understanding of real property as the possession of the kin group rather than the individual.
Testators had limited control over their estates. The strongest rights were reserved for
children, among whom property would be divided equally, without regard to birth
order or gender. Primogeniture (privileging the first-born son) in the inheritance of
property was, thus, forbidden.[5]

By treating all children equally, the law indicated the potential boundaries of
the clan, but simultaneously raised the danger that the estate would be dissipated
through division and sales by individual heirs. The concern with maintaining the
estate intact was especially urgent for families, including the Prados, the Miró Quesadas, and others whose wealth and power rested on a large enterprise—a bank, a
newspaper, a sugar plantation—that could not be split into discrete units. Their solution, a common one among such families in Latin America, was to structure their
shared estate as a joint stock corporation. Family control was maintained by strong
pressures against the sale of stock to outsiders. Despite the egalitarian character of the
law of inheritance, the sizes of individual stakes in the estate diverged over time—in
part because members of succeeding generations produced unequal numbers of
heirs. Some members of the second generation of these two families left no heirs and
their shares passed to other clan members.

Formal positions in clan enterprises were distributed on the basis of lineage (the
line of descent from the founding ancestor), generation, birth order, gender, and, to a
degree, individual talent or motivation. Both families, as chapters 7 and 8 will show in
greater detail, reserved some positions according to lineage. For example, among the
Miró Quesadas, the branch descending from each of the founders' children was allowed
to choose one family member from the third generation to serve at the newspaper.

The organization of oligarchic enterprises was notably patriarchal. Though females inherited equally, executive and board positions were monopolized by males. Female heirs could be represented by their husbands. The leaders of the Miró Quesadas, Prados, and similar clans were commonly referred to as "patriarchs." Mariano Ignacio Prado Heudebert and Luís Miró Quesada, who led their clans in the mid-twentieth century, were worthy of the title. They were commanding figures, feared, and admired within their families and beyond.

The patriarch was the chief administrator of a family's shared estate and, more broadly, its leader in matters economic and political. Primogeniture, proscribed in the transmission of property, was the preferred principle in the selection of patriarchs. Ideally, successive patriarchs were the eldest sons of eldest sons. As a Lima lawyer with many upper-class clients explained, "These families prefer primogeniture, but they will ignore it if they need to." In one powerful family, leadership passed to the second son because the eldest was, in the words of the lawyer, "too easy-going, more interested in hunting than business." In another case, the eldest son was bypassed because he was gay. But the leadership of a third family was conferred on the eldest son, a man of mediocre talents relative to some of his younger brothers, at the insistence of his very traditional father. The Prado patriarchs were all eldest sons, each named for the general, Mariano Ignacio Prado. The history of succession among the Miró Quesadas, as will be seen, was more complicated.

The members of an oligarchic clan viewed themselves and were seen by others as possessing a shared identity. Peruvians thought of the Miró Quesadas, Prados, and the Aspíllagas as collective actors. They regarded *El Comercio*, the Banco Popular, or Hacienda Cayaltí as synonymous with the families that owned them. More obscure families might be referenced as, for example, the Izagas of Hacienda Pucalá.

They learned from childhood that outsiders might not treat them as individuals, but as members of a clan with predictable interests and biases. Children discovered that, with their surnames, they had inherited friends and enemies and that they shared in the glory of their ancestor's achievements, but also the infamy of putative ancestral misdeeds. On the shelves of Peruvian libraries hagiographic accounts of founding ancestors promoted by their descendants confront a debunking literature produced by the clan's political enemies. "What a man most values," remarked patriarch Luís Miró Quesada, toward the end of his very long life, "is his family name."

A 1964 incident involving Luís' nephew Francisco Miró Quesada dramatically illustrated the importance of clan identity. At the time, Francisco was minister of education in the reformist government of Fernando Belaúnde. He was called before the Congress, then controlled by an opposition coalition led by the APRA Party, to face a hostile interpellation examining his ministry. The intention of the parliamentary majority was to censure Francisco, thus forcing his removal. Significantly, APRA and the Miró Quesadas shared a long history of mutual enmity, regularly reflected in the columns of the newspaper. After two hours of aggressive interrogation, Francisco refused to answer further questions, denounced APRA, and prepared to withdraw from the chamber. The session erupted into a welter of screams, applause, and protests that verged on physical violence. Some legislators were likely armed. Francisco feared he would be not allowed to leave. But he managed to escape because the presiding officer—a member of an allied opposition party, who happened to be a friend of the Miró Quesadas—ordered the doors opened. Outside, a mob of enthusiastic supporters greeted Francisco and carried him through the streets to the offices of *El Comercio*, where he was met and embraced by patriarch Luís.

In these events, it is impossible to disentangle Francisco's clan identity from his institutional role. The congressional majority had seized an opportunity to humiliate the government. But Francisco was not just one of a dozen cabinet officers. He was a Miró Quesada and this, rather more than education policy, accounted for his treatment that day by the Apristas, by the sympathetic presiding officer, and by the crowd of supporters who chose to carry him to *El Comercio* instead of the Government Palace, where he might have been embraced by President Belaúde. *El Comercio*, though supportive, was not a government organ, and Francisco, a university professor and distinguished philosopher, was a notably independent person. But, as many members of oligarchic families have discovered, such distinctions between the individual and the clan may not matter.

FAMILY ORGANIZATION: A CATTLE BARON'S DESCENDANTS IN ARGENTINA

For families of the Argentine upper class, as for their Peruvian counterparts, descent was central to family identity and organization. One's lineal ancestors were a vivid presence for a child living in an upper-class Buenos Aires household at the turn of the century. Their portraits hung on the walls; furniture and material objects inherited from them were proudly displayed. Family elders urged children to be worthy of their progenitors (Losada 2008: 102–104).

In the 1950s, anthropologist Arnold Strickon (1965: 334–337) studied a wealthy, politically prominent Argentine family descended from an unnamed, oligarchic-era cattle baron. On the pampas near the family's ancestral estate, where Stricken did field work, there was no doubt whom people meant when they referred to *la familia*. They were "the people who reside in the *palacio*, in which many of them spent their early years. These same people owned, individually and collectively, the ancestral ranch and the 'related ranches' around it." All were descended from the cattle baron "through ancestors of either sex," and descent was central to the family's collective identity.

Although some of the ranches were individually held, they were administered together by a professional manager and, in practice, their legal owners were "not free to dispose of them at will" due to family pressures. At a higher level, a family office in the city (presumably Buenos Aires) directed all the clan's rural estates, whatever their formal ownership, under the guidance of "one or two senior members of the Family."

In Argentina as in Peru, inheritances were divided equally among siblings. Argentine families, Strickon found, adopted varied strategies to prevent fragmentation of their rural and urban properties. One was the joint administration of separate holdings, as described earlier. Another was deferral of probate, sometimes for generations, allowing the heirs to draw income without settling the estate. Yet another was legal incorporation, with heirs receiving stock and family leaders holding corporate offices, an approach especially appropriate for large, integrated urban enterprises, like a bank or newspaper.

FAMILY ORGANIZATION: THE GÓMEZ CLAN OF MEXICO

Leopoldo Gómez climbed from modest origins to become part of the economic and social elite and the founder of an important family fortune in Porfirian Mexico. By 1910, he controlled a diversified empire of textile factories, lumber mills, tobacco mills, banks, insurance companies, and real estate properties, along with a portfolio of shares in many mining, industrial, and commercial ventures. The family suffered significant losses in the Mexican Revolution, and Leopoldo felt compelled to leave the country for two years. But at the time of his death in 1925, the family was recovering its economic position. Led by Leopoldo's successor and second son Pablo, the Gómez continued to expand their interests, so that by 1978, the combined worth of Leopoldo's descendants was conservatively estimated at $100 million (Lomnitz and Perez-Lizaur 1987: 54). Pablo was able to build useful relationships with the leaders of Mexico's new regime and was recognized as a key national representative of the private sector. His funeral in the late 1950s was attended by the president, much of his cabinet, and many other powerful political and business figures.

The Gómez clan is the subject of a book-length study by anthropologists Lomnitz and Perez-Lizaur (1987). According to their account, the Gómez business empire was a family undertaking from the beginning. Leopoldo preferred to work with his brothers, cousins, sons, and other members of his extended kin group. In particular, he leaned on his brother Saul as his legal adviser. Leopoldo is described as an aloof, "patriarchal figure," who distributed jobs to family members, entered into varied business relationships with relatives, and looked after the welfare of his kin, especially older women with limited resources. Pablo would occupy a similar position after his father's death. For decades, the social and emotional heart of the family was Leopoldo's mother, known as "Mamá Inés," the first in a long line of "centralizing women," who reinforced the cohesion of the Gómez clan by bringing their kin together regularly and maintaining the family information network. Myths, transmitted from generation to generation, celebrated family solidarity with stories of filial piety and patriarchs who had generously helped poor nephews.

At Leopoldo's death, his estate was divided among his seven children. Because the estate was not concentrated in a single enterprise like the Aspíllaga plantation, the Prado bank, or the Miro Quesadas' newspaper, the various enterprises and properties could be parceled out among his heirs. The larger firms went to Leopoldo's sons and most of the real estate to his daughters. Enterprises inherited by the daughters were to be managed by their husbands. This pattern was maintained by subsequent generations. The Gómez never wanted to create a family holding company or concentrate their wealth in a few large firms. Though Mexican law required equal division of estates among sons and daughters, Gómez daughters could expect to receive their shares in real estate, jewelry, antiques, and, perhaps, stock in companies managed by their brothers.

By the 1930s, the Gómez clan was differentiating into economically and socially distinct branches. Most of the family fortune and power remained with Leopoldo's line, the Gómez Casés, who were comparable to the descent-based oligarchic clans discussed earlier. Members of the other, smaller lineages, descended from Leopoldo's siblings, were described as middle class, in contrast to the wealthy Gómez Casés. For their part, the Gómez Casés maintained friendly relations with the other branches, especially the Gómez Balbuenas, descendants of Leopoldo's brother and legal adviser Saul (who were also descendants of another brother as a result of a marriage between cousins). Saul and his sons would spend their careers working for the Gómez Casés.

As the family grew larger, the branches further differentiated into what Lomnitz and Perez-Lizaur call "grandfamilies," consisting of grandparents, children, and grandchildren. These kinship units were the centers of family and economic life for the Gómez—more important to their members than the nuclear family or the larger clan. They endured as long as the grandparents were alive. The members of the grandfamily were in more or less daily contact, through visits and phone calls. Attendance at a weekly dinner, often an all-day Sunday affair, was mandatory for all. Ritual occasions, such as baptisms, birthdays, weddings, and funerals, filled family calendars. (These interactions were in addition to regular, but less frequent contacts with other Gómez kin.)

The individual nuclear households of the grandfamily typically clustered in a single apartment house or neighborhood. Brothers worked together. Cousins grew up together. On vacation in Mexico and abroad, members of the grandfamily often traveled together in large groups, led by the grandfather-patriarch. In the hope of carving out a small private space, one Gómez nuclear family purchased a vacation home in Texas. They soon received visits from grandfamily kin, some of whom bought homes nearby for themselves. The grandfamily was, in short, greedy in its demands on members. There was no easy escape.

Business relationships of all sorts connected members of different grandfamilies and lineages. But significant Gómez enterprises were likely to be controlled by a single grandfamily. These firms were led and majority-owned by the grandfather-patriarch. Their formal administrative structure of directors and executives was largely irrelevant, since all power rested with him. The patriarch filled positions with kin, preferentially his sons. If they were too young to serve, relatives, often from the Gómez Balbuena branch, were employed. When the sons came of age, these stand-ins were displaced, but they commonly retained a patron–client relationship with the patriarch. With his help, they might establish a separate business, often as subcontractors, jobbers, or service providers to the main enterprise. The sons rose through the ranks of the firm with age but had little independent authority as long as their father was alive.

For the Gómez, as described by Lomnitz and Perez-Lizaur, business and family were tightly bound. Each existed to serve the other. Sons' careers were seemingly determined at birth. Wives' social activities revolved around cultivating relationships and gathering information useful to the family business. The enterprise was, of course, the source of the family's wealth, power, and prestige. But business decisions were regularly subordinated to family needs. The family leader's personal prestige rested on his ability to freely dispose of the firm's capital and fill positions with relatives and clients (not all of whom were expected to come to work) without regard to training or expertise. The authors suggest that this pattern was common among Mexican firms, at least until the 1960s.

THE OLIGARCHIC CLAN

Underlying these varied accounts of four oligarchic clans from three countries are some common characteristics and concerns. All four families were marked by a collective identity based on descent from a late nineteenth-century ancestor and sustained by a shared estate. The boundaries of the clan were defined by descent through any combination of male and female links from the apical ancestor. Descent was the key to the distribution of shares in the estate and to the staffing of family enterprises. It was underscored by the ritual celebrations that regularly brought the founder's descendants together. Of course, Latin American testamentary laws privileged descent over all other principles.

The organization of the clan was patriarchal. Authority was concentrated in figures like Luís Miró Quesadas, Mariano Prado Heudebert, Leopoldo Gómez, and the Gómez grandfather-patriarchs. Formal rules and organizational structures were of little consequence for clan enterprises. The patriarch was not bound by them. His sons had only so much authority as he cared to grant them. The patriarch was a patron with many clients, often collateral relatives. He was free to use the clan's resources as he saw fit to maintain the loyalty of clan members and friendship of useful outsiders. And the oligarchic clan was patriarchal in another sense: the circumscribed role of women. They did not hold operational roles in the clan's enterprises. Even on corporate boards (which were generally powerless), their interests were represented by their husbands or their brothers. Though women were presumed to inherit equally with their brothers, they might, as the Gómez example suggests, receive their shares in assets that were not central to the clan's fortune, such as jewelry or residential real estate.

Over time, the clan tends toward dissolution. With each generation, the family grows larger, personal relationships become more distant, and demands on the shared estate multiply. By the 1970s, Leopoldo Gómez's descendants comprised 142 individuals in fifty-two separate nuclear families (Lomnitz and Perez-Lizaur 1987:

54). Inevitably the descendants separate themselves into distinctive lineages and "grandfamilies." In the course of successive inheritances, shares in the estate become smaller and, because of differences in the number of children in each nuclear family, more unequal. Individual clan members or segments of the clan may hold separate investments. The clan becomes stratified into the wealthy and the not so wealthy. At some point the clan may lapse into economic and social irrelevance for its members. Hora (2003) has described this process for one of Argentina's wealthiest landed families, the Senillosas.

But there are countervailing factors. One is the unifying presence of strong patriarchs and "centralizing women" like Mamá Inés, who maintain the clan's social bonds. Another is family wealth and prestige that is concentrated in a major enterprise that cannot easily be divided. Oligarchic clans devised varied means of countering the fragmentation of their estates. These ranged from the creation of joint stock corporations (the Miró Quesadas' *El Comercio*) to the shared administration of legally separate properties (the cattle baron's descendants in Argentina). The Argentine and Mexican cases suggest that subgroupings within the clan may hold independent enterprises but also invest in joint ventures of various types. Writing of Peru in the 1960s, Bourricaud (1970: 42) noted considerable variation in clan cohesion. Some remained tightly united, while others split into branches that were more or less independent but coordinated their activities.

These processes of dissolution should be seen in historical context. Since the typical family fortune originated in the last quarter of the nineteenth century, founders and second-generation leaders would have been in charge of these clans through the period of the oligarchic republics. An oligarchic clan, such as the Prados, the Miró Quesdas, and the Gómez in this period, would have consisted of a grandfamily of the type described earlier or a small circle of grandfamilies linked by siblings, one of whom was recognized as the family patriarch. But by the 1950s, as third and fourth generations reached adulthood, an array of centrifugal forces was straining the unity of most oligarchic clans.

MARRIAGE, KINSHIP, AND ELITE SOCIETY

The social world of the oligarchy was held together by bonds of kinship and affinity (marriage) that reached beyond the clan. Inevitably, the oligarchs had keen knowledge of the web of kinship that connected them to others, even to quite distant relatives. A recurrent theme in the early history of the Latin American oligarchy is the transformation of upper-class society by the joining of new and old wealth through marriage. By the beginning of the twentieth century, a dense kinship network joined the families of the oligarchy in each country.

The families of Peru's Oligarchic 29 were linked to one another by numerous affinal ties, as the analysis of oligarchic marriages in chapter 9 will show. However, the oligarchy's social world was not defined by the twenty-nine families but, more broadly, by upper-class society. Nearly all the oligarchic clans were connected by marriage to what I will call the Inner Social Circle, a group of eighty-eight prestigious families at the very center of Lima society.

Similar patterns developed elsewhere under the Old Regime. In turn-of-the-century Buenos Aires, over 60 percent of upper-class marriages joined two members of the social-economic elite (Losada 2008: 30, 44). Among the members of Chile's elite-dominated parliament, 35 percent were closely related to one or more of their colleagues in 1888 (Marcella 1973: 188). The ruling families of Brazil—an enormous, regionally fragmented country—were socially integrated at the state, rather than the national level, a pattern with obvious implications for elite cohesion (Love 1980: 287).

The relatively high level of elite endogamy in Latin America under the Old Regime was not, as might be imagined, the result of arranged marriages, which had been common in the early to mid-nineteenth century. During that earlier period, many families had relied on "strategic marriages," to consolidate their economic position. Cousin marriages and uncle-niece marriages reduced fragmentation of family estates. Marriages between brothers from one family and sisters from another created family alliances, in some cases combining contiguous rural properties. Families sought marriages which promised access to capital or the services of a talented son-in-law.[6]

The atmosphere of patriarchal authority that surrounded such arrangements can be gauged by an 1838 letter from Antonio Prado, a key member of a rising São Paulo family, to his brother-in-law. Antonio explained that he had just forced a marriage between his daughter and his younger half-brother. "I made Veridiana marry Martino and they are very happy and this ought to extend all our people." In fact, the marriages of the Brazilian Prados in this period were generally managed by elders and were often between close relatives (Levi 1987: 35, 37). Four decades later, the world had changed. When, by chance, Joaquim Nabuco encountered the woman he desired at the door to a Petropolis church, he did not hesitate to propose on the spot. Evelina Torres Soares Ribeiro, a wealthy heiress, was strongly attracted to the brilliant young politician, who explained to his future wife that he was not in good health and might not last more than five years. Undaunted, she replied, "That's enough" (Needell 1987: 123). Every element of this encounter—an unmarried upper-class woman alone in public, the intimate character of their exchange, and their independently made commitment—would have been unimaginable a generation earlier.

But if imposed marriage was rare by the oligarchic era, young people could not easily escape the influences of family and class. Joaquim and Evelina were more daring than most, but their engagement could not have surprised either family or the upper-class milieu through which they had become acquainted. Their match had been encouraged by Evelina's godmother, and it was not entirely coincidental that site of their encounter was Petropolis, the Rio elite's summer resort. They and their peers across Latin America inhabited a small world of favored resorts, upper-class neighborhoods, private schools, and exclusive social networks, where they were encouraged to find their mates.

If parents could no longer select spouses for their sons and daughters, they were not irrelevant. Asked about arranged marriage, upper-class Peruvians interviewed in the 1970s laughed at what seemed like an absurdly archaic notion. But several observed that mothers strongly influenced the social lives of their children. Of course, young adults in such families were likely to be economically dependent on their parents and thus vulnerable to parental veto in matters of marriage. A young man from one of the most conspicuous oligarchic families explained,

> My father and mother tried to keep me within a group of families—Olaechea, Rizo Patron, Isola, Miró Quesada. . . . If one goes out with a person not approved by the family, there will be pressure. The person will not be allowed in the house. Not invited to parties. In most families it is the mother who makes out the invitation list. Children of families within the circle are thrown together in the same colegios, parties, visits to each others' homes. You grow up within a circle. I can see it with my nephews, two and three years old. They already go to parties with [the children of] my sister's friends.

SCHOOLS

Aside from kinship and marriage, the most significant connections among the oligarchs and other members of upper-class society were the social ties developed out of shared youthful experience in the schools that served the sons and daughters of the elite. In early twentieth-century Lima, two preparatory schools, La Recoleta for boys and San Pedro for girls, were favored by upper-class families. (Toward the end of the century, Markham and Villa Maria, along with a few others, had attained similar status.) An upper-class Limeña from a prominent family who attended San Pedro during the oligarchic republic remembered the school as "very intimate. My parents were friends of the parents of the other girls." There were students from families of lesser status, and they were "treated equally" but excluded from parties conducted for girls of proper society. Nor were girls from the elite circle permitted by their parents to accept invitations from these students.

In Buenos Aires during the oligarchic era, upper-class children were likely to receive their earliest instruction at home, under the guidance of a European tutor hired for the purpose. There were no local private schools with the exclusive status of La Recoleta or San Pedro in Lima. The boys who, it was expected, would constitute the future ruling class were educated together at a state school, the Nacional Buenos Aires.[7] (In Santiago, Chile, the Instituto Nacional performed a similar function.) They would then enter the University of Buenos Aires, usually enrolling in the elite-dominated school of law. The university was small, with fewer than 1,000 students in the 1880s and no more than 4,000 as late as 1910.

The education of Argentine girls was generally limited to primary school, often at a religious institution. A few families that spent extended periods abroad enrolled their children in European schools and universities. More commonly, young men of elite would study abroad for a limited time after completing their degrees in Buenos

Aires but before beginning their careers. Those who were educated entirely abroad missed the critical friendship-building opportunities available to their peers at home (Losada 2008: 106–127).

In Brazil, as in Argentina, upper-class children received their early education at home. An exceptional few from expatriate families studied abroad. Here also the education of girls was limited, though some were sent to a convent school, the College de Scion in Rio de Janeiro. For boys in the late nineteenth century, the Colegio Pedro II, a state institution in Rio, occupied a position of prestige similar to that of the Nacional Buenos Aires (Needell 1987: 54–63). It educated many of the heirs of the city's privileged class and the state oligarchies. But in Brazil, elite schooling would never be as centralized as it was in the capitals of Peru and Argentina. Not surprisingly, the importance of Colegio Pedro II receded with fall of the Brazilian monarchy in 1889. Under the oligarchic republic that replaced it, fewer than 15 percent of the political elites of São Paulo, Minas Gerais, and Pernambuco attended *colegio* out of state, a figure roughly corresponding to the small minority of each elite that was born out of state. Brazil had no universities until the 1930s. The institutions where the sons of the upper-class were most likely to meet one another were the law schools at São Paulo in the south and Racife in the northern state of Pernambuco. During this period, 63 percent of São Paulo's political elite and 72 percent of their peers in Pernambuco's held law degrees from their own state's law school. Many of their peers from nearby states attended one of these institutions (Wirth 1977: 244–245). In sum, education in Brazil unified the ruling class regionally, a tendency that inevitably undermined elite cohesion on the national level.

NEIGHBORHOODS

Most of the children attending the National Buenos Aires, La Recolecta in Lima, and similar schools by the turn of the century returned home at the end of the day to compact upper-class neighborhoods near the center of the city. By then, even families whose wealth was based in the countryside resided in Lima, Santiago, and other national capitals or major regional centers such as São Paulo or Merida.

At the beginning of the oligarchic era, the cities of Latin America still retained their plaza-centered colonial form and traditional architecture. The main government buildings, the cathedral, and the homes of the leading families were concentrated on or near the principal plaza. The less privileged lived at successively greater distances from the center. But the new wealth generated by the export economy encouraged upper-class families to abandon the area immediately around the plaza— which continued to be the focus of public life—for new neighborhoods nearby, where there was room for the beaux-arts *palacios* favored by the oligarchs. Often the outward movement was along the grand new Parisian-style avenues, radiating out from the center, that were created during the oligarchic era: out the Paseo de la Reforma toward Chapultepec in Mexico City or following the Avenida Rio Branco in Rio de Janeiro. São Paulo's coffee planters built their mansions along the elevated central spine running through the city and traced by Avenida Paulista. Argentina's cattle barons populated the Barrio Norte, a few blocks north of the traditional center, the Plaza de Mayo.

With the increasing importance of the automobile in the 1920s, the elite dispersed still further from the center, often along these same avenues. With the opening of Avenida Arequipa, Lima's upper-class families were drawn southwest toward the ocean. Their peers in Santiago moved eastward into the foothills of the Andes. But even after the oligarchic era, Latin America's upper class remained concentrated in the elite neighborhoods of a few cities, in most cases, the national capital.[8]

SOCIAL CLUBS

One sign of the emergence of national oligarchies in the late nineteenth century was the formation of elite social clubs in Latin American capitals, among them Lima's Club Nacional (1855), Santiago's Club de la Union (1864), and the Jockey Clubs of Rio (1868), Buenos Aires (1882), and Mexico City (1883).[9] Inspired by the European and American clubs of the era, the Latin American clubs were known for their select memberships, prohibitive dues, and sumptuous quarters. The elegant Buenos Aires Jockey Club had a vast wine cellar, an impressive library (where French periodicals might outnumber those in Spanish), and an art collection that included works by European masters. Like many of its counterparts, the club was designed to be a place where men in possession of recent fortunes could feel like deeply rooted aristocrats (Edsall 1999).

Especially during the oligarchic era, when everyone who mattered belonged to the Jockey Club, the Club Nacional, or the Club de la Union, the clubs provided quiet, private settings for ecounters among the rich and powerful—social centers where friendships were cultivated, conflicts negotiated, and strategies refined. As the website of the Buenos Aires Jockey Club now candidly acknowledges, the club was created as "private sphere" for the "ruling class" (http://www.jockeyclub.org.ar/JockeyNeWeb/HISlahistoria.php). Chilean banker Julio Subercaseaux Browne, member of a prominent oligarchic family, recalled midday gatherings at the Club de la Union with a group of "intimates" in the 1890s. Subercaseux's memoir of the oligarchic era names nearly four dozen "friends" he saw regularly at the club, suggesting that his club habit was common among upper-class men of his generation (Browne 1976: 239–240). During the same period, an informal group representing the core of Peru's ruling Civilista elite met Thursday evenings at the Club Nacional to discuss national affairs. Known as "the 24 Friends," the group included representatives of the Miró Quesada, Aspíllaga, Pardo, and other oligarchic clans (Miró Quesada Laos 1961: 354).

If there was any doubt about whom Santiago's Club de la Union represented, it was resolved in 1905, when the government distributed arms to club members and upper-class youths to repress violent working-class protests in the streets of capital (Loveman 1988: 198). Across the Andes, in response to the 1919 labor disturbances in Buenos Aires, the Jockey Club supported the formation of the Argentine Patriotic League, a right-wing paramilitary organization with a distinctly upper- and middle-class membership. In addition to financial support, many of the League's members and about half of its leaders were members of the Jockey Club (Edsall 1999: 122, 174–175).

The clubs became potent symbols of class privilege and, especially after 1930, inevitable targets of populist agitation. The Mexican Revolution compelled the Jockey Club to close its doors. It was reestablished three decades later, but not in the elegant Casa de Azulejos (House of Tiles) it had previously occupied (https:// en.wikipedia.org/wiki/Casa_de_los_Azulejos). In the 1970s, Peru's left-wing military government reportedly attempted to shut down the Club Nacional. The Buenos Aires Jockey Club was destroyed in 1953, in what appeared to be a calculated assault on upper-class treasures and values, by vandals encouraged by then president Juan Perón. The night of April 15, a group of men

> [forced] their way past the majordomo . . . ran up the marble staircase to the main hall and began to destroy paintings by . . . Goya and Velásquez . . . [Other] attackers knocked down the club's prized sculpture of Diana the huntress, breaking off her arms. [The grand staircase and the Diana sculpture are shown in an early photo on the cover of this book]. Someone started a fire fueled by priceless seventeenth-century tapestries. Thousands of books from the club's library collection added to the growing flames. A few of the attackers looted its wine cellar, filled with tens of thousands of bottles of champagne, brandies, wines and hard liquors.

Callers to the fire department were rebuffed. "We have no instructions to put out a fire at the Jockey Club," they were told. Perón's government subsequently dissolved the club and seized its lucrative racetrack and gambling operation. The club did not reopen its doors until 1968 (Edsall 1999: 1–2).[10]

AN INTIMATE WORLD

The upper-class world that the oligarchs inhabited was often described by its inhabitants and observers as "intimate." From childhood, in their neighborhoods, at their schools, at summer resorts, and later at their clubs or in civic and business settings, they were surrounded by people like themselves, people who were their relatives, their friends, often the sons and daughters of their parents' friends—at very least, people who were from "known" families. Adults born in the oligarchic era would later recall visits to their childhood homes by a president or other powerful figure, perhaps at a point when they were too young to grasp exactly who this friendly older man was. Their world was as intimate as a small village in the Andes or the Mayan highland.

The bonds forged in the upper-class social world reinforced elite cohesion based on shared economic and political interests. Upper-class men proposing an investment, pursuing a loan, promoting a candidate, or plotting a coup inevitably depended on others who were their kin, their friends, their former school mates, and fellow club members. As Baltzell (1958: 61) observed in his classic account of Philadelphia's social elite, an upper-class community inculcates and sustains "a mutually understood code of conduct. . . . Upper-class men are especially subject to the norms and sanctions of their peers. A man caught in an act of dishonesty or disloyalty fears, above all, the criticism of his class or life-long friends." Baltzell's comment suggests, on the one hand, an underlying elite consensus rooted in common values and, on the other, a communal mechanism of social control based on the risk of offending one's peers.

The experience of the Miró Quesadas in the late 1950s and early 1960s, examined in chapter 8, suggests both the power and the limits of upper-class communal control. During this period, the editorial policy of the family's influential daily, *El Comercio*, was shifting in a reformist direction that was viewed as "an act of disloyalty" by many of their peers. Some found social ways to express their displeasure. For example, at the Club Nacional, the Miró Quesadas were treated coolly by certain other members. Miró Quesada children in their *colegios* were taunted by schoolmates who labeled the Miró Quesada kids "Communists." That the Miró Quesadas were able to resist such pressures, along with economic and political sanctions that were used to punish them, is a tribute to the clan's unyielding pride and solidarity. It also reflected the family's long-established position at the center of upper-class society. Although the Miró Quesadas successfully defied these pressures, their experience was a loud warning to others, perhaps of less secure social standing, of the price of independence.

The political cohesion of the oligarchy was strengthened, but not guaranteed, by the social bonds of upper-class society. The oligarchs were sometimes divided by conflicting economic interests or political ambitions that social links could not bridge. They might also be divided by social geography. In Peru, Chile, and Argentina, upper-class institutions were, like the oligarchs they served, concentrated in the national capital. But the same was not true in Brazil or Mexico, where, during the oligarchic era, the members of different state oligarchies were less likely to go to school together, join the same clubs, or marry one another's siblings. In these cases, social separation invited political fragmentation of the national elite, as the coming chapters will show.

NOTES

1. For the history of the Pardo, I have drawn on Lasarte Ferreyros 1993: 578; Gonzales 1985: 28; Basadre 1971: 633 and an interview.
2. For details of how the twenty-nine were chosen, see Appendix A. Since the judges were polled in the mid-1970s, their lists would presumably have included families that gained

prominence as late as the mid-twentieth century, but perhaps excluded "early" families whose fortunes were fading by then. A similar list compiled by Quiroz (1988: 78–79) of families prominent between 1890 and 1930 includes many of families in table 1.1. Though referring to an earlier period, it suggests the same social origins and narrow window of opportunity.

3. On Mexico see, González 2000: 672–673; Haber et al. 2003: 47–48, 90–93; Knight 1986: I, 21–24.

4. On this "window" see Hora 2001a: 134–135; Losada 2008: chapter 1; Saragoza 1988: 74–77; Pike 1963: 16; Marcella 1973: 123–125; table 1.1 above.

5. For example, the Peruvian civil code in the late 1970s provided that testators with living first-degree relatives could only freely dispose of one-third of their estates. Children and other descendants had the first claim on the rest. Illegitimate children (who were not uncommon among the descendants of upper-class Peruvian men) were each to receive half as much as each of the legitimate children (Civil Code, Articles 700, 760, 762). See Gilbert 1981: 742; Lewin 2003: 19–20; Hora 2003: 474; Lomnitz and Perez-Lizaur 1987: 140.

6. See Balmori et al. 1984: 5, 100–102, 163–164, 205–206; Freyre 1922: 616–618; Needell 1987: 117–124; Losada 2008: 143–147; Levi 1987: 5–15, 33–36; Lewin 2009.

7. Writing of a somewhat later period, Imaz (1964: 130) finds "no more than five private schools" in Buenos Aires where most upper-class Argentines received their early education.

8. Scobie 1974: 27–28, 1986: 256–261; Love 1980: 82–83; Almandoz 2010.

9. The various Jockey Clubs and Santiago's Club Hípico served the social functions of the other elite clubs but also promoted the sport, favored by the European aristocracy, of thoroughbred horse racing.

10. Sources for this section include Edsall 1999; Needell 1987: 63–77.

2

The Oligarchic Republics

> Men make their own history, but they do not make it just as they please; they do
> not make it under circumstances chosen by themselves, but under circumstances
> directly found, given, and transmitted from the past. The tradition of all the dead
> generations weighs like a nightmare on the brain of the living.
>
> —Karl Marx

A visitor to Buenos Aires in 1912, the British writer James Bryce, found an amal-
gam of New York and Paris. "It has the business rush and luxury of the one, the
gaiety and pleasure-loving aspect of the other. Nowhere in the world does one get
a stronger impression of exuberant wealth and extravagance." Bryce, a well-traveled
observer with easy access to elite circles, noted that the ladies of Buenos Aires graced
themselves with "all the Parisian finery and jewels that money can buy," that the
interior of the Opera house was the equal of "any in Europe," and that the aristocratic Jockey Club surpassed, in its "scale and elaborate appointments," the elegant
the club-houses of New York. Bryce was equally impressed with the busy, modern
port of Buenos Aires, with its miles of docks, enormous warehouses, and converging
rail lines—all comparable, he thought, to other great ports of the capitalist world
(Bryce 1916: 318–320).

Bryce was touring Latin America when oligarchic power reached its zenith.
Oligarch republics had been established in most Latin American countries (Smith
2012: 27). Presidents and other important officials were typically drawn from the
wealthy elites created by the region's flourishing export economy. Their rule faced
little resistance. Export revenue had strengthened Latin American states. The oligarchic republics were better financed, better defended, and more stable than the weak,
postcolonial, caudillo-dominated regimes they displaced.

This chapter compares the oligarchic republics of Argentina, Chile, Mexico, Brazil, and Peru. Table 2.1 profiles these five countries about the time of Bryce's visit. Together, as the table shows, the five accounted for three quarters of the region's exports, population, and land area. Argentina was by far the biggest exporter, producing 30 percent of all Latin American exports. Argentina and Chile were already distinguished from the other three countries by their relatively high levels of GDP per capita, literacy, and urbanization—conditions that were creating the basis for the early emergence of modern working and middle classes. Brazil and Mexico also had large export economies, but like Peru's, they were small relative to the national population, and the social development of these countries was correspondingly retarded.

The export growth that provided the basis for oligarchic fortunes and oligarchic states is tracked in table 2.2. The value of the region's exports in 1929 was more than eight times what it had been in 1870. The typical pattern was slow export expansion

Table 2.1.   Profiles of Five Countries in the Oligarchic Era

	Exports Millions 1912	Population Millions 1912	Area Millions Km. Sq.	GDP/Capita 1913	Percentage Literate 1913	Percentage Urban 1910
Argentina	454.4	7.3	2.8	175.1	60	28
Chile	152.8	3.4	0.8	130.1	44	24
Mexico	152.9	14.3	2.0	72.7	30	11
Brazil	346.8	24.4	8.5	40.8	35	10
Peru	43.0	4.6	1.3	34.6	30	5
% of Latin America	73	70	75	–	–	–

Sources: Exports (three-year averages, current dollars), population, and GDP/capita from Bulmer-Thomas (2003: 413, 412, 425). Bulmer-Thomas' 1913 GDP/capita figures converted to 1913 dollars with "all commodities" wholesale price index. U.S. Bureau of the Census (1975: 200–201). Area from Wilkie (2002: 72). Literacy from Thorp (1998: 354). Urbanization from Clawson (2012: 359).

Table 2.2.   Growth of Exports, 1850–1929
Three-Year Averages in Millions of 1890 US Dollars

	1850	1870	1890	1912	1929
Argentina	11.0	16.8	109.0	369.6	534.9
Chile	11.0	16.8	52.8	124.3	164.5
Mexico	23.7	12.9	50.0	124.4	168.1
Brazil	34.9	51.0	137.0	282.1	268.9
Peru	7.3	15.7	9.9	35.0	79.0
All Latin America	149.7	205.1	592.9	1,247.9	1,713.7

Sources: Bulmer-Thomas (2003: 413), except 1929 from Wilkie (1974: 259–278).
Note: Data for years before and after 1890 were converted from current US dollars to 1890 dollars using "all commodities" wholesale price indexes. U.S. Bureau of the Census (1975: 200–201).

in the middle of the nineteenth century, accelerating especially after 1890. Peru's irregular pattern of export growth reflects its devastating losses in the 1879–1883 War of the Pacific with Chile and its recovery thereafter.

The oligarchic republics endured in these countries for a generation or more and inevitably changed over time, evolving into the contested republics treated in chapter 3. The accounts that follow are far from comprehensive. For the sake of comparison, I have concentrated on the distinctive features of each regime at its maturity. The Peruvian case is treated in greater detail in part II.

PERU: THE ARISTOCRATIC REPUBLIC

During the quarter century from 1895 to 1919, known to historians of Peru as the Aristocratic Republic, an oligarchy of successful sugar and cotton planters, miners, bankers, and import–export merchants dominated the nation's economic and political institutions. They ruled the country through their political vehicle, the Civilista Party.

The Aspíllaga and the Prado clans, introduced in the last chapter, were important players in the economic and political life of the Aristocratic Republic. The Aspíllagas were the owners of Cayaltí, a north coast sugar plantation. In the years following the War of the Pacific, the clan's second generation, the Aspíllaga Barrera brothers expanded and modernized Cayaltí. The ample profits generated by the plantation enabled them to invest in other sectors of the economy, including banking and mining. All four of the brothers held public office at one time or another, but it was Antero, the eldest, who became a leading national political figure during the Aristocratic Republic. Between 1888 and 1919, he served as a finance minister, deputy, senator and presiding officer of the senate, mayor of Lima, and leader of the Civilista Party. He had presidential ambitions.

The Prado Ugarteches, also second generation, were contemporaries of the Aspíllaga Barreras. The eldest of the brothers, Mariano was an energetic entrepreneur who mobilized the export income pouring into the country for investment in urban enterprises. The Aspíllagas and other wealthy planters and miners were conspicuous among the board members and shareholders in the companies Mariano promoted in Lima—including the Banco Popular, which became the center of an economic empire and the key to the Prados' political power. Like the Aspíllagas, the four Prado Ugarteche brothers all held national political office. Though Mariano was more devoted to business, his younger brothers were strongly engaged by politics. Javier, Jorge, and Manuel were successively pushed forward by the clan as presidential candidates. Jorge and Manuel (who finally became president in 1939) were masters of conspiratorial politics.

As the Aspíllaga and Prado examples suggest, the economic, political, and social life of the Peruvian oligarchy was concentrated on the coast and headquartered in Lima, at the coastal midpoint. Except for those invested in mining, the oligarchs had limited connection to the Andean Sierra region, home to most of Peru's population, especially its generally impoverished Indians and mestizos. (The white population was concentrated on the coast, which, outside of major cities, was sparsely popu- lated.) The largest oligarchic fortunes came from the north coast sugar plantations. Others were based on cotton cultivation also on the coast, to the south of the sugar areas. Migrants from the Sierra were, by the time of the Aristocratic Republic, the planters' main source of labor. Only a few oligarchic fortunes were built on Sierra mining, which—in contrast to export agriculture—was increasingly controlled by foreign corporations. The oligarchy's export enterprises were, like Cayaltí, admin- istered from Lima, where oligarchic fortunes based on banking and international commerce developed.

Lima was also the hub of the oligarchs' social world. They lived in close proxim- ity, gathered in each other's drawing rooms, and encountered one another at Sunday mass, at the Club Nacional, at the theater and the racetrack, in business meetings, and at the Congress. Their children played together in the city's plazas, went to the same private schools, and sat in the same university classrooms, where their instruc- tors were drawn from their own upper-class world. Inevitably they married their friends' siblings, strengthening the social network that bound them together. Grow- ing up this way, they could easily believe that the world was their private property.

During the oligarchic era in Peru, power flowed to money. And greater power flowed to bigger money. Thus, the president was usually a sugar planter—if not a sugar planter, someone approved by the oligarchy and protective of its interests. Cabinets were filled with the oligarchs, their relatives, and clients. Oligarchic fami- lies, like the Prados, Aspíllagas, and Miró Quesadas, were well represented in the Congress, but here they were outnumbered by the local, landowning bosses of the Sierra (known as *gamonales*) and their representatives.

If the oligarchy did not fully control the Congress, it hardly mattered. The Con- gress was powerless relative to the executive, and there was little substantive political difference between oligarchs and *gamonales*. Both got what they needed: protection of their property, a generally docile labor force, and control over local affairs in the regions around their land. All members of the Congress were dependent on the presi- dent and his ministers for the vital currency of official appointments that members could bestow on their clients or trade for political favors. From the perspective of the legislators, the government was a great "web of patronage," with the president, at the center, holding ultimate power to appoint (Miller 1982: 113–114).

The local power of the oligarchs was extraordinary. At Cayaltí, for example, the Aspíllagas maintained a private police force and a jail for those they judged guilty of crimes or disruptive of labor discipline. When necessary, they could call in police reinforcements from a nearby town. Local officials also helped the Cayaltí managers chase down indebted peons who had escaped the plantation without working off their obligation (Gonzales 1985: Ch. 7, 1991).

The Sierra landlords exercised similar local powers. The difference between the Lima oligarchs and the *gamonales*—aside from the colossal gap in the scale of their wealth—was that the power of the oligarchy was both local *and* national. The oligarchs controlled not only local officials and congressional delegations but also the national executive. Their investments were diversified, often spanning coastal agriculture, urban industry and finance, and Sierra mining. They possessed a sophisticated understanding of modern technology, business methods, and international markets that the *gamonales* could never match. The nation's economic policy, with its twin emphasis on exports and foreign investment, was their policy.

Most Peruvians, of course, had no place in the political system under the Aristocratic Republic. The right to vote was reserved for males who were both propertied and literate, effectively limiting the electorate to less than 2 percent of the population (Drake 2009: 148). Intimidation of voters and rules that invited falsification of ballots by those who controlled the electoral apparatus muffled the political voice of this circumscribed electorate.

But Peruvian society was changing in response to the economic development promoted by the oligarchy. By the second decade of the twentieth century, a sizable working class had developed in Lima and its port Callao, on the coastal plantations, and in the mining enclaves of the Sierra. The middle class, based on government- and private-sector employment, was still small but growing. The oligarchy was confronting demands for reform, expressed as urban unrest, strikes, student protests, and support for antiestablishment political candidates.

The Civilistas, divided in the last years of the Aristocratic Republic by factional conflict and personal ambitions, were incapable of a coherent response to what came to be known as "the social question." President José Pardo (1904–1908), member of a prominent planter family and son of a nineteenth-century president, introduced a broad reform package that provided, among other things, for the mediation of labor conflicts. The measure was supported by younger, progressive Civilistas but blocked in Congress by the conservative wing of the party. More frequently, however, the intraelite conflicts were over power and personalities, rather than ideology, as the next chapter will show.

In 1912, planter Antero Aspíllaga, the official Civilista presidential candidate, held a very weak hand. The party had split in two, with members of many prominent oligarchic families, including the Pardos and the Miró Quesadas, forming an Independent Civilista Party. Aspíllaga had a formidable opponent, former Lima mayor Guillermo Billinghurst, a wealthy man with a populist message and a large, boisterous following in the streets of the capital. The election was thrown into the Congress, where the Civilista schism worked to Billinghurst's advantage.

In office, President Billinghurst (1912–1914) shocked the oligarchy by tuning his populist rhetoric into concrete proposals and calling people into the streets to support them. After eighteen months in office, he was overthrown with a military coup orchestrated by the younger Prado Urgarteche brothers, Jorge and Manuel. At a postcoup dinner offered by upper-class Lima in honor of the brothers, a speaker voiced the diners' common sentiment: Billinghurst had encouraged the "destructive audacity of the lower classes" and endangered "the ruling class" (Villanueva 1973a: 152).[1]

Billinghurst had managed to reunite the elite. The Aristocratic Republic had been disrupted but was restored, with the help of the Prados. It would endure for a few more years. But the events surrounding Billinghurst's presidency were a harbinger of future elite disunion, lower-class "audacity," and dependence on the military to sustain the Old Regime.

CHILE: THE PARLIAMENTARY REPUBLIC

The power of the Chilean oligarchy, dominant during the period known as the Parliamentary Republic (1891–1925), was rooted in the great estates of the fertile central valley. In 1924, 80 percent of the region's farmland was held by 2.7 percent of central valley estates (Loveman 1988: 210). This concentrated landholding in a compact geographic area provided the basis for a cohesive elite, bound together by shared economic interests and ties of kinship, friendship, and *compadrazgo* (god-parenthood). Landowning families, such as the Ossa, Larraín, Valdéz, Errázuriz, Balmaceda, Echeverria, and Subercaseaux—surnames familiar to generations of their countrymen—were prominent among the wealthiest, most powerful Chileans from the mid-nineteenth to the mid-twentieth century. Even as the weight of agriculture in Chile's exports sank in the late nineteenth century and elite families deserted the countryside for Santiago, central valley landholding remained fundamental to oligarchic power and status.

Their near monopoly of the central valley's best land gave the major landholders control over much of the region's rural labor force. Under what would be known as the "hacienda system," peasants were settled on the estates as *inquilinos*, who were given access to parcels of land in exchange for their labor. Since the estates controlled vast areas of land, much of it uncultivated, the cost of labor was effectively zero. Well into the twentieth century, landowners felt little pressure to use land or labor efficiently. When rising demand beckoned in international or domestic markets, landowners could increase production by intensifying the labor requirements for inquilinos, reducing their privileges, and bringing idle land under cultivation. Chilean agriculture remained backward in comparison with practices in the United States or neighboring Argentina well into the twentieth century.

Charles Darwin, who visited the area in the 1830s, characterized the hacienda system as "semifeudal." An 1861 visitor observed that "Every hacienda in Chile forms a separate society, whose head is the landowner and whose subjects are the inquilinos. . . . The landowner is an absolute monarch in his hacienda" (Collier 1993: 16–17). Such observations are consistent with the example of an especially "patriotic" landowning legislator who volunteered all his inquilinos to fight in the 1879 war with Peru (Collier and Sater 2004: 138). However oppressed the inquilinos appeared to outsiders, they could count themselves lucky relative to the floating population of destitute peons who found only seasonal employment on the haciendas. Bauer, the author of a classic history of rural Chile, concludes that the hacienda

The inquilinos on Chilean estates, such as this family, were tied to the land by a semifeudal arrangement. Like them, most people in the early decades of the Old Regime were poor, illiterate, and powerless. Typically living in rural isolation, they posed no threat to the continent's oligarchs.

Source: Library of Congress, Frank and Frances Carpenter Collection.

system "provided suitable workers in a society where obedience and loyalty were valued over productivity" (Bauer 1975: 560).

In the mid-nineteenth century, the fortunes of the central valley landowners rose with the expanding world market. Chile became an important supplier of cereals to England, Australia, and, for a brief shining moment, California, at the time of the 1848 gold rush. But by the 1880s, growing competition from farmers in Australia, Canada, and the American Midwest had all but eliminated Chilean cereal producers from foreign markets. Mining was the force that drove the country's fast-growing economy in the late nineteenth century. Great new fortunes were made in nitrates (used as fertilizer in European agriculture) and copper mining, in addition to the banking and commercial sectors that thrived with the growth of exports. The nitrate and copper sectors, however, came increasingly under the control of foreign capital.

The central valley landowners benefited in multiple ways from developments that were seemingly adverse to them. Diverted from the global market, they found export-driven markets at home, provisioning the booming mining enclaves, fast-growing Santiago, and its nearby port of Valparaíso. As mineral exports became the main revenue source for the national government, the taxes affecting landowners and other wealthy Chileans, such as property and inheritance levies, were gradually eliminated. The government channeled its expanding export revenue stream toward projects beneficial to the landowners, such as the railroad construction, that enhanced the value of their rural properties by connecting them to markets or the modernization and beautification of Santiago, where most landed families resided.

Many landowners invested in mining and urban enterprises. At the same time, newly affluent miners bought central valley estates—valued as much for the social prestige and political power they conferred as for their economic potential. The landed aristocracy did not long resist the social pretensions of the new rich. Soon the sons and daughters of the new and old elites were joining in marriage. Juan Francisco Rivas, unknown before he accumulated an enormous fortune in mining, bought one of the country's largest estates and married two of his daughters to prominent landed families, the Errázuriz and Subercaseaux. This process of social absorption was nothing new, though it accelerated in the last decades of the nineteenth century. At the beginning of the century, Francisco Ignacio Ossa, a similarly obscure but successful miner, bought two big haciendas, worked his way into upper-class Santiago society, and won a seat in the Senate. By 1887, the Ossas owned fifteen of the country's largest estates.

Among fifty-nine millionaires listed in an 1882 newspaper article, just twenty had fortunes that originated in agriculture, but most of the others—described as miners, bankers, and "capitalists"—had also invested in rural estates. By then, the outcome of this process of social and economic amalgamation was a powerful, blended oligarchy, which, if not perfectly homogeneous, was free of sharp social and sectoral division (Bauer 1975: 41, 179–181; Collier and Sater 2004: 89).

Several decades later, Guillermo de la Cuadra Gormaz, a genealogist nostalgic for a lost world he had never known, wrote, "If an aristocratic great-grandfather of 1850 returned to life and read [the newspaper] society pages of 1934 . . . he would be shocked by the great changes" (Marcella 1973: 99). The resurrected great-grandfather would have searched in vain for some of the old families he had known, and he would certainly have been surprised by the prominence of foreign names like Edwards, Ross, Matte, and Alessandri on the society page.

Chile's nineteenth-century presidents, cabinet ministers, and legislators were drawn from a small world. They were likely to be related to other members of the political elite and were typically owners of large estates. In 1874, for example, 70 percent of senators and 44 percent of deputies were major landowners; by 1902, these proportions had climbed to 73 and 52 percent. Of course, many of these men had other sources of income, as the 1882 list suggests (Bauer 1975: 216).

The key to the political might of the landowners was their control of the peasants who worked their land and could be depended upon to vote as the *patron* decreed. Especially after 1891, the landed oligarchs of a district were likely to be the effective owners of its congressional seat. Their power was enhanced by a system of apportionment that favored rural districts. These political facts of life encouraged successful miners and urban capitalists to invest in rural properties. Julio Suberca-seaux, member of a powerful oligarchic clan, candidly recalled the political advan-tage extensive landowning conferred on the family's bank: "[We] controlled nearly 3,000 votes corresponding to the inquilinos of our estates or those which we rented and administered. Such was the electoral influence which the bank held before its clients." The bank's 3,000 votes (a hefty number in a small electorate) may explain Subercaseaux's own election to a seat in the legislature, where he was able to arrange "the resolution of varied matters of concern to the bank" (Subercaseaux Browne 1976: 234, 283).

From the early years of the republic, Chile had been governed by members of the landed elite, in the interests of that class, but power was concentrated in the hands of the president. The postcolonial regime was a serial autocracy that permitted each president to serve two five-year terms, impose his own policies, and choose his own successor. Although initially satisfied with the stability this scheme brought, the elite grew impatient with its constraints. The intraelite tension inherent in the regime expressed itself as a long power struggle between the executive and the legislature and exploded in armed conflicts in 1851, 1859, and 1891.

The balance of power gradually shifted toward the legislature. The 1891 victory of forces identified with the Congress was politically decisive. That year marked the beginning of the Parliamentary Republic, the era when the government was domi-nated by the legislature and the legislature by the oligarchy. The president was now limited to one term. He lost control over the electoral apparatus (along with the opportunity for electoral fraud) to the oligarchy-controlled localities. The national administration was conducted by the interior minister—in effect, a prime minister responsible to the Congress rather than the president. German Riesco, the first presi-dent elected under the new order, campaigned with a slogan attuned to the times: "I am not a threat to anyone" (Drake 2009: 141).

Ramón Barros Luco, another of the figurehead presidents of the parliamentary era, is remembered for his observation that "there are only two types of problems: those that have no solution and those that solve themselves" (Loveman 1988: 193). In fact, the country had serious problems that the political system steadfastly ignored, but the nation would one day be compelled to confront. One set of problems concerned the socially and economically archaic hacienda system. Another, known here, as in Peru as "the social question," concerned education, poverty, and, especially, the growing militancy of the expanding urban and mining proletariat.

The politics of this era revolved around competition among a half dozen political parties. However diverse their membership, they were generally led by upper-class men. With the exception of church–state issues, the ideological differences among the parties were too modest to be discerned by voters or to become material for leg-islative battles. Because the needs and opinions of the popular classes were irrelevant to the political process, there was little temptation to raise class issues. The govern-ments of the era were not, in any event, inclined to do anything threatening to the interests of the oligarchy. Since no party was dominant, governments were formed by incoherent, transitory coalitions. But the rise and fall of governments presented welcome opportunities for new public appointments. The fundamental concern of politicians was, in fact, control over public money and positions.

Elections were held regularly in the Parliamentary Republic, but there was little competition for hearts and minds. Big landowners owned much of the rural electorate. Large regional companies also controlled blocs of voters. In 1906, for example, two large mining companies supplied votes to elect another member of the Subercaseaux clan, Ramón, to the senate (Vial 1981: II, 587). Government employees were obliged to vote as instructed by the political bosses who provided their jobs. Most of the electorate was controlled by the elite in this fashion. But there was a significant minority, especially in the cities and larger towns, of "free" electors, whose votes were routinely bought by parties and candidates. Political cognoscenti could quote the purchase price of a senate seat, which rose over time to levels beyond the reach of all but the very wealthy. In 1918, for example, a senate campaign required the equivalent of US$100,000 at current exchange rates (Collier and Sater 2004: 192). Parties sometimes evaded vote-buying costs by dividing the available seats with their competitors in advance of an election. But the practice of vote buying was so ingrained that many voters felt cheated by these electoral pacts, supposing that the politicians were stealing the money that the government had provided for electors. When the votes that could be compelled or purchased fell short of victory, local authorities could resort to falsification of returns to produce the desired result.

For the oligarchy, politics was a means to private advantage (as Julio Subercaseaux's comments suggest) and to a cornucopia of public resources with which to maintain their clientelistic networks. The political system was also a mechanism that permitted the oligarchs to work out their differences without violence. For the individual member of an oligarchic clan, politics was an expression of his aristocratic status, an integral and expected part of upper-class life. The legislature would not have been so well stocked with members of the elite if they had not wanted to serve or at least been expected to by their peers. In late nineteenth-century Chile, it could, with little exaggeration, be said, "The oligarchy doesn't just control the state. It is the state" (Barros y Vergara in Fernández Darraz 2003: 35)

But while the oligarchy carried on its accustomed, solipsistic political life, Chile was changing around it. Here, even more dramatically than in Peru, the working and middle classes were expanding in the major cities and export enclaves. If the "social question" was ignored in the legislature, it was finding expression in the streets and the workplace. Protests and strikes, rare through the nineteenth century, were common in the early twentieth century. In October 1905, lower-class protests in Santiago over soaring food prices gave way to days of rioting, later known as "Red Week." In response, the government and private groups armed upper-class youths and members of the elite Union Club, who killed several hundred unarmed protesters. Class conflict had turned into armed confrontation (Loveman 1988: 198).

ARGENTINA'S OLIGARCHIC REPUBLIC

The opulence and industry that British writer James Bryce observed in Buenos Aires in 1912 reflected Argentina at the pinnacle of its oligarchic republic (1880–1916). Argentines have no special name for this time, as Chileans do for the contemporary Parliamentary Republic or Peruvians for their Aristocratic Republic, but they recognize the era as distinct and transformative. The period of the oligarchic republic was framed by two critical dates: 1880 and 1916. In 1880, the national army led by General Julio Roca completed the so-called Conquest of the Desert campaign, clearing the pampas of the nomadic Indians who had constrained the expansion of export agriculture. That same momentous year, Roca's forces put down the rebellion of Buenos Aires Province, settling, once and for all, the status of the country's wealthiest province in the Argentine federation, and Roca was elected president. He became the preeminent political figure of the period. In 1916, the unprecedented election of a popular opposition candidate, Hipólito Yrigoyen, to the presidency marked the end of the oligarchic republic and the beginning of a more competitive political system. In the years between 1880 and 1916, Argentina developed one of world's biggest, most dynamic economies, millions of European immigrants swelled the nation's population, and Buenos Aires grew from a modest commercial outpost into one of the largest cities on the Atlantic. The oligarchic republic was a time of relative calm in the nation's agitated political history and was, above all, an era of elite dominance.

Toward the end of the nineteenth century, an oligarchy of several hundred wealthy families—wealthy even by the gilded standards of contemporary New York or London—had consolidated in the city of Buenos Aires. Its members were large landowners, financiers, merchants, and others who had built fortunes in the rapidly growing trans-Atlantic trade in meat, cereals, and wool. The wealthiest of the oligarchs were the biggest landowners, especially those with holdings on the pampas within Buenos Aires Province. They had taken advantage of land that was fertile and, for much of the nineteenth century, relatively cheap; a booming international market; and proximity to the port and expanding rail system. By improving their herds and farming methods, some had built epic fortunes.

Landownership remained concentrated in Argentina, even though the country was thinly populated and large areas were unsettled through the nineteenth century. Rural estates covering thousands, sometimes hundreds of thousands of acres, were not uncommon, especially on the pampas. Argentine laws devised, like the U.S. Homestead Act, to promote small family farms had limited effect, with the exception of some early farm colonies settled by immigrants in provinces north of Buenos Aires. A study of estate records for the years 1880–1919 found twenty-six decedents with rural land holdings in excess of 25,000 acres. Among them were Juan Anchorena, the scion of a colonial family, who willed his heirs almost three million acres in 1895, and Tomás Duggan, a mid-century Irish immigrant without apparent resources, who left 420,000 acres at his death in 1913 (Hora 2001b: 603–604).

On the pampas, near the end of the oligarchic republic, estates over 2,500 acres, comprising only 4 percent of all holdings, occupied 61 percent of the exploited land area; among these, 584 holdings in excess of 25,000 acres covered nearly 20 percent of the land. These figures, which refer to discrete operational units, underestimate the area controlled by the wealthiest landed families, who often had multiple holdings. At the other end of the scale, rural units under 125 acres accounted for 35 percent of holdings but only 2 percent of the land area (Díaz Alejandro 1970: 152–153).

The tendency toward large holdings was reinforced by Roca's pampas campaign, which opened a vast new territory, some seventy-five million acres, for exploitation (Hora 2001a: 41). The government was anxious to exchange public land at modest prices for badly needed revenue. Those with political influence and money to buy land had obvious advantages, in what became a highly speculative market. As had happened at similar junctures in the past, enormous tracts of new public land fell into the hands of a few, often those who were already large landholders, such as Saturnine Unzué, who obtained 675,000 acres. Tomás Drysdale (800,000 acres), Antonio Cambaceres (300,000 acres), and the Alvears (487,500 acres) (Hora 2001a: 42). Quite frequently, the new land was brought under cultivation by immigrant sharecroppers or tenants, with two- or three-year contracts, who hoped to save enough to become landowners themselves. But few were successful and most moved to the cities, where jobs were abundant and wages were relatively high.

Within a few decades, what may well have been the world's wealthiest landowning class had developed in Argentina. The dominant economic position of the major cattlemen and wheat producers was undeniable. Admired by their compatriots for having modernized export agriculture and energized the national economy, the landowners had achieved an eminence of the sort that Americans reserved for Henry Ford or Thomas Edison. They were regarded, and regarded themselves, as progressive, landed aristocrats. Their social position at the top of upper-class society was unquestioned. But what was the relationship of this economic elite to the political system? Bryce, the ever-inquisitive British visitor, found that the men he met preferred to talk about their estates, cattle, and crops or of horse racing but not of politics. "Politics," he wrote, "is left to the politicians" (Bryce 1916: 344). Similarly, a British MP who visited Buenos Aires in 1894 observed that "Argentine gentlemen of high character, wide culture, great intelligence and large estate, shun politics as the plague" (Hora 2001a: 108).

The oligarchy was not so detached from political life as these comments suggest. But, during the oligarchic era, most of its members, especially the wealthiest landowners, were less politically engaged than their peers elsewhere. Unlike Chile's landed oligarchs, the great landowners of the pampas never benefited from the political power that came with domination over servile hacienda peasants. No cattle baron became president of Argentina at a time when presidents of Peru and Brazil were routinely sugar planters and coffee growers. Under the oligarchic republic, the Buenos Aires elite could not impose itself on the national government as completely as did the oligarchs of the Peruvian coast or Chile's central valley. After 1880, the Buenos

Aires–based oligarchy was forced to share power with the elites of the other Argentine provinces. President Roca, hero of the pampas campaign against the Indians, was himself the son of a prominent family in far-western Tucuman and represented a coalition of interior elites resentful of Buenos Aires.

The political antagonism between the Buenos Aires elite and the elites of the interior provinces that led to the 1880 rebellion was reinforced by a cultural divide separating the traditional, conservative Catholic aristocrats of the interior from the liberal, cosmopolitan, monied gentlemen of the port city of Buenos Aires. The latter were certainly more familiar with Paris than the distant provincial capitals of Salta or Jujuy. Miguel Cané, one of founders of Buenos Aires' elite Jockey Club, would recall the tense, sometimes violent relations between *porteños* and *provincianos* at the preparatory school he attended in the 1860s. The Jockey Club was designed to help bridge such differences (Edsall 1999: 14–15).

These regional tensions tended to fade over time. Some members of leading families of the interior established themselves in Buenos Aires and blended into upper-class *porteño* society, joining elite clubs and intermarrying with prominent Buenos Aires families (Losada 2008: chapter 1). They accumulated land on the pampas; joined the Rural Society, the semiofficial representative of the major landowners; and became part of a renovated national political elite that included both *porteños* and *provincianos*. Among these new landowners from the provinces were Roca himself, his successor Miguel Juárez Celman, and Ramon Cárcano, another prominent politician of the era. Roca bought land and received generous land grants authorized by the grateful Buenos Aires provincial legislature (Hora 2001a: 61–63).

The Partido Autonomo National (PAN), the dominant political organization during the oligarchic republic, was less a party than a shifting coalition of provincial elites, managed through much of the period by Roca. Like his contemporary Porfirio Díaz, Roca was an adroit ringmaster who maintained the system by manipulating competing elites. The key characteristics of the oligarchic regime were decision by *acuerdo* (agreement) and electoral fraud. Important decisions—the governorship of X province or the placement of a rail line—were made by a few men meeting privately and then publically affirmed by pro forma legislative action or predictable election victories.

Suffrage under the oligarchic republic was limited to a small minority of the population. Nonetheless, electoral fraud was required to maintain the stability of a poorly institutionalized system. Votes were bought, voters intimidated, and outcomes falsified. The dead were permitted the vote, and some among the living were permitted multiple votes. Fictional citizens were enfranchised. According to a contemporary observer (whose comment is worthy of Argentine's great writer Jorge Luís Borges), "In the deserted election registration offices one could hear nothing but the scratching pens of the government clerks writing imaginary names."[2]

Roca was, on occasion, candid about his belief that without controlled elections the country would be destroyed by regional and partisan conflicts. He feared intraelite conflict more than the demands that might arise from the masses in a more democratic system (Rock 2002: 166).

Politics was an exclusively elite enterprise. All the presidents of the era were members of the Jockey Club—a good indication of high status, given the club's cost and exclusive membership standards (Edsall 1999: 127). Most presidents, like Roca, were born to traditional upper-class families of the interior—in contrast to the great landowners of the pampas, who were, aside from a few immigrants, typically born in Buenos Aires (Piccirilli 1953–1954). More broadly, systematic research confirms what was long believed: The political elite of the oligarchic republic was nearly identical with the overlapping worlds of wealth and social prestige. For example, almost 80 percent of national and provincial officeholders in 1905 were members of the Jockey Club or other exclusive social clubs in Buenos Aires. The same proportion held important business positions or belonged to major landowing families (Losada 2007: 48–51; Smith 1974: 26–27, 117–126).

Though compelled to share power, the Buenos Aires oligarchs got everything they needed from the new regime: millions of acres of new land, granted in large tracts at generous terms; infrastructure (railroads, in particular) that raised the value of their land; openness to foreign investment for a capital hungry economy; and the promotion of European immigration to meet their labor needs—in short, a development strategy with the landed oligarchy at its center. It is hardly surprising that Buenos Aires cattlemen—many of who had backed Roca's presidential ambitions in 1880—were supporters of the PAN or that the PAN came to be known in Buenos Aires as the "cattle party" (Gallo 1993: 102).

The leaders of the post-1880 regime had no desire to undermine the economic or social standing of the Buenos Aires oligarchs. If anything, men like Roca, Júarez Celman, and Cárcano hoped to imitate them. Politicians representing the interior sought a share in the great bonanza flowing from the pampas. That might mean government positions for them or their clients, infrastructure for their provinces, and tariff protection for provincial products, such as the sugar from Tucuman and wine from Mendoza. But no one wanted to kill the goose that was laying ever-larger golden eggs.

For a generation after Roca's Conquest of the Desert and the creation of a new political system tied to the PAN, the oligarchs could, if they wished, choose to ignore politics because so little was at stake. Their needs would be met without question because their health was deemed vital for the republic. Politics, with its focus on pork and patronage, was generally more important to the provincial elites, who were needier than the Buenos Aires oligarchs. Even the potentially divisive issue of tariff protection proved to be of limited consequence.

But by 1912, when James Bryce visited Buenos Aires, Roca was entombed at La Recoleta, the preferred cemetery of the oligarchy, and the regime he had created was facing new problems. The vibrant city that so impressed Bryce was home to forces that threatened the oligarchic social order. With a population near 1.5 million, Buenos Aires was many times larger than it had been before the parallel surges of export growth and immigration of the oligarchic era. The city was home to a large, unruly proletariat and a rapidly expanding, increasingly demanding middle class. By the early years of the twentieth century, strikes were common, sometimes resulting in violent confrontations.

A more explicitly political challenge came from Hipólito Yrigoyen's Radical party, which was beginning to attract middle-class support. The party's ideology was nebulous except for an unyielding insistence on democratic elections. Frustrated by the impossibility of gaining power at the polls, the movement that evolved into the Radical party had staged unsuccessful armed rebellions in 1890, 1893, and 1905—with support from younger military officers.

The oligarchic regime was slow to respond to these social and political challenges. Though Argentina had the region's most developed labor movement, there was no legal framework for unions and no mechanism for mediating labor conflict. Argentines were generally literate (65 percent in 1914) and increasingly urban, but they might as well have all been peasants subject to the wishes of the *patron* as far as the electoral system was concerned.

The ruling elite was divided in the face of change. A group of reformers within the PAN, alarmed by the resilience of the Radicals and signs of growing working-class militancy, favored opening the political process. Their efforts were resisted by conservatives who feared the loss of power and social instability that might result from democratization. They shared the opinion of the PAN president who declared, "To consult the people is always an error, since the people have only confused and muddy opinions" (McGann 1957: 30). But in 1912, the reformers succeeded in passing the decisive Sáez Peña laws, which extended the franchise to all male citizens, made voting mandatory, provided for a secret ballot, and established a more credible system of administering elections.

The guiding assumption of these oligarchic reformers was that they could win free elections, gain legitimacy, and preserve the status quo by building a conservative party, with middle- and upper-class support. This was not an entirely fanciful notion, since many middle-class Argentines shared the elite's fears of social upheaval. But, as subsequent events would demonstrate, the men of Argentina's oligarchic political elite had little capacity for competitive electoral politics. Their political expertise, in the best of times, was limited to elite coalition building and *acuerdo* making behind closed doors. As the 1916 presidential elections approached, a divided PAN was not even capable of coalescing around a presidential candidate.[3]

BRAZIL: THE OLD REPUBLIC

With the fall of the Brazilian monarchy in 1889 and the creation of what we now know as the Old Republic, Brazil became more perfectly what it already was: a society dominated by an exporter elite. Emperor Pedro II (1840–1889)[4] had presided benignly over a regime devoted to "progress" through export development—a policy whose main beneficiaries were the planters, financiers, and marketers of coffee. Early in the century, coffee had eclipsed sugar, traditionally Brazil's leading export. The country's center of economic gravity shifted with coffee production, away from the sugar-producing Northeast. Strong world demand and the soil-exhausting character of coffee cultivation as then practiced in Brazil drew planters southward in search of new land, successively into the provinces of Rio de Janeiro, Minas Gerais, and São Paulo. By the 1880s, coffee was providing most of Brazil's export income; São Paulo was the country's biggest coffee producer; and the Paulista coffee oligarchy was, by far, the wealthiest, most dynamic sector of the national elite.

Political power did not immediately follow economic fortune. Power, under the empire, was, to a degree unusual in Brazilian history, centralized in Rio de Janeiro, where the landholding elites of the Northeast and the older coffee-growing regions carried the greatest weight. Their power was amplified by Rio's permanent cadre of well-educated bureaucrats, magistrates, and professional politicians—many of them connected to traditional landed families of these same regions. This national power structure was to the obvious disadvantage of São Paulo's coffee planters.

In 1889, Pedro II was forced from the throne by a bloodless military coup. The abolition of the monarchy had been favored by the São Paulo oligarchy and by sectors of the military, the intelligentsia, and the country's nascent middle class. But in the wake of the coup and even after the promulgation of a republican constitution in early 1891, it was not at all clear what kind of political system would replace the empire. A period of instability followed. Military officers controlled the government during the first presidential term. But the military was itself divided. A monarchist-leaning rebellion in the far south, backed by the Navy, threatened the survival of the republic in 1893. The São Paulo oligarchy seized this opportunity to consolidate its own national position, while pushing aside other groups that backed the republic. São Paulo's strategic position between the capital in Rio and the rebellion in the South made its loyalty critical. The Paulistas agreed to support the government with their "fat coffers and well-trained militia" in exchange for scheduling a presidential election they expected to control (Burns 1993: 245).

Prudente de Morais, a former governor of São Paulo with strong ties to the state's coffee oligarchy, was Brazil's first civilian president. His election to the presidency in 1894 marked the true beginning of the Old Republic. De Morais' immediate successor was a São Paulo planter, Manuel Ferras de Campo Salas. Coffee interests would dominate the Old Republic. In 1907, an American diplomat reported that "All the Northern States are bitterly opposed to the hold the planters have over the Government. . . . The executive, however, clings to the purpose of doing everything to please the coffee interests. The President realizes that he was elected by the planters and he must now return the favor" (Burns 1980: 305, 1993: 265).

The political system of the empire was aptly described as "centralized, oligarchical, and unrepresentative" (Da Costa 1989: 171). The new political system would be *decentralized*, oligarchical, and unrepresentative. Under the 1891 constitution,

Brazil became a federation, in which states enjoyed an independence-approaching sovereignty. Governors, previously appointed from above, were now elected locally. States gained the exclusive right to tax exports, a lucrative revenue source for the major coffee-producing states. Brazilian states could contract foreign loans, run their own immigration programs, and even maintain military forces. São Paulo fielded a well-equipped professional army, trained by French officers and capable of challenging the national army. The central government, though not powerless, was much diminished.

The constitution described a democratic polity, with representative institutions and popularly elected officials, that bore no relation to the political realities of the Old Republic. National politics was generally controlled by the allied elites of two coffee-producing states: São Paulo, Brazil's wealthiest state, and Minas Gerais, its most populous. Presidents were selected by agreement between Paulista and Mineiro leaders in consultation with the outgoing president. Among the eleven presidents "elected" under the Old Republic, six were from São Paulo and three from Minas. In Congress, their representatives depended on São Paulo's cash and Minas' large delegation to assure that coffee interests were favored. Between them the two delegations held the critical congressional posts and controlled other delegations with the credentialing process. They were not above bribing members or paying for favorable coverage in the Rio press. As a fictional character of the era sardonically observed, "The 20 states of Brazil are two: Minas Gerais and São Paulo" (Burns 1993: 343; Love 1980: 188).

In sum, in the transition from empire to republic, power at the national level was displaced away from the capital and the declining Northeast, toward the dynamic Southeast and South. But little changed at the state or local levels. The states were controlled by the same landed elites, with power structures that varied from state to state. In some northern and northeastern states, a single clan dominated. In other states, power was dispersed or the object of contention between competing elite factions. In the advanced states, such as São Paulo, power was typically more institutionalized and representative of class interests rather than those of a family or small group. São Paulo's coffee oligarchy ruled the state and exercised national influence through the well-organized and amply funded Paulista Republican Party (PRP).

Joseph Love's study of São Paulo during the Old Republic records a telling statistic: 60 percent of the members of the PRP's executive committee were major landowners (Love 1980: 165). This body—the planter-dominated directorate of the most powerful party, in the most powerful state, in a republic controlled by its wealthiest coffee-producing states—was (to appropriate a phrase from the *Communist Manifesto*) "a committee for managing the common affairs of the whole bourgeoisie."

Love's portrait of the broader Paulista political elite reveals a leadership representative of the state's capitalist class, homogeneous in background and experience; united by kinship and marriage; and, though cosmopolitan in outlook, surprisingly isolated from the elites of other states. Love collected data on the 263 Paulistas who had held

President Manuel Ferraz de Campos Sales of Brazil (1898–1902) was, like many chief executives of the oligarchic republics, a wealthy planter.

Source: Public Domain.

significant political positions at home or in Rio, under the republic. He found that 43 percent had close family ties to some other member of the São Paulo political elite. (Presumably, broader kinship data and information on godparenthood would have revealed an even thicker network of relationships). All but a few came from upper or upper-middle class families, and over 60 percent held degrees from the state's law school. Drawing on comparable data from studies of Minas Gerais and the northeastern state of Pernambuco, Love determined that the Paulistas were significantly less likely to be related to members of other state elites or to have pursued professional careers in the national capital (an attractive alternative for sons of states in economic decline). But the Paulistas were more likely to have traveled outside Brazil. One third of the Paulista leaders had lived abroad for at least six months—most likely in Europe.

Republican São Paulo was, as the prominence of planters at the top of the PRP suggests, ruled by a plutocracy. Forty percent of the state's political elite was economically connected in some way to export agriculture. Many political leaders also had interests in other sectors, including banking, railroads, and manufacturing. (Paulista planters' investments in manufacturing, often in collaboration with immigrant entrepreneurs, set the stage for the industrial powerhouse that the state would become [Dean 1969].) The majority, 56 percent, were apparently dependent on capitalist sources of income (profit, interest, or rent) rather than professional sources. Common background and shared economic interests strengthened political discipline. Love determined that members of the elite had, almost unanimously, supported the state establishment's position on three critical issues related to coffee and presidential succession (Love 1980: 152–175, 283–287; Love and Barickman 1986).

In the countryside, still home to the vast majority of Brazilians during this period, the republic probably strengthened the traditional political bosses Brazilians call "colonels." These men were typically important local landowners. Many commanded private armies of gunmen. Their value to the statewide oligarchies rested on their ability to deliver the votes of the local population through some combination of patron–client influence, violence, and fraud. In exchange for this service, state and national authorities allowed the colonels access to government resources and a free hand in the conduct of local affairs.

The 1891 constitution expanded the potential electorate by eliminating the property qualification, though women and illiterates were still denied the vote. But whatever value the franchise might have had was vitiated by the nonsecret ballot—the colonel was watching—and by the meaningless candidate choices offered. It is said that a naive, young voter in Pernambuco once asked the colonel, "Chief, now that I have done just what you told me to, who did I vote for?" and the colonel replied, "Son, never ask me that kind of question and don't forget that the vote is secret"—which, in fact, it was not (Hagopian 1996: 49, n18). Few Brazilians who had the right bothered to vote.

The overweening power of the colonels and the corruption of the electoral system under the republic preserved the deep cleavage that had existed since colonial times between a privileged minority and the powerless majority. Slavery was not a distant memory. A French diplomat who served in Brazil toward the end of the Imperial era recalled that, in the national capital, "One *bought* [people of color] as one would buy a horse, a sheep, a cow or a dog" (Pinheiro 2009: 181). Slavery had been slowly declining in the late nineteenth century but was not abolished until 1888, the year before Pedro's forced abdication. Servile labor relations, sustained by violence, persisted long after abolition. It is one of the great ironies of the country's history that the Brazilian elite managed the transitions from colony to independence in 1822 and from empire to republic in 1889 without the violent upheavals that attended analogous transitions in Spanish America, all the while violently imposing itself on the day-to-day lives of Brazilians.

No provision was made for former slaves, many of whom continued to work under unchanged conditions in the same areas, even on the same plantations, as they had before abolition. Massive, government-subsidized immigration of European workers, vigorously promoted by the coffee oligarchy, undercut the economic bargaining power of both the former slaves and the large free black and mulatto population that had grown up before abolition.

Land presented a related set of issues. The republic, like the empire, did little to change the extreme concentration of farmland inherited from the colonial regime. The newly empowered state governments were quick to legalize, without cost to the beneficiaries, the holdings of those who had occupied large tracts of public land during the empire. But small farmers who opened land on the agricultural frontier in the Southeast were likely to lose it to land-hungry coffee planters, backed by lawyers, hired gunmen, and accommodating officials. In 1920, only 3 percent of the rural population held land titles; a fraction of a percent held three-quarters of the land recorded by the census (Dean 1989: 234). The exceptions to the general rule were the southern states of Rio Grande de Sul and Santa Catarina, where the empire, eager to populate a frontier region, had favored settlement by smallholders.

Despite such issues, Brazil's oligarchic republic never faced a significant challenge to its stability from below. Perhaps this was because Brazil remained, even in the contemporary Latin American context, a backward country. In the 1920s, its population was still overwhelmingly rural (84 percent), largely illiterate (76 percent), and mainly agricultural (70 percent of employed males) (Fausto 1989: 279; Topik 1987: 8). Except for the period of World War I, organized labor was not especially active. There was no national opposition party comparable to Argentina's Radical Party—in fact, no national party at all, except the tiny Brazilian Communist Party, organized in 1922. This is not to say that the Old Republic enjoyed anything like broad support. Elites in most states were resentful of a regime that marginalized them and subordinated their interests to coffee. Many intellectuals and middle-class Brazilians, especially in Rio, were critical of a system they saw as undemocratic, unpatriotic, and corrupt.

The military was increasingly disenchanted with the republic. The officer corps felt underpaid and disrespected by civilian authorities. Having defended the country in the Paraguayan War (1865–1870) and abolished the monarchy, the military had a sense of itself as the guardian of the nation, standing above a government that they regarded as barely legitimate. In the early 1920s, there were several unsuccessful revolts led by reformist younger officers, known as the *tenentes* and admired by many middle-class Brazilians. But the Old Republic, with its jerry-rigged political structure and dwindling support, would endure until 1930.

MEXICO: THE PORFIRIATO

There was no Mexican national oligarchy in the period of interest to us here, when Mexico was dominated by Porfirio Díaz. During the long years of the *Porfiriato* (1877–1910), Mexicans were subject to the rule of a privileged few, but power was dispersed across the country, among a disparate array of provincial elites.

In the far south, Yucatan was controlled by planters and exporters of henequen fiber—in particular, a tight-knit circle of thirty families known locally as the *Casta Divina* (Devine Caste), whose sumptuous mansions lined Mérida's Paseo de Montejo. First among them, by 1900, was the Molina-Montes group, led by Olegario Molina, who would become governor and serve in the national cabinet.

At the other end of the country, Chihuahua was dominated by the Terrazas clan, linked to other prominent Chihuahua families by a series of strategic marriages. The Terrazas had built an export-oriented fortune on cattle-ranching, mining (often in partnership with American investors), and banking on both sides of the border. They were the world's largest landowners and cattlemen, with holdings totaling ten million acres (Wasserman 1984: 48). Family patriarch Luís Terrazas was governor of the state for most of the period 1860 to 1884. He was forced from office after an extended political duel with Porfirio Díaz, who backed a competing Chihuahua clan. But the Terrazas' separation from political power did not halt the growth of their economic empire. After 1902, when they reconciled with Díaz and regained control of the state government, their power in Chihuahua was, as described by historian Friedrich Katz, nearly absolute.

> Anyone wishing to hold a government position, weather at local or state level, had to go through [the Terrazas]. Anyone going to court had to appeal to judges appointed by them. Anyone needing credit had to turn to banks controlled by them. Anyone seeking employment with a foreign company probably had to depend on their mediation. Anyone losing his land to a *compañía deslindadora* (surveying company) could blame them (Katz 1981: 16).

In neighboring Coahuila, three oligarchic factions competed, often violently, for statewide power. Further east in Nuevo Leon, the Monterrey oligarchy, bound together by kinship and shared investments, maintained a lower political profile. The Monterrey elite preferred to exercise its power indirectly, through alliances with sympathetic political figures, such as General Bernardo Reyes, who presided over the state, at various times, from both military and civilian positions. Taking advantage of a national economy driven by expanding international trade, the Monterrey oligarchy built a local economy that was uniquely industrial, independent of foreign capital and largely oriented toward domestic markets.

In states such as Yucatan, Chihuahua, and Nuevo Leon, the oligarchs sought political leverage to bolster entrepreneurial fortunes. The leading figures among them were shrewd investors; technological innovators; and creators of modern plantations, railroads, and factories. Governors Olegario Molina and Luís Terrazas were self-serving rulers of their states, but the Molina and Terrazas fortunes did not depend on holding formal political power—as was clearly demonstrated in the latter case by the continued success of the Terrazas in exile from politics. Elsewhere political office itself was often the path to personal wealth, as it was for General Mucio Martínez, the governor of Puebla through much of the Porfiriato. Brutal, arbitrary, and corrupt in his exercise of power, Martínez operated illegal gambling houses, pocketed money from the sale of meat and pulque monopolies, collected large kickbacks on public works projects, and looted state and municipal treasuries. He reportedly left office with close to one million pesos of state funds (LaFrance 1984: 80).

In Mexico City a powerful metropolitan oligarchy of overlapping intellectual, political, and business cliques emerged during this period. Its leading members were regime insiders, many of them identified with the *científicos*, the Porfirian brain trust led by Finance Minister José Yves Limantour. Included were Olegario Molina and Enrique Creel, a key member the Terrazas clan, who both served in the national cabinet during the late Porfiriato. From government positions, the cientificos shaped national economic policy around a vision of Mexican development that emphasized foreign investment but also, especially after 1900, favored selective tariffs to promote domestic industry. They wrote the legislation that structured banking and other important economic sectors.

Their extensive government and business connections provided the metropolitan oligarchs with ample opportunities to build personal fortunes. They were well rewarded by foreign investors, whom they served as advisors, attorneys, brokers, and board members. The financial system they created joined their own interests, as shareholders and directors of the two main national banks, to the government's fiscal requirements. The banks received a valuable monopoly over the national financial sector, and the government, in turn, got a needed line of credit. Unsurprisingly, the banks' directors, shareholders and their relatives were the institutions' principal borrowers. In the manufacturing sector, which was growing in the late Porfiriato, those with close ties to the regime were favored by easy credit, low tariffs on their inputs, and prohibitive tariffs on competing finished goods from abroad.

The cientificos had political ambitious. Above all, they hoped that one of their own might succeed Díaz. But they were technocrats with limited political talent and—with the notable exceptions of Molina and Creel—little connection to Mexico beyond the limits of the national capital. Some likely knew Paris better than any second city in their own country. These were talented men, but their political influence and business prospects hung on a single thread of uncertain strength—the connection to Porfirio Díaz.

Porfirio Díaz was the "ringmaster" of this multifaceted power circus of oligarchies, clans, and strongmen. A shrewd man of modest background and outsized ambitions, he was known to his countrymen as the general who won a celebrated victory over occupying French forces on May 5, 1862. He seized national power in 1876 with the stated intention—ironic in historical hindsight—of restoring the integrity of the electoral process.

Though his own authority over the nation was never quite absolute, Díaz was, for thirty-five years, more successful than any of his republican predecessors at imposing order on a disorderly nation. The members of the national legislature were chosen by Díaz and summarily elected. The Supreme Court was, as one contemporary critic described it, "more courtesan than court" (Knight 1986: I, 20). The governors, putatively elected in the states, were often selected by him. By conducing tightly controlled statewide elections without audible objection, governors demonstrated to Díaz and a wider elite audience that they were in command.

Díaz was a master of divide and conquer politics, using appointments to counterbalance threats to his own power and setting clans and political factions against one another, as he did with the Terrazas in Chihuahua. Toward the end of the Porfiriato, Díaz manipulated two competing national-level factions: the Cientificos and the supporters of General Reyes, a regime loyalist who had served in diverse military and civilian positions. Both groups hoped to control the succession to the aging ruler by claiming the vice presidency. Díaz undercut both but in the process encouraged other potential successors with more radical agendas.

Porfirio Díaz presided over the first sustained period of political stability and economic growth in the country's republican history. He was Mexico's president continuously from 1877 to 1911, with the exception of one term (1880–1884) served by a stand-in figure selected by him. In the preceding period of the same length, Mexico ran through some twenty presidents; almost none of whom served a full term. During the Porfiriato, GDP per capita more than doubled and exports increased sixfold. Railways increased from a negligible 570 kilometers to 20,000 kilometers with the help of foreign capital, assiduously courted by the Porfirian regime. Mining, commercial agriculture, and even manufacturing grew impressively. But in Mexico, as elsewhere in Latin America during the oligarchic era, the benefits of growth were narrowly distributed. Real wages declined and infant mortality increased. Many Mexicans, especially rural people, were the victims rather than the beneficiaries of Porfirian prosperity (Moreno-Brid and Ros 2009: chapter 3).

In the end, the Porfiriato was undone by its own achievements: economic modernization and political order. The robust expansion of commercial agriculture stimulated by growing demand and improved transportation destabilized rural society. According to a revealing study, a trail of conflicts between landowners and peasant communities ran parallel to new railway lines (Coatsworth 1974). The Porfirian state offered no protection to the rural poor. It permitted the division and sale of communal land held by peasant communities and allowed survey companies to claim untitled public lands without regard to the rights of small cultivators who had occupied them, sometimes for generations. In densely populated central and southern Mexico, powerful landowners, such as the sugar planters of Morelos, appropriated most of the communal land that had sustained peasant villages since colonial times. The result in the south was the 1910 peasant uprising led by Emiliano Zapata that began in Morelos and soon spread to nearby states. In the north, the rebellion led by Pancho Villa was set off by the growing capacity of well-funded, federal and state governments to impose themselves in previously remote areas. Especially in Chihuahua, under the restored Terrazas regime, rising taxation, land issues, and unwelcome interference in local government had provoked a traditionally independent rural people, who were already armed and comfortable in the saddle.

In 1907, a sharp economic downturn had contributed to a gathering crisis. Mexico's bigger, more integrated, more export-oriented economy was inevitably more vulnerable and turbulent than it had been in the early days of the Porfiriato. At the same time, a growing sector of the elite, excluded from power—especially in the north—was turning against the regime. The source of this elite alienation was the concentration of power in the tight, unchanging circle of men around Díaz in Mexico City and the governors he licensed to run their states as private fiefdoms. Middle-class support for the regime was also waning.

Díaz resisted advisers who urged him to find a way to institutionalize his regime and assure its continuity beyond his own lifetime. In a candid letter to Díaz, Education Secretary Justo Sierra warned, "There are no institutions in the Republic of Mexico. Only a man" (Krauze 1998: 231). Díaz, who in 1910 at age eighty, was a candidate for an eighth presidential term, obviously intended to hang on to power until called to eternal rest. Political stability rested on a narrow, precarious foundation.

DEFINING OLIGARCHY

I have portrayed the "oligarchies" in five countries, without defining the term beyond the observation in the Introduction that this was the label contemporaries applied to them. Classical understanding of oligarchy emphasized connection between wealth and power—in particular, the domination of the many poor by the wealthy few.[5] In a recent, influential book, titled simply *Oligarchy*, Winters (2011) defines extreme concentration of wealth as the essential basis of oligarchic power. His concept is relative. The material wealth of the oligarchs is colossal in comparison with that of average people in their society. In his conception, the oligarchs may rule directly and openly or exercise their power less visibly. They may act collectively to defend their interests or more individually. Historical situations vary. But oligarchy exists, according to Winters, wherever there are vast differentials in wealth, as there certainly were in Latin American during the Old Regime.

In the mid-1970s, I asked some well-informed Peruvian observers to define the oligarchy and name the oligarchs. Their responses, which are the basis of the list of oligarchic families in the last chapter (table 1.1), revolved around the idea of small group of families who built political power on economic power. One interviewee whose own family was generally counted as part of oligarchy defined the oligarchs as people who employ economic power politically and use politics to get rich.

For the purposes of this book I want to adopt an ad hoc definition, which is consistent with Winters' but more specific. The Latin American oligarchies were (1) the region's ascendant classes in the late nineteenth and early twentieth centuries that (2) accumulated great wealth in this period by direct or indirect connection with the export economy and (3) had a privileged relationship to the state. There is leeway in phrases like "direct and indirect connection" and "privileged relationship." This is intentional and points to dimensions on which these five oligarchies differed and changed over time. More problematic is the matter of boundaries: How big were the oligarchies? Who was rich and powerful enough to be considered part of the oligarchy? From country to country, the number of oligarchic families ranged from a few dozen to a few hundred. The Peruvian oligarchy was on the low end of this scale. The Argentinian and Chilean oligarchies were likely on the high end. There were surely families in every country that were on the margins of the oligarchy, perhaps because they were just consolidating their fortunes or in the process of losing them. But, especially in the early years of the oligarchic republics, even those at the lower limits of oligarchic wealth and power were, as Winters would note, sharply distinguished from the impoverished, politically irrelevant mass of the population.

COMPARING THE OLIGARCHIC REPUBLICS

The oligarchic republics were built on the wealth that flowed from the production of primary products for the industrializing nations of the North—wealth that became the basis of large family fortunes, revitalized economies, and more powerful states. They prevailed in Latin America in the interval between the postindependence era of weak states and languishing economies and the time of contested republics, when the oligarchs faced significant challenges from below.

Table 2.3 profiles the five oligarchies and oligarchic republics. The dates given refer to the political events—crises, coups, elections, new constitutions—that framed the era of oligarchic ascendance. They indicate that the typical oligarchic republic (defined earlier as the period when the oligarchs ruled openly, directly, and more or less exclusively) endured for around thirty-five years, beginning in the late nineteenth century and ending in the early twentieth. Chapter 3 will compare developments that brought each of the oligarchic republics to an end and trace the continuing influence of the oligarchs in the contested republics.

SOURCES OF OLIGARCHIC WEALTH

Land exploited for export production was the key to most oligarchic fortunes. The Aspíllagas' north coast sugar plantation, the Terrazas' vast cattle ranches in Chihuahua, and the Anchorenas' extensive holdings on the pampas are prime examples. Latifundismo, the polarized distribution of land, was a legacy of the colonial era carried into republican times and exacerbated by renewed competition for land in the oligarchic era. In all but a few areas, family-sized farms were the exception. Under the impulse of growing external demand and improved transportation, new land was opened for commercial exploitation across the region in the late nineteenth century. This was accomplished in Argentina through the forced removal of the nomadic

Table 2.3. The Oligarchic Republics

	Sources of Wealth	Rural Society	The Oligarchic State
PERU 1895–1919 "Aristocratic Republic"	Control of coastal land and water. Sugar, cotton plantations. Banks. Mines.	Concentration of plantations on coast insulates oligarchy from conflict with land-holding Indian communities in the Sierra.	Oligarchic control of executive. Powerful president. Congress shared w/ Sierra landowners. Small electorate. Elections managed by intimidation and fraud.
CHILE 1891–1925 "Parliamentary Republic"	Central valley land. Also, mining, banks.	Central valley land-holding highly concentrated. Quasi-feudal control of inquilinos. Floating population of seasonally employed peons.	Oligarchic control of government via Congress dominated by central valley land owners. Weak presidency. Institutionalized competition among (elite controlled) parties. Blocs of voters controlled by landowners and regional firms. Urban vote buying.
BRAZIL 1894–1930 "Old Republic"	Land. Coffee plantations. In São Paulo oligarchs invest in urban, industrial economy.	Land-holding concentrated, especially in newer coffee areas. Servile labor relations, a legacy of slavery. Immigrants reduce bargaining power of rural labor.	Oligarchies of wealthiest states, especially São Paulo, dominate central government. "Colonels" manage patron-client relationships, deliver local vote.
MEXICO 1877–1910 "Porfiriato"	Land (henequen, cattle, sugar, etc.). Banks. Manufacturing in Monterrey.	Tensions over appropriation of Indian communal land for commercial ag. Seizures of untitled land under survey laws. Abusive authorities alienate people in rural north.	National government dominated by Díaz. Powerful state and metropolitan oligarchies, clans, and strongmen. Highly controlled elections—even elite competition minimized.
ARGENTINA 1880–1916 Oligarchic Rule	Land on the pampas. Cattle, cereals, wool. Finance, trade.	Indigenous population eliminated from pampas, opening new land for cultivation, but land concentration remains high. Transient rural labor force of immigrant tenants and sharecroppers.	Pampas/Buenos Aires oligarchy shares national power with provincial elites. Rule through PAN, a loose coalition. Powerful presidency. Roca dominant figure until 1904. Elections managed by governors. Votes bought, voters intimidated, outcomes falsified.

indigenous population from the pampas (Roca's "Conquest of the Desert") and in central and southern Mexico by the appropriation of Indian communal land. In Brazil, public land on the southern agricultural frontier was titled to coffee planters, often after it was brought under cultivation by small farmers.

Chile presented a revealing variation on the usual pattern. In the second half of the nineteenth century, the landed families of the central valley were insulated from the continuing struggle against nomadic Indians in the South and able to take advantage of new export opportunities. Even after they withdrew their own production from the increasingly competitive international market, they continued to benefit from the export economy.

Some oligarchic clans built their fortunes in mining, among them the Fernandinis, Mujicas, and Rizo Patróns in Peru and the Ossas and Cousiños in Chile. Landowning families often invested in mining, even if it was not their primary economic base. Over time, foreign capital came to control the largest mining operations, most notably the enormous iron and copper mines in Peru and Chile. But the oligarchs were not eliminated from the sector. They continued to operate smaller mines, profited by selling their claims to foreign companies, and invested in foreign-controlled mines. Members of oligarchic families served foreign mining firms in various lucrative capacities.

A few oligarchic fortunes were based on urban enterprises, prospering indirectly from the export-driven economy. Especially important were the banking families, including the Prados in Peru and the Subercaseaux family in Chile. The prominence of planters on the board of the Prados' Banco Popular and the extensive landholdings of the Subercaseaux point to the importance of land and exports to banking in the oligarchic era. The wealth of the Monterrey oligarchy, an exceptional case, was built on manufacturing, largely for the domestic market, but that market would certainly have been much smaller, and the Monterrey fortunes correspondingly reduced, without the stimulus of Mexico's rapidly growing export sector. Over time, the oligarchs tended to become more and more invested in the urban economy, as the Chilean landowners did after the export potential of their land declined. In São Paulo, a vibrant industrial sector developed out of collaboration between coffee planters and immigrant entrepreneurs. Social ties, reflected in club memberships and marriages, also linked oligarchic families with urban and rural fortunes.

THE RURAL SETTING

The character of the rural setting was critical for oligarchic wealth and power. For better or for worse, the oligarchs were subject to the raw facts of geography and demography in the countryside. The expansion of commercial agriculture during the Porfiriato was a destabilizing force in the countryside, especially in densely populated central and southern Mexico, where the appropriation of Indian communal land ultimately provoked a violent revolt.

The consolidation of plantations on the Peruvian coast in late nineteenth and early twentieth centuries engendered disputes with local farmers and communities over land, water rights, and other issues. It is no coincidence that APRA, the populist party that would later challenge oligarchic power, was strongest in the areas dominated by export agriculture—especially the northern sugar-producing region. But the coast was thinly settled. Peru's population and its Indian communities were concentrated in the Sierra, so planters were spared the conflicts over communal land that were so explosive in Mexico. For the same reason, the planters could not meet their labor needs locally and were compelled to depend first on African slaves, then on Chinese coolies ("semislaves," as the Aspíllagas described them), and finally on peasants recruited from Sierra.

In Argentina, after the 1880 "Conquest of the Desert," landowners on the pampas were wholly free of indigenous resistance to their expansion. They had to depend on immigrant labor, but their labor needs, especially for sheep and cattle raising, were modest. The inquilinos on the estates of Chile's central valley provided a near captive source of labor and a political base that bolstered oligarchic political power well into the twentieth century.

As chapter 3 will show, differences in access to land, labor, and electors in the countryside influenced the histories of the oligarchies, with outcomes as varied as Mexico, where revolution swept away the oligarchic order, and Chile, where oligarchic power endured into the 1960s.

THE OLIGARCHIC STATE

In the oligarchic republics, rising export revenue empowered and stabilized governments. With the resources to support standing armies (more on this topic in chapter 3) and vastly improved internal communications, they were no longer vulnerable to caudillo upstarts and better able to impose themselves on unruly populations. The oligarchic republics had three other basic features in common: (1) They were committed to export-driven development, (2) they favored the interests of the oligarchs, and (3) they excluded all but a tiny elite minority from political participation.

But there were consequential differences in their political structures. Peru could be considered the ideal type: The Aristocratic Republic was dominated by exporters, and presidents were typically chosen from the wealthiest of the export producers, the sugar planters. In Brazil's Old Republic, presidents were most often coffee planters, but they were selected by the oligarchies of just two states, São Paulo and Minas, much to the resentment of other state elites. In Chile's Parliamentary Republic, presidents were relatively powerless; the landed oligarchy of the central valley (formerly exporters who continued to benefit from the export economy) ruled from the Congress. Argentina's Buenos Aires/pampas oligarchy and Mexico's disparate state elites did not monopolize power. In these cases the oligarchic state was organized by sympathetic but independent figures drawn from the military, who ruled in close collaboration with the oligarchs.

The oligarchic republics maintained the trappings of liberal democracy. The press was relatively free and not infrequently critical of governments. Opposition parties were typically represented in the legislature. The armed forces usually remained aloof from politics. Elections were held regularly. But their outcomes were, in most cases, foreordained and popular participation was minimal and meaningless. By various formal mechanisms, such as the exclusion of illiterates, women, and immigrants (who comprised the larger part of the working class in Argentina and southern Brazil), most people were legally denied the vote, leaving only 2 to 6 percent of national populations enfranchised during the oligarchic era (Drake 2009: 146). Whatever small, independent influence these voters might have claimed was thwarted by a variety of informal mechanisms, including the control of whole blocs of voters through patron–client relationships, intimidation and violence, vote buying, voting by persons dead or fictitious, the manipulation of voter lists, and fraudulent reporting of results.

But elections were not irrelevant. They represented a more or less peaceful form of competition among oligarchic factions and provincial elites and provided a basis, however questionable, for claims of legitimacy by the elected leaders of oligarchic regimes. Such claims strengthened the potentially subversive notion that popular election was the legitimate basis for power in a republic. Over time, governments came under increasing pressure—especially from the growing middle class—to widen the franchise and eliminate the practices that had debased it. But the oligarchic republics rested on political exclusion. They could not survive electoral reform, as the political transformation of Argentina in the wake of the 1912 Sáez Peña laws would soon demonstrate.

NOTES

1. These events are presented in more revealing detail in chapter 4.
2. McGann 1957: 25. See also Botano 174–189 and Rock 1975: 27.
3. Rock 1975, 2002; Gallo 1993; Remmer 1984.
4. Pedro II was a vestige of Brazil's unique path to independence In 1807, the Portuguese monarch Pedro I, Pedro II's father, threatened with imminent invasion by Napoleon's army, transferred his court to Rio de Janeiro, with the help of the British navy. In 1822 he severed his official ties to Portugal and established an independent Brazilian monarchy.
5. See Winters 2011: 26–27 and Adler et al. 1952.

3

The Contested Republics

It is impossible to govern with the masses.
Every government must neutralize them.

—Peruvian oligarch

History is a graveyard of aristocracies.

—Vilfredo Pareto

The medieval towers that rise over many northern Italian cities are relics of the oligarchic republics that once predominated in the region and reminders of their political fragility. For all their charm, they are military structures built, not to defend the city-state against its external enemies but to protect oligarchic families and factions from one another. Intraelite conflict was endemic and destabilizing in these cities. The level of distrust was such that often the only solution was to hire a dictator-administrator known as a *podesta* to impose order. The typical podesta was a "citizen noble" with legal training, from another city-state, free of any connection to internal factions. He served for a limited contractual period, but the demand was so great that some men made a career of *podesteria,* moving from post to post (Waley 1969: 66–74, 170–182).

Men like Porfirio Díaz and Julio Roca might be compared to podestas presiding over divided elites. Oligarchic republics are fragile polities. Most of the Italian republics gave way to "tyrannies," rule by a self-serving strongman or dominant clan. The oligarchic republics of the Old Regime in Latin America were similarly vulnerable.

THE PASSING OF THE OLD REGIME

To observers of Latin America in 1900 or even 1912, when the English writer James Bryce toured South America, the oligarchic republics must have appeared impressively strong. The oligarchs were wealthy, cultured, and confident. They controlled critical resources and were sustained by robust economies and well-financed states. But the oligarchic regimes were threatened both from within and without. From within, because of conflict among the oligarchs. From without, because new political actors gradually emerged to challenge them.

As the last two chapters have shown, elite cohesion in the oligarchic republics was rooted in the social bonds of elite society and in shared material interests, but increasingly endangered by factional conflict and individual ambitions. Division among the Peruvian oligarchs in 1912 had split the Civilista Party, opening the way to the short-lived presidency of protopopulist Guillermo Billinghurst. In Brazil, the state oligarchies of São Paulo and Minas Gerais dominated the national government to the inevitable resentment of the other state elites. The Paulistas were drawn together by a dense kinship network, but socially isolated from elite peers elsewhere. In northern Mexico, out of power elite families were resentful of their treatment by Díaz. The Argentine elite was divided over how to respond to pressure to open the political system.

By the second decade of the twentieth century, the power of the oligarchs over their societies was not quite what it seemed. Power is relational—a political actor is powerful in relation to potential opponents. Initially, the oligarchs were all powerful, because others were weak. They were like animals set loose (in this case by the world economy) in an environment devoid of natural predators. In the beginning, their world was largely populated by Indians, mestizos, and ex-slaves, living in isolated rural communities, on haciendas or on plantations—people who were poor, illiterate, and effectively disenfranchised. An odor of political illegitimacy hung over this world, as a result of the gross disparity between liberal constitutions and illiberal practice, but no one who mattered seemed to notice.

Over time, the export development promoted by the oligarchs was creating a new world, more urban, more literate, more interconnected. With it came expanding middle and working classes and professionalized, independent militaries, all potential threats to oligarchic power. The political tensions that arose in this transformed environment exacerbated divisions among the oligarchs and opened alluring paths to power for some among them.

By the early 1930s, the oligarchic republics had been displaced by new systems of power as varied as the right-wing military regime in Peru and the Mexican Revolution. As this chapter will show, oligarchic power did not vanish with the oligarchic republics, but survived in a new, more contentious world here labeled the contested republics. In this era, the power of the oligarchs, though still formidable, was challenged by organized opposition and was necessarily exercised less overtly. The life spans of the contested republics varied from two years to several decades. But finally, under circumstances that differed from country to country, the oligarchy ceased to be a significant force in affairs of these nations, marking the end of the Old Regime in Latin America.

CHANGING CLASS STRUCTURE

By 1930, Buenos Aires, Rio de Janeiro, and Mexico City, each over a million inhabitants, were among the world's largest cities. The populations of Santiago, Lima, and São Paulo were in the hundreds of thousands and growing rapidly. Nationally, Chile and Argentina had attained levels of urbanization comparable to the United States and Western Europe; nearly 40 percent of Argentines and one third of Chileans lived in a city over 20,000 (United Nations 1969: 106, 112). Urbanization and export growth propelled economic diversification. The era saw rising employment in transportation, commerce, finance, government, and, by the early twentieth century, manufacturing. Hundreds of thousands of miners, plantation workers, railway men, meatpackers, stevedores, construction workers, textile workers, bakers, and tailors were added to the working class—its expansion in Argentina and southern Brazil accelerated by policies encouraging large scale immigration. At the same time, a modern middle class was taking form, with growing numbers of white-collar workers, including civil servants, teachers, journalists, merchants, lawyers, doctors, engineers, and other professionals.

The old postcolonial class structure of *gente decente* and *pueblo*—a tiny elite of "decent people" and an impoverished, generally rural majority—was being replaced by something more complex and less predictable. Early on, members of the developing working and middle classes had little sense of belonging to distinct social classes with defined interests. Many middle-class men and women, distinguished from the popular majority by their superior education and relatively higher income, identified with the elite. Workers might identify with the common people (*el pueblo*) or the "poor" or think of themselves in ethnic terms, especially if they worked in small scale, informal settings and were not connected to militant labor or political organizations. Over time, however, large sectors of these new groups would become more class conscious and demanding. Their concentration in distinctively middle-class and working-class neighborhoods, mining areas, and transportation hubs contributed to this process.

From the perspective of the oligarchs, the growth of the working and middle classes potentially threatened the established order—all the more so because they were clustered in the cities. Urban people are harder to control. The literate middle sectors of society, including the rising numbers of middle-class students at the region's universities and the recently professionalized officer corps, formed a growing audience for critical discussion of the status quo. Workers in the biggest cities or massed around mines, ports, railyards, and plantations were natural targets for labor organizers and often participants in strikes and street protests. The oligarchs were increasingly concerned with, and often at odds over, "the social question."

THE WORKING CLASS[1]

Workers associated with the export economy, including meat packers, miners, and rail workers were prominent in the early development of the Latin American labor movement. The 1890s and the initial years of the twentieth century saw the first wave of working-class protest, often inspired by militant European movements and ideologies such as anarchism and anarcho-syndicalism. (Later, Marxism and pragmatic concern with workplace and wage issues would shape the Latin American labor movement.) A second wave swept across the region during and just after World War I, a period of large-scale, often violent labor confrontations, set off by a wartime wage-price squeeze and the example of the 1917 Russian Revolution. Labor activism generally waned in the 1920s but recovered in the 1930s.

Argentina, followed by Chile, had the largest working-class and the most formidable labor movement. By the 1890s, there were at least two dozen unions in Buenos Aires and many others in smaller cities. A national labor confederation was organized in 1901. The labor movement was aggressive, growing rapidly, and often successful. During the period 1907–1913, workers in Buenos Aires won at least partial victories in 40 percent of 1,082 strikes (Hall and Spalding 1986: 345). Sometimes local strikes with limited objectives turned into paralyzing general strikes that spread from city to city.

A tragic chain of events in Buenos Aires beginning with the 1909 May Day demonstration revealed Argentina's potential for violent class conflict. The May Day observance, which brought out tens of thousands of workers, was violently repressed by the police. In retaliation, an anarchist assassinated the city's chief of police. When labor activists subsequently threatened to disrupt the independence centennial celebration with a general strike, mobs of mainly upper-class youth smashed union and leftist newspaper offices and rampaged through Jewish neighborhoods. Then a bomb was set off at the Buenos Aires opera, without doing great damage, but providing justification for repressive new regulation of union activity. A similar series of violent confrontations culminated in the 1919 *Semana Tragica* (Tragic Week), when hundreds were killed and thousands injured in the streets of Buenos Aires.

Chile's working class, large in relation to the country's modest population, was notable for its militancy. The country's early labor history, centered in mining enclaves and transportation hubs, was marked by frequent strikes and deadly confrontations. In 1903, Army and Naval troops crushed a dock workers strike in Valparaiso, with a loss of a hundred lives. The death toll was several times higher in 1907, when the army machine-gunned striking nitrate miners and their families in the port of Iquique. Despite these brutal tactics, labor won some victories. Unions were successful about half of the two hundred strikes between 1902 and 1908 (DeSchazo in Collier and Sater 2004: 196). Labor activism surged in Chile after 1917. For two months in 1919, Santiago and the port of Valparaiso were under a state of siege declared by the government to contain union-organized protests over high food prices. But the protests, which had already spread to other cities, continued. The Chilean labor movement had gained a momentum that carried it well beyond the crisis created by the Great War.

Brazil, Peru, and Mexico were backward countries relative to Argentina and Chile, with lower per capita incomes, lower literacy rates, and lower levels of urbanization (see table 2.1). Their early labor movements were correspondingly smaller and less sustained, but not insignificant. The Brazilian labor movement was strongest in Rio, São Paulo, and its port Santos, especially during the first two decades of the twentieth century. Labor militancy and state repression peaked during and immediately after the war, but union activity dropped off sharply in the 1920s. Peruvian labor unions were active from the 1890s in Lima and the port of Callao, but weak in the mining and plantation enclaves where they would flourish a generation later. In the last months of the oligarchic republic, striking workers in Lima forced the government to establish an eight-hour workday. A general strike in the wake of the disputed 1919 election contributed to the collapse of the Aristocratic Republic.

The Porfiriato brought notable expansion of employment in mining, railroads, and manufacturing (especially textiles) in Mexico. Despite official repression, labor unions were active in these sectors. Brutal responses to strikes in 1906 and 1907 undercut the regime's legitimacy. When workers in the American-owned Cananga copper mine went on strike in 1906 over multiple grievances, authorities imported armed Arizona Rangers from across the border to defend the company. Subsequently, a contingent of Mexican Rurales arrived, rounded up the presumed leaders of the strike, and summarily hung them. It seemed to many Mexicans that the government was more intent on protecting the interests of foreigners than the lives of its own citizens. A few months later, troops fired on strikers at the Rio Blanco textile mills in Veracruz state, killing dozens of workers.

The Brazilian, Peruvian, and Mexican cases all suggest that even where modern working classes were small relative to the national population, their concentration at sensitive locations and their actions at critical historical junctures could magnify their influence.

The oligarchic republics regarded union activity as criminal and thus "a matter for the police" or, in the worst cases, the military. Governments were especially sensitive to activity that threatened the export economy, such as strikes in mining, meatpacking, or transportation.

Because the Argentine working class was largely immigrant and its leadership identified with exotic foreign doctrines, elite propaganda could brand labor activity as unpatriotic and incite violent, xenophobic attacks on workers and their organizations. The antiworker rampage that grew out of the 1909 May Day demonstration was a prime example.

Occasionally governments attempted informal mediation of strikes, but, during this period, none created a regulatory framework for labor matters. As the examples above suggest, the most typical regime response to working-class protest movements was repressive violence. Quieter measures included the infiltration of working-class organizations by police spies and *agents provocateurs*, summary deportation of foreign-born leaders deemed subversive, and (especially in Mexico and Brazil) the internal exile of activists to remote work-detention camps, from which many would never return. Depending on where and when, these policies continued into the contested republics.

In none of these countries did working-class movements contribute directly to the demise of the oligarchic republic. But disagreement over how to manage "the social question" contributed to conflict among the oligarchs, which weakened their rule. In Argentina, and Chile, elites divided over proposals to open the political system in the hope of countering the working-class threat with middle-class support. In Peru and Mexico, labor crises in the period preceding the end of the oligarchic republic added to a sense of impending collapse that inevitably encouraged enemies of these regimes. Nothing like that happened in Brazil, where the labor movement had still not recovered the momentum of the war years when the Old Republic crumbled in 1930.

THE MIDDLE CLASS[2]

By the early years of the twentieth century, thriving economies, growing state sectors, and swelling cities had created the basis for a modern middle class in the more developed countries of Latin America. Argentina and Chile had the region's largest middle classes. In these two countries, reformist politicians would draw on middle-class electoral support to challenge the oligarchic republics. The other three countries had much smaller middle classes and closed political systems that still shielded oligarchic rule from any electoral challenge.

The Argentine middle class, by one estimate, accounted for one third of the labor force in 1914 (Smith 1974: 8), but its political presence was only starting to be felt. One area of growing tension was higher education. Enrollment at the universities in Buenos Aires and two other cities climbed from 3,000 to 14,000 between 1900 and 1918 (Rock 1993b: 152). The universities were run by and for the upper class, with archaic curricula, and faculties that reflected elite nepotism. But the typical student was the son of a shopkeeper or petty industrialist, who aspired to professional status and was frustrated with the institutional status quo. In 1918, a student reform movement at the University of Cordoba succeeded in making the university more democratic and autonomous. The success of the Cordoba movement inspired students in universities across the region.

The Chilean middle class was, by reputation, more interested in imitating the elite than in challenging it—so much so, that the Chilean lexicon evolved a special disparaging term for middle-class people who assume upper-class airs: *siúticos* (Pike 1963: 22). But, in the early twentieth century, many middle-class Chileans were both unhappy with oligarchic domination of the political system and frightened by working-class militancy. The oligarchy could not control the largely urban middle-class electorate as it did the rural poor. The growing political influence of the middle class was reflected in the successful campaign to secure passage of a 1914 municipal reform law designed to reduce electoral fraud. The law produced mixed results, but probably had the effect of increasing the political weight of the middle-class vote. Chilean university students, increasingly radicalized, were becoming a political force. In 1906, the national student federation forced the resignation of the head of the medical school at the University of Chile and in 1910 compelled the unpopular papal nuncio to leave the country. In what must have been an alarming development for the ruling elite, students began supporting the labor movement. In September 1919, the student federation backed a one-day general strike in Santiago.

The growth of Peru's middle class was reflected in the creation of a white-collar workers' union in 1903 and the rapid increase of university and normal school enrollments. Militant white-collar unionists and university students pressed the government and employers for reforms in the last years of the Aristocratic Republic. In Mexico, by the turn of the century, 8 percent of the population could be considered middle class, and distinctly middle-class neighborhoods had appeared in Mexico City. In 1907, Porfirio Díaz told an American reporter that Mexico had developed a middle class, which he considered the key to the country's future (Iturriaga 1951: 28, 65–66). While many middle-class Mexicans credited Díaz with bringing peace and progress to Mexico, middle-class enthusiasm for the aging dictator was waning by the early 1900s. Similarly, much of the Brazilian middle-class, concentrated in Rio, was unhappy with a regime that was corrupt, exclusionary, and narrowly based on one or two state oligarchies. In both Brazil and Mexico, growing middle-class disaffection was articulated by middle-class intellectuals. Their critiques helped prepare the ground for a decisive coup in Brazil and an armed revolution in Mexico.

THE MILITARY[3]

The export revenue of the oligarchic era enabled Latin American countries to build their first truly national armies. State financed, standing armies replaced the destabilizing caudillo-led forces of the early nineteenth century. Initially, the officers were men with limited formal preparation, recruited and advanced on the basis of family or personal connections. Socially and politically close to the ruling elite, they could be relied on to defend oligarchic rule. Later, the officer corps would become more professional and independent.

By the early twentieth century, the oligarchic regimes were modernizing their militaries, at a pace that varied from country to country. As they often did, the oligarchs looked to Europe for models of modernity. Advanced weaponry was imported from Germany and France. New military schools were established, and German or French missions were contracted to create a professional, technically proficient officer corps. Armies were transformed into rule-driven, pyramidal bureaucracies, in which advancement presumably depended on professional competence, determined by military superiors, free from the influence of civilian outsiders. That, at least, was the guiding ideal. As militaries modernized, officers increasingly became identified with their institution, isolated from civilian life, and inclined to regard themselves as the true, patriotic, representatives of the nation. The early modernizing Brazilian military acted on this presumption when it toppled the monarchy in 1889, inaugurating the oligarchic republic. Officers saw themselves as morally superior to the corrupt, self-serving civilian elites of the Old Regime, an attitude epitomized by the backhanded compliment a Chilean military officer offered to a cabinet member in a 1924 letter:

> Even though you . . . represent for us the most disgusting element in our country—politicians—that is, all that is corrupt, the dismal factional disputes, depravities and immoralities, in other words, the causes of our national degeneration, we recognize that you, despite the fact that you must defend sinecures, hand out public posts and support avaricious ambitions, that you are one of the few honest politicians (Loveman 1988: 192).

Although military leaders generally regarded themselves as apolitical or above politics, they were increasingly drawn into political affairs. In some cases militaries defended the oligarchy, as when they toppled reformist governments in Peru (1914 and 1948) and in Argentina (1930). In others, they supported the enemies of oligarchic power, as they did in Chile (1924–1925) and Brazil (1930–1932). Ambitious politicians, especially the leaders of emerging middle-class parties, courted military support, often fomenting division in the officer corps. In Argentina, Chile, Brazil, and Peru groups of younger officers conspired against oligarchic rule, usually without success. From 1890 to 1905, small groups of the Argentine officers supported a series of failed insurrections organized by the emerging Radical Party. In Brazil during the 1920s, a group of reform-minded younger officers known as the *tenentes* (lieutenants) revolted repeatedly against the Old Republic. On occasion—most notably in Peru in 1968—the military intervened with the intention of imposing its own program of national transformation.

Mexico was a special case. Porfirio Díaz, a military man who became president by armed rebellion, kept his army on a short leash. Loyalty counted more than ability. Díaz banished his talented minister of war, General Bernardo Reyes, to a comfortable civilian post, apparently to separate him from a growing following in the officer corps. He reduced the size of the army and cut the military budget. The Porfirian army, with the help of a mounted constabulary, the *Rurales*, was sufficient for the routine maintenance of order, but would prove inadequate to counter a national rebellion with multiple fronts. The army was destroyed in the 1910 Revolution and replaced by multiple, competing revolutionary forces. It would be years before a modern, centrally controlled, national army would emerge.

FIVE HERETICS AND THE END OF THE OLIGARCHIC REPUBLICS

As they aged and the world changed around them, the oligarchic regimes did not adapt. Attempts at reform from above proved divisive and generally failed. The labor reforms promoted in Peru by Pardo during his first term (1904–1908) might have dampened the labor conflicts that later undermined the Aristocratic Republic, but they were blocked in the Congress by conservatives from his Civilista Party. Argentina's 1912 electoral reform laws were passed after a long struggle that strained the oligarchy's already factionalized political vehicle, the PAN. In 1916, PAN was not even able unite behind a candidate to run against opposition leader Hipólito Yrigoyen, who won the presidency under the new rules. In Mexico, an aging Porfirio Díaz seemed oblivious to the strains the regime's rural policies were creating the countryside. He installed governors, like the heavy-handed Pablo Escandón in Morelos, who only exacerbated social tensions, and rehabilitated the abusive Terrazas family in Chihuahua. In 1909, approaching eighty and certain of reelection, Díaz spurned the best chance he would ever have to assure the survival of the regime beyond his own lifetime, by suppressing the movement to nominate General Bernardo Reyes for his vice president (and likely successor). Reyes was an able administrator, a shrewd politician, and, most important, the one Porfirian stalwart with a national middle-class following. But he was opposed by the Científico faction and unwilling to confront Díaz.

Reyes would not take the step that his compatriot Francisco Madero would take, as would Augusto Leguía in Peru, Arturo Alessandri in Chile, Hipóito Yrigoyen in Argentina, and Getúlio Vargas in Brazil. These men broke with the oligarchic regimes to become presidents of transformed, more inclusive republics. Ironically, each of them had a stake in the system he helped to destroy. They were men with private fortunes ranging from comfortable to colossal. Judging by kinship and marriage ties and elite club memberships, most, if not all, were connected to upper-class society prior to entering politics. With the exception of Francisco Madero, all had held high political office under the oligarchic republic. Yet all were, in some way, socially or politically marginal to the world of the oligarchs. They were from an out of favor family, a marginalized region, or an inferior (middle-class, provincial, or immigrant) background. And all came to understand that their societies were changing and that social change was opening new political opportunities. They were political innovators and opportunists who courted popular support and became enemies of their own class, despised by their peers. None sought a radical transformation of society, but they radically changed national politics.

Clockwise from the upper left, Presidents Vargas, Madero, Yrigoyen, and Alessandri, who undermined their countries' oligarchic republics. Leguia, the fifth of the renegade presidents, is pictured in chapter 4.

Source: Public Domain.

MEXICO: MADERO

In his 1908 political manifesto, Francisco Madero confessed, "I belong by birth to the privileged class. [N]either I nor any other member of my family have cause for complaint against General Díaz" (Kandell 1988: 393). The Maderos were certainly among the wealthiest families in Mexico. Their relations with the regime were overtly friendly. But there was, in fact, some cause for complaint. In the early 1880s, Diaz had consolidated his power in the North by forcing several regional clans, including the Terrazas and the Maderos, out of power in their states. Like the Terrazas, the Maderos continued to prosper. Unlike the Terrazas, they had never been returned to office. There were other northern oligarchs who had been similarly marginalized. Some would become revolutionaries. Madero, in other words, emerged from a family and elite ambience colored by resentments toward the Porfirian regime. His presidential campaign attracted the middle-class Mexicans who had recently been drawn to General Reyes. Maderismo, observes historian Alan Knight, "was the expression of a rising middle class . . . demanding its place in the political sun" (Knight 1986: I, 63). Madero did not, however, represent the more radical, agrarian side of the opposition to the regime. Jailed for daring to run against Díaz in 1910, Madero escaped, fled to Texas, and called for armed rebellion. The dictator's resignation and Madero's election to the presidency in 1911 signaled the end of the oligarchic republic, but only the beginning of the Mexican Revolution and a long fight against the remnants of oligarchic power.

PERU: LEGUÍA

Augusto Leguía was a self-made man of provincial middle-class origins, who had won his way into oligarchic circles by talent and charm. Admitted to the elite Club Nacional before the age of 30, he had married well, and accumulated a sizable fortune in the key oligarchic sectors of coastal agriculture and finance. He saw his daughters married into prominent upper-class families, the Ayulos, the Chopiteas, and the Larrañagas.

At the beginning of his political career, Leguía was a protégée of José Pardo. He sided with Pardo on the issues dividing the Civilistas, served in Pardo's cabinet, and was Prado's chosen successor in 1908. Some of the conservative old guard, proud of their aristocratic lineages, were displeased with the nomination of this parvenu. For his part, Leguía had never felt comfortable with these men, whom he openly scorned. But Leguía had been an effective finance minister and loyal party member. With Pardo's support, he was easily elected.

During his presidency (1908–1912), Leguía alienated most of the Civilista elite by his personalistic, self-aggrandizing methods. By the time he launched his candidacy for second presidential term in 1919, he had cut himself off from the men who had once been his companions at the Club Nacional. He now presented himself as the antioligarch.

Leguía had seen the popular street protests that helped bring Billinghurst to power in 1912. He had learned a valuable lesson from the striking workers and the increasingly politicized middle-class university students. Here were fresh social bases for political power, on which he could build a new regime. His Civilista opponent in 1919 was Antero Aspíllaga, a man with limited popular appeal, who, it will be recalled, had lost to Billinghurst in 1912. The election took place in the turbulent wake of World War I, a period of massive, sometimes violent strikes in Lima, paralleled by a radicalized student protest movement at the national university. Leguía found sympathizers among the workers, the students (who named him their 1918 "Mentor of Youth"), and, as it turned out, among the soldiers. When Leguía's victory was questioned in a series of court decisions, he seized power in a coup d'état. During his eleven year dictatorship (known to Peruvians as the *Oncenio*), members of many oligarchic families including the Aspíllagas, the Prados, the Miró Quesadas, and Pardos were forced into exile. Those who remained were barred from politics.

CHILE: ALESSANDRI

Arturo Alessandri's grandfather was an Italian immigrant who had come to Chile in 1821 and accumulated a healthy fortune. His father was a wealthy landowner, and Arturo grew up on the family estate. Despite the family's success, the Alessandris could not claim a secure position within the Chilean elite: Their roots were not deep enough, their money not big enough, and their social connections not exclusive enough (Vial Correa 1981: V. 3, 38–41). Nonetheless, Arturo married into an aristocratic Santiago family, became a successful lawyer, and served several unremarkable terms as a deputy with one of the traditional oligarchic parties. In 1915, he won a northern senate seat in an upset victory, by appealing to working-class and middle-class voters. In the wake of this unexpected triumph, Alessandri made no secret of his presidential ambitions, in violation of the discretion expected of gentleman politicians in the oligarchic era. He was the one national figure who grasped the political opportunity created by a changing society. Alessandri must have been encouraged by the passionate responses he evoked from audiences during the senate campaign. He is remembered as a mesmerizing speaker, who presented himself as the champion of the unrepresented masses. "I want to be a threat to the reactionary spirits," he proclaimed, ". . . to those who resist all just and necessary reforms" (Loveman 1988: 215). But his antioligarchic rhetoric suggested more than he could or likely intended to deliver. As president, Alessandri backed modest social reforms, including legislation that would legalize labor unions, though his government would use bloody force against striking workers, just as his predecessors had.

During his tumultuous first term (1920–1925), Alessandri saw his initiatives blocked by a hostile, conservative congress. In 1924, the army, impatient with the stalemate and with the failure to resolve certain issues directly affecting the military, intervened to force change. Among the measures passed under intense pressure was a long-delayed labor reform bill. The bill was backed by an officer corps weary of its repressive role in labor relations and troubled by the radicalization of the workers. A high-ranking officer later wrote that Communist influence was infecting "the consciousness of all workers, awakening in them feelings of greed and vengeance, stirring the lower instincts of the popular masses" (Bergquist 1986: 68).

In the wake of the army's intervention, Alessandri felt compelled to resign his office and go into exile, but he returned several months later with the support of the younger reform-minded officers, who declared their intention to "show . . . that the oligarchs are not the masters of Chile" (Loveman 1988: 219). The most important outcomes of this period were the labor measure and the promulgation of a new constitution, approved by national plebiscite in 1925. Together they would shape Chile's contested republic.

ARGENTINA: HIPÓLITO YRIGOYEN

When Hipólito Yrigoyen died in 1933, the elite club to which he had belonged since he was a young man acknowledged the event with a brief, cool note in its annual bulletin: "It falls to the Jockey Club to honor the official mourning period decreed due to the passing away of the ex-president of the Republic, Dr. Hipólito Yrigoyen, member of this institution since 1887" (Edsall 1999 144). This for a man who had been the dominant political figure of his time. He obviously was not a favorite of the Argentine elite.

Yrigoyen was born to a middle-class family in provincial Buenos Aires. After serving a term in Congress in the early eighties, he bought land and started raising cattle. Within a few years he had gained the wealth and status to claim membership in the Jockey Club and help fund a political movement that developed into the Radical Party. Though rather different in style, Yrigoyen was, like Alessandri, a charismatic figure who appealed to the middle- and working-class people who had been shut out of the oligarchic political system. His followers, frustrated by a corrupt electoral system, had staged unsuccessful armed rebellions since 1890. But Yrigoyen won the presidency in 1916 with the help of a divided oligarchy and the 1912 Sáez Peña electoral reform law that broadened the electorate and reformed the balloting process. Yrigoyen had built an odd coalition of political "outs." His supporters included dissident elements of the elite, members of the rapidly growing middle-class, native-born sons of immigrants, and, perhaps unexpectedly, farm tenants, and some working-class voters. All that these people had in common was political marginality, but, together, they represented the end of the oligarchic republic and beginning of a new, uncertain political era.

BRAZIL: GETÚLIO VARGAS

Getúlio Vargas, the last of the five heretics who presided over the dismantling of the oligarchic republics, was born to a prominent landowning family in the far southern state of Rio Grande do Sul. One of the larger, wealthier states, Rio Grande do Sul was distinctively oriented toward food production for the domestic market rather than export. The state was, for this reason, relatively marginalized in a national political system dominated by coffee-producing states. Vargas had represented his state in the Congress and served as finance minister in the oligarchic government headed by the Paulista Washington Luís Pereira de Sousa. He was governor of Rio Grande do Sul when he ran for president in 1930. Vargas and his vaguely reformist platform appealed to middle- and working-class Brazilians in the cities, as he discovered during the campaign. But Brazil was still an overwhelming rural society, the least urbanized of the five countries. Vargas' ultimate victory—and the collapse of the oligarchic regime—had less to do with the modernization of Brazilian society than with an oligarchic schism and a bad economy.

The dominant São Paulo-Minas alliance unraveled when Luís imposed another Paulista as the regime's presidential candidate. Political tensions were amplified by a sharp economic downturn brought on by the world depression and plunging coffee prices. The oligarchic political network, led by São Paulo's Republican Party managed, in the usual fashion, to round up enough votes to claim victory for the official candidate. But Minas, Rio Grande do Sul, and several other states that had backed Vargas rejected the results, mobilized their own forces, and marched on Rio. They were supported by elements of the national military, including many of the rebellious *tenente* officers of the 1920s. As rebel columns converged on Rio in October 1930, senior military officers, hoping to avoid a civil war, forced the president to resign and formed a ruling junta. But, within a few days, the generals felt compelled, by Vargas' apparent popular appeal and armed support, to transfer provisional power to him. The Old Republic ended as it had begun, with military intervention, but this time, under circumstances imposed on the generals, rather than initiated by them. In 1932, the army helped Vargas consolidate his power by defeating an armed revolt by São Paulo, a final attempt by the Paulista oligarchy to regain its position by force. In and out of office, Vargas would be the dominant figure in Brazilian politics until his death by suicide in 1954.

IN THE LIVING MUSEUM

In the 1960s, political scientist Charles Anderson memorably described Latin American politics as "a living museum" in which old forms of political power and the actors associated with them are preserved even as new ones arise. In the living museum, wrote Anderson, the old and the new interact in "a pageant that seems to violate all the rules of sequence and change."

Thus, the masters of semifeudal estates and military caudillos may coexist with industrial entrepreneurs and the leaders of mass political parties. The contending parties have disparate power capabilities. Since no single source of power is accepted as legitimating by all parties, there is always a tentativeness to political arrangements.

New contenders must force their way into the political arena by demonstrating their unique power capability—staging a coup, organizing a general strike, mobilizing voters, and so on. They may gain acceptance when (1) they have proven their capacity to threaten the interests of established parties and (2) they are "perceived by other contenders as willing to abide by the rules of the game, to permit existing contenders to continue to exist and operate in the political system." In the living museum, modest change is possible, but sweeping transformation is unlikely, since that would imply the elimination of one or more of the existing players. According to Anderson, political movements that win a following with promises of radical change are almost inevitably tamed by the system, whose rules they must accept as the price of admission (Anderson 1967: 104–105).

Anderson's living museum is an apt metaphor for the politics of the contested republics in the decades after the collapse of the oligarchic republics. Under changing social and economic circumstances, new contenders had entered the political arena. As the national accounts that follow will show, the oligarchs were, in varying degrees, successful in dealing with the challenge they posed. But, even as Anderson wrote, the living museums were closed or closing. Oligarchic power, overwhelmed by change, became politically relevant.

CHILE'S CONTESTED REPUBLIC: A POLITICAL BARGAIN[4]

Alessandri served two presidential terms (1920–1925 and 1932–1938). The entire period was marked by violent social conflict and political upheaval, exacerbated by the devastating impact of the Great Depression. Between Alessandri's presidencies, there were numerous transfers of power, none of them constitutional, installing governments ranging from a short-lived "Socialist Republic" to a more resilient military dictatorship that was at once reform-minded and repressive.

Yet Alessandri's election to a second term in 1932 began four decades of constitutional succession, free of military intervention. Chile was moving, in fits and starts, toward a new, durable sociopolitical regime that made concessions to new contenders, while preserving much of the power of the oldest specimens in the museum, the landed oligarchy. The new contenders were the liberal and leftist political parties and labor unions that appealed to working- and middle-class Chileans. Elections, involving varying coalitions of left, center, and right parties, were competitive during Chile's contested republic.

The two major achievements of Alessandri's first term, the 1925 constitution and the labor code, were the keys to the social and political order of the contested republic. The new constitution shifted the balance of power away from the Congress and toward the president, undermining the institutional basis of the oligarchy-dominated Parliamentary Republic. The labor law recognized, for the first time, the right of workers to form unions, obligated employers to deal with them, and gave the state the power to regulate labor relations. The law also imposed important restrictions on union activity. Strikes were, for example, limited to a single firm, and could be ruled illegal.

Gradually implemented by succeeding administrations, the 1925 labor code was the answer to the "social question" that had haunted Chile for decades, but the protections it provided were denied to one sector of the labor force, rural workers. At first this was done informally and extralegally. For example, rural labor organizing was "temporarily suspended" for long periods by authorities. Sometimes carabineros (well-armed national police) were sent to evict peasant activists and their families from the estates where they had long worked and lived. Subsequent legislation effectively prohibited union activity in the countryside and destroyed the existing rural labor organizations. Though labor conditions on rural estates deteriorated during this period, there was little protest, in part because the inquilinos were kept isolated from outsiders who might have stirred their resentments and encouraged organization. The price of progress on the urban social question was the preservation of the retrograde hacienda system. Reformers, along with leftist parties and labor organizations, felt compelled to accept the exclusion of rural labor in exchange for an implicit political bargain that benefited them and the people they represented.

Behind this arrangement lay the traditional power of the landed oligarchy, amply represented in the legislature and vigorously defended by the semiofficial National Agrarian Society, which lobbied successive governments on rural labor issues. Land in the central valley remained highly concentrated. Most of the region's labor force lived on large estates, whose owners typically controlled their votes. As a result, the legislature was still dominated by landowners, whose power was enhanced by an archaic system of apportionment, which favored rural districts over the rapidly growing cities. Of course, there was little distinction between major landowners and urban capitalists in Chile's blended oligarchy. They were tied to one another by shared investments and kinship. Many urban capitalists, like the bank-owning Subercaseaux clan retained rural properties especially for their political and prestige value.

If rural workers were the sacrificial lambs of the new order, the growing urban working and middle classes were its special beneficiaries. Public policy favored a growing role for the state, expansion of education at all levels, and the promotion of manufacturing—all creating new employment opportunities for white- and blue-collar workers. Statistics from the 1940s and 1950s show that the real wages of industrial workers were rising at the same time that the earnings of rural workers were declining (Loveman 1988: 235). Mindful of past conflicts in the cities over the cost of living, governments struggled to keep food prices low. This was a politically problematic endeavor. On the one hand, food costs consumed the greater part of urban working-class budgets (Bauer 1975: 221). On the other, the suppliers of food to the cities were the powerful landowners. The solution was a system of generous subsidies to agriculture, financed with taxes on mining exports—which by this point were largely controlled by foreign corporations. Landowners also had the advantage of low, in fact, declining labor costs.

Under Chile's contested republic, when new contenders for power were gaining ground and presidents were constitutionally stronger than they had been in the previous era, the key to sustaining oligarchic power was legislative power based on control of rural labor. But the oligarchy was compelled to accept new political actors, representing urban middle- and working-class Chileans. This was the kind of political arrangement described by Anderson's living museum. The Old Regime would endure in Chile until 1962, when as a result of a 1958 election reform law, the landed oligarchy lost its legislative veto. The critical provision in the legislation was the secret ballot, which made it impossible for the rural *patron* to control the votes of his clients.

ARGENTINA'S CONTESTED REPUBLIC: FROM YRIGOYEN TO PERÓN[5]

In the three decades of Argentina's contested republic, from Yrigoyen's election in 1916 to Juan Perón's in 1946, middle- and working-class Argentines were drawn into the political arena, long monopolized by elites. The period began with three successive democratic transitions—a first for Latin America. But it was marred by angry polarization and the emergence of the military as a key player in national politics. Oligarchic attitudes toward Yrigoyen, relatively benign in the beginning, soon hardened. By 1930, when his second term was cut short by a military coup, the propertied classes were solidly united against him.

From Radical Party's formative years, large landowners were prominent among its leaders. In the decade before Yrigoyen won the presidency, two thirds of the party's parliamentary deputies were from "aristocratic" social backgrounds (Smith 1974: 31–32). Yrigoyen's first cabinet could have been taken for an oligarchic era government. The majority of the ministers were cattlemen or otherwise connected with the export sector. His minister of agriculture was a major landowner. The new finance minister, a banker, was a former president of the Rural Society, traditional defender of landed interests. Nine of the ministers who served during Yrigoyen's first term were members of the Jockey Club (Edsall 1999: 144). In Congress, the great majority of the party's representatives were landowners. Of course, Yrigoyen was himself a rancher and Jockey Club member. There was little change in economic policy or, as it turned out, labor policy. Yrigoyen first courted and then repressed labor. At the same time, Yrigoyen engaged in a bitter struggle for power with conservative opponents in Congress, including disaffected members of his own party, and provincial governments.

Prohibited from serving consecutive terms, Yrigoyen left office in 1922 but was easily reelected in 1928. His second-term appointments had a very different complexion from his earlier choices. The Rural Society and the Jockey Club were barely represented (Edsall 1999: 160). Key ministerial positions were now held by men of middle-class origins, and the party's congressional delegation was typically drawn from middle-class, often immigrant, families. After the first term, the Radical Party had split between a majority faction controlled by Yrigoyen and a minority faction known as the Anti-Personalistas, which included most of Yrigoyen's former upper-class supporters. Although Yrigoyen had won the second term with an imposing 60 percent of the vote, the oligarchs were already in contact with officers plotting a military coup.

How had Yrigoyen so thoroughly alienated the elite? Not so much by any fundamental shift in policy as for reasons that were largely political. The Radicals had won the presidency in 1916 without gaining control of most of the interior provinces or of either chamber of the legislature, which remained under the control of conservatives. For Yrigoyen, these remnants of the oligarchic republic were illegitimate, and he was determined to consolidate his own power by all means available to him. Much more than his predecessors, Yrigoyen exercised the executive's power to take over provincial governments or annul elections won by his opponents. The Radicals exploited government resources to woo middle- and working-class voters, and built a personality cult around Yrigoyen, who did not doubt his own messianic mission.

The Radical government responded to middle-class aspirations for social mobility by broadening educational opportunities and expanding government employment. Both policies strengthened the Radicals' middle-class base, but threatened the interests of the upper class, including some of the party's earliest supporters. The government backed the university reform movement discussed earlier and widened access to higher education by founding new institutions. These policies transformed a sector that had traditionally been controlled by the upper class and opened competition for professional and bureaucratic positions to graduates who were neither sons nor clients of the elite. Patronage employment was the party's basic means of rewarding its leaders and supporters. As a result, public spending grew markedly, as did public debt. Landowners found themselves competing with the government for credit, especially during periods of economic downturn, when their credit needs were greatest. The oligarchs worried that the government might be forced to default on the country's international debt. Excessive spending, for what they took to be political purposes, became a key part of elite's indictment of Radicalism.

Yrigoyen's approach to labor was ad hoc and politically calculated. He did not propose a labor code to regulate workplace relations as his contemporary Alessandri would in Chile. But, initially at least, the government avoided the repressive tactics regularly employed by the Old Regime and intervened selectively to mediate strikes. The fundamental objective was to win over workers who were potential Radical voters. Early on, the government helped settle maritime and railroad strikes on terms relatively favorable to workers, but did not hesitate to send troops to guard meatpacking plants against strikers. In the latter case, there was little to be gained in siding with workers: The plants were located in areas of no political interest to the Radicals, since they were solidly controlled by the conservatives, and many of the workers involved were noncitizen immigrants.

What the Radicals regarded as a moderate, conciliatory approach to labor relations, appeared threatening to the oligarchy, in part because some of industries involved, like the railroads, were critical to the export economy. Moreover, Yrigoyen's first term, coincided with the wave of labor protest across Latin America that accompanied World War I and the outbreak of revolution in Russia. A revolution in Argentina, with its large, militant, heavily immigrant working class, now seemed a real possibility to many upper and middle-class Argentines. From their perspective, siding with the workers, even selectively as the government did, was inviting disaster. Even for the Radicals, the government's labor policy was becoming politically problematic, because it was undermining the government's moderate middle-class base.

Whatever promise this initially moderate labor policy may have held died with the January 1919 *La Semana Trágica* (The Tragic Week). A failed strike by metal workers, turned into a riot-plagued general strike, which provoked a violent response from armed, right-wing vigilante brigades. Organized with the help of the military and the Jockey Club, the brigades consisted of upper- and middle-class civilians, who imagined they were fighting an incipient Bolshevik revolution. Led, as in quotidian life, by their upper-class members, the brigades attacked working-class immigrants and Jews—the presumed wellsprings of subversion. Hundreds died in the fighting. After these events, the vigilantes were formally organized, with continuing upper-class support, into the Argentine Patriotic League, which became a powerful antiimmigrant, antilabor force in the streets and in Argentine politics. Another important conservative group that emerged during this period was the well-financed National Labor Association, formed in May 1918 by leading private sector representatives to combat unions and break strikes. Its members shared a deep animosity toward Yrigoyen and his party.

Yrigoyen had achieved something uncommon in Argentine history: He had united (against himself) all sectors of the elite, including the landed oligarchy, urban industrial, financial and commercial elites, provincial elites, the conservative politicians of the oligarchic era, and the estranged patrician wing of his own party. He had also alienated much of the officer corps by compromising professional standards with politically oriented advancements and by repeatedly using the army to impose Radical rule on the interior provinces via numerous federal interventions.

The Great Depression, arriving early in Yrigoyen's second term, weakened his government and undermined his popularity. By then in his late-seventies, he appeared weary, and many thought him senile. The September 1930 military coup that deposed him likely surprised no one. It was supported by two groups, united mainly by their dislike of Yrigoyen: Conservatives in the mold of the oligarchic regime and ultranationalists of varied inspirations, ranging from European fascism to militant Catholicism. The first group was dominant for most of the period from the September coup to a second, critical coup in June 1943.

The new regime was based on an alliance of conservative parties formally known as the *Concordancia*. Its leading figure was Agustin Justo, a retired military officer and wily politician with an elite family background and strong links to the propertied classes. Justo served as president from 1932 to 1938. The governments of the Concordancia were again well staffed with members of the Rural Society and the Jockey Club. An analysis of cabinets in the second half of this period leaves no doubt about whose government this was: "[A]lmost all of the ruling team came from . . . the upper class. There was little co-optation: One simply belonged in government by right of ascription" (Imaz 1964: 15). Electoral corruption (now glorified as "patriotic fraud") was, as it had been during the oligarchic republic, essential to the political system. The Radical Party was, by various mechanisms, prevented from competing. Such practices inspired the name by which this period is remembered: the Infamous Decade.

These years were difficult for the landed oligarchy. Export volume, prices, and profits declined. Credit was hard to obtain. Some of the wealthiest old families were compelled to sell their Buenos Aires mansions, which became embassies and government ministries. After three generations, fortunes dating from the mid-nineteenth century, divided among many heirs and strained by the Depression, were often inadequate to maintain upper-class living standards. More than a few young men learned that they could not expect to be gentlemen of leisure but would have to prepare for active professional careers. One of the great *palacios* sold during this period was the Buenos Aires home of the Senillosas, who had been among the wealthiest, most influential families of the landed oligarchy. Years earlier, Pastor Senillosa had warned his children that the family fortune could not support them all in the style they had known growing up. He chose a cattleman's metaphor to make the point: "[S]uckling two each teat . . . either the calves die or the cow becomes exhausted." Senillosa advised his sons to "pursue a career whose capital is in its academic qualification, such as law or engineering," the path that several them took (Hora 2003: 475).

Affluent families that could were shifting their wealth out of the countryside and into the cities, investing in the expanding manufacturing sector, in real estate, construction, publishing, and other urban enterprises. At the same time, families that had accumulated urban fortunes were beginning to buy rural properties, mainly for the social prestige that still adhered to them. These developments were closing the economic and political distance between the old landed families and the new urban bourgeoisie. They provided the basis for a broader oligarchy of the propertied classes, unified in the face of resistance from below and strongly supportive of the Concordancia.

Despite appearances, the Concordancia was not the reincarnation of the oligarchic republic. It differed in fundamental ways. The most important was, of course, the transformation of the political arena by actors who had been of little significance during the oligarchic republic: the middle and working classes and their representatives, the unions and the Radical Party, in addition to the military. The Concordancia could for the time being keep the popular classes at bay with the help of the army and a good deal of unacknowledged violence, but the continuing appeal of Radicalism was demonstrated by the thousands of mourners who jammed the streets of Buenos Aires when Yrigoyen died in 1933.

Argentina's economy was also fundamentally and irreversibly altered. Within a few years, the country had recovered from the Depression. But the international economy had changed. The extraordinary export growth of the late nineteenth and early twentieth centuries, which had driven the economy and created the wealth of the oligarchy, would not return. Argentina was becoming an industrial society, with a rapidly growing urban proletariat. Its members were immigrants, their offspring, and increasingly, migrants from the interior, who together would provide the social base for Juan Perón's rise to power.

The Concordancia collapsed in the early 1940s. At the outbreak of World War II, the regime's supporters had split between those, especially among the traditional elite, who wanted the country to side with British, and the nationalists, including many in the military, who favored the fascist states. Argentina assumed a neutral stance, but the issue remained contentious and contributed to conflict over the choice of a presidential candidate in 1943. It must have long been obvious to thoughtful observers that the rule of the propertied classes after 1930 could last only so long as the regime retained the united support of the military—which was waning by 1943. The officers who plotted against the regime that year feared that a new Concordancia government would side with the Allies, who seemed to be losing the war. They were also, as they had been under Yrigoyen, tired of imposing the central government's authority on recalcitrant provinces.

A military junta of uncertain direction assumed power in June. Over the coming months, one of the plotters, Colonel Juan Perón, from the minor post of labor secretary in the new government, quietly devoted himself to building a following among industrial workers and union leaders. The urban working class was much bigger and more Argentine that it had been in the recent past. Between 1935 and 1943, the number of blue-collar workers in manufacturing had almost doubled (Horowitz 1999 27). Many workers were the native-born sons and daughters of immigrants, that is, Argentine citizens. A growing proportion were people who had migrated from the countryside for what they hoped would be a better life in the city. Perón built a power base for himself by winning higher wages and more dignified working conditions for workers, at the same time that he imposed himself on the union leadership, rewarding his allies and repressing those who were less than cooperative. By the time his military colleagues had grasped what was happening, he was unstoppable.

Perón's election to the presidency in 1946 marked the end of the Old Regime in Argentina. The oligarchy had become irrelevant. National politics would, in the future, revolve around Peronist populism and the military's futile attempts to control it.

BRAZIL'S CONTESTED REPUBLIC: BURNING SÃO PAULO'S FLAG ON THE NATION'S ALTAR[6]

A diverse—in fact, incoherent—coalition backed Getúlio Vargas in the March 1930 election that he officially lost and in the October 1930 revolution that placed him in power. Its members included (1) the oligarchic establishments of Minas (which felt cheated of its proper place in the presidential rotation), Rio Grande do Sul (Vargas' home state), and some smaller states also resentful of São Paulo's dominant position in national politics; (2) the tenentes and the so-called civilian tenentes allied with them, who saw in Vargas the political and economic modernizer the nation required; (3) the Democratic Party, recently created by dissident members of the Paulista elite and committed to liberal constitutional reforms, such as the secret ballot, for which Vargas had expressed support; (4) coffee planters, many of them backers of the Democratic Party, unhappy with the incumbent government's response to the depression era collapse of coffee prices.

The members of this coalition had little in common besides illusions about Vargas. There were big differences in the scope of their grievances and the implied remedies. The discontented coffee planters and regional oligarchies were hoping for some modest adjustment to the structure or policies of the oligarchic regime—better support for coffee prices or a more inclusive (among oligarchs) system of picking presidential candidates. The tenentes, in contrast, were proposing the fundamental transformation of a backward society, imposed from above. Somewhere in-between were the liberal constitutionalists of the Democratic Party, who, like Argentina's oligarchic reformers, seem to have imagined a conservative regime, bolstered by elite and middle-class support and democratic legitimacy. Vargas would use these groups and finally disappoint them, one by one.

The makeup of the opposition coalition also shows, above all, that the conflict surrounding the 1930 election was a struggle among elites and even within the Paulista oligarchy. None of these groups and none of those that backed the official candidate of the oligarchic regime represented the urban middle and working classes or the rural poor. They were as irrelevant to the end the Old Republic as they had been to its creation in the 1890s. The words of a French observer fifty years earlier still rang true: "Brazil has no people" (Bethell 2008: 4).

Vargas moved quickly to consolidate his victory and centralize power in Rio. In November, his provisional government assumed broad powers after dissolving the Congress, state legislatures, and municipal councils. State governors were dismissed and replaced with "interventors," many of them tenentes, appointed by Vargas and personally loyal to him. His intention to dismantle Brazil's oligarchic regime was now obvious. The only mystery was what would replace it.

São Paulo, which had the most at stake, soon responded. In 1930, the Paulista elite had lost national power and state autonomy, in part because it was divided, most notably between the dissident Democratic and the establishment Republican parties. In July 1932, a reunited Paulista oligarchy led the state in a doomed, three-month revolt against Vargas. The state's well trained 10,000 man force posed a formidable challenge to the national military. But expected support from Rio Grande do Sul and Minas did not materialize and the navy blockaded São Paulo's critical port of Santos. If the Paulista oligarchy were to reassert its power, it would not be by force of arms.

In 1933, elections were held for a constituent assembly, under a new election law that provided for a secret ballot and other reforms. The results were surprisingly favorable to candidates aligned with state oligarchies and demonstrated the continuing power of the elites in the key states of São Paulo, Minas, and Rio Grande do Sul. The assembly produced a new constitution and elected Vargas to a four-year presidential term. As national elections approached in 1937, the São Paulo elite made a final attempt to reclaim national power by promoting one of its own as a presidential candidate. In reply, Vargas, who could not succeed himself under the provisions of the new charter, dissolved the legislature and assumed dictatorial powers, with the support of the military. Many of his elite opponents were jailed or forced into exile. This "auto-coup" established a new regime Vargas called the Estado Novo and marked the definitive end of the Old Regime in Brazil. The contested republic had lasted only seven years.

Shortly after the declaration of the Estado Novo, Vargas presided over a "Flag Day" ceremony in which state flags were burned on the "Altar of the Patria." São Paulo's flag was the first to be sacrificed. Vargas was determined to reduce the independence of the states and the power of the state oligarchies.

Vargas is credited by historians with creating a stronger, more autonomous, and, especially, more centralized Brazilian state; with accelerating the process of industrialization; and with creating a legal basis for labor relations. In Rio he built a larger, more technocratic, more engaged federal bureaucracy. Vargas made import substitution industrialization a national priority. He turned industrialists, who had not supported his candidacy in 1930 into allies of the Estado Novo and gave the military a significant role in the program.

Vargas created a corporatist framework for urban labor, designed to bring unions and employers together under firm state control. Independent unions, especially those with radical political agendas, were suppressed. Social legislation extended benefits such as minimum wage pension and disability payments and health care benefits to many urban workers.

Equally important, Vargas appealed directly to common people in personal appearances across the country and by the new medium of radio with the message that he understood their struggles and was concerned with their welfare. He was the first leader of Brazil to celebrate the country's multiracial, multicultural heritage. The image he created of himself as "The Father of the Poor" tapped the most traditional, patriarchal Brazilian notions of authority, but the effect was revolutionary. No national figure had ever reached out to the majority of Brazilians in this fashion. Although he never created a mass political movement, as his contemporary Perón did in Argentina, he had opened the path to populist politics for his successors.

Though Vargas displaced the oligarchic political system, he was protective of the traditional elite's economic interests, and, once he had established his authority, open to political compromise with regional elites. His government defended the depressed coffee sector, as best it could, by buying and destroying a portion of the annual crop, limiting plantings, and negotiating agreements with other coffee-producing countries. A landowner himself, Vargas showed no interest in land reform or in extending the new labor and social benefits to the great majority of the labor force still employed in the countryside. Landowners, like the industrialists, supported the Estado Novo. They had, it was said, an implicit *pacto de compromisso* with Vargas (Bethell 2008: 52).

The country had experienced what Brazilian historian Boris Fausto describes as "an exchange of elites. . . . The traditional oligarchies fell from power. Their place was taken by military men, technocrats, young politicians, and, a little later by industrialists" (Fausto 1999: 196). Brazil would be governed by a broadened elite, which would not be quite as free to ignore the rest of the population as the oligarchs had been.

MEXICO'S CONTESTED REPUBLIC: FROM MADERO TO CÁRDENAS[7]

The overthrow of the ringmaster who had held Mexico's oligarchic republic together left the future of the country's disparate oligarchic elites unresolved. That would require the better part of three decades, each of which, roughly speaking, represented a different phase of the revolution: a decade of violent upheaval, a decade of economic reconstruction and political struggle, and a decade of radical transformation. The period of the contested republic in Mexico can be dated from the departure of Díaz to the transformative presidency of Lázaro Cárdenas in the third decade.

At the beginning of the first decade, Madero was elected president. He filled his administration with prominent businessmen (Camp 1989: 16) and resisted demands from Zapata and others for land reform, all of which must have been reassuring to the oligarchs. But Madero's murder in 1913 plunged the country into a decade of brutal civil war—at first, between the revolutionaries and remnants of the Porfirian regime, but soon among the revolutionaries themselves. The fighting involved the large-scale mobilization of the rural poor, who would return home from war with heightened expectations of change and less deferential attitudes toward their traditional *patrones*. Though Zapata and Villa were both defeated on the battlefield and later assassinated, the radical currents in the revolution that they had inspired did not disappear.

By 1920, the military phase of the revolution had ended in favor of rule by the more conservative, development-oriented faction, whose leaders were typically northerners of middle- to upper-class origin. In the 1920s, they created a strengthened, stable, state and a new army under political control—at least at the national level. They presided over governments focused on promoting capitalist economic growth, while making limited concessions to popular demands for social reform. To some, it seemed that the Mexico's revolutionary government was in the process of resurrecting the Porfiriato.

In late 1923, Finance Minister Alberto Pani called a "bankers' convention" with the objective of restructuring the financial system. As an indication of what he had in

Zapata (holding large sombrero) and Villa (in presidential chair) in 1914, when their armies temporarily occupied Mexico City. They represented the radical forces, rooted in rural discontent, that give the revolution its explosive energy.

Source: Library of Congress.

mind, Pani recruited two of the Porfiriato's most prominent bankers, Enrique Creel and Miguel Macedo, to "advise" the convention. Both men had held national political office under Díaz. Creel, it will be recalled from chapter 1, was a key leader of the ruling Terrazas clan in Chihuahua, where he was remembered as an especially rapacious governor in the last years of the Porfiriato. The financial system that emerged from the convention, much like the Porfirian system before it, was designed to support the government, while enriching the bankers (many with familiar Porfirian names) and regime insiders (Haber et al. 2003: 104–106).

During the same period, a gala wedding was held for the governor of Chihuahua, Jesús Antonio Almeida, and his bride, Susanna Nesbitt Becerra. The Almeidas were a middle-class family that had seized the economic and political opportunities offered by the turmoil of the revolution. In the years to come, they would build one of the country's leading economic groups. The Becerras had been stalwarts of the prerevolutionary regime in the state. Amply represented on the guest list were Terrazas, Creels,

Lujáns, Falomirs, and other leading families of Porfirian Chihuahua. After a decade of bloody popular revolution, "revolutionary generals ate, drank and danced with scions of the dictatorship they had overthrown" (Wasserman 1995: 10–11).

The banking convention, the Almeida-Becerra wedding, and comparable moments of the second decade raised inevitable questions. Had anything really changed? Were the new and old elites simply merging, as had often happened in Latin American history, to produce a new oligarchy? But while the bankers parleyed in Mexico City and the celebrants danced at blended weddings, a more contentious process was unfolding in across the country. Revolutionary factions, organizations, and ambitious individuals were struggling, often violently, for political advantage. A new mass politics, expansive, vital, chaotic, often corrupt, had replaced the claustrophobic political world of the oligarchic republic. At the same time, the old elite, which had retained much of its wealth, was fighting to regain political influence. In the countryside, agrarianists demanding land reform battled hacendados, defended by private armies, friendly politicians, and once revolutionary generals who had become landowners themselves. In the cities, union activists fought one another (and successive governments) for control of the growing labor movement. Nationally and locally, competing political factions formed alliances with the labor and agrarian movements, exchanging material concessions for organized popular support.

In the third decade, President Lázaro Cárdenas (1934–1940) confronted the social issues that had continued to agitate the country and laid a foundation for the stable postrevolutionary regime that replaced the uncertain contested republic. The effects of the worldwide depression, fading as Cardenas took office, intensified popular militancy, helping him to overcome conservative resistance and pursue a program quite radical by the standards of what came before and after. His candidacy had been promoted by the agrarianists. Cárdenas carried out a sweeping agrarian reform that redistributed much of the country's arable land and, in the process, broke the power of the landed elite. Cárdenas strongly backed the labor movement, openly favoring workers over employers. He consolidated the revolutionary state by incorporating the major labor and peasant organizations into the official party, later known as the PRI (Partido Revolucionario Institutional). Thus, the popular movements unleashed by the revolution gained benefits for their adherents but came under the firm control of an increasingly conservative ruling party that would dominate the country for decades to come.

How did the Porfirian elite fare under the new regime? Political cliques that had dominated a state, like the Terrazas clan in Chihuahua, the Molinas in Yucatan, and the sugar barons of Morelos, would never regain their prerevolutionary power. Families with fortunes largely dependent on rural land were the biggest economic losers, while those with urban and diversified interests were the most likely to prosper in the new order. The ruling party, committed to capitalist development, needed their entrepreneurial talents and their capital—especially as industrialization became a national priority in the late 1930s and 1940s. Thus, the tight-knit Monterrey industrial elite survived the revolutionary period intact, even though its leaders abandoned the low political profile they had maintained under Díaz and, from time to time, openly resisted government policies. In Mexico City, the Legorreta family and the Banco National de Mexico, in which they held a large share, survived the upheaval, in part because Agustín Legorreta and his bank provided the revolutionary governments a critical link to foreign credit (Hamilton 1982: 82–84, 288–290). The Gómez clan, profiled in chapter 1, rebuilt a large family fortune, while developing friendly, mutually useful relations with the new regime. When Pablo Gómez, a key member of the clan, died in the late 1950s, the president and much of his cabinet were among those who attended his funeral.

Camp, who has collected systematic data on Mexican elites, concludes that "a large group of Mexican entrepreneurs trace their familial and economic origins to antecedents in the Porfiriato." But it appears that only six of the twenty-four on his list of leading entrepreneurial families in the 1980s held fortunes that predated the 1910 Revolution (Camp 1989: 76, 199–205).

The revolution replaced the Old Regime with a new system of elite rule that differed in two critical ways. First, the ruling party could not be as indifferent to the welfare or wishes of the popular classes as the Porfirian rulers had been. The PRI was not above electoral fraud or violent repression, but it wanted, needed, and courted popular support. Second, the new regime, in sharp contrast to the late Porfiriato, separated economic and political power. Under Díaz, men like José Yves Limantour, Enrique Creel, and Olegario Molina served as cabinet officers and governors. One in five "leading" Porfirian politicians, according to Camp, had been an "important businessman." They made and, in many cases, enforced (or failed to enforce) the laws and regulations that affected their enterprises. In the 1920s, there were reasons to believe that a similar situation might emerge from the revolution. But it did not. In later periods, elite circulation between the private sector and the postrevolutionary state was limited (Camp 1989: 78–79). Contributing to this pattern were the distinct political and business cultures that developed in the wake of the revolution. The populist, anticlerical ideology of the official party clashed with the generally conservative, Catholic entrepreneurial culture. Politicians and businessmen came from different families, went to different schools, and were tied to different social networks. Those who might cross between the two worlds faced resistance from those closest to them.

Cárdenas, the least business-friendly of revolutionary presidents, created a state-controlled mechanism for private sector representation: sectoral business chambers with mandatory membership. While this structure provided business with a communications channel, it was politically inferior to the representation of workers and peasants provided by the new party organization.

Whatever their differences, leaders of the new regime and the private sector understood that they needed one another. The official party depended on the private sector to deliver the economic growth that was critical to sustaining popular support. The private sector needed the state to regulate labor and was, in fact, vulnerable to the pressure that the state could impose through its control of labor. The private sector also depended on the state for credit, tariff protection, and other policy favors.

What had emerged from the revolution was a new urban capitalist order that held capitalists at a distance from the state. In this respect, the regime reflected its populist origins—especially the effects of the violent upheaval in the countryside and agrarian reform of the 1930s. One has only to look at Chile after 1925 to see a different conceivable outcome. There the oligarchy retained significant institutional power for decades after the oligarchic republic because it retained political control of the countryside and the rural vote. The 1910 revolution did make a difference.

PERU'S CONTESTED REPUBIC: FROM LEGUÍA TO THE REVOLUTION OF THE ARMED FORCES

Augusto Leguía assumed power in 1919, promising to "liquidate the old state of things" (Capuñay 1951: 51–52). He did put an end to oligarchic rule, but oligarchic *power* reemerged in a contested republic that endured for several decades. Part II of this book presents a detailed history of the Peruvian oligarchy, but, for the sake of comparison with the other national cases, this section provides a brief sketch of the period after 1919.

In 1919, Leguía acted decisively against his oligarchic opponents. Prominent members of the old elite were imprisoned and exiled. Some saw their property attacked by government orchestrated mobs. The Aspíllagas, Prados, and Miró Quesadas were among the victims. But Leguía was a champion of capitalist development, who did not threaten economic interests of the oligarchs. In fact, he opened up some new opportunities for them. And by stifling the labor movement, he protected the sugar and cotton planters whose operations were heavily dependent on the large wage-earning rural proletariat. For their part, the oligarchs despised Leguía. Only later would they see the value of what he had given them in exchange for power.

The World Depression ravaged Peru's export dependent economy and undermined Leguía by cutting off the international loans that had sustained his regime. After many failed plots, Leguía was toppled in 1930 by military coup led by Colonel Luís Sánchez Cerro. The following year, Sánchez Cerro ran for president, with strong backing from the oligarchy. His main opponent was Victor Raúl Haya de la Torre, leader of the *Alianza Popular Revolucionaria Americana* (APRA), a relatively young populist party that posed a direct threat to the coastal elite. APRA's ideology singled out the oligarchy as the class enemy. The party's program proposed nationalization of the coastal plantations. Its election propaganda featured attacks on the "the barons of sugar and cotton." Worst still from the oligarchy's perspective, APRA was strongest in plantation areas and among plantation workers.

The Apristas refused to accept the apparent victory of Sánchez Cerro in the strongly contested 1931 election. What followed was one of the most violent periods in Peruvian history, notable for brutal confrontations between armed Apristas and security forces, and for the assassinations of prominent political figures including

Antonio Miró Quesada, head of the family's newspaper, and of Sánchez Cerro himself. Sanchez Cerro was replaced by General Oscar Benevides, an officer with long-standing ties to the oligarchy, who had helped the oligarchs remove protopopulist president Billinghurst from power in 1914.

The oligarchs had learned from experience that they could no longer rule the country directly and openly as they had done during the Aristocratic Republic. But they could rule indirectly with the support of the military and the continued political backing of the landed gamonales of the Sierra. In this fashion, they could resist popular demands and retain a political veto over the matters they considered critical.

The typical regime of the three decades following Leguía's removal was a military dictatorship with strong ties to the oligarchy that suppressed APRA and labor activity. But over time, APRA moderated its ideology and political behavior. The party assumed a less combative stance in labor relations and sought an understanding with receptive sectors of the oligarchy and certain military figures. The question of how to handle APRA often divided the oligarchs.

In some periods, APRA was granted quasilegal status in exchange for electoral support. In the late 1950s, APRA was finally legalized and entered a pact known as the *Convivencia* (coexistence) that supported an oligarchy-led government. These developments recall Anderson's living museum of Latin American politics, in which the admission of new players to the political arena depends on their ability to threaten the vital interests of established players and their ultimate willingness to play by rules that allow for the survival of the established players.

In 1962, APRA's Haya de la Torre, with significant oligarchic support, won a three-candidate presidential race by a thin plurality. It seemed that the Peruvian political system had evolved to an ironic, once unthinkable, conclusion: an oligarchy-backed Aprista government. But Haya was prevented from taking office by a military coup, justified by supposed electoral irregularities. He would never become president.

Peruvian politics and society had changed in fundamental ways since the 1930s. The national economy was bigger and more diversified. The population was more urban. The middle class was larger. One result was the emergence of new middle-class, reformist parties, the most important of which, Acción Popular, had run a close second to APRA in 1962. In a surprising way, the military had also evolved. The officer corps remained staunchly anti-Aprista, as it had been since the 1930s. But military leaders were tired of fighting to defend elite interests on the plantation coast and in the semifeudal Sierra. They had come to see Peru as a desperately backward country in need of a modernizing, reformist, nationalist leadership. That could not come from the oligarchs or from APRA, much less from an alliance between them. In 1963, new elections were held. This time Acción Popular's presidential candidate, Fernando Belaúnde Terry, narrowly defeated Haya.

Belaúnde's government would accomplish little, in part because the reforms he promoted were continually blocked or watered down by an APRA-oligarchy congressional alliance. On October 3, 1968, the military intervened to end the political stalemate. At first, many members of the oligarchy thought that the new military regime would serve its interests as military governments of the past had done. But they, like many observers, had misjudged the intentions of the armed forces. The new president, General Juan Velasco Alvarado was not a traditional strongman, but an institutional leader representing a military that was determined to transform Peru from above. Velasco would soon describe the oligarchy as "the irreducible adversaries of our movement." In the next few years, the self-styled Revolutionary Government of the Armed Forces carried out a radical program that directly attacked the bases of oligarchic power.

Leguía's Oncenio had marked the end of the oligarchic republic. A half century later, military revolutionaries destroyed what remained of the Old Regime.

THE CONTESTED REPUBLICS AND THE END OF THE OLD REGIME

In retrospect, the eclipse of the Latin American oligarchies seems all but inevitable. The oligarchs were ultimately reduced to political irrelevance because they, like the sorcerer's apprentice, could not control the forces they had unleashed and because they were, not infrequently, divided in the face of change. The export development promoted by the oligarchs fostered the growth of cities, the transformation of the class structure and, as a result, the rise of new, challenging political actors. The professionalization of the military, part of this broad process of modernization, created an institutional wildcard, whose influence on events could be surprising and decisive. The divided responses of the oligarchs to these challenges reflected their differing strategic assumptions (e.g., what will happen if we open up the political system?), personal ambitions and the conflicting interests of economic sectors, regions, and oligarchic clans.

The account of the Old Regime presented in this book distinguishes two stages of historical development: the oligarchic republic and the contested republic. Chapter 2 described the oligarchic republics in their maturity, when the oligarchs exercised more or less exclusive national power. Chapter 3 has focused on the collapse of the oligarchic republics and the subsequent withering of oligarchic power in the contested republics. This section and the national profiles in table 3.1 summarize the key factors that shaped the distinctive histories of the contested republics. (Readers may want to refer back to table 2.3, for a baseline description of the oligarchic republics.)

Chronology The dates given in table 3.1 and the durations in table 3.2 reveal big differences in the timing of the contested republics. Is there a systematic pattern to this variation? The level of domestic development (judged by the socioeconomic indicators in table 2.1) seems irrelevant: The period of the contested republic was longest in "backward" Peru and "advanced" Chile. It was, by far, shortest in Brazil, the country most like first-place Peru. The external economy was influential but not predictive. The Old Regime owed its existence to the growth of the global economy.

Inevitably, the effects of the World Depression in the 1930s were felt across the region—but in very different ways, ranging from the collapse of oligarchic power in Brazil to its resurgence in Argentina and Peru. The one consistent factor in the persistence of the contested republics was related to elite cohesion. The contested republics, and the Old Regime more generally, endured longest where there was a geographic basis for cohesion, as explained below.

Elite Cohesion

In each country the strength of elite cohesion varied over time, but depended, especially on the geography of oligarchic life and economic interests. Until the last years of the oligarchic republics, the ruling elites faced limited resistance from below. Usually politics revolved around rivalries among oligarchic factions or between the oligarchs and other elites. Since oligarchic political systems were not well institutionalized, political stability hung insecurely on informal understandings among the players. In four of the five countries—Chile was the exception—intraelite conflict contributed to the breakdown of the oligarchic republic. And in all five, the contested republic was inaugurated by an ambitious, maverick member of the elite.

In Peru, Chile, and Argentina, a geographically concentrated productive base, coupled with a common business, political, and social center in the capital, provided a structural basis for elite cohesion. At very least, the oligarchs in these countries were likely to share economic interests and a dense network of social ties, binding them to one another. Nonetheless, in the last years of Peru's oligarchic republic, disagreements over labor policy and especially over Leguía's personal ambitions divided the oligarchy and the Civilista Party. The Argentine oligarchy split over electoral reform and was unable to unite behind a candidate to oppose Radical Party leader Yrigoyen in 1916. But after the fall of the oligarchic republics, these three national elites were probably more cohesive and politically effective than they had ever been.

There was, in contrast, no structural basis for elite cohesion in Brazil and Mexico. In Brazil oligarchic economic power was not concentrated in the political capital, Rio, but regionally disbursed. Evidence presented in chapter 2 indicates that the Paulistas, in particular, had only limited social ties to elites in other states. The oligarchies of São Paulo and Minas, the two wealthiest states, controlled national politics, marginalizing the elites of lesser states. This inherently weak system collapsed in 1930, when the São Paulo-Minas partnership broke down in the midst of an economic crisis.

Similarly, in Mexico, economic power was regionalized. There is no indication that the Porfirian oligarchs had developed the kind of centralized, cohesive social world that bound their peers in Lima, Santiago, or Buenos Aires. Politically, Porfirio Díaz had imposed himself on the country's separate state oligarchies and provincial strongmen, creating a regime that was precariously dependent on his choices and his health. By the end of the Porfiriato, a significant sector of the northern elite, including Madero's own family, was alienated from the regime and open to revolutionary

Table 3.1. The Contested Republics

Period of Contested Republics	Politics of the Contested Republics	Elite Cohesion	Class Factors	Military
Chile 1925–1962	1925 constitution undermined Parliamentary Republic. But oligarchy's political base in central valley landholdings and strategic concessions to urban labor sustained oligarchic power for decades, until the oligarchy lost legislative veto in 1962.	Oligarchy united by concentration of economic, political, and social life in central valley and Santiago.	Large middle class (MC) in cities. Large working class (WC) in cities and northern mine enclaves. Strong, militant labor movement. Alessandri's appeal to MC/WC against oligarchy was key to his victories and later political strength of reformist and leftist party coalitions.	Critical military support for Alessandri, 1924–1925. Military dictatorship 1927–1931. But military does not intervene from 1932 to 1973.
Argentina 1916–1946	In 1930, with help of the army, the oligarchy put an end to Yrigoyen's protopopulist rule and regained power for more than a decade, only to lose it, in 1946, to a broader, more deep-rooted populism under Perón.	Oligarchy's economic, political, and social life concentrated in BA and Pampas. Power shared with interior elites. Divided over 1912 election reform. United behind Concordancia regime after 1930.	Largest MC and WC and strongest labor movement in Latin America. MC support for Radicals key to 1916 victory. Continuing growth of working class provides base for Perón.	Young officers support failed Radical movement insurrections, 1890–1905. Army topples Radical government, in 1930 and Concordancia regime in 1943. High command unable to stop Col. Perón.

Peru 1919–1968	After 1930 fall of Leguía, oligarchic power sustained by decades-long dance among the oligarchs, APRA, and the army, until a transformed military stopped the music in 1968.	Oligarchic economic, political, and social life concentrated on the coast and in Lima. Before 1919, Civilistas divided over labor reform and Leguía's ambitions. After 1930, some differences surrounding APRA, but planter core of oligarchy generally united.	Early WC, MC, and labor movement concentrated in Lima. Later, unions at plantations and mines. In 1919, sectors of WC, MC, and students back Leguía. After 1930, APRA with large MC/WC support challenges oligarchy. In 1960s, expanded MC is base of Belaúnde's reformist Acción Popular.	Oligarchy-supported military regimes protect elite against APRA most of period 1930 to 1956. Velasco's coup ends Old Regime in 1968.
Brazil 1930–1937	Inherent weakness of a regime based on one or two state oligarchies permitted Vargas to seize power in 1930, displace the oligarchs, and recentralize national power.	Separate state oligarchies with limited connection. Northern elites resentful of national dominance of São Paulo and Minas.	Modest WC and MC concentrated in Rio and São Paulo. Some MC support for tenentes & Vargas.	Tenente revolts in 1920s. Military helped Vargas consolidate power 1930–1932.
Mexico 1911–1934	Revolution, with diverse class support, destroyed the Porfirian regime and opened the way for a sweeping transformation of politics and society, culminating under Cárdenas.	Separate state oligarchies and strongmen. Northern elites resentful of Porfirian regime. Little basis for national elite cohesion against emerging revolutionary state.	Under Díaz, growing WC and labor movement in industry and mining. Strike wave at the end of Porfiriato. MC small, but expanding. 1910 rebellions of rural poor led by Zapata and Villa. Agrarianist support for Cárdenas.	Federal army tightly controlled by Díaz and displaced by the revolution. 1920–1934, revolutionary generals struggle for presidency.

Table 3.2. Duration of the Old Regime

	Duration of the Contested Republic (Years)	Total Duration of the Old Regime (Years)
Peru	49	73
Chile	37	67
Argentina	30	66
Mexico	23	57
Brazil	7	43

Source: Tables 2.3 and 3.1

appeals. Wealthy families would later sustain their fortunes as best they could, sometimes by forming ties with members of the revolutionary elite. In their corner of Mexico, the Monterrey elite maintained its traditional cohesion. But there had not been a cohesive national oligarchy before the revolution and there would not be one in its wake.

In sum, the contested republics endured the longest in the three countries, Peru, Chile, and Argentina, which had the strongest structural basis for elite cohesion. The contested republic passed quickly in Brazil and might have done so in Mexico were it not for the unresolved issues dividing the factions of the revolution.

Class Factors

The growth of the working and middle classes was a destabilizing force in the last years of the oligarchic republics. The oligarchs were often divided over how to respond to challenges from below. Labor protest, middle-class disaffection, the critical assessments produced by middle-class intellectuals, and the increasingly radical student movements in the universities contributed to a sense of regime precariousness at critical moments.

In Mexico, Madero found support for his challenge to Díaz in the still small middle class. But it was the rural poor, victims of Porfirian modernization, who give the Mexican Revolution its explosive energy in 1910 and, under Cardenas in the 1930s. In this, Mexico was unique. Elsewhere, in the oligarchic republics, there was no challenge from the countryside, either because the rural population was still under firm elite control, as in Chile, or because it tended to be small and transient, the Argentine case (see "Rural Society" in table 2.3 and related text in chapter 2).

During the contested republics, class became more consequential, especially in Argentina and Chile with their more advanced class structures. Elite support for the Concordancia in Argentina reflected fear of both the middle-class supported Radical Party and the large, militant labor movement. Perón brought the contested republic to a close by mobilizing urban working-class support. In Chile, coalitions of middle-class and working-class parties reshaped parliamentary politics in the contested republic and ultimately gained sufficient strength to overcome the veto of the landed oligarchy in 1962. In Peru, middle- and working-class support for APRA and later for Belaúnde's Acción Popular challenged the oligarchy. In contrast, it was not class politics, but intraelite politics drove the transformation of the Brazilian state from 1930 to 1937.

The Military

The modernization of the armed forces in Latin America did not separate officers from politics. It generally made military interventions more institutional and purposeful, though hardly more predictable. The military contributed to the demolition of the oligarchic republics in Chile and Brazil by backing the political initiatives of Alessandri (in 1924) and Vargas (in 1930 and 1932) at key moments, but sustained oligarchic power in Argentina and Peru during long stretches of the contested republics. Ironically, in both of these countries, decisive military intervention (1943–1946 and 1968) subsequently undermined oligarchic power and brought the Old Regime to an end.

Transitions

Table 3.3 summarizes the role of the three elements discussed above—elite cohesion, class issues, and military power—in the two regime transitions that frame the history of the contested republics: from oligarchic to contested republics and from the contested republics to the end of the Old Regime. The starred and double-starred items are judged, respectively, to be significant and highly significant influences at the time and place indicated. Generalizing broadly, problems of elite cohesion weighed heavily in the first transition, while the class and military factors were more substantial in the second. In the first period, elite cohesion was undermined by conflicts among

Table 3.3. Transitions

	Cohesion	Class	Military
Oligarchic Republic to Contested Republic			
Peru	**	*	*
Chile		*	*
Argentina	**	*	
Mexico	**	**	
Brazil	**		*
Contested Republic to the End of the Old Regime			
Peru			**
Chile		**	
Argentina		**	**
Mexico	*	**	
Brazil	*		

the oligarchs; in the second, intraelite conflict was less important than the weak structural basis for unity in two cases. Class became more important in the second period as the popular classes grew and political movements based on them became more powerful. In the first transition, the military intervened in Chile and Brazil in support of civilian reformist initiatives; in the second transition, the military intervened decisively to impose its own vision.

THE LONG LIFE OF THE PERUVIAN OLIGARCHY

As this and previous chapters have suggested, the Peruvian oligarchy was not terribly different from its peers elsewhere in the region. But in one important sense, it was different: It lasted longer. Well after oligarchic power had faded as a consequential factor in the politics of most other Latin American nations, the oligarchs remained a force in Peru. Part II will show how this happened. While part I has described, in broad strokes, the changing structure of oligarchic power in five countries, part II presents fine grained description of the exercise of oligarchic power in one country and by three families.

NOTES

1. The broad characterizations of the working class here and in table 3.1 are based on Collier and Collier 1991, Hall and Spalding 1986, Spalding and Crites 2008, Alexander 1962, Bergquist 1986, Roxbourgh 1998, Alexander 2003 (on Argentina), and the general literature for each country in the separate country bibliographies.

2. The broad characterizations of the middle class in this section are based on Johnson 1958 and Portales 2004: 354–368, Parker 1919 (on Peru), and Iturriaga 1951 (on Mexico), in addition to the general literature listed in the separate bibliographies and the information in table 2.1.

3. The characterizations of national militaries here and in table 3.1 are drawn from Rouquié 1982, 1998, North 1966, Johnson 1964, McAlister et al. 1970, Poppino 2008 (on Brazil), Young 2008 (on Brazil), Rath 2013 (on Mexico), Masterson 1991 (on Peru), and the general literature for each country listed in the separate country bibliographies.

4. This section draws on Loveman 1988, Bauer 1975, Lagos 1965, Zeitlin and Radcliff 1988, and Vergara 2014 and other sources listed in the Chile section of the bibliography.

5. Besides the general sources for Argentina listed in the bibliography, this section has drawn on Rock 1975a, 1975b, Falcoff and Dolkart, 1975, Potash 1969, Deutsch 1993, Dolkart 1993, Hora 2001a, 2001b, 2014, and Horowitz 2008.

6. This section has drawn on Bethell 2008, Burns 1993, Fausto 1999, Conniff 1999, Font 2010, Levine 1998, Love and Barickman 1986, Skidmore 2007, 2010, Woodard 2006, and Young 1967. Wolfe 2014, and other sources in the Brazil bibliography.

7. In addition to the general sources listed in the Mexico section of the bibliography, for this chapter I have drawn on Hamilton 1982, Wasserman 1995, Meyer 1991, Knight 1991, Camp 1989, Smith 1979, and Nutini 1995.

II

THE OLIGARCHY AND THE OLD REGIME IN PERU

Selective Chronology of the Old Regime in Peru

1840–1875	**Guano Age**. Earnings from exports of nitrate-rich guano create new fortunes and strengthen Peruvian state.
1872	**Manuel Pardo**, descendent of colonial family and wealthy guano trader, elected Peru's first civilian president as candidate of oligarchic Civilista Party.
1879–1883	**War of the Pacific**. Peru defeated, occupied, and stripped of valuable southern provinces by Chile.
1895–1919	**Aristocratic Republic,** Peru's oligarchic republic. Rebirth of Civilista Party and return to civilian-oligarchic rule.
1908–1912	Presidency of **Augusto Leguía** divides oligarchs and Civilista Party.
1912–1914	Presidency of proto-populist **Guillermo Billinghurst,** cut short by oligarchy-promoted coup, led by Colonel **Oscar Benavides** and **Prado** brothers. Oligarchic rule restored.
1919–1968	**Contested Republic**. Oligarchy challenged by new political actors.
1919–1930	**Leguía**'s eleven-year dictatorship, the *Oncenio*. Prominent oligarchs separated from politics, jailed, and deported. But their interests protected.
1930	**Colonel Luís Sánchez Cerro** topples Leguía. Gains oligarchic support.
1931	**Sánchez Cerro** victorious over APRA leader **Victor Raul Haya de Torre** in hard-fought, sometimes violent election campaign. Repression of APRA by new government.
1931–1968	**Trilateral Politics.** State of national politics varies with relationships among oligarchy, APRA, and the military.
1932	**Aprista Uprising in Trujillo** ends with execution of several dozen military prisoners by Apristas. Thousands of Apristas killed in reprisal.

1933	**Sánchez Cerro assassinated** by young Aprista.
1933–1939	**Benavides** appointed interim president. Remains in power beyond Sánchez Cerro's term. Initially pursues more moderate policy toward APRA under "Peace and Concord" cabinet led by **Jorge Prado**.
1935	**Antonio Miró Quesada**, director of *El Comercio* assassinated by young Aprista.
1939–1945	**Manuel Prado** elected president with help of Benavides and some Aprista support, but party remains illegal during his term.
1945–1948	**José Luís Bustamante** elected president in alliance with APRA, which soon falls apart. Term is marked by growing political and economic instability.
1948–1956	**General Manuel Odría**, backed by oligarchy, overthrows Bustamante, inaugurating eight-year dictatorship.
1956–1962	**Manuel Prado** elected to second presidency, with open APRA support in *Convivencia* arrangement.
1962	**Military coup** blocks Haya election victory and prevents extension of *Convivencia*.
1962–1963	Reform-oriented **military junta** rules.
1963–1968	**Fernando Belaúnde** elected president. His reform initiatives blocked in Congress by oligarchy-APRA opposition.
1968–1975	**General Juan Velasco** leads coup installing the "Revolutionary Government of the Armed Forces." ***End of Old Regime in Peru.***

4

Peru's Oligarchic Republic

I have come to liquidate the old state of things, but also to detain the advance of communism. . . .

—Augusto Leguía

The Aristocratic Republic, Peru's oligarchic republic, took form in the 1890s, under the control of a small group of wealthy men with interests in exports, finance, and international commerce. They would govern the country's politics for a generation. But by the end of this first phase of the Old Regime in Peru as in the other four countries studied here, oligarchic power was threatened by intraelite conflict and popular challenges from below.

THE GUANO OLIGARCHY[1]

The Aristocratic Republic had its roots in the Guano Age (1840–1879), a period of sudden wealth, corruption, and extravagance that ended in economic collapse and military disaster. Yet many of the fortunes, political alliances, and social connections that would shape the Aristocratic Republic can be traced to this period. The three families of special interest to us here—the Aspíllagas, the Prados, and the Miró Quesadas—begin their rise during the Guano Period.

The years following independence from Spain (1821) were not especially propitious for the emergence of a new national ruling class. The destructive wars of independence had delivered the coup de grâce to an already struggling economy and undermined the fortunes of the colonial elite of crown officials, wealthy merchants, and others. Many members of this class had fled to Spain. Those who remained were, as a class, economically weak and politically inconsequential. But they possessed valuable cultural and social capital: education, social prestige, and useful social networks. Some owned land. A few colonial families survived and could, more than a century later, be counted among the wealthiest and most powerful Peruvians (see table 1.1, chapter 1).

The postcolonial period was the time of the caudillos, a succession of men on horseback, who continually challenged Lima governments with their private armies. Once in power, the successful caudillo was forced to devote much of his energies and treasury to fending off new challenges.

Guano changed things. Guano is the accumulated manure deposited over centuries by sea birds on certain small islands off the Peruvian coast. Rich in nitrogen, it is a valuable fertilizer, prized by the Incas, but largely forgotten after the Spanish conquest. By no accident, guano was rediscovered in Peru at a time when Europe was industrializing, its population growing rapidly and in need of increased agricultural productivity. These factors and concurrent improvements in international transportation launched Peru back into the world economy.

The Peruvian government controlled the guano deposits and licensed a changing mix of national and foreign consignees to exploit them in exchange for a percentage of the expected revenue. Guano flowed out and millions in hard currency flowed back. Soon a new class had emerged whose members had built large fortunes on some combination of guano and political influence. By the end of the period, Peruvians were referring to them as "the oligarchy" (Basadre 1964: V, 2196).

As early as 1853 the guano rich appeared on the stage of Lima society at the Victoria Ball, an event recorded by Ricardo Palma, a contemporary social chronicler, in tones swelling with contempt for the parvenus. He recalls that the women of the "genealogical aristocracy" appeared at the dance wearing silver jewelry in order to distinguish themselves from the *nouveaux riches*, who sported gold jewelry, the only type then available in Lima shops. But the women of the aristocracy, according to Palma, were unable to match the luxurious dresses that adorned their competitors (Palma 1953: 1126–1127).

In fact, some colonial families managed to insert themselves into the guano trade, and many took one course open to a decaying aristocracy faced with a rising moneyed class: They married their sons and daughters to families with new fortunes. The foundation in this period of the elite Club Nacional reflected the social consolidation that came with the new economy.

The guano trade and the new class it created were responsible for profound changes in the Peruvian political system. Guano revenue was a source of corruption, but it also supported the creation of a stronger central government in Lima to fill the vacuum left by the departing Spanish. A civil bureaucracy and, even more important, a standing army could now be maintained. One result was a shift of power from the provinces to Lima, which was no longer dependent on them for revenue. These developments mark the beginning of one of the dominant trends in modern Peruvian political history: the centralization of political power in Lima governments sustained by the export economy and dominated by export interests. The accompanying reciprocal trend was the decline of provincial elites.

In 1872, Peru elected its first civilian president, Manuel Pardo, grandson of a colonial official, guano consignee, and founder of one of the most important oligarchic lineages. He was the nominee of the new Civilista Party, organized with the backing of most of upper-class Lima. As the party's name suggests, its founders wanted to escape the military-caudillo tradition that had dominated Peruvian politics since independence from Spain. They also were anxious to assert their own control over the guano trade.

Pardo's election marked the apogee of the Guano Age and the plutocracy it created. Guano income was flowing into Peru at record levels. In Lima and the nearby summer beach resort of Chorillos, the guano rich were becoming accustomed to an opulent style of life based on contemporary European models. But the guano deposits were depleting, and the trade had not created a basis for sustained economic development. The guano rich speculated in securities and urban real estate. Their names appeared on the boards of the banks that existed to facilitate the guano trade and provide credit to the government against future guano earnings. The one productive area the oligarchs did promote (through direct participation and by extending credit) was export-oriented coastal agriculture. The main crops were cotton and sugar. Among those who entered the sugar industry at this time were President Pardo's family and the Aspíllagas, who took over the plantation Cayaltí in partnership with a guano consignee.

In the mid-1870s Peru's fragile national economy began to stall. The guano deposits were nearly exhausted, and other fertilizers were successfully competing with guano on the international market. Peru was deeply indebted. The government was finally forced into bankruptcy, and the banking system, built on guano, collapsed. The financial crisis, in turn, undermined the heavily mortgaged sugar industry, which was already suffering from declining international prices.

As the guano boom faded, Peruvian economic and political elites shifted their attention to the southern coastal desert region, where there were abundant deposits of nitrate, another exportable fertilizer. However, Bolivia and Chile were also interested in the region, and the prospect of a second fertilizer boom was cut short when war broke out among the three nations in 1879.

The War of the Pacific (1879–1883) found Peru economically weak and politically divided. Peruvian forces had no hope of defeating the well-trained, better-equipped Chilean army and navy. Parts of the country, including Lima, were occupied by Chilean troops, and a valuable piece of southern Peru was lost to Chile. It would take the country over a decade to recover economically from the devastation of the war. A sense of national humiliation and anger over these events would linger for generations. It would, as we will see in chapter 7, especially affect the history of the Prado family.

The Guano Age left little of enduring value for Peru. But there was some continuity between the guano rich and the renewed oligarchy that emerged at the end of the century. Among the twenty-nine oligarchic clans of the mid-twentieth century named earlier (table 1.1), three had participated directly in the guano trade (Pardo,

Barreda, Ayulo), and at least five were descended from European immigrants who established themselves as merchants during the guano boom (Berkemeyer, Gildemeister, Larco, Wiese, Picasso). Most of these families would become, if they were not already, involved in plantation agriculture.

THE ARISTOCRATIC REPUBLIC: ECONOMY[2]

The Peruvian oligarchy reemerged in the last decade of the nineteenth century with the revival of the export economy. Expanded coastal agriculture and mining in the sierra provided a more dependable basis than guano for building and sustaining oligarchic fortunes and the national economy. The reincarnated oligarchy proved more entrepreneurial than its predecessor.

Most of the families of the twentieth-century oligarchy (the Oligarchic 29, listed in table 1.1) made or renewed their fortunes during this period. The elite families referred to here and in coming chapters are, in almost all cases, members of this small group.

The planters were the dominant economic and political actors of this period. They filled the boards of the newly created banks and insurance companies. They provided the leadership of the Civilista Party and frequently held elective and appointive political office. The semiofficial National Agrarian Society founded in 1896 and controlled by the major planters gained powerful influence over national economic and social policy—an influence that it maintained to the last years of the Old Regime.

Cotton and sugar were again the principal export crops. Each provided the basis for oligarchic fortunes, though sugar proved more significant, both economically and politically. In the 1890s, the sugar industry was still recovering from a string of disasters that begin with the financial collapse of the 1870s and culminated in the damage suffered at the hands of occupying Chilean troops during the War of the Pacific. Those who survived had to contend with tight credit, antiquated equipment, labor shortages, and a volatile international market. One result of these conditions was a process of concentration in the industry as the strongest survivors extended their dominions. Another was increased dependence on foreign sources of credit. Nonetheless, most of the industry remained in Peruvian hands. Those who remained (among them, the Aspíllagas and the Pardos) were modern capitalists in two important senses. They regularly upgraded their technology in order to remain competitive in an unforgiving market, and they employed a large, permanent, free (waged) labor force. During the Aristocratic Republic, modern sugar mills, private railroads, and new port facilities were built on the major plantations. Foreign industrial and agricultural methods were carefully studied and applied by the Peruvian planters. Having lost access to imported labor (first slaves and later Chinese coolies), growers were forced to recruit workers from among the peasantry of the Sierra. Despite these difficulties, sugar cultivation was lucrative for those who survived. World War I was a particular bonanza for the industry, transforming a family like the Aspíllagas from merely rich to extraordinarily wealthy.

The revival of coastal agriculture was paralleled by a renaissance in Peruvian mining for the first time since the colonial period. The sector attracted the attention of many oligarchic families and would contribute significantly to some large oligarchic fortunes. However, from the turn of the century, initiative in mining, in Peru as in Chile, passed to foreign capital. Many Peruvian mine owners, including the Bentins and Gildemeisters, sold their properties to foreign companies at advantageous prices. A turning point came in 1902, when the American Cerro de Pasco Mining Company, after losing a long, bitter battle in Peruvian courts, was forced into an onerous settlement with a Peruvian mining syndicate controlled by the Aspíllagas, Pardos, and other oligarchs. Many families would continue to hold mining stocks in their portfolios, but only a few, including the Fernandinis, Mujicas, and Rizo Patrons, continued to work in the sector.

The oligarchs also invested in the urban economy, which blossomed in the 1890s. Cotton textiles—a logical extension of local cotton production—led industrial boom. Other light consumer goods industries followed. Utilities, including electricity, water, and public transportation (electric tramways), also developed in this period. The Prados, one of the few oligarchic families whose interests were primarily urban, played a central role in these developments.

A key to the diversified economic expansion of this period was the revival of the financial sector. The banking system provided an effective mechanism for transfer among sectors of capital originating in exports. Inevitably, the names of export oligarchs appeared frequently on the boards of banks and insurance companies; among them were Aspíllagas, Mujicas, Gildemeisters, Pardos, and Fernandinis (Portocarrero 1995: 152–153; Yepes 1972: 175–180).

In the course of the Aristocratic Republic, the oligarchy's position within the Peruvian economy was defined and would remain unaltered to the very end of the Old Regime in 1968. The economic interests of the oligarchy continued to be concentrated in exports, especially coastal agriculture, and finance. Oligarchic involvement in the urban sectors other than finance would be minimal. The urban boom that the oligarchs fueled with indirect and some direct investment of export earnings had waned by the late 1910s. Manufacturing, by and large small scale, would be led by immigrant entrepreneurs. The utility sectors came increasingly under foreign control. As Thorp and Bertram (1978: 118–132) have shown, the oligarchs withdrew from the urban sectors for the simple reason that they had become less profitable in a changed economic environment. A modest exception was real estate, which proved lucrative for families including the Prados and the Aspíllagas in periods such as the 1920s when Lima was expanding.[3]

THE ARISTOCRATIC REPUBLIC: AN OLIGARCHIC POLITY

As in the Guano Age, so in this period an economic boom presaged the emergence of a new oligarchic political regime. After the War of the Pacific, Peru reverted to military rule. The more or less constitutional order they created would endure for a quarter century, the longest period of political stability Peru had enjoyed since independence. For most of that time, the government was in the hands of the Civilistas, whose control was reinforced by an 1896 electoral "reform law" enabling the manipulation of election results by those in power.

The Civilista Party was, according to Carlos Miró Quesada, son of one of its best-known figures, the party of "big landowners, bankers, merchants, rural bosses, rentiers and lawyers" (Miró Quesada Laos 1961: 356). It was now possible to speak quite literally of oligarchic rule in Peru. The party was controlled by the same small group of families that dominated the economy. In contrast to the situation that existed after 1930, this elite conducted the affairs of state in person. For almost the entirety of the Aristocratic Republic, the president, in a regime that favored presidential power, was a sugar planter or member of a sugar family. Such was the case for presidents Eduardo López de Romaña, José Pardo, who served two terms, and Augusto Leguía. Key cabinet ministers were drawn from similar backgrounds.

The core of the ruling elite participated in an informal group known as the "Twenty-four Friends," which met at the Club Nacional Thursday evenings to discuss national affairs. Over time, this select group of wealthy planters, bankers, merchants, and their associates included two presidents, at least eight cabinet ministers (five of whom held the key treasury portfolio), three presidents of the senate, and the publishers of Lima's two major newspapers (Karno 1970: 62–63; Miró Quesada Laos 1961: 354).

Members of oligarchic families served in the legislature, alongside representatives of the landowning families of the Sierra. During this period, 16 of the Oligarchic 29 families of the oligarchy listed in table 1.1 were represented in the Congress, most of them by more than one member.[4] Of the remaining thirteen families, five had still not consolidated their economic and social positions at the end of the Aristocratic Republic, 1919.

THE ARISTOCRATIC REPUBLIC: ELITE SOCIETY

As the oligarchy was reemerging economically and politically, it was integrating itself socially. During the Aristocratic Republic, many families with new fortunes, including families of recent immigrant origins, were absorbed into the social elite. It was important to such families to validate their elite status through marriage with families of unquestioned social prestige. Thus the parvenu Wiese brothers of German origin married into the Osma and Montero families, whose high social position dated from colonial times. Elite renewal through "blood and gold" marriages, evident in the Guano Period, was back in motion. At the same time, it is probable that many colonial and guano era families who failed to sustain their fortunes fell into social obscurity. The net outcome of this process, as will be shown by an analysis in chapter 9, was the thick web of family ties connecting the oligarchs to each other and the inner circle of upper-class Lima society.

Peruvian historian Jorge Basadre would later evoke the intimate world of the elite during the Aristocratic Republic:

> Marriages were made among a small number of families, endogamously. Their children's education began in exclusive schools. Playmates continued as schoolmates and as classmates in the universities . . . they greeted each other ceremoniously, they went to Sunday mass together, they dined, drank and chatted together in the Club Nacional, they occupied preferred seats at the bullring, race track and theatres, they also met each other in the Congress, the charity organizations, the university faculties, the Chamber of Commerce, the directors' lounges of the large banks or industrial enterprises and the parties and discussion groups held in the same drawing rooms, and they saw their names in the social pages of the same newspapers. Families were generally large with an abundance of servants, who were sometimes treated as if they belonged to the same family circle. There were . . . families before which one knelt in respect awe and adulation. The daughter of one of these once said in Europe, "In my country I am like a princess" (Basadre 1968: XI, 127. Translated by Klaren 1986: 613).

The oligarchs' overlapping kinship ties, neighborhoods, schools, elite clubs, political associations, and business connections created a social foundation for elite cohesion. Consider the links between the Pardo and the Aspíllaga clans. Pardo and Aspíllaga children attended La Recolecta together. Both families owned major sugar estates and were leaders of the National Agrarian Society. Members of the two families participated in the Cerro de Pasco syndicate. Antero Aspíllaga and José Pardo were key figures in the Civilista Party. Aspíllaga and two Pardo brothers participated in the weekly gatherings of the Twenty-Four Friends at the Club Nacional. Inevitably, multiple members of both families belonged to the club.

To an outsider it must have appeared that the families of the elite had reserved for themselves every significant social institution. When Luís Alberto Sánchez, an ambitious man who would become one of Latin America's leading intellectuals, entered San Marcos University, Mariano Ignacio Prado Heudebert (later head of the family's Banco Popular) was among his fellow students. Prado's uncle was president of the university, and his father was dean of the very important law faculty. The university was under the domination of what Sánchez later described as the "Civilista clan." Three families in particular—the Miró Quesadas, the Pardos, and the Prados—held most of the important university positions (Martin 1949; Sanchez 1969: I, 135, 143).

Sánchez had already encountered this elite at the exclusive La Recoleta boys school, where his classmates included two of the Aspíllaga Barrera brothers and members of the Pardo, Lavalle, Bentín, and Beltrán clans. Sánchez, who was apparently from a middle-class family, must have felt out of place. He later described the period of his attendance (1908–1916) as a time when La Recoleta was just beginning to admit a few students who were not among the social elect (Sanchez 1969: I, 99, 105). Sánchez would have a long, shifting relationship with one of his classmates, Pedro Beltrán. The two worked together on the school paper. Both became prominent public figures: Sánchez as a scholar, ideologue, and key leader of the populist APRA party; Beltrán as a cotton grower, political leader of the planters, and publisher of the right-wing daily, *La Prensa,* known for its relentless attacks on APRA. Years later, in a much transformed Peru, Sánchez would himself become president of the university and write for *La Prensa.*

THE DISINTEGRATION OF THE OLIGARCHIC REPUBLIC

In 1904 a generational rift developed within the Civilista Party. That year there was a struggle for control of the Central Committee between partisans of the presidential candidacy of Isaac Alzamora and that of José Pardo. Pardo's "young Turks triumphed and forced Antero Aspíllaga, and others off the committee" (Miró Quesada Laos 1961: 364). This was a purely *intraelite* struggle representing a changing of the guard. Isaac Alzamora and Aspíllaga had participated in the Twenty-Four Friends' weekly gatherings but so would Pardo and his then ally Augusto B. Leguía. If the younger group was in some ways more progressive in its thinking, it still represented the same basic interests. Aspíllaga and Pardo were, of course, both from sugar planter families.

One goal of the progressive wing was the enactment of protective labor legislation. Shortly after taking office, Pardo's government commissioned the drafting of legislation to cover such problems as compensation for industrial accidents, regulation of female and child labor, working hours, work contracts, and industrial safety. It is notable that this initiative was taken before a significant working-class movement had developed. Such legislation was a particular concern of two politician-intellectuals, José Matias Manzanilla and Luís Miró Quesada. But little came of these early efforts. The only piece of legislation enacted was a law establishing the firm's liability in work accidents, which did not apply to agricultural field workers or miners and therefore did not much affect the oligarchs.

The tension between generations within the Civilista Party did not precipitate an enduring split within the party or otherwise transform the political system. The same cannot be said for the ambitions of Augusto Leguía. I have already described Leguía as an outsider who accumulated a considerable fortune and won his way into elite economic and social circles with a combination of talent and charm. He was incorporated into the leadership of the Civilista Party.

Leguía was Pardo's protégée; had sided with him in the central committee fight; served him as finance minister; and was elected, with Pardo's support, as his successor. Once in power, however, Leguía alienated much of the Civilista elite, in part for policy reasons, but mainly because of Leguía's obvious desire to substitute his own rule for the democracy among plutocrats, which had been the hallmark of the Aristocratic Republic. From the beginning, Leguía excluded most of the party's established leaders from his cabinet and surrounded himself with men of his own making. His manipulation of the 1911 congressional elections precipitated violent confrontations in the legislature over the seating of the candidates he had favored.

His Excellency Dr. D. José Pardo
President of Peru

Sr. D. Augusto B. Leguía
President of the Cabinet and Minister of Finance

José Pardo (with presidential sash) and Augusto Leguía. The politics of the last years of the Aristocratic Republic were reflected in the shifting relationship between these two men.

Source: Garland, Peru, in 1906 (1908). Public Domain.

In the wake of these events, Leguía's opponents (among them the Pardos, Miró, Quesadas, and members of many other oligarchic clans) split from the party to form the Independent Civilista Party.

The Civilista schism contributed to the victory of the protopopulist Billinghurst in 1912. But two years later, alarmed by Billinghurst's radical talk and fervent popular following, the oligarchs came together to topple him. The Prado brothers, Jorge and Manuel, were the civilian leaders of the coup d'état and the personal links in an alliance between the elite and Colonel Oscar Benavides, military leader of the coup (Gerlach 1973: 75; Sanchez 1969: I, 122–124). Benavides served as provisional president for eighteen months and relinquished power to José Pardo, who was elected after a convention of political parties chose the former Civilista president as their common presidential candidate.

The return of José Pardo to the presidency represented the restoration of the Aristocratic Republic, at least for the time being. The elite had overcome its divisions to remove Billinghurst and reinstall one of its own. However, these achievements had required the help of the military. The events of 1914 and 1915 foretold the system of Peruvian politics, which emerged after 1930, when the oligarchy was compelled to rely on the military to overthrow reformist regimes and repress popular movements.

Pardo's second term saw the enactment of a few pieces of social reform legislation of the sort that he and other second-generation Civilistas had favored during his first presidency. Most notable was a law regulating the labor of women and children. However, the labor movement had far outrun the modest proposals of the young Civilistas of 1904.[5] Pardo's government had to face widespread strikes and frequently responded with bloody repression. During this period a radically inclined labor federation and Peru's first socialist party appeared. At the university, a student movement developed, demanding reform of the institution's archaic, elite-dominated organization and a more democratic admissions policy. The students were sympathetic to the workers and supported them in some of the more serious strikes.

Labor militancy was fed by the special economic conditions created by World War I. Highly favorable markets for Peruvian exports such as sugar, cotton, copper, and petroleum brought a new bonanza for the oligarchy and foreign-owned firms exploiting these products. At the same time there was a precipitous rise in domestic prices. The effects on the lower classes were aggravated by the expansion of export crops onto land normally devoted to the production of basic foodstuffs. The inability of Pardo's government to deal with this situation only increased lower- and middle-class disaffection with Civilista rule. It was, after all, the oligarchic elite that controlled the party, who most profited from wartime conditions. (Note, for example, the spectacular profits of the Aspíllagas' sugar plantation during this period in table 6.1.)

The most serious labor troubles came in 1919. In January there was a short general strike, supported by university students, which demanded the reduction of food prices, the enforcement of existing labor legislation, and the enactment of the eight-hour day. The city was virtually paralyzed, and Pardo was forced to call out the army to impose order. Despite some resistance within his administration and among the oligarchs, Pardo capitulated to the demand for an eight-hour day, which he imposed by degree. A second, grimmer general strike broke out in May. Again Pardo resorted to armed force. The city was under martial law from May 27 to June 5, and repression was particularly brutal, resulting in many deaths. The industrialists, bankers, and merchants of Lima were so grateful that social order had been reestablished that they raised a considerable sum of money as a gift to the army.

In the midst of these difficulties, presidential elections were held. The candidates were Leguía and the official candidate, planter Antero Aspíllaga, now backed by Pardo. Leguía, who had spent the years following his presidency in exile, had carefully prepared his return by building a national political network and propagating a new image of himself. Unpopular when he departed, he now reappeared as a fresh face, the progressive anti-Civilista, the un-Pardo. Thus when Pardo responded unsympathetically to student pressures for badly needed university reforms, the university students turned to Leguía and, hoping to gain his support, bestowed on him the honorary title "Mentor of Youth," usually reserved for outstanding university professors. Since the social basis for Civilismo was narrow indeed, Leguía could draw an ample following with vague appeals. He presented himself to certain upper-class supporters as a modernizer, a cautious reformer who knew how to stave off revolution through minor changes in the system. At the same time he led workers and students to believe that he favored far-reaching reform measures. His main strength came from a populist alliance of "students, store clerks, public employees, soldiers and low ranking officers, artisans and workers" (Basadre 1964: VIII, 3931).

Leguía swept the 1919 election. But convinced that the Civilista-oligarchs were maneuvering to nullify the vote and award the presidency to Aspíllaga, he seized power in a preemptive coup d'état, sent Pardo into exile, and dismissed the Congress.

Leguía's Oncenio[6]

Upon taking office, Leguía announced his intentions clearly: "I have come to liquidate the old state of things, but also to detain the advance of communism. . . ." (Capuñay 1951: 151–152). During the *Oncenio,* Leguía's eleven-year dictatorship, the families of the Civilista oligarchy were banished from the political arena. At the same time, his government resisted the radical forces that threatened their privileged existence.

The election of a new Congress at the beginning of Leguía's presidency represented a definitive break with the Civilista past. Since 1895 a series of overlapping congresses had maintained the unbroken continuity of the Aristocratic Republic, even through the critical transitions of presidential power in 1912, 1914, and 1915. By displacing the entire Congress in the wake of the 1919 coup, Leguía consolidated his power and put an end to Civilism's patrician democracy.

Leguía's efforts to solidify his political position went beyond the exclusion of his enemies from the formal exercise of power. For example, shortly after assuming power, he unleashed a campaign against the oligarchy-controlled press. One evening in September 1919, mobs, with the apparent encouragement of the government, attacked the offices of Lima's principal dailies, *La Prensa* and *El Comercio,* and the homes of their respective publishers. At *El Comercio* the attackers were driven off by gun fire, but they did manage to burn down the home of its publisher, Antonio Miró Quesada, a leading Civilista figure. The nongovernment press learned self-censorship, a lesson that was reinforced by the periodic jailings and deportations of journalists.

Prominent Civilistas, suspected by Leguía of conspiring against him, were also imprisoned or deported. Members of the Aspíllaga and Miró Quesada families and the Prado clan (which had initially supported Leguía) were victims. Anti-oligarchy rhetoric suffused the columns of the regime's press and the speeches of its politicians.

What Leguía wanted from the oligarchs was clear. As Ramon Aspíllaga Barrera explained in a letter, "With respect to politics . . . as if we were foreigners in our own land" (RAB 11–22–19).

But if the oligarchs were politically marginalized, their economic interests were respected by Leguía. This was a period when many wealthy Civilistas lived comfortably in European exile on the earnings of their Peruvian properties. Some of Leguía's policies opened new opportunities for the oligarchs. For instance, certain families earned considerable sums in real estate speculation in greater Lima, whose rapid expansion during this period was promoted by Leguía's government.

The oligarchy had little reason to be unhappy with Leguía's attitude toward labor.[7] He had, of course, taken advantage of the labor unrest of the late Pardo years to promote his own return to the power and backed a new constitution allowing for official recognition of labor unions and mediation of strikes. But, in practice, especially after the first two years, Leguía pursued labor policies that were more repressive than those of his predecessor. Rather than dealing with labor conflicts as they arose (Pardo's approach), Leguía sought to stifle organizing activity itself. In 1922, for instance, Leguía forcibly disbanded the militant and well-organized labor movement that had grown up on the sugar plantations of the Chicama valley (Klaren 1976: 107–108). The regime's brutal 1927 campaign against labor and radical organizations brought enthusiastic praise from the Miró Quesadas' paper (*El Comercio*, June 10 and 12, 1927).

Leguía has been portrayed as the champion of the middle class. He did significantly expand state employment and promote legislation that protected white-collar employees. But those who gained most under Leguía were new men of power associated in one way or another with his regime. Many were friends or relatives of the dictator. Some accumulated considerable fortunes in ways that depended on government contracts or special concessions. Others were associated with American capital, which received especially generous treatment from Leguía, whose regime was highly dependent on U.S. investment and loans from American banks.

A new oligarchy was emerging parallel to the old. Its members were from relatively affluent families, but not drawn from the Civilista elite or its clients and frequently of provincial origins. Unable to penetrate the aristocratic Club Nacional, they took over the second-ranking Club de la Union and engaged in a style of conspicuous consumption that recalled the guano years.

The Civilista oligarchy despised Leguía and those around him. Yet he remained in power for more than a decade. Historian Basadre (1931: 185) attributes this in part to a lack of cohesion within the oligarchy. However, there were many plots against him and at least some of the numerous oligarchic figures who were jailed or deported by Leguía were involved in such activities.[8] Leguía was able to resist these efforts because he strengthened and adroitly managed the security forces. Until the end of Leguía's long reign, his machinery of repression proved as effective against elite subversive movements as it was at crushing union activity on the sugar estates and Indian revolts in the Sierra.[9]

It took the impact of the World Depression to weaken the regime to the point that it succumbed to rebellion led by Lieutenant Colonel Luís Sánchez Cerro in August 1930. Sánchez Cerro, who was later elected president, was supported by many professionally oriented, younger officers who were alienated by Leguía personal corruption of the military.

The oligarchy survived Leguía and would survive the depression. As table 1.1 clearly shows, nearly all the families that would comprise the mid-twentieth-century oligarchy had attained elite economic and social status well before the 1919 coup that inaugurated the Oncenio. The Leguiista parvenus did not exhibit the same powers of survival. Relatively few managed to sustain their position beyond 1930 (Basadre 1968: XIV, 8–33).

In the early thirties formal and informal efforts were made to purge former Leguiistas. A special tribunal was set up to deal with those who had profited illegally in their dealings with the state. At the same time the Civilista oligarchy maneuvered to eradicate whatever residual political influence the Leguiistas might have.[10] Many had depended on a continuous flow of political largesse from the regime. Not infrequently they had spent income as it was earned. The dual shock of the political shift and the depression proved devastating for most. A few families close to Leguía's regime did manage to sustain their positions after his fall. But these were, by and large, families such as the Wieses and de la Piedras that had achieved substantial fortunes before the Oncenio and had never become wholly dependent on the regime.

Leguía and the End of the Oligarchic Republic

The 1919 coup marked the end of the Aristocratic Republic. Leguía united in his person the twin forces that were undermining oligarchic power in Peru: intraelite conflict and growing social challenges from below. His ambition was the primary cause of the schism that destroyed Civilism. At the same time, he had recognized the power in early popular resistance to elite rule and had channeled it against his enemies.

Leguía's fall in 1930 freed the oligarchs of the constraints long imposed by his regime. But they soon learned, if they did not immediately understand, that they could not hope to rule as they once had. They needed to find new ways to defend their interests in an era of mass mobilization, playing out in the midst of an economic disaster.

NOTES

1. Yepes 1972, Bonilla 1974, Maiguasha 1967, Levin 1960, Sater 2007, and Garland 1895, in addition to general sources for Peruvian history.
2. In addition to general sources on Peruvian history, this section draws on Thorp and Bertram 1978, Yepes 1972, Portocarrero 1995, Bollinger 1971, Burga and Flores Galindo 1984, Klaren 1976, Gonzales 1985, and Garland 1895.
3. Other families with real estate investments include Brescias, Rizo Patrons, Benevides, and Gildemeisters (Portocarrero 1995: 183–191).
4. Families represented in the legislature during this period included Aspíllaga, Prado, Miró Quesada, Pardo, Benavides, Olaechea, Picasso, Chopitea, Mujica, Barreda, Beltrán, Bentin, de Lavalle, Carrillo, Larco, and Malaga (Echegaray 1965; Senado 1961).
5. On labor and labor legislation in this period, Levano 1967; Basadre 1964: VIII, 3896–3934; Martínez de la Torre, 1949: 11–52.

6. Capuñay 1951, Basadre 1931, Miró Quesada Laos 1957 and 1959, Stein 1980, Dagicour n.d.

7. For labor in the 1920s and 1930s, I have drawn on Martínez de la Torre 1949, Payne 1965, and Drinot 2014.

8. On the involvement of the Prados in such plots, see chapter 7.

9. Villanueva 1962: 53–59; Gerlach 1973: chapter V, 158; Masterson 1991: 30–34.

10. There are numerous letters to this effect in the Aspíllaga correspondence of the period, for example, LAA, 9–9-30; IAA 1–4-32.

5

Peru's Contested Republic

> I only govern with my friends.
>
> —Colonel Luís Sánchez Cerro, 1931

> It is the historical destiny of any true process of transformation to confront the beneficiaries of the status quo. Ours is no exception. The irreducible adversaries of our movement will always be those who feel their interests and privileges under attack: the oligarchy.
>
> —General Juan Velasco Alvarado, 1969

The Depression struck Peru's export-oriented national economy with blunt force. By 1932, the value of Peruvian exports had fallen to a third of the 1929 level. The plunge in the oligarchic sugar and cotton sectors ran close to this overall figure (Thorp and Bertram, 1978: 151–152). Peru's biggest bank, Banco del Peru y Londres, collapsed, to the misfortune of stockholders including the Aspíllagas, the Chopiteas, and the Ferreyros. Foreign exchange flowed out of the country as the relative value of the local currency tumbled. Unemployment rose to alarming levels. Peru would recover more quickly than most of its neighbors, but in the early 1930s conditions could not have been worse.

Leguía's fall and the Depression unleashed political forces that had long been held in abeyance by his repressive state apparatus. Militant new labor and political groups had emerged. In the 1920s the ideological tendency among them was away from the early anarchist orientation and toward a Marxist perspective. One of the new groups was the American Popular Revolutionary Alliance (APRA). It would transform Peruvian politics.

THE RISE OF APRA

APRA was founded in 1924 in Mexico by Peruvian exiles but was probably unknown to all but a few Peruvians until it burst onto the national political scene with explosive energy in 1931, under the direction of a group of talented young leaders. It would become Peru's largest, most enduring political party.

The party's founder and central figure for decades was Víctor Raúl Haya de la Torre. The son of middle-class north coast family, Haya first attracted national attention as a student political leader at San Marcos University between 1918 and 1923. There he played a key role in the student-worker movement that gained the eight-hour day for industrial workers, organized a popular university where student volunteers led classes for workers, and led protests that forced Leguía to abandon plans to secure church support for his regime by dedicating the country to the Sacred Heart of Jesus.

The ideology that Haya developed for APRA after visits to revolutionary Mexico and the Soviet Union in the 1923 was Marxist in inspiration but differed from official Communism in significant ways. Haya argued that European models could not be applied to Latin American conditions. He saw Latin American societies as essentially "feudal" in nature and dominated by national oligarchies allied with "imperialist" interests operating in their own countries. (The imperialist interests Haya had in mind were basically large-scale, foreign-controlled enterprises, typically engaged in export-oriented mining or agriculture.) Most important, industrialization had hardly begun in Latin American countries, and therefore they did not have proletariats of significant size or developed national bourgeoises.[1]

While Haya accepted Marx's notion of the long-term historical significance of class conflict, he contended that under contemporary conditions in Latin America, single-class parties would not be effective in promoting change. "It is necessary," he wrote, "to abandon the idea of a class party" (Alexander 1973: 109). In opposition to the Communist strategy, he proposed an alliance of exploited classes including the workers, the peasantry, and the middle class.

He also differed from the Communists regarding further development of national capitalism as a necessary prelude to socialism. While he wrote of "the progressive socialization of wealth under the control of the state . . . and by . . . means of a vast system of cooperatives," this was intended as a long-range ideal (Alexander 1973: 123). The immediate goal was a developmentalist state, installed by electoral means and dedicated to a planned pattern of capitalist growth. Such an Aprista government would carefully control the conditions under which foreign investment entered the country to insure that it was compatible with national economic goals. The government's supporters would form a "united front" with the incipient national bourgeoisie, which, like the country as a whole, was threatened by imperialism. A technically competent bureaucracy would develop and carry out a national economic plan. Popular participation in economic planning would be insured through the medium of a National Economic Congress.

APRA leader Victor Raúl Haya de la Torre haranguing a crowd in 1931.

Source: Wikimedia Commons.

APRA's philosophical differences with Communism involved the party in end-less bitter ideological debates with its rival, the Peruvian Communist Party. But the subtleties of their polemics were lost on APRA's oligarchic enemies, especially when party spokesmen in 1931 were talking of economic planning, progressive taxation, regulation of wages, rent controls, agrarian reform, and, however vaguely, of social-ization of the economy. For years the oligarchic press insisted on labeling APRA "communist."

APRA rhetoric singled out the oligarchy as its special enemy. The party claimed to be engaged in "a great class struggle of productive classes against a plutocratic minor-ity, the accomplice and instrument of imperialism" (Basadre 1968: XIV, 145). Many elements of the party's program threatened the oligarchy, such as suggestions that the coastal plantations be nationalized. Party propaganda featured attacks on "the barons of sugar and cotton." As it happened, APRA's support was strongest in the areas where the oligarchy's export enterprises were located and among their workers.

APRA leaders would spend years walking back the party's most radical positions, which many Peruvians found alarming: No, they really didn't intend to expropriate the sugar plantations and mines and weren't against foreign investment. But the APRA leadership could not always control the message coming from activists, and the leaders were often inconsistent or vague. Haya and other party officials who met with American diplomats over the years convinced them that APRA posed no threat to U.S. interests. The oligarchy was inevitably more skeptical about the party's intentions.

Almost continuously from 1932 into the 1960s, APRA was deprived of the right of full, peaceful participation in the political system. In periods of intense repression, Apristas were exiled, jailed, beaten, and murdered. But the party was also a source of violence. ARPA used gangs of young toughs, known as "búfalos," to intimidate its enemies. It was never clear how much control the top leadership had over the lower ranks of the party. Aprista militants—perhaps acting on their own, perhaps not— were responsible for three high-profile assassinations. APRA staged a series of armed rebellions, with the help of dissident military officers. All failed, in part because of the inconsistent support they received from the leadership. For his part, Haya was personally ambivalent and publically ambiguous on topic of political violence (Pike 1986: 152–153, 159–161, 185, 237–238).

THE OLIGARCHY AND SÁNCHEZ CERRO

Leguía's fall in August 1930 precipitated a tumultuous political situation, aptly described by historian Geoffrey Bertram (1991: 411):

> [Within days of] Sánchez Cerro's triumphant entry into Lima . . . anti-Leguia *civilista* leaders, hungry for power and revenge, returned from exile. Out from underground came the organized cadres of APRA. Into the streets of Lima came delighted mobs to loot the homes of the leguiistas. In factories, plantations, mines, labour unions emerged. . . . The army command was uneasy. . . . APRA was feverishly recruiting support; and government finances were sliding towards collapse, as revenues from taxes on exports and imports fell with the depression.

Whatever thoughts the oligarchs may have initially had of restoring the patrician democracy of the Civilista years were quickly abandoned. They understood that the social upheaval of the period was more than the benign Civilista-style governments could handle. Some form of dependence on the military was inevitable. Further, the oligarchs had discovered, during the Leguía years, that open participation in national politics was risky. The Aspíllaga letters from this period are full of relevant warnings. In one, Ramon Aspíllaga Anderson urges on his brothers the political example of the Pardos "who are involved in everything, but visible nowhere" (RAA 1–25–32).

In the course of the year after the August 1930 coup, the oligarchy gravitated toward Luís Sánchez Cerro, the officer who had led the revolt. The relationship of the oligarchs to the coup is unclear, though it is known that some, including the Miró Quesadas, had been in contact with him regarding Leguía's overthrow. After the coup there was a struggle for Sánchez Cerro's allegiance in which APRA itself vainly participated (Miró Quesada Laos 1947: 3; Sánchez 1969: I, 332–333).

By the end of the year the U.S. ambassador was reporting to Washington, "Sánchez Cerro is about to be appropriated by the very reactionary old Civilista Party, representing the landowning aristocracy and vested interests and headed by Antonio Miró Quesada, editor of *El Comercio*" (Gerlach 1973: 276). At the time, the Aspíllagas were finding Sánchez Cerro, then provisional chief executive, very receptive to them. When they complained of a leftist group that was disseminating propaganda attacking the planters, he asked for more information so he could "proceed in the proper way to eliminate those jerks" (RAA 9–11–30). Informed of pending strikes on the plantations, he assured the Aspíllagas that the government would support no concessions to the workers and urged that the workers be quietly informed of this (RAA 11–23–30).

The oligarchs cultivated Sánchez Cerro. To a degree that is somewhat surprising given his dark mestizo features and modest provincial middle-class origins, the colonel was welcomed into elite social settings. One of the Miró Quesadas later noted that he "liked society and frequented the Club Nacional" (Miró Quesada Laos 1947: 34). Sánchez Cerro did, in fact, become a member of that most exclusive of Lima men's clubs, and it was even said that he was engaged to a blond young lady from one of the city's most prestigious families (Osma 1963: 125; Sanchez 1955: 184). Such attention must have been heady wine for a man of Sánchez Cerro's background. It served not simply to win him over but also to create an atmosphere of informality that eased discussion of political matters.

In the 1931 presidential election, the oligarchy generally backed Sánchez Cerro against APRA's Haya de la Torre, for reasons that are unambiguously outlined in the Aspíllaga family correspondence of the period. Haya posed a threat "to the established order in all things." Sánchez deserved the support of "those of us who have interests to preserve and protect. . . . His principles and program of government are conservative, as are those who surround him. There is no other candidate with his popularity" (RAA 8–27–31). "Above all, he has the army which is essential" (IAA 1–26–31). Sánchez Cerro's candidacy was unstintingly promoted by the Miró Quesadas' *El Comercio*, the traditional voice of the oligarchy. The oligarchs recognized that they needed a popular candidate (not an Aspíllaga or a Pardo), who was sympathetic to their interests and backed by the military.[2]

The 1931 election set two charismatic figures against one another. Both were able to draw tens of thousands of supporters to rallies and both sought mass support with national campaigns on a scale unprecedented in Peruvian history. But Sánchez Cerro had unique advantages. He was the fearless "Hero of Arequipa," a man of action, who had launched the movement from that city to overthrow an unpopular dictator. He could speak the language of the streets and dance the *marinera*. His dark features made him—in a phrase that was heard frequently—"a cholo like us," with whom Peru's poor majority could identify. Ironically, his political instincts were, as the Aspíllagas correctly perceived, fundamentally conservative. The oligarchy would never again find a candidate who combined Sánchez Cerro's politics with his enormous popular appeal (Stein 1980: 82–128).

After a nasty, sometimes violent campaign, Sánchez Cerro triumphed with a convincing 51 percent of the vote to Haya's 35 percent. While Haya was favored by the organized working class and sectors of the middle class, Sánchez Cerro drew support from the urban poor—market venders, construction workers, street cleaners, and laborers in small artisan shops, many of them recent migrants to the city. Sánchez won the south and central regions, including greater Lima. Haya won the coastal north, home to the oligarchy's sugar plantations and for years to come, APRA's geographic base (Stein 1980: 188–202; Werlich 1978: 195–196).

In power, Sánchez Cerro did not disappoint his oligarchic backers. He appointed a cabinet that was strongly Civilista and anti-APRA. One of his ministers was a Miró Quesada. Four had served in Pardo's cabinets. Sánchez Cerro resisted pressures to soothe political tensions with a unity government, saying "I only govern with my friends" (Basadre 1968: XIV, 18).

Sánchez Cerro's sixteen month presidency was a period of severe, often violent social and political confrontation. The Apristas were resolutely convinced that their loss had been the result of electoral fraud (a view that finds little support among contemporary historians).[3] Haya considered himself the "Moral President of Peru." Party members engaged in violent public confrontations with their opponents, while the leadership began to plot the overthrow of Sánchez Cerro's government. Labor conflicts continued unabated in response to economic conditions and efforts of Aprista and Communist organizers (Alba 1968: 268). This was a matter of obvious concern to the sugar planters, who were involved in a common effort to offset declining income by lowering labor costs with reduced wages and increased work demands (RAA 5–27–32).

From the beginning, Sánchez Cerro responded with hash measures, which only stiffened resistance and pushed the country toward civil war. The most important instrument of government repression was the 1932 Law of Emergency. Under its provisions, the government had twenty-three Aprista legislators arrested and deported, suppressed union organizing, shuttered opposition publications, and closed universities whose campuses had become bases for Aprista activity. In May, Aprista sailors seized two naval ships, which were quickly retaken by loyal forces. Authorities randomly picked eight of the 300 mutineers to be executed by a firing squad while the others watched (Werlich 1978: 197). Haya was arrested, tried, and sentenced to death by a military tribunal.

Events culminated with a July uprising in Trujillo, the largest city in the northern Aprista heartland. The action was part of a larger plan by APRA and sympathetic officers—chief among them, Lt. Colonel Gustavo Jimenez, Sánchez Cerro's most prominent military rival. Their strategy anticipated a national revolution that would begin in Trujillo and spread across the north and into other parts of the country. The rebels easily seized the local garrison and took control of the city. But they had acted prematurely, before their allies in other areas were ready.

A considerable deployment of government forces was required to retake Trujillo. In the last hours before the city was recaptured, the rebels killed several dozen captive officers and enlisted men. The army avenged these murders with a massacre of more than a thousand Trujillo Apristas, before firing squads at the ruins of the ancient city of Chan Chan. Jimenez would later kill himself to avoid capture.[4]

The political repercussion of these events was an enduring enmity between the officer corps and APRA. This served the interests of the oligarchy, which could only see the possibility of an alignment between APRA and the military as a supreme threat. For decades after Trujillo, memorial ceremonies were held annually by officers from all the services at the graves of the military men killed by the Apristas. These observances were prominently reported in Miró Quesadas' *El Comercio*. APRA similarly memorialized its own fallen.

Perhaps at no time in Peruvian history did the government so closely approximate the Marxist notion of a bourgeois state defending class interests as it did in these years. At Trujillo the regime faced a movement that posed a significant threat to the planter oligarchy. In fact, the sugar workers on nearby plantations, among whom APRA was particularly strong, rose in support of the Trujillo rebels the Chopiteas, owners of one of these plantations are reported to have played an important role in organizing the government's counterattack. The Lambayeque sugar planters, including the Aspíllagas, Pardos and de la Piedras, were protected by their distance from Trujillo. But the support the nearby sugar workers gave the Trujillo rebels was a frightening demonstration of their own vulnerability.

In the aftermath of the revolt, oligarchs were concerned with preparedness for the next battle with APRA. A special committee was formed to take up a collection to improve armaments and fortifications. Consisting of Luís Pardo, Eulogio Fernandini, Francisco Fernandini, and Ramon Aspíllaga Barrera (all members of prominent oligarchic families), the committee met with Sánchez Cerro soon after Trujillo (RAA 7–19–32).

This ugly period came to a violent end on April 30, 1933, with the assassination of Sánchez Cerro as he emerged from the race track, by a seventeen-year-old Aprista, who was killed on the spot. Sánchez Cerro had been wounded in an earlier attempt on his life in a Lima church, also by a young Aprista. The party would deny responsibility for these episodes and at least two other high-profile assassinations, apparently involving Aprista perpetrators.

TRILATERAL POLITICS

Within hours of the assassination of Sánchez Cerro, General Oscar Benavides was selected by the Congress to complete his term. Benavides, a man with family and per-

sonal connections to the elite, had served as provisional president after the removal
of Billinghurst in 1914. But what kind of political regime would Peru have? Under
conditions of mass mobilization, moving back to direct oligarchic rule or ahead to
a popular democracy seemed—from the perspective of the oligarchy—equally unvi-
able. Instead, the oligarchy would promote and guide governments, usually military
governments, that could be depended upon to protect its privileges. Politics came
to revolve around relationships among three key political players: the oligarchy, the
military, and APRA. The state of the system at any given time depended on relations
among the three and the manner in which APRA was controlled or integrated. This
trilateral system, whose evolution is outlined in table 5.1, endured from the Sánchez
Cerro's government until the 1968 coup that marked the end of the Old Regime.

The trilateral political system allowed the oligarchs to defend their interests without taking direct responsibility for governing the country. But there were inevitable
tensions in this system. One source of tension was the varied possible alignments
among the three. How would a third player react to an alliance between the other

Table 5.1.   Peruvian Regimes of the Trilateral System

Years	President	Type of Regime	Status of APRA
1932–1933	Sánchez Cerro	Oligarchy-backed, military-led government	Violently suppressed
1933–1939	Benavides	Oligarchy-backed, military-led government	Remains illegal but milder treatment, especially in early years
1939–1945	Prado	Civilian oligarchic government created with help of military predecessor and factional APRA support	Illegal, but allowed to operate clandestinely
1945–1948	Bustamante	Civilian reformist, national front government, elected with APRA support and without oligarchic participation	Legal. Initially in cabinet and Congress; allowed to organize workers
1948–1956	Odría	Oligarchy-backed, military-led government	Suppressed
1956–1962	Prado	"Convivencia," oligarchy-APRA alliance	Informal partner of government
1962–1963	Junta	Interim military government	APRA electoral victory aborted by military, but party remains legal
1963–1968	Belaúnde	Reformist government	In opposition parliamentary alliance with oligarchy
1968	Velasco coup	"Revolutionary Govt. of the Armed Forces"	Political parties banned

two? How, for example, might the military respond to a political alliance between APRA and the oligarchy? Such an alignment was inconceivable in the 1930s but became a reality in the 1960s. Another source of strain was factionalization of any of the three parties. As Trujillo revealed, there were APRA sympathizers in the army. Factions among the oligarchs had contributed to the breakdown of the Aristocratic Republic. In the early 1930s, the oligarchs were united against the threat posed by APRA. But there would be some, such as the Prados, who believed that aligning with APRA or some Aprista faction could be to their own advantage. The party's capacity to mobilize voters, workers, protestors, or fighters was always a powerful temptation to the politically ambitious.

The trilateral system would endure until the end of the Old Regime. The evolution of the key trilateral relationships, described in terms of varying types of national regimes, can be seen in table 5.1, which lists three "oligarchy-backed, military-led governments." They account for much of the period covered by the Tripartite System. These governments share important characteristics, which are summarized here.[5]

1. *Strong ties to the oligarchy.* The military figures who lead these regimes are brought into politics with the support of the oligarchy and maintain close ties with particular oligarchic figures. Oligarchs and their clients serve as cabinet ministers and advisers to officer-presidents.

2. *Dictatorial rule.* These regimes are what Peruvians called *regimenes de fuerza* (government by force). The press is controlled, special laws free the regime from the obligation to observe due process, the political opposition (including but not limited to APRA) is intimidated and its leaders are jailed and exiled. Elections, when held, are not credible, if only because the biggest political party is denied participation. The obvious exception was 1931 when Sánchez Cerro triumphed over Haya de la Torre.

3. *APRA is suppressed.* The party is denied legitimate access to the political arena and forced to operate underground. The degree of repression may vary, from Sánchez Cerro's campaign of political extermination to the more benign policies of his successor, Benavides. During some brief periods restrictions on party activity are relaxed, but at no point is the party allowed to openly present its own candidates in an election.

4. *Union activity is suppressed.* Union organizers are subject to the same sort of forceful treatment that the political opposition receives. Unions and union leaders are manipulated by the regime for its own purposes. During some periods the Communists are given freedom in union organizing in order to oppose the superior strength of the Apristas in the labor movement. But the general level of union activity remains quite low in striking contrast to the 1945 to 1948 and post-1956 periods when unions would flourish under civilian governments.

5. *Economic Orthodoxy.* An exporter-oriented laissez-faire political economy is maintained by these regimes. Industrialization is not a significant goal.

This last point deserves elaboration since it reflects the basic orientation of the oligarchic economy. Under both military and civilian governments, the oligarchy was remarkably successful in holding the country to open economy, laissez-faire economic policies. On the rare occasions when governments strayed from this true path, they were, almost without exception, forced back by the oligarchs. Economist Rosemary Thorp (1967) observes that Peru was outstanding among Latin American countries for strict adherence to this policy regime. The official economic response to the depression of the 1930s was, for example, modest and orthodox in proportion to the magnitude of the crisis and very different from the aggressive, innovative responses of most other Latin American nations. Only after the 1968 coup was the traditional economic faith definitively abandoned.

"Creole Liberalism," as Bourricaud (1970: 201) labeled Peru's traditional economic orthodoxy, was based on the classical view of the economy as a self-equilibrating system, the maintenance of which is dependent on free private pursuit of economic gain and the unfettered operation of "natural economic laws." Any government interference with this mechanism, particularly if it threatens returns to private investment, inevitably leads to economic chaos. Thus, the Creole Liberals insisted on private ownership of all productive enterprises; low taxes and tariffs; monetary stability; and freedom from government regulation of prices, wages, or currency exchange. They welcomed foreign investment.

Economic planning, even in the mildest of forms, was an anathema to Creole Liberalism. Pedro Beltrán, a cotton grower, leading spokesman for planter interests, and publisher of the Lima daily *La Prensa*, asserted that

> authoritarian planning would do the country incalculable damage. It would inevitably lead to inflation, the collapse of the currency, a soaring cost of living, thousands out of work, the shrinkage of the national and per capita income, the flight of capital, universal poverty and the enslavement of the country to a corrupt clique which would fatten on it behind the shelter of the laws (quoted by Bourricaud 1970: 197).

Clearly these doctrines were in direct opposition to APRA's official ideology, which stressed state intervention to promote economic growth and protect the exploited, along with careful regulation of foreign investment. At the same time, Creole Liberalism's emphasis on an open economy characterized by free trade and unrestricted currency markets was a direct reflection of the oligarchy's export orientation.

Tied to the demand for a laissez-faire political economy was the assumption that national economic health is highly dependent on the maintenance of *confianza*, investor confidence. Julio de la Piedra, member of a planter family and a key political representative of the oligarchy, put it quite simply in a Senate speech. "Private enterprise depends on investment. Let's not forget that confianza brings forth investment" (*La Prensa*, November 6, 1967). Behind the frequent reminders of this sort from oligarchic sources is an implicit threat: Government tampering with the economy will lead to a crisis of confianza, declining investment and rising unemployment. This prospect gave the oligarchy a powerful veto over national economic policy.

Pedro Beltrán, political leader of the planter core of the oligarchy and publisher of La Prensa.

Source: Wikimedia Commons, Archivo "El Comercio."

FROM BENAVIDES TO PRADO

General Oscar Benavides, like his predecessor, generally followed the policy prescription just outlined. But Benavides was a more subtle and independent figure than Sánchez Cerro, and his relationship with the oligarchy was accordingly more complex. Historian Fredrick Pike describes him in these terms: "Socially prominent himself and at home in the salons of the most wealthy and cultured Peruvian families, Benavides exhibited a certain aloofness in his dealings with most people" (Pike 1967: 268). Benavides had gained national fame in 1911 as the hero of a brief border conflict with Colombia. His participation in the Billinghurst coup was apparently the beginning of his close ties to the Prado family. As provisional president, he aligned himself with the anti-Leguiista Civilistas, thus helping to return the country to oligarchic rule under José Pardo.

The Benavides family, whose progenitor in colonial Peru was a crown official, had formed part of the Arequipa aristocracy (Lasarte 1938). Branches of the family that established themselves in Lima became part of the most exclusive stratum of Lima society and were listed by informants consulted for the Oligarchic 29 (see table 1.1). But according to one of the general's descendants, Benavides' personal background was relatively modest—in fact, "lower-middle class." The same informant indicates that Benavides had begun his career as a "mere soldier" and whatever culture he possessed had been assimilated much later when, as an officer, he was sent on military-diplomatic missions abroad. He did not become a member of the Club Nacional until he was over thirty-five and had attained the rank of colonel.

A key to Benavides' rise was his marriage to a distant cousin, Francisca Benavides Diez Canseco, member of an affluent and socially prominent branch of the family. The close ties to upper-class Lima that Benavides developed through her apparently influenced the success of his early military career, during the Aristocratic Republic. Benavides' more confident relationship to the elite that had guided Sánchez Cerro probably contributed to the tactical independence that crops up periodically in his political career.

Soon after assuming power in 1933, Benavides' appointed a new cabinet led by Jorge Prado of the banking family. The government pursued a more conciliatory policy toward APRA designed to calm a situation that had verged on civil war during Sánchez Cerro's presidency. Under Prado's "Peace and Concord" government, Haya de la Torre and other Apristas were released from prison, and the party was allowed some freedom of expression. However, promised congressional elections—which would have allowed APRA to regain seats Sánchez Cerro had taken away—were never held, and the more temperate attitude toward APRA was abandoned under severe pressure from the Miró Quesadas, Aspíllagas, and other fervent anti-Apristas.

Toward the end of 1934, Benavides easily defeated a series of small scale Aprista revolts. A few disloyal officers and Aprista leaders were deported. (Haya remained in Lima, living clandestinely but monitored by authorities, who, perhaps, felt it was easier to keep track of him in Lima than in exile.) "The government," Ramon Aspíllaga assured one of his sons, "with the support of honest people and we who call ourselves rightists . . . despite the pacification notions of Mr. Benavides . . . continues persecuting the Apro-Leguiista-communists. Many are in jail and some have been deported" (RAB 1–21–36).

Although Benavides never lifted the party's illegal status, jailed or deported most of its leaders, and suppressed its press organ and unions, he was still regarded with suspicion by some of the oligarchs. His most prominent enemies were the Miró Quesadas. They had been unhappy with Benavides even before the 1935 assassination of Antonio Miró Quesada, the director of *El Comercio*, and his wife by a young Aprista militant. Benavides' refusal to have the assassin put to death, won him the enmity of the family and their newspaper.

In 1936, Jorge Prado, former head of the "Peace and Concord" cabinet was the official candidate, backed by Benavides. This election cycle has been commonly portrayed as a demonstration of the inability of the oligarchy to unite and rule the country. There were, as it happened, three candidates on the right competing with Prado, ranging from a relative moderate to self-declared fascist. Haya de la Torre was not permitted to run, but when a contender with presumed Aprista backing appeared to be winning the ballot count, Benavides halted the process and, with congressional approval, extended his own rule. Some suspected that this was his intention all along.[6]

What 1936 demonstrated was not the inability of a divided oligarchy to win elections, but, as I will argue in chapter 9, the impossibility of their winning in an era of mass mobilization without some support from the one mass party.[7]

New elections were held in 1939. Benavides backed another of the Prado Ugarteche brothers, the more able Manuel. Haya was again prevented from running. With some Aprista votes purchased by the Prados[8] and heavy handed help from the government, Manuel was the declared winner. The Aspíllagas took a pragmatic attitude toward this outcome, which was probably typical of the oligarchy at that point. They were not unhappy with Benavides and had positive expectations for his chosen successor. The important thing, Ramon Aspíllaga Barrera wrote one of his sons, was that "Prado had the total support of the armed forces, which fortunately have not been corrupted" (RAB 11–14–39; 12–13–39).

Though Manuel Prado was, in practice, somewhat less repressive than his military predecessors, he did not stray far from the pattern of government they had established. APRA remained illegal. Union activity was constrained. But by 1945, the political atmosphere created by the impending victory of the western democracies (supported by Peru) over Hitler's Germany, favored a national turn toward democracy.

Prado's successor would be José Luís Bustamante, a respected lawyer, drawn from the aristocracy of Arequipa, the southern city that had often been the source of challenges to governments in Lima. Bustamante ran for office as the candidate of a reform-oriented National Democratic Front backed by APRA. In exchange for its support, APRA was permitted to present congressional candidates, under the hastily improvised label "Party of the People." Bustamante was pledged to legalize the party, and it was assumed that APRA would be allowed to present its own presidential candidate in 1951.

Benavides was the godfather of the new political arrangement, having worked out its cautious terms in direct negotiations with Haya and Prado.[9] His support, which guaranteed the military's neutrality, reflected APRA's recent ideological moderation. The party's leaders were anxious to gain the political legitimacy that had long eluded them. By 1945 they had abandoned their most radical positions along with their attacks on the "barons of sugar and cotton" and "Yankee imperialism." On May 20, shortly after Prado had lifted most legal restrictions on the party, Haya addressed a crowd of over 100,000 supporters in Lima's San Martin Plaza. One of his observations was seemingly directed over the heads of his supporters to listeners in the nearby Club Nacional: "It is not necessary to seize the wealth of those who possess it but rather new wealth should be created for those who not have it" (Masterson 1991: 82).

Bustamante and the 1948 Coup

With APRA's support, Bustamante was easily elected. The Apristas won a majority of the seats in the legislature and were assured of some cabinet positions. The oligarchs had, for the moment, lost control of events, but many were cautiously hopeful.[10] Shortly after the election, the Lima elite honored Haya with extravagant (if unimaginable) dinner at the home of Pedro de Osma Gildemeister.

Bustamante's government lasted three years, half the term prescribed by the constitution. During that period, Peru slid into economic and political chaos. Inflation, which had developed during the war, wildly accelerated after 1945 because of international scarcities of basic food commodities that Peru was importing. At the same time Peru's own exports were declining in value, and foreign exchange was fleeing the country in anticipation of a devaluation. Shortages forced the government to resort to unpopular rationing.

These economic difficulties exacerbated Bustamante's political problems. An inexperienced politician, without a political base of his own, the president was soon caught in a trap between APRA and the oligarchy. The party's leaders, ambitious and in control of Congress, were unwilling to cooperate with the president, whom they regarded as a mere figurehead, placed in power by their followers. Aprista influence grew in the public bureaucracy and the schools. In the streets, the Apristas were becoming involved in frequent violent clashes.

Bustamante's government had abandoned the policy prescriptions that had been observed by the conservative regimes the oligarchy had supported since Sánchez Cerro. The sacred economic precepts of creole liberalism were abandoned. Civil liberties were restored. APRA was legalized, allowed full freedom to organize, and even held cabinet posts for a time. Union activity flourished.

The oligarchy soon felt the effects of this shift. APRA conducted an extensive and successful campaign of labor organizing, which particularly concentrated on the major plantations of the north coast.[11] The government employed price, import, and currency exchange controls that favored import interests over exporters. The oligarchic response to the new government took shape gradually. Bustamante would later recall that early in his administration he received discreet offers of support from the oligarchs on the condition of his turning publicly against APRA. But Bustamante felt honor-bound to hold to his pact with the party. On a number of occasions Bustamante offered posts to individuals in the oligarchic camp, but such minority representation was unacceptable to them and the offers were rejected. There emerged what Bustamante later described as a progressively expanding "boycott" of his government (Bustamante 1949: 87–88).

A critical aspect of the boycott was the refusal of cooperation from the business and financial community. For instance, Bustamante tried unsuccessfully to get banks to restrict credit, especially for speculative purposes (Bustamante 1949: 215). The country's currency problems deepened as foreign exchange flowed out of the country. Economic historian Geoffrey Bertram concludes that, by 1947, the oligarchy had "turned definitively against the Bustamante regime and [had] set about subverting its economic policies" (Bertram 1991: 435–436). In April 1948, exporters, led by Augusto Gildemeister, began to withhold foreign exchange (hard currency) earnings from the central bank. The government then issued regulations that forced exporters to surrender 65 percent of their earnings at the overvalued official rate—in effect, a heavy tax on exports. Exporters, anticipating a devaluation, responded by delaying acceptance of payments from abroad. Whether they were acting with political intent or out of purely self-serving economic motives is unknowable and less relevant than their effect, which was to undermine the economy and the government.[12]

For their part, the Apristas were divided, with many members disenchanted by the party's conservative ideological shift and seeming opportunism. The APRA's militant wing, over which Haya exercised only tenuous control, turned to increasingly brutal tactics. In April 1946, Apristas invaded the offices of *El Comercio* and *La Prensa*, which had relentlessly attacked APRA and the government. In January 1947, Francisco Graña Garland, director of *La Prensa*, was murdered by (a lengthy, independent investigation would later conclude) two APRA militants, one of them a member of congress.[13] Graña was a cotton planter and member of a prestigious family with many ties to upper-class Lima. His assassination inevitably recalled the murder, a decade earlier, of Antonio Miró Quesada, to whom the Grañas were related. If the oligarchy needed another reason to plot against Bustamante's government, here it was. Bustamante, committed to democracy, had refused to outlaw APRA and seemed unable to control the violence.

By 1948 both APRA and the oligarchy were both conspiring against Bustamante's debilitated government with sympathetic members of the military. APRA discussed Bustamente's removal with Generals Juan de Dios Cuadros and José del Carmen Marin, among others. Bustamante's government learned that General Manuel Odría (who had recently resigned from the cabinet) and Pedro Beltrán, political leader of the planters, were also plotting a coup. On October 3, Apristas launched the largest civil-military revolt since 1932, at Lima's port of Callao. Led by army major Victor Villanueva but centered on navy personnel, the movement was quickly defeated, in good part because the party's top leadership wavered, as it often did on such occasions, and finally withdrew its support for the rebellion. In the wake of the Callao revolt, APRA was outlawed, its leaders driven underground, and hundreds of officers and enlisted men were arrested.[14]

The October 3 revolt was a pivotal event for both APRA and the military. Callao left APRA badly divided. Disaffected Apristas came to see their leaders, including Haya, as craven, opportunistic, and self-serving. Many, especially the more radical and militant cadres, deserted the party. APRA, once again operating clandestinely and from exile, would have to find a new path to power. Callao was party's last significant attempt to gain power by armed rebellion.

Callao convinced the majority of the officer corps that APRA posed a grave threat to the discipline and unity of the armed forces, which could not be overcome under Bustamante. Many officers did not wish to see the country fall under another

General/President Manuel A. Odría seized power in a 1948 military coup supported by the oligarchy.

Source: Columbus Memorial Library OAS.

strongman. However reluctantly, they backed Odría's coup, which triumphed on October 29 without a single shot being fired (Masterson 1991: chapter 6).

The apparent aim of the coup was the restoration of oligarchic power. As Beltran's participation suggests, Bustamante's removal was especially important to the planters. Prominent among the conspirators were members of planter families, including the Gildemeisters, the Aspíllagas, and the Pardos. Their main concern, according to close observers, was the loss of control over the foreign exchange earned by their exported crops. The Prados also participated, contributing, along with other conspirators, to a "bolsa" (purse) of several million soles to finance the coup. The fund was used to gain the active support or at least acquiescence of officers and enlisted men in critical positions. The liberality of the conspirators may help explain the bloodless outcome of the revolt. The Miró Quesadas, steadfast enemies of APRA, also supported the coup, to no one's surprise. It is not clear whether they were in touch with Odría, but they had been connected to an earlier right-wing military revolt against Bustamante led by an Odría ally.[15]

ODRÍA AND THE OLIGARCHY

General Manuel Odría, who would be Peru's president for eight years, was "shrewd, politically tough, and a good judge of personalities" (Masterson 1991: 99). He had been among the army's most resolutely anti-APRA soldiers. An ambitious, well-trained career officer, Odría had studied at advanced military schools in the Peru and the United States. Like Benavides before him, he became a military hero by leading troops in a successful border war (against Ecuador in 1941) and was subsequently named army chief of staff. From a prosperous provincial family, he never had Benavides' easy social connection to upper-class Lima. Odría's name would not appear on the rolls of the Club Nacional.

The 1948 coup, had for the moment at least, turned back the clock. The oligarchs were more unified in their support of the regime. In Odría, they had, once again, the kind of leader they were comfortable with. Oligarchs were prominent in the new regime. Pedro Beltrán was appointed president of the central bank, a position from which he presided over a tough monetary stabilization program. Julio de la Piedra served as head of the official party and leader of the Senate in Odría's politically disciplined congress. A Prado presided over the Chamber of Deputies. The Aspíllagas and Miró Quesadas were also known to be close to the regime, at least in the early years of Odría's rule.

Peru returned to the conservative military-led model of government whose chief characteristics were set out earlier. Political rights and personal constitutional guarantees were jettisoned under a 1949 Internal Security Law. APRA was treated more severely than at any time since Sánchez Cerro. Party leaders were hunted down, jailed, or sometimes shot when discovered in their hiding places. Apristas were rooted out of the military, the unions, and the universities. Military officers whose loyalty was suspect were seized in their homes, subject to lengthy interrogations and sent to prison. Haya de la Torre, who had been permitted a barely disguised clandestine existence under Benavides, was forced to seek refuge in the Colombian embassy, where he would remain for six years, while well-armed Peruvian troops monitored the building. Union activity was suppressed and nowhere so brutally as on the oligarchy's plantations. A tragic episode on the Aspíllagas' plantation, Cayaltí, left over a hundred sugar workers dead. Peru returned to a laissez-faire political economy, with Odría proclaiming the glories of "a liberal economic regime which allows the free operation of the law of offer and demand, which brings as a natural consequence the rejuvenation of our currency, prosperity, and the general welfare" (Odria 1950: 10). Once he had consolidated his control over the country, Odría had himself elected president in 1950. He was the sole candidate on the presidential ballot, which offered a choice of "yes" or "no."[16]

While maintaining conservative policies and preserving ties to certain members of the oligarchy, Odría sought a degree of independence for his government. After the initial period, he carefully removed from positions of influence those who thought they could control him. Thus, Beltrán was soon eased out of his position. Odría found additional bases of support for his government outside the oligarchy. His extremely welcoming attitude toward foreign capital brought new investment from abroad. A Peruvian businessman later commented, ' "Odría flung back the doors so wide that the hinges fell off" ' (Ballantyne 1976: 86). A generous mining code (1950) based on American models, with ample guarantees for foreign companies, attracted massive American investment in iron and copper mines (Ballantyne 1976: 21–40). Odría formed close ties with certain officials of the American mining firms. These new American interests were not in conflict with the oligarchy. In fact, some of the oligarchs took advantage of Odría's mining code to invest on their own or in association with foreign capital. But the growth of the foreign mining sector, beholden to the regime, provided Odría with alternative sources of support.

With the new mining activity and favorable conditions on international markets during the Korean War, Peru's export economy came back to life. The planters, who were additionally blessed by the regime's repression of union activity, prospered. Ironically, the thriving national economy enabled Odría to court lower-class support with assistance to the urban squatter settlements called *barriadas*, created by the growing numbers of migrants from the countryside, and with large-scale public works programs, which provided employment opportunities. These programs also favored some of his wealthy supporters, who, like Max Peña Prado, received lucrative public works contracts.

But the end of his eight-year reign, Odría's support among the elite was waning. Some families apparently had been pressured into making extravagant gifts to the dictator and his friends (Payne 1968: 21). In 1954, the regime's relations with the Miró Quesadas soured when Odría, bowing to intense international pressure, allowed Haya de la Torre to end his years of asylum in the Colombian embassy and go into exile. Carlos Miró Quesada Laos, Odría's ambassador in Rio de Janeiro, resigned in protest on hearing the news (Chirinos 1962: 101–102). The end of the Korean War about this same time meant the collapse of the export boom, and the beginning of a period of difficulties for the Peruvian economy. Probably because he hoped to have himself reelected, Odría insisted on maintaining an extensive, job-creating, construction program, while ignoring pointed criticism about government spending from *La Prensa*, managed by Pedro Beltrán since the death of Graña. Only after deterioration of the exchange rate and an apparent crisis of business confidence did Odría appoint a new finance minister who cancelled the more elaborate projects and shrank the budget.

As the 1956 elections approached, both the oligarchs and military leaders were troubled by indications that Odría intended to perpetuate himself in power. In mid-1955, an anti-Odría manifesto appeared in *La Prensa*. The signers included Beltrán, Ramon Aspíllaga Anderson, and Manuel Mujica Gallo, all high-profile members of the oligarchy (Chirinos 1962: 107). Mujica and Beltrán were among the leaders of a political movement, the National Coalition, which grew out of this initial gesture and began to hold antigovernment meetings around the country. The coalition attracted considerable popular support, which grew as the government responded with repressive measures.

When a military revolt broke out in February 1956 in a distant province, repression was directed at the oligarchs. Suspecting that the planter owners of *La Prensa*[17] were behind the conspiracy (they probably were not), Odría's police invaded the paper's office and carted off forty people, including Beltrán, who was placed in El Fronton, the country's maximum security prison. Even more remarkable, authorities invaded the august Club Nacional. Among those jailed was club president Miguel Mujica Gallo, brother of Manuel. Surely the oligarchy had felt nothing like this since Leguía, and even he would never have done anything quite so ungentlemanly, but then Leguía was a member of the club and Odría was not. (Of course, imagining that the oligarchy would plot the overthrow of a government with members of the officer corps was not a fanciful leap for Odría.) The defection of oligarch-politician Julio de la Piedra and other leaders of Odría's official party only confirmed what was already obvious: Having lost the support of both the oligarchy and the military, he could not continue in office.

THE CONVIVENCIA

The years of Odría's dictatorship were a time of reassessment for the Aprista leadership. Living in exile or holed up in the Colombian embassy, the party's leaders had ample time to consider their options. In the 1930s and 1940s, APRA's leaders had learned that they could not gain power in opposition to the oligarchy or by armed rebellion. The party would need to find allies among the oligarchs, and to do so, the party would need to become more conservative and less militant. By then, many of the party's more radical cadres had departed.

By the mid-1950s a growing rapprochement between the party and many of its one-time oligarchic enemies was evident. Pedro Beltrán had gone so far as to hire young Apristas at his once virulently anti-APRA paper. When two oligarchic figures emerged as presidential candidates, both sought APRA support. The two were former president Manuel Prado and banker Hernando de Lavalle. (Of course, Prado had his own family connections with banking.) Odría initially supported Lavalle.

As the 1956 election approached, a third candidate emerged: Fernando Belaúnde, an American-trained architect and the son of a highly respected family of the Arequipa aristocracy. Charismatic, running on a reformist, anti-Odría platform, Belaúnde was drawing strong support. With him in the race, Prado seemed unlikely to win without help from APRA. Lavalle, weighted down with the burden of being the "official" candidate of an unpopular regime, was the weakest of the candidates.

For his part, Odría feared that a Belaúnde victory would mean an investigation of corruption in his government. He began to allow APRA greater freedom to organize and invited Prado and APRA leaders to his home in Monterrico. There, an unwritten agreement remembered as the "Pact of Monterrico" was worked out. Odría would transfer his support from Lavalle to Prado, APRA would deliver votes for Prado and support his government, and Manuel would legalize APRA, which could expect to win power for itself in 1962. This arrangement came to be known as the *Convivencia* (coexistence). There was, apparently, also agreement that the new government would conduct no investigation of its predecessor. Prado won the election with 45 percent of the vote. Belaúnde was not far behind.[18]

The Convivencia did not involve the APRA's formal participation in Prado's government. The party would hold no cabinet posts or prefectures, as it initially had under Bustamante. But the Apristas gained a considerable number of posts in the public bureaucracy. APRA controlled a large block in the Congress, which allied itself with the representatives of Prado's personal party. APRA leader Ramiró Prialé, served as "superminister," meeting frequently with Prado to coordinate the party's relations with the government.

Most important, the Convivencia opened the country to Aprista political activity and labor organizing. On taking power, Prado immediately abrogated Odría's Internal Security Act, restoring Peruvians' political and personal rights. The party's paper *La Tribuna* returned to regular circulation, and there was a virtual explosion of union organizing in Peru by APRA and others. The Apristas were particularly successful on the sugar plantations, which they made the target of a well-coordinated national campaign.[19]

Largely because it gave APRA such freedom, the Convivencia had many enemies among the oligarchs, including the Miró Quesadas, the Ayulos, the Picassos, and the de la Piedras. However, Prado's elite cabinet appointments, the generally conservative caste of his government policies, APRA's support for them, and the party's circumspect behavior, all tended to allay oligarchic fears of the Convivencia. When the government was unable to contain an economic and fiscal crisis midway through his presidency, Prado called on the high priest of criollo orthodoxy, Pedro Beltran, who would be finance minister and prime minister for two-and-half years.

APRA, looking toward the 1962 elections, was determined to avoid the political and social instability that had attended their earlier experience in alliance politics. In Congress, the Aprista bloc gave the government its full cooperation. Haya spent most of the period lecturing abroad. In spite of their union organizing campaigns, APRA's leaders strove to minimize labor strife. The party's labor organizations pursued limited economic objectives without raising fundamental political issues. *Tribuna* looked forward to the emergence of "a new spirit between employers and workers, an economic convivencia, which calls them to their common responsibility to augment production and national prosperity" (Cevallos 1972: 38). The sugar planters discovered that they could live with such bread-and-butter unionism by granting wage raises while reducing their labor requirements through increased mechanization. (This process took place in a period of generally good prices on the international sugar market.)

The public statements of Aprista leaders showed how anxious they were to placate their conservative enemies within the oligarchic and military elites. As the 1962 election approached, Manuel Seoane, a top party leader, declared that APRA was opposed to economic planning, which would be "contrary to private initiative. We need a torrent of investment and thousands of investors. If we thought of engaging in authoritarian planning, we would scare away foreign capital" (Aguirre 1962: 200). Beltrán could hardly have said it better. At the same time, Haya de la Torre was proclaiming his agreement with Beltrán in areas as diverse as agrarian reform and fiscal and monetary policy (Aguirre 1962: 199). "Haya de la Torre," commented one of Beltrán's closest political associates, "is the conservative that we need" (Aguirre 1962: 10). The radical and combative APRA of the 1930s and 1940s was indeed long gone.

In 1962 the Prados, Beltrán, and other important oligarchic figures backed Haya for the presidency. Pradista leader Augusto Thorndike boldly predicted a fifty-year convivencia (Payne 1968: 37). His confidence did not seem totally unwarranted. The Convivencia represented the logical culmination of the trilateral system of Peruvian politics, the resolution of its contradictions. Oligarchs and Apristas were allied. The military, APRA's implacable enemy, was apparently held in check through its ties to the oligarchy. The Prados, in particular, were famous for their ability to manage the military.

But Haya would not then or ever become president. The fifty-year convivencia was thwarted by a concatenation of factors: division in the oligarchic camp, the emergence of a new middle-class reformism as a force in Peruvian politics, and a surprising ideological realignment of the Peruvian military. Behind these factors were a series of important changes in Peruvian society that would shape the politics of the 1960s.

SOCIAL CHANGE IN THE 1950S AND 1960S

The most obvious changes were economic and demographic. In the 1950s and 1960s, Peru experienced unprecedented economic expansion. By 1968, real GNP was almost two-and-a-half times what it had been in 1950 (Thorp and Bertram 1978: 258). Much of this growth was in the export sector, traditional focus of the Peruvian economy. The expansion of mining under Odría has already been mentioned. Beginning under Prado, the production of fishmeal for export grew at boom rates to become the country's leading export by the early 1960s. Peru also experienced a significant level of industrial growth during the 1960s, for the first time since the turn of the century (Bertram 1991: 391).

One notable effect of these economic developments was the reduction of the relative weight of the oligarchy's interests within the larger economy. As metal mining and fishmeal production expanded the contribution of sugar and cotton to total exports sank from 26 percent in 1958 to 8 percent by 1969 (Banco Central de Reserva del Perú, n.d.). Oligarchic involvement in the most dynamic sectors of the revitalized economy was limited. Metal mining continued largely under the control of foreign capital. The fishmeal industry was pioneered by a new group of Peruvian entrepreneurs[20]; later the industry attracted substantial foreign investment. Multinational firms dominated the expansion in manufacturing.

Economic expansion was paralleled by a demographic revolution of the sort felt throughout Latin America in the postwar period. The annual rate of population growth, relatively constant from 1876 to 1940, ascended to 3 percent in the 1960s, a pace at which a population doubles every twenty-five years (Larson and Bergman 1969: 95–96). Population growth triggered a process of mass migration from the Sierra region to the coast and from rural areas to the cities, especially the capital. The most visible evidence of these movements was the ring of barriadas, which had grown up around Lima, beginning in the 1950s. By the late 1960s, they contained a quarter of the city's population (Powell 1976: 150).

Associated with the economic and demographic shifts of these years were important political developments.

1. *The creation of a new political constituency in the barriadas.* Initially regarded as a threat to social stability, this population was open to appeals from anyone willing to meet their needs for basic amenities such as electricity, water, and transportation and wooed by politicians of varied stripes from conservative Odría to the left-wing ruling generals of the early 1970s (Collier 1976; Doughty 1976; Powell 1976).

2. *An expanding, self-aware middle-class constituency.* Between 1950 and 1972 the proportion of professionals and white-collar workers in the labor force rose from 10.7 to 15.9 percent. Workers in these categories came to think of themselves as "middle class" people with distinctive values and class interests. They would provide a social base for a reformist, development-oriented politics, and especially for Belaúnde's Acción Popular party (Oliveira and Roberts 1998: 312; Parker 1998; Pereyra 2015).

3. *The reduction of rural isolation.* As a result of improvements in communications and the movements of migrants back and forth, the countryside was brought economically, politically, and culturally closer to the city. In the Sierra, new political, bureaucratic, and economic elites challenged the traditional hegemony of the landed gamonales. Peasants were coming into contact with radical political ideas, especially in the wake of the Cuban revolution, that would spawn the rural rebellions in the 1960s (Alberti 1976; Cotler 1970c; Quijano 1968).

These sociopolitical developments, like the expansion of the nonoligarchic sectors of the economy, were diluting the oligarchs' control of Peruvian society. But to a remarkable degree, the oligarchy was able to outmaneuver its enemies and sustain its power until the late 1960s.

THE 1962 AND 1963 ELECTIONS

The 1962 elections were, for reasons that will be explored below, aborted by a military coup. New elections were held in 1963. The same three major presidential candidates competed on both occasions.[21] Haya de la Torre, the Convivencia candidate, was permitted to run for the first time since 1931. This time he had the support of a substantial part of the oligarchy, especially those closest to Prado and Beltrán. Another candidate was former president Manuel Odría. He was supported by a second group of oligarchs, consisting particularly of those who had profited from their close relations with his 1948–1956 government and some oligarchic families that remained suspicious of APRA. Odría also retained some of his following in the barriadas, cultivated during his presidency (Collier 1976: 55–66).

Fernando Belaúnde was again a candidate. He presented himself as the anti-oligarchy reformer, claiming ideological terrain apparently deserted by the Apristas. Belaúnde and his Acción Popular Party attracted the middle-class Peruvians who were frustrated by the nation's continuing economic and social backwardness and tired of watching the country's political life run by the oligarchy, the military, and a now conservative APRA. These middle-class voters would have been frightened by a program of radical change but were reassured by Belaúnde's emphasis on solutions to national problems based on technology and economic development.

Belaúnde had the support of a small group of oligarchic families including the Ferreyros and the Bentins. Francisco Miró Quesada was a key Popular Action leader. The oligarchic supporters of Belaúnde tended to have predominantly urban, rather than agrarian interests. Some of these families felt they had little to lose and might even gain through a moderate reorientation of national social and economic policies. Interviews with several members of oligarchic families that supported Belaúnde's candidacy revealed a pragmatic belief that gradual, peaceful change now would prevent a more violent, radical transformation in the future.

The division of the oligarchic camp in this election was even evident within families. The Aspíllagas were split between Odría and Haya. The Miró Quesadas were divided between Belaúnde and Odría, though they would all reject Odría in 1963. Evidence from interviews suggests that personal ties and the pursuit of private advantage were more significant than differences in political philosophy in explaining divisions among the oligarchs in these elections.

Haya de la Torre received a plurality of the votes in the 1962 presidential election and the party secured a plurality of the seats in Congress. But he narrowly missed obtaining the one third of the vote legally required for election. This meant that the election would have to be decided by the Congress that was required to choose among the top three candidates.

A period of maneuvering for support in Congress followed the inconclusive balloting. Haya sought the backing of both of the other principal candidates until he was informed that the armed forces were prepared to "veto" his election in this manner. At that point Haya negotiated an agreement to throw his congressional support to Odría, the man who as president had relentlessly prosecuted APRA. Before this new, broader Convivencia could be consummated, the military intervened with a coup d'état, which they justified on the questionable grounds that there had been electoral fraud.

The military's action was unprecedented and, more important, indicative of the beginnings of a major shift in the attitudes of one of the three actors of the trilateral system. Observers stressed that the coup had been conducted by the military as an "institution" rather than being the work of some particular *caudillo* or clique within the military, as had been typical in the past. It was also notable that the military was not acting on behalf of the oligarchy (or even with the approval of some sector of the oligarchy), as it had in 1914, 1930, and 1948. Formally the 1962 coup was against a sitting oligarchic president, Prado, and against a fraudulent election. Actually it was against APRA, against a political deal between the Haya and Odría, and in support of the reformer Belaúnde. The latter would triumph in the presidential elections the following year with the "obvious, but reasonably discreet" help of the military government (Pike 1967: 310).

THE TRANSFORMATION OF THE MILITARY[22]

Certain measures and pronouncements of the interim military government (1962–1963) in areas such as agrarian reform and economic planning also suggested a shifting military mentality. This transformation, begun in the 1950s, continued through the following decade and culminated in the 1968 coup and General Juan Velasco's antioligarchic regime of the early 1970s.

Dependence on the military had long been a quiet fault line running beneath the edifice of oligarchic power in the contested republic. The oligarchs assiduously courted key military figures, but officers could not ignore the social gulf separating them from the oligarchy. The oligarchs rarely sent their sons into the armed forces. At the turn of the century officers were, nonetheless, often drawn from respectable families a step below the oligarchs. That had changed, and the military had come to function as a mobility path for ambitious young men of more modest middle class and provincial origin.

Until the last years of the Old Regime, the oligarchy could depend on the loyalty of the officer corps. "[F]aithful watchdogs of the oligarchy" is how one general would later describe the traditional role of the armed forces.[23] At critical historical junctures, the oligarchy had recruited Sánchez Cerro, Benavides, and Odría to lead authoritarian regimes that suppressed threatening social and political forces and maintained a prescribed set of conservative policies. These officers ruled in association with the oligarchy (although each had a slightly different set of oligarchic families with whom he maintained close ties).

Though the oligarchy could generally depend on its "faithful watchdogs," its control over them was imperfect, as this chapter has shown. Odría's presidency illustrates what was more subtly evident with Benavides: The oligarchy could place a general in office, but its control was uncertain once he was there. The very qualities that enabled such men to dominate the military establishment suggested that they would not be simple puppets. On occasion, Odría and Benavides were pressured into abandoning policies the oligarchs disliked.[24] But, in the end, the oligarchy depended on the fact that the military elite had no desire to present an ideological alternative to the dominant system. The essential elements of the political and economic program shared by Sánchez Cerro, Benavides, and Odría, as outlined earlier, reflected deference to oligarchic interests. It was the transformation of the officer corps into an elite with an independent social and political project that endangered oligarchic control.

Ironically, this process began under Odría. During his presidency the officer corps became better paid and more professionalized. Military pay had been so modest that even high ranking officers hardly earned enough to afford a house or a car. Some depended on oligarchic largesse to bolster their standard of living. Gains in military salary and benefits in the late 1950s made the officer corps more independent of the oligarchy. At the same time, officers began to travel to the United States for special training. In Lima a Center for Advanced Military Studies (CAEM) was created to provide an advanced course of studies for colonels and generals that included consideration of major national problems.

Improved education broadened the intellectual perspective of high ranking officers. In particular there was growing conviction that the country could not build modern and effective armed forces under conditions of severe underdevelopment. For instance, Peru's weak national manufacturing sector implied a precarious dependency on foreign arms suppliers. The largely illiterate pool of potential recruits was not a promising human material for a modern military. A preoccupation with the social and economic bases of national security became increasingly evident in military journals of the 1960s. CAEM and the army's Intelligence Service were sources of the new thinking that was becoming widespread among officers.

The concern of the officer corps with problems of national development was reinforced by the 1959 Cuban Revolution and its political reverberations throughout the region. Events in Cuba showed that a military establishment backing a reactionary regime ran the risk of being swept aside by revolution. The American military missions and stateside courses for foreign officers stressed the need to meet the Castroite threat with counterinsurgency tactics and military civic action programs in affected areas.

Such matters did not remain abstract in Peru. In the mid-1960s, the military had to confront a widespread peasant guerrilla movement. In the course of this conflict, the United States refused to supply Peru with napalm (an incendiary that the United States was then employing against insurgents in Vietnam). Although arrangements for local production of napalm were subsequently made with the American-owned International Petroleum Company, this refusal only reinforced the Peruvian military's awareness of the nation's military-industrial dependency (Villanueva 1973a: 303–304). The counterinsurgency experience of this period also impressed on the military leadership the precariousness of the political and social system. As an intelligence officer observed after the 1968 coup, "The army was getting tired of being called in to put down the revolts of the starving peasants. We were worried about Communism. . . ." (Gall 1971: 310).

In the 1950s and 1960s, then, the Peruvian armed forces were developing a modernizing ideology that moved them beyond the bounds of the narrowly conceived social and economic order led by the oligarchy (now backed by APRA) and the traditional military. It was this tendency that brought them into an implicit alliance with Belaúnde and his similarly inclined middle-class supporters.

THE DEFEAT OF MIDDLE-CLASS REFORMISM

Belaúnde's victory in 1963, with strong middle-class backing and the clear approval of the military, left the oligarchy in an apparently weakened position. Yet the oligarchs showed a remarkable ability to control political events during the five years of Belaúnde's presidency. They were generally able to veto reform efforts. The key to their success was control of congress by the opposition alliance of APRA and General Odría's personalist party, the National Ordriista Union (UNO).

The fate of agrarian reform under Belaúnde illustrates the political dexterity of the oligarchs and their allies. Belaúnde's campaign had raised expectations of a thorough-going agrarian reform law, a potential threat to the interests of the planter core of the oligarchy. The apparent strategy of the oligarchs and their allies was to subvert the reform with meaningless legislation. Oligarchic organs never denied the need for legislation. To counter a reasonably strong administration bill, UNO introduced a bill that had the backing of the oligarchy-controlled National Agrarian Society and of Pedro Beltrán's *La Prensa*, traditional spokesman for the planters. The legislation that finally passed was quite close to the UNO bill. Crafted so as to be difficult to put into practice, the legislation exempted the major cotton and sugar plantations of the coast. The oligarchy had, observers noted, sacrificed the interests of the large land-holders of the Sierra to protect their own. The legislation had little effect anywhere.[25]

While the agrarian reform bill was being dismembered in the Congress, peasant land seizures and finally guerrilla warfare fomented by urban radicals were breaking out in the provinces. Under pressure from the oligarchic press and the army, congress approved legislation providing stern penalties for those giving assistance to the guerrillas and authorizing a large bond issue to finance the military response. Pedro Beltrán bought the first million soles of these "Bonds for the Defense of the National Sovereignty." The counterinsurgency campaign that followed was massive, brutal, and successful. But many officers were convinced that the rural issues behind the insurgency would not go away.

The capacity of the oligarchy and its allies to stifle the efforts of the reformers was aided by a growing ideological split within the Popular Action party. Belaúnde himself seems to have been more conservative personally than the role in which he was cast in the campaign suggested (Jaquette 1971: 140–142). He came increasingly under the influence of advisers drawn from the party's right wing, many of whom had close business and kinship ties to the oligarchy. His need for their support grew under difficult economic conditions toward the end of his presidency. One of his worst defeats came in 1967 when the oligarchy-led export and banking interests forced the government to accept a severe currency devaluation despite the determined resistance of industry and importers, who were hurt by the measure (Astiz 1969: 118–120; Jaquette 1971: 148–162).

Belaúnde's defeats were not, in the end, APRA's victory. The party's collaboration with the oligarchic UNO to stifle reform, suggested that party leaders wanted nothing more than power for its own sake. They would pay a price. APRA's weak showing in the 1963 municipal elections, even in areas of traditional strength, was a sure sign that disillusioned Apristas were deserting the party.

THE 1968 COUP AND THE END OF THE OLD REGIME

The immediate cause (or perhaps pretext) of the 1968 coup led by General Juan Velasco Alverado was the political crisis generated by negotiations over claims by the International Petroleum Company, a subsidiary of Standard Oil of New Jersey, to a vast north coast oil field. Belaúnde had promised to resolve the long-festering issue, which had become a focus of nationalist passions. He had failed in a way that exacerbated the controversy. The nationalization of IPC's properties a few days after the coup won wide public support for the new military government.

At the time of the coup, the military must have anticipated the election of Haya de la Torre, backed by the oligarchy, in 1969. An expanding oligarchy–APRA alliance had been the basis of Prado's Convivencia government, of the failed attempt to extend the Convivencia in 1962, and of the UNO–APRA congressional opposition to Belaúnde's reforms. But an oligarchy-supported, APRA-led government was a step too far—intolerable to the army, both because of the institution's traditional suspicion of APRA and, ironically, because the officer corps had become more progressive as APRA had grown more conservative. Moreover, many officers, as a ranking general had once explained to the American ambassador, were unwilling to serve under a man, Haya de la Torre, whom they believed to be a homosexual.[26]

But the motives of the officers who planned the October 3 coup went beyond these immediate concerns with the IPC, Haya, and the 1969 elections. The defeat of Belaúnde's middle-class reformism and coincidental eruption of a peasant insurgency in the Sierra had given the military palpable evidence of the precariousness of Peru's backward society. The military conspirators of 1968 intended to remain in power to lead a program of modernization from above.

The oligarchy had defeated all attempts to modernize Peru. Central to the program of the Revolutionary Government of the Armed Forces, as the new regime titled itself, would be an attack on the bases of oligarchic political power. Ironically, General Velasco and his allies had notable oligarchic collaboration in carrying out their coup and received support from oligarchic quarters for at least the first year of the new government.

The Prados, according to several knowledgeable sources, including one family member, gave the conspirators a considerable sum of money to help finance the coup, just as they had in 1948. On the eve of the October 3 coup, Valasco conferred with Mariano Prado Heudebert and members of at least three of the most important oligarchic families, though the nature of the discussion is not known. Another prominent oligarchic family, which was among the chief supporters of the new regime in its first months, is said to have held meetings with key officers before the coup and assured them of support for a military government.

In the days immediately after the October 3 coup, the Banco de Credito, whose top ranks included several prominent members of the oligarchy,[27] helped to stabilize the new regime by stemming the outflow of foreign exchange. Credito was the country's largest bank. A lawyer close to banking circles suggests that Credito acted out of fear that the Prados' Banco Popular, the nation's second largest bank, was so close to the revolutionaries that it was gaining advantages over the Banco de Credito.

There are varied indications that the oligarchs were well-disposed toward the new government through much of its first year of existence. Members of several oligarchic families who attended a dinner shortly after the coup were "ecstatic" with this turn of events, according to one of the participants. "They thought they had a second Odría, that the era of the fat cow had returned. I asked them about the radical manifesto the military had issued. They didn't take it seriously. They said that revolutionary manifestos always contain such talk."

Relations between the oligarchy and the military were outwardly friendly. There were informal meetings between oligarchs and top military officers at Ancon, the oligarchy's favorite summer retreat. The Prados had easy access to the new president, General Juan Velasco.[28] The Miró Quesadas' paper *El Comercio* was enthusiastic about the regime's early policies. Richard Goodwin, who visited Peru during this period to do a piece for *The New Yorker* (May 17, 1969), came away convinced that country's conservative banking and commercial families were behind Velasco.

Whatever the reason for such support, the oligarchs had badly misjudged the intentions of the military. If Velasco's own statements are to be believed, those intentions were elaborately spelled out in a secret plan formulated *before* the military moved on October 3 (Velasco 1974). Among the key features of the plan were three radical measures, which had already been executed when a version of the plan was released in 1974. These measures struck directly at the bases of oligarchic power: a decisive agrarian reform decree, which was inaugurated with the dramatic seizure by military forces of the major sugar plantations on June 24, 1969; government takeover of the principal Lima dailies, carried out in the early morning hours of July 2, 1974; and state consolidation of control over the financial system through a series of measures including the strengthening of government power over the Central Reserve Bank, government purchase of controlling interests in three commercial banks, and the imposition of government regulation of all exchange transactions. The families that are the subjects of the next three chapters of this book were directly affected. Within the space of a few years, the Aspíllagas lost their plantation Cayaltí, the Prados lost the Banco Popular, and the Miró Quesadas lost *El Comercio*.

The changes in the financial system, the institutionalization of economic planning, and the rapid expansion of government ownership of most of the major export enterprises amounted to a repudiation of Creole Liberalism.

In a speech on the first anniversary of the October 3 coup, Velasco proclaimed, "It is the historical destiny of any true process of transformation to confront the beneficiaries of the *status quo* against which it rebels. Ours can be no exception. The irreducible adversaries of our movement will always be those who feel their interests and privileges under attack: the oligarchy" (Velasco 1973: 65). The military government's rhetoric often described the oligarchy and "imperialism" as the enemies of progressive change—a formulation that ironically echoed APRA's early ideology.

The oligarchy, according to Velasco, was a narrow stratum at pinnacle of Peruvian society. He carefully distinguished between the oligarchs and the national bourgeoisie or "small and medium industrialists" whom the government hoped to encourage (Velasco 1973: 78). The oligarchy controlled the banks, the plantations, and the national press. Watching Belaúnde recapitulate Bustamante's failure convinced the military that the severance of the oligarchy from these bases of its power was a political prerequisite to modernizing Peru (Velasco 1973, 1974).

By 1974, the oligarchy had been eliminated as an effective force in national affairs. The political and economic power that had been tentatively established during the Guano Age, institutionalized in the Aristocratic Republic, and maintained through adroit alliances in the years of trilateral politics had finally been shattered.

THE END OF THE OLD REGIME IN PERU

The last several chapters have revolved around the idea that the fall of the Old Regime in Latin America was the result of the failures of elite cohesion and rise of new social forces related to the development the oligarchy had set in motion.

In the case of Peru, it was primarily division within the Civilista elite that destroyed the oligarchic republic. But during the subsequent contested republic the main threat to the oligarchy was not so much intraelite conflict as the challenge from below, arising initially from an expanding working class, the labor movement, and the APRA party, and later from a growing middle class, Acción Popular, and a transformed officer crops. Reviewing the history of the contested republic, one might conclude, to the contrary, that the oligarchs were often at one another's throats and that this was what undid them. But the oligarchs came together whenever they perceived serious threats to their class interests, as they did when they united behind Colonel Sánchez Cerro in the early 1930s, when they supported the overthrow of the Bustamente's reformist government in 1948, and when they backed the UNO-APRA opposition to another reformer, Belaúnde, in the 1960s. Ironically, the same might be said of oligarchic support for Velasco's 1968 coup, which the oligarchs collectively and happily imagined was in their interest.

The question that did sometimes divide the oligarchs was how to contain APRA. Division over this issue is hard to ignore because two of the most prominent and powerful families, the Prados and the Miró Quesadas, had opposite and unchanging attitudes toward APRA. The coming chapters on these families will show that the reasons for their, respectively, soft and hard stances toward the party were idiosyncratic reflections of their own family histories. In contrast, the planter core of the oligarchy seems to have been, as the Aspíllaga chapter will show, politically cohesive and active in defense of its interests. The planters took a collective hard line on APRA in the 1930s, which evolved into a collective accommodationist stance toward a tamed APRA in the 1960s. The first phase found them on the side of the Miró Quesadas and the second on the side of the Prados. Chapter 9 will return to these issues and the question of elite cohesion.

The oligarchy did not directly rule Peru in the contested republic, but it retained a generally effective veto over national policy and was able to manage the threat from APRA within the framework of a trilateral system. The oligarchic veto was evident in the capacity of the exporter oligarchs to force wayward administrations (including Odría's and Prado's) back to the economic policies of creole liberalism, in the 1948 coup, and, literally, in the legislative veto that the oligarchs exercised in alliance with APRA in the 1960s. The trilateral system enabled the oligarchs to contain and finally to reshape APRA. But the system was precariously dependent on the use or threat of military force and, obviously, on the loyalty of the armed forces.

By the time of the 1968 coup, newer social and political forces had arisen to challenge the oligarchs: an enlarged and demanding middle class, a dynamic new middle-class party, and a transformed military. The economy, once dominated by the oligarchs' export enterprises, had grown beyond their control. The Peruvian oligarchy, having survived well beyond its peers in neighboring countries and resisted the forces of change in the 1960s, was finally an archaic species unfit for survival in a radically altered environment.

NOTES

1. For APRA and Haya, I have drawn on Cossio del Pomar 1961 and 1969, Sanchez 1955, Klaren 1976, Alexander 1973, and Pike 1986.

2. Nonetheless, support for Sánchez Cerro was not universal among the elite in 1931. For reasons that may include anticipated private advantage, some contributed to Haya's campaign, including plantation owners Rafael Larco Herrera and the de la Piedras (Stein 1980: 170; LAA 10–27–31).

3. See especially Stein 1980: 188–197. Also see Pike 1986: 158 and Klaren 2000: 274, who notes that Peruvian historian Basadre considered the 1931 contest one of the fairest in the country's history.

4. Masterson 1991: 49–52; Pike 1967: 265–266; Basadre 1968: XIV, 235–236; Gerlach 1973: 400–408; Kenashiro and Rueda 1972: 89–90.

5. Klaren 2000, Werlich 1978, North 1973, Sánchez 1969, Hilliker 1971, Payne 1965, Alba 1968, Chirinos 1962, Gerlach 1973, Pike 1967 and 1986.

6. Bertram 1991: 417–419; Klaren 2000: 279–281; Pike 1967: 272–275; Miró Quesada Laos 1961: 480; Tuesta Soldevilla 1998. See also discussions of this election from varied perspectives in chapters 6–9.

7. The one notable exception to this generalization was 1931, when the oligarchs won with an extraordinary candidate under special circumstances. They would never find another Sánchez Cerro.

8. See discussion of this election in chapter 7.

9. Benavides had reportedly hoped to run himself but encountered resistance from sectors of the oligarchy and the officer corps.

10. Pedro Beltrán, political leader of the planters, seems to have taken this view according to his 1945 exchange of letters with Gildemeisters discussed in chapter 10.

11. Payne 1965: 48–49; Rodriguez Pastor 1969: 111–112; Kenashiro 1972; 96–97; Cevallos 1972: 5–10.

12. According to a Lima attorney knowledgeable about monetary matters, during this period the Caja de Depositos, the official tax-collecting agency controlled by the banks, reduced the flow of funds to the Bustamante government. The oligarchy, he claims, "turned off the faucet" and brought down the government.

13. Masterson 1991: 101; Werlich 1978: 230–231.

14. The best account of these events is Masterson's (1991: 111–127). A Bustamante cabinet officer I interviewed in 1974 said that he informed the president of the Odría/Beltran plot and unsuccessfully urged their arrest. In his own account, Bustamante says the conspirators were under government surveillance (Bustamante 1949: 240–241, 349–351).

15. This account of participation in the 1948 coup is based on a series of interviews conducted with members of oligarchic families, high-ranking security officials of the Bustamante government, and several other individuals who had knowledge of these events. It is in agreement with published accounts including Bustamante 1949; Montagne 1962: 218; Payne 1968: 21; Villanueva 1962: 212–215; Bourricaud 1966: 26; and Masterson 1991: 123, 127, n56.

16. On these aspects of the Odría period, see Werlich 1978: 248–249; Pike 1967: 290–295; Masterson 1991: 129; Payne 1965: 50–51; Alba 1968; 268–269; Cevallos 1972: 12; Plaza 1971: 8–14; Rodriguez Pastor 1969: 112; and the discussion of the Cayaltí massacre in chapter 6.

17. *La Prensa* was the planters' mouthpiece. On the paper's ownership, see the section on the press in chapter 10.

18. On the 1956 election, Sanchez 1969: II, 1060–1084; Miró Quesada Laos 1959: 177–214; Chirinos 1962: 111–126; Payne 1968: 25–31; Klaren 2000.

19. Payne 1965: 47; Alba 1968: 296; North 1973: 229–230; Cevallos 1972; Plaza 1971: 14–25; Kenashiro 1972: 100.

20. One of them was Luís Banchero, listed among the oligarchs in table 1.1, but only beginning to emerge as an important figure in this period.

21. Klaren 2000: 318–322; Sanchez 1969: III, 1217–1234; Astiz 1969: 101–105; Payne 1968: 4–9; Pike 1967: 300–310.

22. Masterson 1991: 159–264; Villanueva 1972 and 1973a; Einaudi 1969 and 1976; Jaquette 1971: 125–127; North 1966: 51–56.

23. The phrase, which had by then become a cliché, was used by General Jorge Fernandez Maldonado, interviewed by Masterson (1991: 248).

24. Benavides had been compelled to abandon his "Peace and Concord" policy toward APRA in the early 1930s. Toward the end of his presidency, Odría had been forced to cut back spending and appoint a new conservative finance minister. Pressure from both the oligarchy and the military had blocked Benavides and Odría from seeking new presidential terms in 1945 and 1956, respectively.

25. Astiz 1969: 200–203; Jaquette 1971: 135–138; Bourricaud 1970: 325–339; Malpica 1973; Kuczynski 1977: 62–70.

26. Whatever the truth of this notion of Haya's sexual orientation, it was widely believed by Peruvians in and outside the military (Masterson 1991: 170; Pike 1986: 237).

27. The bank's president was Enrique Ayulo Pardo. Its board included members of the Berkemeyer, Brescia, Ferreyros, and Graña families, but the largest blocks of the bank's stock were apparently held by European banks.

28. In April 1969, when the government was apparently in the midst of an effort to gain investor confidence, Mariano Prado led a group of bankers that publicly declared its support of the regime. For a more detailed description of the Prado's relations with Velasco, see chapter 7.

6

The Aspíllagas: North Coast Planters

[W]e hope the lesson will be like the rebellion—bloody, very bloody, to put a definitive end to this damned Aprista party. Immediate punishment without waiting for trials and other idiocies.

—Luís Aspíllaga, responding to the July 1932
Trujillo rebellion (LAA 7–11–32)

Of the three oligarchic families studied for this book, the Aspíllagas are the least extraordinary and the most representative. The Aspíllagas were not driven by family tragedies or passions. But their fortunes and politics were representative of the planter core of Peruvian oligarchy—the largest, most coherent, and, for many decades, the most powerful sector of the oligarchy. The Aspíllagas' central concern, as will be clear in this chapter, was the control of labor, both on the planation and in national policy. It shaped their relations with successive governments and with the APRA party. Labor and other issues, in particular, the maintenance of an exporter-friendly political economy, drew them into a continuing alliance with other planters and exporters generally.

The political trajectory of the Aspíllagas was typical of oligarchic clans in the course of the Old Regime. Prominent among the post-1895 Civilistas, they were politically banished by Leguía in the 1920s, ardently anti-Aprista and supporters of Sanchez Cerro in the early 1930s, backers of Odria's 1948 coup and his eight-year dictatorship in the 1950s, and, ironically, moving toward APRA in the 1960s.

As this chapter will show, the capacity of the Aspíllagas' and other planters to control labor was tied to their political fortunes. In the late nineteenth century, when the Peruvian state was weak, they exercised unlimited power over the lives of their Chinese coolie workers. In the early twentieth century, they ruled their now native labor force with the help of a state that they dominated. With the advent of the contested republic, control of labor become more problematic and the methods of control varied with the political climate, from brutal armed force to lawyerly negotiations over union recognition.

ORIGINS

Peru was in the last years of Spanish rule when Catalina Ferrebú de Aspíllaga arrived at Lima's port of Callao from Chile. She brought with her a small son, Ramón. A second son, Antonio, was born shortly after her arrival. It is not known why she came, though one version has it that her husband Aspíllaga, who apparently remained in Chile, had deserted her for another woman.[1]

Some years later the Aspíllagas were supporting themselves hauling freight by wagon between Lima and Callao. But their progress was rapid. In the early 1850s Ramón's name appears as the owner of an eighty-five-ton ship, licensed to engage in commercial shipping, probably among Peruvian ports.[2] The Aspíllagas' first agricultural investment, Palto, a small cotton plantation, located in Pisco, dates from this same period.

At the time of Peru's 1866 conflict with Spain, Ramón Aspíllaga Ferrebú felt prosperous enough to make a 2,000 peso donation to the national treasury accompanied by a guarantee of another 200 pesos in credit each month until the end of the war. In a letter to the Minister of the Interior, Aspíllaga declared, "I have formed a small fortune in Peru and having passed my youth [here] since Independence was declared and having a wife and children born on this soil, I cannot do enough for Peru [at this time of peril]" (*El Peruano*, February 16, 1866). An intriguing bit of evidence from the period suggests that despite his economic success, Ramón was burdened socially by his past as a wagoner. In 1862, *El Comercio* rejected criticism of the appointment of a former silversmith to a diplomatic post with the comment, "[J]ust a few years ago they said to the worthy and honorable Don Ramón Aspíllaga, 'you are a wagoner and therefore worthless'" (May 21, 1862).

Ramón's sons, the Aspíllaga Barreras (box 6.1 and figure 6.1) would be among the most conspicuous members of the economic, social, and political elite of the Aristocratic Republic. The source of family's wealth and influence was their ownership of the north coast plantation Cayaltí. The plantation defined the family's politics. They needed a tame labor force, an export-oriented political economy, and an ample supply of water. The Aspíllagas would generally be allied with other planters, especially the sugar growers, who formed the core of the oligarchy.

Box 6.1. Generations of the Aspíllagas

I. **Ramón Aspíllaga Ferrebú** (died 1875)
    Purchased plantation Cayaltí in 1860 with partner Zaracondegui, merchant and guano trader. Developed plantation with his sons.

II. The Aspíllaga Barreras (born 1849–)
    Sons of Aspíllaga Ferrebú. Built up Cayaltí, active in Civilista politics.
      Antero Aspíllaga Barrera (1849–1927), leading political figure in Aristocratic Republic. Forced into exile by Leguía in 1923 and sold his interest in Cayaltí to brother **Ramón Aspíllaga Barrera** (1851–1940). Ramón key backer of Sanchez Cerro in early 1930s.

III. The Aspíllaga Andersons (born 1897–)
    Sons of Ramón Aspíllaga Barrera. **Ramón Aspíllaga Anderson** (1897–1973) and brothers **Luís** and **Ismael** ran Cayaltí. Backed 1948 coup against Bustamante.

CAYALTÍ

One key to the early success of the Aspíllagas was the close business relationship that they developed with Julian de Zaracondegui, a wealthy Lima merchant and leading figure in the guano trade. Zaracondegui provided the capital to put the Aspíllagas (Ramón and his sons) to work at Cayaltí in 1860.

Ramón Aspíllaga Ferrebú and Zaracondegui purchased Cayaltí as equal partners. The exact purchase price is not known. However, subsequent litigation revealed that Zaracondegui put up $119,860 for Aspíllaga, which was to be paid out of profits at 12 percent interest. Aspíllaga managed the plantation on a salary. The contract between the two men provided that one of the partners was to buy out the other at the end of ten years (Alzamora and Arrospide 1890; Argumaniz ms.).

Cayaltí is located on the Zaña River, on which local agriculture is precariously dependent, near the north coast town of Chiclayo. (Sugar is a thirsty crop, the coast is arid, and access to the limited water supply is crucial for growers.) The main plantation consists of some 9,000 acres, though the Aspíllagas would eventually increase their holdings to 19,000 acres, mainly through three major purchases made in the 1920s and early 1940s and the rental of a fourth parcel.[3]

The colossal expansion of Cayaltí was sustained by the family's growing political power. The Aspíllagas, like other planters, used their influence over the local water board to manipulate irrigation allotments and compel Cayaltí's neighbors to sell their land to them. When land disputes arose they were likely to be decided in the Aspíllagas' favor. Should protests arise, the family could generally depend on the support of local authorities appointed with their approval (Gonzales 1985: 52).

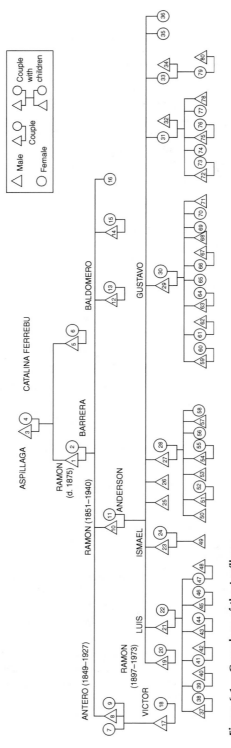

Figure 6.1. Genealogy of the Aspillagas.

1. Ramón Aspíllaga Ferrebú
2. Melchora Barrera
3. —— Aspíllaga
4. Catalina Ferrebú
5. Antonio Aspíllaga Ferrebú
6. Rosa Taboada
7. —— Negrete
8. Antero Aspíllaga Barrera
9. Ana Argote
10. Ramón Aspíllaga Barrera
11. María Agripina Anderson
12. Baldomero Aspíllaga Barrera
13. Julia Sotomarino
14. Ismael Aspíllaga Barrera
15. Damacita Cereña
16. Sofía Aspíllaga Barrera
17. Victor Aspíllaga Negrete
18. Carmen Delgado Gutierrez
19. Ramón Aspíllaga Anderson
20. Sara María Larrabure
21. Luis Aspíllaga Anderson
22. Luzmila Dammert Muelle
23. Ismael Aspíllaga Anderson
24. Luísa Larrañaga
25. Carlos Aspíllaga Anderson
26. Antero Aspíllaga Anderson
27. Rafael Aspíllaga Anderson
28. Aurora Plenge Washburn

29. Gustavo Aspíllaga Anderson
30. Luísa Menchaca Blacker
31. Victoria Aspíllaga Anderson
32. Carlos Ferreyros R.
33. Melchora Aspíllaga Anderson
34. Augustin Gutierrez
35. Sofía Aspíllaga Anderson
36. Adelina Aspíllaga Anderson
37. Luis Aspíllaga Dammert
38. Bertha Banchero
39. Luzmila Aspíllaga Dammert
40. Luís Ferrand Cilloniz
41. Ana Rosa Aspíllaga Dammert
42. Alfonso Noriega Plascencia
43. Jaime Aspíllaga Dammert
44. Carmen Seoane Weiss
45. Gonzalo Aspíllaga Dammert
46. Carmen Baracco
47. Cecilia Aspíllaga D.
48. Eduardo Burbank
49. Ramón Aspíllaga Larrañaga
50. Rafael Aspíllaga Plenge Washburn
51. Carlos Aspíllaga Plenge Washburn
52. Margarite Stille
53. Jose Antonio Aspíllaga Plenge Washburn
54. Juan Alfonso Aspíllaga Plenge Washburn
55. Luz María Freire Sarria

56. María Eugenia Aspíllaga Plenge Washburn
57. Iñigo Aspíllaga Plenge Washburn
58. María de Rocio Aspíllaga Plenge Washburn
59. Gustavo Aspíllaga Menchaca
60. Rosa María Santos
61. María Luísa Aspíllaga Menchaca
62. Leopolo Pflucker
63. Alejandro Aspíllaga Menchaca
64. Rosario de Bracamonte Orbegozo
65. Patricia Aspíllaga Menchaca
66. Ines Aspíllaga Menchaca
67. Kenneth Blekey
68. Felipe Aspíllaga Menchaca
69. Susana Aspíllaga Menchaca
70. Helena Aspíllaga Menchaca
71. Hernando Aspíllaga Menchaca
72. Carlos Ferreyros Aspíllaga
73. Maggie Saligman
74. Victoria Ferreyros Aspíllaga
75. Ramón Ferreyros Aspíllaga
76. Mariella Pomar
77. Ana Teresa Ferreyros Aspíllaga
78. Jaime Ferreyros Aspíllaga
79. María Victoria Gutierrez Aspíllaga
80. Francisco Madalendoitia Cavero

Figure 6.1. (Continued)

At the time the Aspíllagas began working Cayaltí, cotton was the principal crop of the area. Cotton prices were high because of the American Civil War. But by 1870, Cayaltí had been converted to sugar cane production. Ramón Aspíllaga Ferrebú and his sons imported machinery from England and mounted a modern sugar mill on the plantation. This, in itself, was a nearly heroic feat, given the primitive character of the plantation's transportation links to the coast (*Cultura Peruana* 1960). The plantation was worked with indentured Chinese coolie labor.

As Cayaltí prospered, Zaracondegui's own enterprises faltered. In 1873 he was badly in need of money. In the last month of that year, the partners took out a $338,700 mortgage. Zaracondegui received this sum, signing over his share of the estate to the Aspíllagas. Shortly thereafter Zaracondegui went into bankruptcy and committed suicide (Alzamora and Arrospide 1890; NSS 2–12–46).

THE ASPÍLLAGA BARRERAS: ECONOMICS

From the beginning, the Aspíllagas saw Cayaltí as the door through which they would enter the national elite. In a 1871 letter, Ramón's eldest son Antero remarks, "All I want is that this plantation be ours and the three of us [apparently Antero and his brothers Ramon and Ismael] administer it in complete independence; this is my dream . . . this is our fortune and future."[4] A few months earlier he had predicted, "[Cayaltí] will establish us socially and commercially." To this he might have added, *politically* (AAB 7–9–1871, 1–8–1871).

To consolidate their control of Cayaltí the Aspíllagas had to overcome a series of formidable challenges. The first involved the title to Cayaltí itself. Zaracondegui's heirs refused to accept the 1873 transfer. His death set off a long legal battle and it was not until 1899 that a final settlement was achieved, leaving the family in complete control of the plantation (Alzamora and Arrospide 1890; NSS 2–12–46).

Before the title question could be settled, the War of the Pacific presented the Aspíllagas with a very different sort of threat. As the Chileans advanced, they imposed tribute on Peruvian plantations. Many estates were burned by the invaders, often with the help of Chinese workers who welcomed the Chileans as liberators. At Cayaltí, Antero acted adroitly to minimize the consequences of the invasion. Having noted that the Chileans were less likely to inflict serious damage to plantations belonging to foreigners, he had documents drawn showing that Cayaltí was owned by its major creditor, the American firm Prevost & Company. When the Chileans occupied Cayaltí in October 1880, some food and a few oxen were stolen and three Chinese workers escaped. The Aspíllagas were forced to pay a tribute of 4,000–6,000 paper soles per month. But no physical damage was done to the plantation and production was not interrupted.[5]

Like the other planters who managed to survive the successive national disasters of the 1870s, the Aspíllagas faced difficult circumstances in the postwar period. Cayaltí, to which they had a still questionable title, was, like many such enterprises, heavily

The Aspíllagas owned this oft-rebuilt colonial mansion in Lima from 1897 to 1954.

Source: Wikimedia Commons, courtesy of Miguel Angel Chong.

indebted. There was a real possibility that they could lose the estate. The Aspíllagas endured because they were able to find new financing and were successful in modernizing the operations of the plantation and solving their labor supply problem. In the 1880s the family initiated its long and intimate relationship with the English commercial house Henry Kendall & Sons. Between 1884 and 1910 the Aspíllagas negotiated three mortgage loans with the firm. Kendall also acted as Cayaltí's commercial agent and provided frank, often critical business advice that was received with appreciation by the Aspíllagas (Gonzales 1985: 35).

The relationship was crucial for Cayaltí's postwar modernization, which began with a series of improvements in the sugar mill that increased its capacity and yield while reducing labor costs. In 1911 a new mill was built with financing from Kendall (Gonzales 1978: 89). Several years earlier the Aspíllagas had built a twenty-two mile rail line between Cayaltí and the port of Eten, freeing Cayaltí of its dependence on costly and inefficient mule trains to move sugar to the coast. Integral to Cayaltí's modernization program was a determination to keep the estate abreast of developments in sugar technology. Antero, in particular, read extensively in the field and was well acquainted with technical aspects of Cayaltí's operations. He assumed personal responsibility for the selection of equipment for the new mill.[6]

In the years immediately following the war with Chile, Cayaltí did not produce profits for its owners. But as the Aspíllagas solved their financing and labor problems and modernized the estates' operations, Cayaltí's balances steadily improved. By the early 1890s, the plantation was showing substantial earnings (Gonzales 1978: 59), which climbed to spectacular levels during World War I when prices on the international market rose steeply (table 6.1). By 1916, the Aspíllagas were able to retire mortgages dating from 1884 to 1903 which they had with Kendall and Sons (RAB

Table 6.1. Cayaltí Earnings after Taxes (in 1967 dollars)

Year	Profits	Losses	Year	Profits	Losses
1911	781,700		1935		26,400
1912	857,100		1936		n.a.
1913		295,200	1937		9,600
1914	1,296,600		1938		n.a.
1915	1,182,600		1939–1945	High wartime profits	
1916	1,381,400		1945–1949		n.a.
1917	1,645,200		1950	6,679,700	
1918		n.a.	1951	225,900	
1919	2,240,200		1952	227,500	
1920		n.a.	1953	122,600	
1921	778,600		1954	150,400	
1922	516,300		1955	224,600	
1923	1,775,600		1956	517,600	
1924	1,013,100		1957	544,600	
1925	253,600		1958	140,200	
1926		n.a.	1959	180,600	
1927	559,000		1960	768,400	
1928		309,900	1961	362,600	
1929		Loss	1962	87,900	
1930		Loss	1963		n.a.
1931	Profit		1964		408,100
1932		164,200	1965		n.a.
1933		Loss	1966		785,000
1934		Loss	1967		403,800

n.a. = not available.
Sources:
   1911–1915, 1921–1925: CDA, "Projecto de Constitucion de la Sociedad Anomina denominada Negociaciones Agricolas Cayalti y Palto, Anexo no. 1," December 20, 1926.
   1916–1919: Personal communication from Professor William Albert, August 30, 1975. Data based on Aspíllaga correspondence in CDA.
   1927: CDA, "Finanzas del Señor Ramon Aspillaga . . . enero a junio de 1928."
   1928: Huertas 1974: 107.
   1929–1937: CDA, Aspíllaga correspondence.
   1940–1945: Interview with AAHSA executive.
   1950–1961: AAHSA, "Carta abierta al Señor Ministro de Agricultura," *La Prensa*, August 22, 1969.
   1962–1967: CDA, "Balances, 1962–1967."
Deflator based on U.S. Bureau of the Census 1975: 224.

4–10–16). Cayaltí showed almost continuous annual profits until the mid-1920s when a combination of falling prices and, in some years, drought conditions hit the industry.

The Aspíllagas used the profits generated by Cayaltí to modernize the plantation as described earlier and to expand their interests into other sectors of the economy. By the turn of the century, they were appearing on the boards of directors in companies engaged in banking, insurance, real estate, and mining. The Aspíllagas profited handsomely, in 1902, when the Peruvian mining syndicate, in which they had a major interest, won its long-running legal fight with the American Cerro de Pasco Mining Company in 1902. By the early twenties, the Aspíllagas were the largest stockholders in the important Banco de Peru y Londres.[7]

A listing of securities owned by Ramón Aspíllaga Barrera in 1927 reveals a typically oligarchic pattern of investment. Nearly 60 percent of the investment is in banks and insurance companies. On the other hand, only a trivial proportion of the portfolio is dedicated to industry and none to metal mining.[8] Early in 1929, Ramón estimated his personal fortune, excluding his interest in Cayaltí, at $1.2 million (RAB 1–5–29).

CONTROLLING LABOR

In the 1880s the Aspíllagas remained dependent on the Chinese laborers with whom they had worked the plantation prior to the war. At Cayaltí, as on other estates, the Chinese were low-paid, cruelly exploited, and subject to a private system of justice administered by the planters. The Aspíllagas maintained a jail on the hacienda and arrogated to themselves the right to order workers imprisoned or whipped. Gonzales (1985: 106–109) records several occasions on which the family members actually ordered executions for murder, and one incident in 1875 in which an escaped Chinese worker was killed by a search party of Cayaltí overseers sent out to recapture him. In family correspondence the Aspíllagas admitted that their Chinese laborers were "semi-slaves" and "very badly treated." Nonetheless, they were ready to justify their actions with racist characterizations of the Chinese as "barbarians," "devils," and "semi-men" (Gonzales 1985: 114). An 1878 letter dismisses "slavery" with the following extraordinary observations:

> . . . it exists for but short periods of time, besides we are not the only ones, although they say that to follow the bad example of several is to take the advice of fools, but some need others and this brings us forward as heroes who search for a sure death in order to live eternally in the pages of history (Gonzales 1985: 115).

Not all Peruvians viewed the exploitation of the Chinese as "heroic." Four years before this letter was written the government had yielded to domestic and international pressure and ordered a halt to the importation of indentured Chinese laborers. However, this action did not put an end to exploitation of the Chinese. The initial response at Cayaltí as elsewhere was to extend the contracts of indentured workers already in the country.

Later Cayaltí came to depend on "free" Chinese employed on a daily basis and Chinese laborers supplied by Chinese contractors. Although not indentured labor, these categories of workers could be bound to the plantation by their accumulated indebtedness. They were not, however, sufficient to meet the needs of coastal agriculture, especially as the work capacity of the aging Chinese population steadily declined. As late as 1885, the Aspíllagas were convinced that the renewal of Chinese immigration was both politically feasible and essential to the survival of export agriculture. But the Coolie trade was never reopened and in the course of the 1890s Cayaltí and other plantations were forced to turn to the peasantry of the northern Sierra to fill their expanding labor needs. By 1899, Cayaltí's workforce of 1,000 men was largely Serrano (Gonzales 1978: 234).

The Serranos were brought to Cayaltí with the help of labor contractors under a system called "enganche" (literally "hooking"). A peasant agreed to work on the estate for a specified period of time in exchange for a cash advance. Many workers chose to remain and a community of resident Serrano workers and their families gradually developed at Cayaltí. The Aspíllagas encouraged family settlement, on the theory that "this is the tie which makes them more permanent" (Gonzales 1978: 270).

The material conditions of this new labor force were somewhat better than those that the Chinese had experienced, and they were subject to more subtle forms of control. By the end of the century the Aspíllagas had yielded the right to imprison or execute workers to public authorities. In the twentieth century, the Peruvian state would play an increasingly important role in controlling labor. This change had one important advantage for the Aspíllagas: They could employ paternalistic means to manage their labor force while depending on impersonal (and formally independent) authorities to apply violent force when this became necessary. Under these conditions, of course, the Aspíllagas and their fellow planters were compelled to take a more active interest in the management of the state.

THE ASPÍLLAGA BARRERAS IN THE ARISTOCRATIC REPUBLIC

The economic success of the Aspíllaga Barreras earned them access to upper-class Lima society and the ruling circles of the Aristocratic Republic. They were able to achieve the social position that had eluded their father. Aspíllaga Ferrebú's sons were educated in Lima's best private schools, such as La Recolecta where they mixed with children from prominent families including the Pardos, the Beltráns, the Riva Agueros, and the Ortiz de Zevallos. By 1890 all four brothers had been admitted to Lima's Club Nacional. When the eldest of the four, Antero, died in 1927, a local paper noted, "In Lima he occupied the highest rung. His noble mansion has been a great aristocratic center."[9]

Aspíllaga Ferrebú had been politically active in his later years. He was an enthusiastic supporter of the candidacy of the first Civilista president, Manuel Pardo, in

1871 (RAF 10–16–1871) and is said to have had "close friendships with prominent politicians and most especially with Don Mariano Ignacio Prado" (*Cultura Peruana* 1960). That would be General and sometime President Mariano Ignacio Prado, whose family is the subject of the next chapter. The elder Aspíllaga was never, however, a notable political figure. That distinction was reserved for his sons.

All four of the Aspíllaga Barrera brothers served at one time or another the Civilista-dominated congresses of the Aristocratic Republic (Echegaray Corea 1965; Senado 1961). But as happens in many oligarchic families, one individual—in this case Antero—becomes *the* family politician.[10] (Julio de la Piedra and Manuel Prado were later examples.) Antero was a leading public figure during this period. He participated in the "Twenty-four Friends," the elite core of the Civilista Party that met regularly at the Club Nacional. He was allied with the conservative wing of the party that resisted young liberals like José Pardo and the Miró Quesada brothers in the opening years of the new century.

For eighteen years, Aspíllaga represented Lima in the Senate, for four of these years as presiding officer. He was twice the Civilistas' presidential candidate, in 1912 and 1919, losing on both occasions, under circumstances described in chapter 4. Antero had the misfortune to run in a period when the elite was divided and popular mobilization was beginning to challenge oligarchic control. Planters were no longer the sure candidates they had once been. Historian Pike (1967: 214) writes of Antero's 1919 candidacy, "The lackluster Aspíllaga, however good his intentions and however widely recognized his integrity, was too staunchly conservative to be able to win the confidence of the masses or even the moderately reform-minded political and intellectual leaders."

In 1912 Antero had the half-hearted support of President Leguía, who probably hoped to perpetuate his own power. The election was thrown into the Congress, where Guillermo Billinghurst, with strong backing from the streets of Lima, was declared the winner, after a deal was struck in Congress. Like their peers, the Aspíllagas were pleased with the overthrow of Billinghurst two years later, not simply because they felt that Antero had been cheated out of the election, but because they saw Billinghurst as a threat to social stability and control of labor (AAB 1–27–13; RAB 2–15–14).

One incident of the period suggests that, whatever their relationship to Billinghurst's government, the Aspíllagas were still powerful enough in Lima to be sure of maintaining control where it mattered most: In Lambayeque, where Cayaltí is located. In 1913 a final decision was handed down in a long-standing land dispute between Cayaltí and the little town of Zaña, which is completely surrounded by the plantation. The decision, favorable to the Aspíllagas, provoked an attack on property in the town owned by the family and the burning of the disputed land. At the Aspíllagas' request, Zaña was occupied by the army, which imposed a curfew, banned public meetings, and prohibited the sale of liquor and the possession of firearms. The army restored order but in the process killed two Zañeros and inflicted injuries on several others. Subsequently the Prefect of Lambayeque (equivalent of governor, a presidential appointee) filed a report on these events, describing the army's action as a "massacre" and asserting that all of the hills around Zaña had been stolen by nearby plantations, especially Cayaltí. Antero saw the report and, within a week, was able to have the prefect replaced with someone more sympathetic to the interests of the Aspíllagas (Gonzales 1985: 52).

From the perspective of later years, one of the more significant political events of this era was the founding of the National Agrarian Society in 1896 with the participation of Antero and his brother Ramón (*Lima* 1935). The Society, a semiofficial body, was to be the pressure group for the major landed interests on the coast and, on occasion, a forum for political conspiracy. The Aspíllagas were associated with it throughout its history (which ended under the Velasco government), frequently serving as officers and on the board of directors.

UNDER LEGUÍA

Antero had run against Leguía in 1919. Leguía's preemptive coup following the election was a decisive political turning point for the Aspíllagas, as it was for the entire Civilista elite. It marked an end to the family's formal and open participation in politics. In the short run, the coup encouraged popular protest and quickly brought troubles down on Cayaltí and the Aspíllagas. A potentially violent strike broke out at the Eten port facility where the plantation stored sugar and alcohol for shipment. Workers at the sugar mill went on strike, and in September cane cutters conducted a work stoppage to support demands for higher wages and lower food prices. Aside from Leguía's coup, principal cause of these actions was the rapid rise in the cost of living during World War I. The increase during 1919 alone was estimated at 73 percent (Gonzales 1985: 183).

Also in September, the new regime claimed to have discovered a plot to overthrow the government. Antero's house in Lima was set on fire by Leguía partisans, and his brother Ramón was jailed. In Chiclayo there were demonstrations against Cayaltí and Tuman (a nearby plantation owned by the Pardo family) and proplanter newspapers were attacked.[11]

But the situation was not as bleak for the Aspíllagas as these events suggest. The problem at Eten was resolved when the prefect, in response to Cayaltí's request for help, sent eighty armed men to the port and informed the workers that they would be jailed if they refused to go back to work. The mill workers had been demanding a pay increase that would bring their wages to the levels being paid at other plantations; they were given a raise. When the cane cutters refused an offer from the Aspíllagas, the prefect was asked for twenty-five men; he sent fifty and the cutters went back to work.

Leguía wanted to intimidate his oligarchic enemies. The message was clear: Leguía intended to rule without the participation of those who had come to regard ruling as their right. But it was equally obvious that he had no intention of upsetting the established social order. Leguía's attack was on power, not on property. The response to the Cayaltí strikes was preliminary evidence of that.

The Aspíllagas gave Leguía the response he wanted: withdrawal. Several months after the coup, Ramón Aspíllaga Barrera spelled out the new rules for his nephew Victor (Antero's son), then administrator of the plantation: "With respect to politics, neither national nor departmental, nor provincial, nor local—as if we were foreigners in our own land—so as to give no pretext for gossip and calumny . . . " (RAB 11–22–19). In 1920, Ramón took his family to Europe where they remained until 1923 (supported of course by continuing income from Cayaltí).

Where Antero spent this period is not clear. But early in 1923, by then in his mid-seventies, he was deported and sailed for Europe. Shortly thereafter, he ordered Victor, his illegitimate son and only heir, to leave his position at Cayaltí and bring his wife and children to Europe. Victor was replaced at Cayaltí by Ramón's sons Ismael and Carlos Aspíllaga Anderson (CDA, "Aspíllaga historia familiar").

Before the end of the year Ramón had agreed to buy Antero's one-third interest in Cayaltí and Palto for $760,350, leaving Ramón as the sole owner (RAB 10–29–23; IAA 11–19–23). Baldomero Aspíllaga Barrera, considerably younger than his brothers, Antero and Ramón, had sold his interest some time earlier to dedicate himself to the good life, particularly racing horses, a favorite sport of Lima's upper class. He is remembered in Lima for the Baldomero Aspíllaga Classic, an annual thoroughbred race, run for the hundredth time in 2013.

The remainder of this family history concerns Ramón and his lineage, the Aspíllaga Andersons, that is, the branch of the family that remained in control of Cayaltí. They have had little or nothing to do with the other major surviving branch, the Aspíllaga Delgados, Antero's grandchildren through Victor. The Aspíllaga Delgados, who apparently inherited Antero's fortune, became important figures in Lima business circles.[12]

REORGANIZING THE FAMILY

The Aspíllagas had long conducted their affairs guided by patriarchal principles, with authority concentrated in eldest sons, and females wholly excluded from decision making. Antero was the eldest and the leader among the Aspíllaga Barrera brothers, a year older than Ramón. Shortly after their father's death, he had asserted his authority in a lengthy memorandum to his brothers. The 1876 document describes "the by-laws that our father left us" for the management of the family estate, which recognized Antero as general manager of the family enterprise and obliged his brothers to "obey all his orders" (reproduced in Macera 1973: 6–11).

With the departure of Antero from the family enterprise almost fifty years later, his brother Ramón Aspíllaga Barrera emerged as a willful patriarch. He had eleven children. On his birthday in 1925, he wrote his sons, "Today I am 75 years old and my most important and affectionate thoughts are of you my dear sons. Carry my name with honor and be united so that you will be respected and powerful" (RAB 9–14–25). He endured to the age of ninety. Even after he had re-organized the family holdings into a new firm, making his children stockholders and giving them formal responsibility, the old man was never reluctant to intervene or give orders in both business and political matters. For instance, a year before his death, he put an end to suggestions from his sons that the firm incur new obligations in order to carry out a capital development program in preparation for wartime demand, as neighboring plantations were doing. "I do not wish . . . nor do I authorize you, and neither do I wish to know anything about what our neighbors are doing."[13]

The new firm, Aspíllaga Anderson Hermanos, S.A. (AAHSA), was organized with a stated capital of $2.64 million to run both Cayaltí and Palto (RAA 6–6–28). At Ramón's insistence, his eldest son, Ramón Aspíllaga Anderson, became chief executive and ran the company from its offices in Lima. Brothers Luís and Ismael served as administrators of Cayaltí, living for long periods, singly or together, on the plantation. None of the younger Aspíllaga Anderson brothers ever served for a significant amount of time in a position with operating responsibility for AAHSA. Their sisters never held positions in the company, nor were they, to judge from correspondence, involved, even informally or indirectly, with its management.

As responsibility for the management of Cayaltí passed to a new generation, the family enterprise entered a period of severe economic difficulties, which would soon be exacerbated by the general economic and political crisis of the 1930s. The available profit and loss data for the period 1925–1937 indicate nearly continuous losses (table 6.1). This state of affairs reflects problems faced by the entire Peruvian sugar industry during this period. In the late 1920s prices on the international sugar market declined, as European sugar beet production, curtailed during the war, revived. The industry was also affected by both droughts and floods during this period (Bertram 1974a: 71–88).

THE CRISIS OF THE 1930S: LABOR

Nothing could have pleased the Aspíllagas more than "the fall of the traitor and felon, Leguía—the news we have hoped for so many years" (LAA 8–26–30). They were less delighted with the political problems left in his wake. The rise of APRA, as shown in the last chapter, especially threatened the sugar planters, because the party was strong in sugar-growing areas and gaining strength among sugar workers.

In the months before the 1931 election, Cayaltí seemed to be surrounded by a sea of political hostility. "In Zaña," wrote Ismael Aspíllaga Anderson, "they are absolutely all Apristas" (IAA 8–25–31). Luis complained that a local paper, "daily insults Civilismo, us, the planters. And there are anonymous wall posters (*pasquines*) talking of Pardo and Aspíllaga. . . ." (LAA 10–27–31).

The Aspíllagas were also uneasy over strikes and signs of labor and political organizing on other estates (IAA 5–28–31). In June, Luís wrote Lima of "an attempted assault by workers from Tuman and Patapo-Pucala [neighboring plantations] which was repelled by forces under the prefect at the entrance to Chiclayo with a point-blank barrage of gunfire they say left eleven dead and a similar number wounded." Such conditions were ominous even though the labor situation at Cayaltí remained peaceful during this period. "Happily, at our Cayaltí, we live in great tranquility and have not even had token indications of discontent" (Huertas 1974: 71).

In this period, labor control was a matter of crucial concern to the Aspíllagas, who were trying to meet the economic crisis by intensifying their exploitation of the workforce. To achieve this they resorted to varying combinations of wage cuts, increases in the daily piece-work (*tarea*) required of each worker, and reductions in the plantation's workforce. These were delicate matters, requiring considerable discretion. "We must try to obtain the maximum amount of work per *tarea* [task] within the limits of what is humane, practical and therefore free from the risk of generating conflicts with the working class."[14]

Under these conditions, the Aspíllagas favored strong repressive action by authorities against the emerging labor movement. Luis approved of the prefect's "energetic gesture" in the bloody incident cited earlier and was pleased that the "ringleaders" had been jailed and *El Trabajador,* a labor movement paper that had been circulating on the haciendas, had been closed down in the aftermath (Huertas 1974: 71).

At the same time, the family strove to treat its own workers as moderately as possible. Their approach was described by Ismael, who criticized the administrator of a nearby plantation for this rough treatment of the workforce: "The era of beating people has passed. More can be gained with justice, but with severity when necessary" (IAA 6–16–31). At Cayaltí, the Aspíllagas depended on maintaining close contact with the workers, careful isolation of the plantation from "subversive" influences, and activities designed to keep laborers distracted. They presented movies on the plantation and encouraged such activities as interplantation sporting events, "everything which, without diminishing our authority and position, gives us the opportunity to be in contact with our people, to treat them with moderation, so as not to show the least fear . . . and finally to keep them distracted and content" (RAA 1–6–31).

The Aspíllagas consulted continuously with other sugar planters, such as the Pardos and the de la Piedras, about the evolving labor situation. These contacts took place both locally and in Lima. They urged the others to resist worker demands and, in particular, to refuse to recognize unions. At the same time, they were careful to maintain discretion about these interchanges. On one occasion they resisted a call for a meeting of planters because they feared that workers would get the idea that the sugar growers were organizing and they should do the same.[15] The family's policy regarding collaboration with other planters was, as Ramón characterized it, "cooperation where ideas are concerned, but without personal participation in any overt measure . . . I will sign nothing" (RAA 1–6–31).

THE CRISIS OF THE 1930S: NATIONAL POLITICS

The Aspíllaga clan's attitude toward national politics post-Leguía paralleled (and in fact was closely tied to) their labor strategy. While they wanted a government that would take stringent, even brutal measures against their enemies, they wanted to maintain their own distance from such repression where at all possible. They favored "a good dictatorship which would treat the Apristas with the lash" (IAA 4–9–31). The family, Ramón wrote his brothers, should help the government to maintain order, but discretely, "avoiding the creation of hatreds around us beyond those already in existence. All efforts toward social and public order should seem to come from the authorities and nowhere else. Here, as in many other attitudes, Machiavelli imposes himself" (RAA 4–18–32). The Aspíllagas, he urged in another letter, should follow the example of the Pardos, made their influence felt, while maintaining a low political profile (RAA 1–25–32).

Even within conservative circles, the family wanted to avoid presenting an "ultrapartisan" image. They tried to maintain discretion about the financial backing they were giving Sánchez Cerro's campaign, saying that they had "a moral commitment and nothing more." Above all they wanted to avoid a repetition of the experience they had with Leguía when they were trapped, "with neither voice nor vote," an ever-present danger given the capriciousness of national politics. But Ismael ran for Congress on Sanchez Cerro's ticket, an obvious violation of these principles, which was regarded as a mistake by family members.[16]

The decision to back Sanchez Cerro in 1931 was made for reasons quite explicitly laid out in the letter quoted in the last chapter: APRA represented a threat to "the established order" and Sanchez Cerro merited the support of "all who have interests to preserve and protect" (RAA 8–27–31). Also important was the simple but crucial fact that Sanchez Cerro would have the support of the army (LAA 1–26–31).

Although there is no indication that they participated in any way in the coup against Leguía, the Aspíllagas were in close contact with Sanchez Cerro thereafter. In October 1930, Ramón wrote his brothers about two lengthy interviews with the colonel, who proved quite receptive and promised strong action to halt the activities of radical political agitators who had been attacking the plantations. Informed of pending strikes on the north coast, Sanchez Cerro assured Ramón that the government would support no concessions to the workers and urged that they be discretely warned of this (RAA 9–10–30).

After he was elected, Sanchez Cerro consulted frequently with the Aspíllagas regarding appointments of local officials in Lambeyeque, matters of supreme importance to them.[17] Relations between the family and the president were warm, with family members often receiving invitations to be presidential palace and Sanchez Cerro paying frequent visits to the Aspíllagas. "I see," Luis wrote one of his brothers, "that the president has become a constant visitor at the family mansion at La Punta, and what good talks he must have with father, who can give him very good advice with his experience. It is gratifying to see that the chief has an affinity for good society and is gracious to those who have helped him so much."[18]

The day-to-day cooperation that developed between the Aspíllagas and Sanchez Cerro's government suggests the extent to which the regime made itself an instrument of the oligarchy. The Aspíllagas, as quietly as possible, supported government efforts to repress political and labor organizing activity that threatened Cayaltí and the other major estates. A 1932 memo from Luis to Ramón shows how direct the collaboration was. The document lists certain expenses related to "public order and tranquility in the department, something to which we cannot be indifferent," which were being charged to the family firm. Among these were "payment made to Sub-Prefect Morante to contribute to the deportation of undesirables" and "payment made to Sub-Prefect José M. Maldona do to contribute to the imprisonment and deportation of eight communists sent to Madre de Dios [a jungle province] by order of the Director of Government [sub cabinet official in Lima]" (undated). Such deportations were a way of putting an end to the agitation against the planters and "Civilismo" of which the Aspíllagas complained in their letters.

On several occasions Cayaltí provided facilities to the army to aid in the suppression of "subversive movements." Most important in this regard was the use of the Cayaltí railroad to move troops from the coast to the interior.[19] The elder Ramón met with Sanchez Cerro in the wake of the Trujillo rebellion and agreed to join members of the Pardo and Fernandini families on a committee to raise funds for the armed forces (RAA 7–19–32). As the army returned from Trujillo, forty officers and three hundred enlisted men were honored with lunch at Cayaltí and "a patriotic demonstration attended by all the workers and employees" (LAA 7–30–32). One advantage of controlling a sizable workforce was the capacity to organize successful political demonstrations on demand, something the Aspíllagas did on many occasions.

Aside from their direct connections with a succession of national governments, the Aspíllagas' exerted political pressure in collaboration with other major planters through the National Agrarian Society. In the 1930s the SNA sought government relief for the sugar industry. These efforts were most successful in the early 1930s when reductions in irrigation and guano (fertilizer) payments, and the establishment of an agrarian bank were granted (RAA 8–25–31). The Aspíllagas benefited from these measures, as they did from the devaluation of the Peruvian sol in 1932, also a result of pressure from the Society. But the most important contribution the government made to the economic survival of the Aspíllagas and other sugar growers was surely the continuing repression of APRA and other radical elements that threatened their control of labor.

Another important area of political collaboration among the planters was management of the press. The Aspíllaga correspondence indicates the devotion of considerable time and money to insure coverage supportive of oligarchic interests generally and the sugar industry in particular. Inevitably, the media they influenced backed right-wing governments and attacked APRA and the labor unions. In the 1930s the Aspíllagas participated in the conduct of press campaigns, "which we manage from the National Agrarian Society," pressuring the government to allow a monetary devaluation (RAA 7–5–32). "We have at least two newspapers, *La Cronica* and *La Prensa*. . .," " wrote Ramón Aspíllaga Anderson in 1934 (Huertas 1974: 205). As part of such efforts, members of the family wrote anonymous articles for the papers arguing the planters' point of view or arranged to be interviewed by reporters from sympathetic publications (RAA 10–21–35; LAA 10–13–34).

In Lambeyeque, the Aspíllagas were as interested in silencing newspaper attacks on the planters from the left as they were in arguing their own point of view. When *La*

Hora, a radically inclined local paper began to publish articles by a Spanish journalist attacking the planters and the Aspíllagas in particular, the family had the Prefect order the paper to cease publication of such articles and took other steps designed to force the journalist to leave the area (IAA 5–28–31). The closing of the antiplanter *El Trabajador* was referred to earlier.

In 1931 the Aspíllagas and other Lambayeque planters developed an elaborate plan to get favorable coverage in the local press. The key to this effort was a $280/month stipend, which was to be paid to the editor of *La Hora.* This amount, which represented what a plantation worker might earn in three years, was to be raised by monthly subscription among the planters. The campaign was to be organized from Lima to minimize the chance that its sponsorship would be detected locally (RAA 11–5–34). While it is not clear whether this plan was ever carried into action, there are other indications in the correspondence that the Aspíllagas and other Lambeyeque planters did find ways to subsidize sympathetic publications.[20]

The Aspíllagas' most important journalistic association was with *La Prensa,* of which they were still shareholders at the time it was nationalized in 1974. Ramón Aspíllaga Barrera took a special interest in *La Prensa* when it was revived in the 1930s to serve as the organ of the major land-owning interests on the coast. At the time, he wrote "[W]e are interested in the life of *La Prensa,* its circulation, and its—political program of order and, above all, service to national agriculture and other influential national interests. . . ." Aspíllaga was part of a group from the National Agrarian Society that was subsidizing the paper until it could be made self-supporting (RAA 8–26–35).[21]

Though the Aspíllagas worked with other planters to defend what they regarded as their vital common interests, the family correspondence also provides evidence of conflicts among the planters over matters including water and tax policies. Cayaltí had to compete with neighboring plantations over access to water. In the 1950s, Aspíllagas clashed with other producers over the sugar export tax, which was based on volume rather than profit, placing a relatively inefficient producer like Cayaltí at a disadvantage. The Aspíllagas despised the de la Piedras, owners of the nearby Pomalca estate, who had been close to Leguía. One Aspíllaga letter describes them as "great enemies of the name Aspíllaga" (IAA 9–8–30). Another suggests that the de la Piedras that they were behind attacks on the Aspíllagas during the 1931 campaign (LAA 10–27–31). The family suspected Pomalca of diverting irrigation water and saw the hand of the de la Piedras behind a decision that demoted the status of the Cayaltí's port of Eten, depriving them of mail deliveries. Nonetheless, they were, as noted earlier, regularly in contact with the de la Piedras over shared labor concerns.

THE CRISIS OF THE 1930S: AFTER SANCHEZ CERRO

Sanchez Cerro was assassinated in 1933. The Aspíllagas would never again be as close to a national administration as they had been to his. Although the family (especially the elder Ramón) remained politically active through the 1930s and beyond, they were never part of General Benavides' inner circle and he dominated the politics of the later 1930s.

In 1936, Benavides promoted the presidential candidacy of Jorge Prado, who was known to favor a more conciliatory policy toward APRA. The Aspíllagas joined fellow planters and other anti-APRA conservatives to support Manuel Villarán, a distinguished lawyer with Civilista roots, who proved to be a very weak candidate. The Aspíllagas were not unhappy when Benavides decided to annul the election and perpetuate himself in power. They saw this as "[T]he only possible solution at the moment. If he counts with the support of the army he should have little difficulty in the government of the country and we ought to have three more years of internal rest and progress" (GAA 1–12–36).

The family was most uneasy with Benavides when he appeared to be heading toward some sort of *rapprochement* with APRA, which particularly seemed to be the case early in his first term. But as long as he kept APRA at bay they were satisfied.[22] In 1939, they gave financial support to Jorge's brother, Manuel Prado, who also had the backing of Benavides.

In a letter to one of his sons, the old man recognized that there had probably been some fraud in Prado's election, but "[A]s I told President Benavides, it is the outgoing president that makes the incoming one" (RAB 9–11–39). In a second letter, he remphasized the importance of "the fact that Engineer Prado has the effective support of the armed forces, which is, unfortunately, the only thing that matters now" (RAB 11–14–39). Implicit in these observations is the recognition that the oligarchs no longer chose presidents (though they needed to be consulted in their selection) and that the military strongmen they backed tended to escape their control.

The Aspíllagas may have harbored some suspicions that Manuel, like his brother, was inclined to open the political system to APRA, but they were apparently reassured by his connection to the (generally anti-APRA) military. Also reassuring were their own long-standing ties to the Prados. The connection between the two families dated from Ramón Aspíllaga Ferrebú's political support of General Prado in the nineteenth century. From 1924, Ramón Aspíllaga Barrera had served on the board of the Prado-owned Banco Popular. After 1940, the bank became increasingly involved in the financial affairs of AAHSA. The cordial social relations between the families were demonstrated early in Manuel's presidency when his wife was entertained at Cayaltí and invited her hostess to visit her at the presidential palace (RAA 9–12–40).

THE CRISIS OF THE 1930S: ECONOMICS

AAHSA managed to survive the long crisis of the 1930s through a combination of political and economic measures. By political means, they maintained control over labor, the preservation of a political economy favorable to exporters, and policies specifically designed to aid the ailing sugar industry. The economic efforts were directed at the internal functioning of the firm. While they waited for a break in the market, the Aspíllagas strove to keep their losses to a minimum by increasing productivity and holding down costs, by, for example, intensifying the exploitation of labor. The letters of the period are full of exhortations to cut expenses by any means possible. New capital investments were to be shunned, except for the drilling of some new wells and the purchase of new tractors. These investments were part of a drive, which included experimentation with new cane varieties, to increase production by intensifying cultivation and increasing the total area planted.[23]

In spite of these efforts, AAHSA accumulated substantial debts during the 1930s. By 1935 they owed the equivalents of $196,431 in pounds sterling and $175,241 in soles (RAB 8–3–35). This debt had to be guaranteed by the old man's security holdings (RAA 1–28–35) and only the boom years on the sugar market during World War II allowed them to amortize it. Wartime profits also allowed the Aspíllagas to make substantial new investments in Cayaltí in the postwar period.

By and large, the nonagrarian part of the Aspíllaga fortune fared better in the late 1930s than Cayaltí. By 1936, as the old man observed bitterly in a letter to Ismael, only sugar was still in a depression. The entire urban economy and even cotton were enjoying prosperous times (RAB 12–21–35). The elder Ramón's stocks were producing far more income than he could spend (GAA 1–26–36). Some of the money was channeled into the gold mining boom, the one major area of expanding oligarchic investment during the 1930s. The Aspíllagas were represented on the boards of three gold mining companies, along with other oligarchic families and some British investors. All three ventures were failures.[24]

In 1940 Ramón Aspíllaga Barrera died at the age of ninety. By law, both legitimate and illegitimate children had a claim on his estate. This meant that the Aspíllaga Andersons and their mother (who retained a 50 percent interest in the family holdings) had to come to terms with "E. & B. Aspíllaga Navarrro," the old man's illegitimate children (RAA 4–7–41). At the same time they had to pay a national inheritance tax.

At this point the family's friendly relations with the Prados and their bank proved helpful. Ramón, who had replaced his father on the board of the Prado bank, wrote Luis, "[W]e have a generous offer of money and in my position of director of the Banco Popular I am anxious to increase our commercial relations with that bank" (RAA 4–17–41). The Banco Popular agreed to loan the family $154,000 at 7 percent, to pay the inheritance tax of $90,007 and settle with the Aspíllaga Navarros (RAA 4–7–41). The Aspíllagas had another kind of help from the Prados. Manuel, it appears, applied presidential influence to assure a low appraisal of the estate (RAA 1–6–41).

The character of the elder Aspíllaga's estate can be inferred from an "Inventory-Balance" sheet prepared a little over a year before his death, the details of which can be seen in table 6.2. The pattern of investment revealed here is quite similar to that which was evident in the 1927 portfolio mentioned earlier. The emphasis is on the typically oligarchic areas of finance, real estate, and, of course, export activities. There is virtually no involvement in industry with the exception of shares in a glass factory in which the Aspíllagas had invested along with the Bentins and others.

Table 6.2.   Ramón Aspíllaga Barrera: Balance Sheet, January 1, 1939

ASSETS		
Agriculture		
Shares AAHSA	$1,411,200	
		$1,411,200
Real Estate		
Land and Buildings	317,327	
Shares, Cia. Urbana Cocharacas	14,000	
Shares, Cia Urbana Av. Magdalena	8,400	
Financial Stocks		
Banco Internacional	13,317	
Banco Popular	39,474	
Banco Italiano	90,037	
Cia. de Seguros La Nacional	5,063	
Cia. Internacional de Seguros	22,040	
Cia. de Seguros Rimac	3,261	
		339,727
Other Stocks		
Cia Manufacturera de Vidrios	8,960	
Edificio Club Nacional	224	
Empresa Electricas Asociadas	7,050	
Empresa Periodictica, S.A.	4,480	
Cia. Adm. de Guano	3,260	
Certificates of Deposit		
Banco Central Hipotecario at 7%	57,786	
Banco Central Hipotecario at 71/2 %	11,034	
		68,820
Bonds		
Beneficencia de Lima	36,736	
Hospital Arzobispo Loayza	2,240	
		38,976
Receivables		
Maria A.G.A. de Aspíllaga	2,609	
Ramón Aspíllaga A.	1,608	
Ismael Aspíllaga A.	46,462	
Luis Aspíllaga A.	1,120	
Rafael Aspíllaga A.	1,680	
Gustavo Aspíllaga A.	1,680	
Alfonso G. Anderson	2,738	
Other Loans	4,343	62,312
"Ramón Aspíllaga-Private"	64,493	
		64,493
Cash	103	103
Other Assets	4,709	
		4,709
LIABILITIES	Total Assets	$2, 187,525
Short and Long-term debt		
Banco Italiano "Current Account"	12,746	
Banco Popular	4,416	
Fundacion M.B. de Aspíllaga	4,408	
AAHSA	64,494	
		86,063
	NET WORTH	2,202,462
	Total Liabilities & Net worth	$2,187,525

Source: Huertas 1974: 139–141.

POSTWAR POLITICAL AND LABOR PROBLEMS

The Aspíllagas were in good financial condition by the end of World War II, but they were confronted with a troubling political situation. APRA had gained admittance to the legitimate political arena as part of Bustamante's National Democratic Front government. General Benavides had brokered the political deal that made this possible. Somehow, out of office, he had done just what the Aspíllagas had feared from him when he was president. The family had no point of contact with the new government. Moreover, the restoration of political rights for the first time since the brief period after the fall of Leguía meant a return of long-suppressed leftist political activity and labor organizing. It was also apparent from the beginning that the new government was not committed to the orthodox economic policies that favored the Aspíllagas and other exporters.

Bustamante's government brought with it a sudden upsurge in union activity reflecting political liberalization and the APRA party's commitment to labor. In 1945 the first national union of sugar workers was created, affiliated with the APRA-controlled union confederation, the C.T.P. (Confederation of Peruvian Workers) (Sulmont 1974: 48). Workers at Cayaltí were organized for the first time in 1945.[25] The Cayaltí union received the required recognition from the Labor Ministry, even though it may not have fulfilled all the legal requisites; this was possible, according to Ramón, because of pressure applied on the union's behalf by Aprista congressmen from Lambayeque. Nonetheless, the Aspíllagas decided not to resist, apparently regarding the union as what their administrator at Cayaltí described as, "an evil in tune with the epoch through which we are living" (RN 8–11–47).

The union generated a seemingly endless series of demands (some of which were met) and work stoppages until maneuvers by AAHSA lawyers compelled the Labor Ministry to withdraw the Cayaltí union's official recognition. This was achieved in 1947 and resulted in the closing of the union's headquarters and the removal of its officers from the estate.

During this same period the character of labor relations at Cayaltí was changing for reasons not entirely related to the union. A semipaternalistic mode was being abandoned for a more formal and abrasive contest between contending parties. This shift reflected the social and political atmosphere of the period, but also a change in management. For the first time since Ramón Aspíllaga Ferrebú came to Cayaltí in 1860, the plantation was being run by a nonfamily employee. Luis left Cayaltí in 1943, after nearly two decades there. Thereafter the Aspíllagas ran Cayaltí from Lima, supplementing phone and mail contacts with occasional visits. "What a shame it is that the Aspíllagas don't go to their plantation," lamented an unnamed old employee of Cayaltí, "because the Superintendent [a hired manager] and this new one at Cayaltí, Elias head of the union, are ruining the plantation and in the long run it is the poor workers who will pay the consequences." As this man saw it, "Don Gustavo," youngest of the Aspíllaga Anderson brothers, thought he could handle labor problems by hiring lawyers to deal with the union instead of the way

Ismael and Luis had always done, settling problems "with the workers of Cayaltí . . . without any need for lawyers or taking money from the people" (CDA, Cayaltí Archive 2–22–47).

The labor difficulties that hit Cayaltí in the Bustamante period were not unprecedented. Gonzales (1985: 170–188) notes periodic labor disputes at Cayaltí beginning in 1912. However, with the exception of the 1919 strikes, the plantation had escaped the serious conflicts that had plagued many other north coast plantations. The early forties had seen increasing labor unrest in many parts of the country, in part a reaction to rising wartime prices. But the new situation seemed more threatening. The Aspíllagas had not particularly wanted a union, but they had hoped that it might provide a channel for the orderly settlement of labor problems. Instead the union seemed to continuously create new problems, upsetting the smooth functioning of the plantation. The Aspíllagas were most disturbed by a work stoppage at Cayaltí in support of a strike at the nearby plantation Pomalca on orders of the Chiclayo union federation. (On this occasion the union had almost total support of the Cayaltí workforce.) There had been a similar incident earlier in the support of some government officials in the department who had been dismissed.

This all meant that labor was more than ever a political problem. The Aspíllagas had always worried at least as much about labor relations in Lambayeque generally or, Lima for that matter, as they had about the situation at Cayaltí itself. During the 1930s they had supported intense labor and political repression even though relations at Cayaltí remained relatively amicable. Now, even though the Aspíllagas had for the moment eliminated the union through legal maneuvers, the situation outside the plantation that was responsible for its creation remained unchanged. This concern is reflected in the mutual defense pact, which was in effect among the Lambayeque sugar growers during this period. According to the agreement, to which the Aspíllagas were party, any sugar planter would be reimbursed by his peers in the department for expenses incurred while resisting "any difficult social situation, demands, work stoppage or strike" (RAA 5–1–48). But even this approach was not equal to the problem. The only long-range security, it seemed, lay in a national political solution.

During this period, the Aspíllagas were almost certainly hurt, as were other exporters, by Bustamante's economic policies.[26] As the account in chapter 5 showed, oligarchic opposition to Bustamante's government was galvanized by questions of monetary policy and exporter control of foreign exchange earnings. The Aspíllagas were closely tied to two organizations that became foci of resistance to his government. They were stockholders in *La Prensa* and members of the National Alliance, a rightist political party organized by Beltrán. The family allowed Cayaltí to be used as a base for the National Alliance activities in the Chiclayo area (RN 5–7–47; RAA 3–7–47). *La Prensa* was a relentless critic of the Bustamante's government and APRA.

The Aspíllagas were among the main organizers of the 1948 coup and backed the military dictatorship that resulted from it.[27] After the coup, Cayaltí continued to be used as an organizing base for the National Alliance, which was supporting General Odría's bid for the presidency in 1950. On one occasion Cayaltí delivered 700 workers to swell the attendance at an NA rally in Chiclayo. The Cayaltí contingent was organized by the plantation's managers on family orders. Food was provided attending Cayaltí workers (RAA 6–7–49; RN 4–7–49).

CAYALTÍ: NOVEMBER 1950

Odria's election brought with it an abrupt shift in national labor policy and contributed to a tragic episode at Cayaltí, in November 1950.[28] That year salaries had been raised by a national decree intended to compensate workers for the rapidly rising cost of living. However, AAHSA had in effect neutralized the raise by increasing the price of certain basic commodities at the plantation markets. Cayaltí workers protested, but the Aspíllagas, from Lima, staunchly refused to rescind the increases. A tense situation developed as the workers went out on strike and the managers of the plantation called in extra police to reinforce the Civil Guard post at Cayaltí.

An initial confrontation between police and workers resulted in the death of a worker, followed by a series of arrests. The strikers were reportedly on the verge of capitulating, when a second confrontation provoked an extreme reaction from the police. Officers fired on workers who had gathered at the Civil Guard post, and then pursued them through the company town, firing wildly at those attempting to escape. At least 120 persons were killed (Plaza 1971: 10). Many workers fled the plantation for their homes in the mountains. Cane fields were burned.

"That night," a Cayaltí worker recalled years later, "[T]hey gathered the dead and wounded with company trucks and took them directly to La Guitarra Mountain where a pit had been dug and there they were thrown." One of this man's friends was a driver, who, he said, "became ill from the horror of what he had seen and died without ever recovering" (Plaza 1971: 11).

Another informant remembered, "afterward, all was calm. The company had the support of all the authorities. They threatened the people who complained with being dismissed or shot. The police took the leaders away and nothing more was heard of them. The only thing heard was the crying of many old women, daughters and wives asking about their dear ones. In the end, it was a thing like an earthquake: senseless. There was calm, but, yes, there was this hate" (Plaza 1971: 10).

Aspíllagas had long preferred to resolve their labor problems peaceably, but they had lost touch with their own enterprise and had responded intransigently to worker demands, exacerbating tensions. They and their oligarchic allies had installed a military dictatorship because they wanted a regime that could impose "social peace," if necessary by violent means. Their inflexibility reflected their sense that they now had the "support of the authorities." They would likely have responded very differently a few years earlier under Bustamante. Ironically, the workers later blamed Cayaltí's refusal to rescind the price hikes on the plantation's administrators and were convinced that the matter would have been settled satisfactorily if they could have deal directly with the plantation's absentee owners (Huertas 1974: 288).

There is, unfortunately, no record of the Aspíllagas' reaction to these terrible events. They must have had a good idea of what had happened from the long, candid, contemporaneous letter they received from their manager at Cayaltí (Huertas 1974: 286–289). They would not, however, have read about it in *La Prensa*, the paper they co-owned or in any other Lima daily. Public knowledge of the 1950 massacre at Cayaltí was buried with the victims, so that it became politically irrelevant. In contrast, the assassination a few years earlier of Francisco Graña, publisher of *La Prensa* and member of another land-owning family, became a major political issue. The oligarchic press concentrated on the crime for weeks, placing the blame directly on APRA, and turning it into a critical test for the Bustamente administration. The cabinet resigned and the government felt compelled to call in an expert foreign investigator to guarantee an impartial inquiry. By some accounts, the Graña case marked the beginning of the end for Bustamente's government.[29]

Labor relations at Cayaltí, already troubled, never recovered. At the time of the agrarian reform in 1969, they were known to be worse than on any other sugar plantation in Lambayeque,[30] a sad fate for an estate that had passed relatively peacefully through the difficult years of the depression, under the careful guidance of its owners.

LABOR AND POLITICS AFTER 1956

The shield that had protected the Aspíllagas through Odría's eight-year reign fell away when Manuel Prado's returned to the presidency with APRA support in 1956. Prado's Convivencia government brought legalization of the party and of union activity. APRA embarked on a determined campaign of labor organizing, especially on the sugar plantations. The political environment, though not as chaotic as the 1945–1948 period, posed many of the dangers that the Bustamante administration had represented. But the Prado government could not so easily be swept aside by the oligarchy.

Within months of the inauguration of the new government, union activity had revived at Cayaltí with strong support from the APRA-dominated national sugar workers union (FTAP) (Cevallos 1972; Plaza 1971). A bitter three year struggle followed for recognition of the Cayaltí union. The Aspíllagas resisted with tactics that included dismissal of union sympathizers and the purchase of votes in union representation elections. The workers responded with two month-long strikes.

The final victory of the union would have been impossible without the strong backing the Cayaltí organizers had from APRA and the FTAP and the participation of national labor authorities to guarantee a fair representation election. The most powerful weapon the FTAP used was secondary strikes on other sugar plantations, especially the two largest, Casa Grande (Gildemeister) and Cartavio (Grace Co.). These two had, ironically, arrived at amicable solutions with their own unions. Even if the other producers wanted to support the Aspíllagas, the country was having serious monetary difficulties and the government was loath to sacrifice foreign exchange by allowing a decline in sugar exports. Prado's administration—which, after all, was presided over by a member of a family long close to the Aspíllagas—did not interfere.

The establishment of a union at Cayaltí was only possible because political circumstances had changed. Toward the end of the recognition struggle, Cayaltí's lawyer was quoted as saying, "The APRA party gets rulings from the Labor Ministry because it has power, but the day the cake gets turned over, the unions will disappear" (*Tribuna*, October 11, 1959). But if the Aspíllagas and their lawyer were waiting for another right-wing military dictatorship, it was in vain.

In spite of this recent union battle and a history of brutal conflict with APRA stretching back to the 1930s, the family began to move toward friendly relations with the party in the 1960s as did much of the oligarchy. The younger brothers were most open to the party. Under Belaúnde, the family apparently supported the APRA-Odriista opposition alliance in the Congress. At Cayaltí in the mid-1960s, the Aspíllagas strove to promote Aprista sympathies among their workers (one can imagine their father turning in his grave at this) and even fired some who had been sympathetic to Belaunde's Popular Action (Cevallos 1972: 26–27 and interviews). It does not, in any event, appear that the Aspíllagas were politically consequential during these last years of the Old Regime.

ECONOMIC DECLINE IN THE 1950S AND 1960S

The political decline of the Aspíllagas was paralleled by the economic deterioration of AAHSA. Although Cayaltí showed profits throughout the decade of the 1950s, earnings were meager (table 6.1). In the period 1950 through 1961, the family company paid taxes (based on quantity of sugar exported) equivalent to 201 percent of its net after-tax profits. During Odría's presidency, when AAHSA's taxes were running about three times their profits, the Aspíllagas attempted to exploit their close ties to the regime to get the whole basis of taxation shifted from output to profit (*La Prensa*, August 22, 1969). But this initiative was unsuccessful because it was resisted by other planters, a sure sign that the rest of the industry was producing sugar more efficiently than Cayaltí.

In the fifties the Aspíllagas were investing much of the capital they had accumulated during the war. A number of improvements were made in the plantation, most notably a new $3.2 million sugar mill, built in England and set up at Cayaltí in 1952. The mill never functioned properly. Ramón blamed its "deplorable performance" on the manufacturer, who replied that the problems stemmed from improper operation. To maintain output, the decrepit old factory was pressed back into production alongside the new plant. By the end of the year AAHSA was having serious cash flow problems and had fallen behind on many credit obligations. It was another full year before production had risen to satisfactory levels.[31]

The Aspíllagas were more successful as partners in a Peruvian group, including the Bentins and Olaecheas, that bought out the English owners of Backus and Johnston, Peru's major beer producer in 1955. Backus and Johnston did quite well under Peruvian ownership. In the early 1970s, the Aspíllagas were represented on the company's board and collectively held about 8 percent of its stock—probably their largest single investment after the loss of Cayaltí, and a source of substantial income.[32]

The family made a few smaller, by and large unsuccessful, investments in the domestic economy during this period. Alongside the renewed commitment to sugar production, they not greatly change the shape of the family portfolio. Nor did the Aspíllagas abandon their espousal of an export-oriented political economy. They continued their support of an "open economy" in such matters as monetary and tariff policy (Miró Quesada 1953: I, 546–548). For example, in 1956 Gustavo Aspíllaga Anderson resigned from the board of directors of the National Society of Industries in a disagreement over broad protectionist tariffs that the society was pressuring the government to adopt at the time (*La Prensa*, September 14, 1956).

The Aspíllagas' continuing commitment to Cayaltí was unfortunate for them. Despite the enormous capital investment they made there during the 1950s, the financial condition of the firm deteriorated further in the 1960s. World sugar prices were low and Cayaltí's production costs were high. AAHSA began to sustain heavy annual losses (table 6.1) and ran up enormous debts. By 1967 the situation had deteriorated to such an extent that the Aspíllagas were forced to admit that the net worth of their firm was in the vicinity of zero.[33]

WHAT WENT WRONG?

In 1965, the Aspíllagas ordered a technical and financial study of Cayaltí by a Hawaiian consulting firm. The American team that visited Cayaltí that year formulated a plan for the rejuvenation of the plantation that called for a drastic reduction in the size of the workforce, approximately $2.0 million in capital improvements, and a series of administrative and technical reforms. They found the 1952 sugar mill to be fairly modern, but poorly run (American Factors 1965). The Aspíllagas had wanted to reduce their payroll since the 1950s, but had apparently been unable to overcome union resistance. In contrast, labor force reductions coupled with mechanization were enabling other planters to survive unionization and a depressed world market. The de la Piedras at Pomalca had cut their labor in force in half between 1960 and 1965 (Horton 1973: 21).

Cayaltí's problems were obviously interrelated. AAHSA had failed to carry out the sort of reforms that could increase yields and cut costs, especially by shrinking labor requirements. At the same time, low sugar prices and the loss of the power over labor, which had helped the Aspíllagas get through the 1930s, made it difficult to carry out such a program. Yet other producers faced similar problems with better results.[34]

"Cayaltí is probably the worst managed Hacienda in the country. . . ." That was the explanation for the situation of AAHSA given by the head of Henry Kendall & Sons, Cayaltí's English factors and a firm with long experience in the Peruvian sugar industry.[35] Cayaltí may not have been so much mismanaged as unmanaged. The elder Ramón had warned his sons, "The devil takes plantations which are not managed and administered by their owners. The family and children of many planters are left as vagrants because the planters haven't known how to protect their patrimony, trusting it to strangers." The Aspíllaga Andersons agreed on this point, but particularly after the death of the old man, none was willing or able to take over operating responsibilities at Cayaltí.[36] Their trips to the plantation often took on the character of leisure outings. The children of the Aspíllaga Andersons showed even less interest in working at Cayaltí.

In Lima in the early 1970s, one frequently heard the observation that the Aspíllaga Andersons were not equal in ability and ambition to their father and uncles. The Aspíllaga Barreras, particularly Antero and Ramón, were not born to great wealth. They had worked closely with their father and, after his death, together, to build up Cayaltí. Their letters, quoted earlier, show a determination to build up a secure family fortune. The Aspíllagas Andersons, in contrast, were born to affluence and a gracious style of life. The older Aspíllaga Anderson brothers successfully faced the challenge of guiding the family firm through the economic and political crisis of the depression. However, after Luis left the plantation in 1943, he was not replaced with a family member.

Family dynamics seem to have also contributed to the Aspíllagas' decline. Ramón did not endeavor to provide the family leadership that his father had. In Lima he was regarded as something of a *bon vivant*. Enmities among certain of the brothers and personal problems undermined the management of the family enterprise. Ismael, perhaps the most talented of his generation, was haunted for years by severe depression and finally committed suicide. He was not the only member of his generation debilitated by psychological troubles.

Generational succession is inevitably problematic for wealthy families. It is difficult for a generation born to wealth to duplicate the ambitions and attitudes of those who established the family fortune. Granick (1964: 303–320) concluded on the basis of a study of business enterprises in four European countries that few family firms are able to survive three generations. If the Aspíllagas illustrate this principle, so may the Prados who are the subject of the next chapter.

LAST CHANCE

The 1965 report had been ordered by the Aspíllagas in the hope that it could be used as a basis for recapitalizing AAHSA. In 1967 a European group organized by Cuban businessman Rafael Gonzalez agreed to invest in Cayaltí. The Gonzales group agreed to provide $5 million in credits and carry out needed capital improvements.

They would receive 65 percent of the stock in the firm. Another 10 percent would go to the Prados' Banco Popular, Cayaltí's largest creditor, in return for cancellation of their share of the plantation's enormous debt. Gonzales would take complete executive control of the enterprise, which he would run with the help of Cuban technicians (CDA, "Plan de financiación").

In August 1968 a memorandum from Ramón notified the family that the agreement with Gonzales was being carried into effect. Cayaltí was being transformed from a family enterprise into a modern corporation. As Ramón informed his kin,

> [F]rom this date AAHSA has ceased to operate as a family corporation and becomes in every sense a corporation with a strictly commercial character. The stockholders, therefore, must strictly subject themselves to this new established order. All facilities or services which previously were provided them by the company, especially economic ones, however small, are abolished. The plantation house and its domestic service organization must also lose their family residence character . . . and its use by the stockholders for vacation or rest purposes will be provided . . . subject to the requirements of the operation of the enterprise and rules which shall be established opportunely ("Plan de financiacion").

If it ever had a chance, the Gonzales plan did not operate long enough to succeed. It was not helped by the worst drought in 50 years, during the 1967–1968 harvest season.[37] When Cayaltí was taken over by the agrarian reform in 1969, a century after the Aspíllagas had begun their work there, AAHSA was declared bankrupt.

NOTES

1. *La Prensa*, March 12, 1951; Lasarte 1993: 78; interviews. Lasarte seems to contradict this account, in part. He writes, at the beginning of his meticulous Aspíllaga genealogy that "Nicolás Aspíllaga" and his wife "se establicieron en Callao hacia 1823." A family member, who has taken an interest in the clan's history, says that, according to family lore, she arrived without him.

2. "Patente de Navigacion," October 13, 1852

3. Malpica 1973: 78–79; RAA 6–6–28, 12–24–30, 11–25–41, 12–1–41; *Cultura Peruana* 1960. (From internal evidence, it is likely that this anonymous article was prepared with the help of the Aspíllaga family.)

4. A fourth, much younger brother, Baldomero, had only limited involvement in Cayaltí. Two sisters included in a genealogy, Sofia and Melchora (Lasarte 1993: 82), seem have had none at all. They may, in fact, have died before reaching majority. An 1876 document, which refers to living family members does not mention them (Macera 1973: 6–11).

5. Gonzales 1978: 43, 153; Gonzales 1985: 32, 202 n41.

6. Gonzales 1985: 31, 51–59; *Cultura Peruana* 1960; Espinoza 1905: 51–55.

7. Yepes 1972: 175–180; Basadre 1968: X, 294–5; RAB 6–7–16; Quiroz 1993: 77.

8. Banco del Perú y Londres, Señor Ramón Aspíllaga, Relación de Valores . . . 1927.

9. *La Cronica*, December 10, 1927; Sanchez 1969: I, 93–104; *Cultura Peruana* 1960.

10. Prior to the return to civilian rule, Antero had served as finance minister in the government of General Caseres. On his career see *La Cronica,* December 9, 1927; Basadre 1968: IX and other standard accounts of the period.

11. The account of these events is based on Cayaltí correspondence. Since the relevant volume of letters ("Cartas Administrativas, 1919") was unavailable. I have depended on notes taken by Bill Albert, who was kind enough to make them available to me.

12. Positions held by them are listed in Vernal Consultores (1968).

13. RAB 11–20–39, see also RAB 11–10–38; RAA 2–1–31.

14. RAA 6–2–32. Also "Aviso" 8–16–30; IAA 4–5–30, 2–21–30; LAA 10–27–34; GAA 2–9-35; RAA 1–24–36.

15. IAA 5–28–31; IAA 5–30–31; RAA 6–1–31; RAA 6–6-31; Aspíllaga historia familiar.

16. RAA 10–1–31; LAA 12–8–30; RAA 1–2–31; RAA 8–27–31.

17. RAA 12–16–31; RAB 3–8–32 and similar letters from this period.

18. LAA 9–3–32; RAA 6–28–32, 3–8–32; IAA 3–9–32.

19. LAA 7–30–32; GAA 5–11–33; LAA 8–8–34.

20. LAA 1932, undated; RAA 4–3–35; IAA 3–12–47.

21. It is impossible to determine the size of Aspíllagas' interest in *La Prensa.* The publishing shares in the elder Ramon's 1939 portfolio (table 6.2) are probably *La Prensa.* Later Ramón Aspillaga Anderson held a very small block of shares and his brother Gustavo was an officer in a holding company with 16 percent of *La Prensa's* stock (*La Prensa,* June 6, 1971: 243; Vernal Consultores 1968). From 1947 to 1957, Ramón Aspíllaga A. served as president of the paper's board (*La Prensa,* February 23, 1973), but according to one of the paper's top editors in the postwar years, from the time Pedro Beltran took over as publisher in 1947, he ran the paper just as he wished, pretty much ignoring Aspíllaga. However, when APRA-backed unions began their organizing drive at Cayaltí in the late 1950s, the Aspíllagas got determined editorial support in *La Prensa* (see editorials August 10 and 12, 1958).

22. RAB 11–21–34; LAA 8–18–34; RAB 11–14–39.

23. On problem of increasing yields, frequent comments in early 1933 correspondence and RAA 5–31–35; 2–1–33. On expenses and investments RAA 2–1–33; RAE, 3–13–35. On the tractor purchase decision including careful weighing of all related technical and economic considerations, see "Cartas Reservadas Lima-Cayaltí, 1936–1939."

24. GAA 2–21–36, 8–31–36, 12–1–36. Correspondence in the folder titled "Cia Aurifera Benditani."

25. The following account of labor relations at Cayaltí during the 1940s is based primarily on correspondence from the Centro de Documentacion Agraria reproduced in Huertas 1974: 208–285 and on Cevallos 1972: 5–10.

26. This problem is not discussed in the Cayaltí correspondence. Unfortunately, after 1943 when the plantation was not under the direct management of family members, the correspondence between Cayaltí and Lima ceased to deal with broad political and economic problems.

27. This conclusion is based on interviews with a security official of the Bustamante regime, a former cabinet minister close to certain oligarchic circles, an Aspíllaga family member.

28. This account is based primarily on Plaza 1971: 8–11 who interviewed Cayaltí personnel twenty years after the events described, and Huertas 1974: 286–289 who reproduces a long and frank letter written to Ramón Aspíllaga shortly after the strike by R. Neumann, "Superintendent" of Cayaltí, at the time. An account that appeared in *Expreso,* April 7, 1970, was also consulted.

29. Pike 1967: 285–286; Chirinos 1962: 72–73; Bustamante 1949: 107–113.

30. According to an agrarian reform official, native to the area and long familiar with Cayaltí.

31. Cartas Administrativas, 1953–1957; interview with AAHSA executive; RAA 8–25–53; Huertas 1974: 137.

32. In 2005 Backus and Johnston become part of international beer giant SABMiller. It is not clear whether the Aspíllagas still retained shares at that time.

33. RAA 9–7–59; American Factors 1965; "Plan de Financiacion . . . Gonzales"; "Memorandum No.1" in "Plan de Financiacion."

34. At the time of the agrarian reform in 1969, only AAHSA among the sugar companies was found to be bankrupt. *La Prensa*, October 29, 1969. On the condition of other producers at this time I consulted the *La Prensa* Archive folders entitled "Reforma Agraria."

35. R.M.M. Pryor, October 12, 1966, Correspondence on American Factors 1965.

36. RAB 5–2–29; LAA 12–12–36; RAA 12–21–36.

37. Comisión Creada para la Resolución Suprema No. 400. 1968. Informe Sobre la Sequia en el Norte del Pais.

7

The Prados: Bankers and Politicians

Peru has no navy, has no army, has no money: it has nothing for war.

—General Mariano Ignacio Prado

The type of banking created by the Prados was a creole type. Mariano was no banker, but he knew people—who to talk to, who to pay off.

—Lima attorney

The first of the Prados that historians remember was General Mariano Ignacio Prado (1826–1901), a sometime military hero, who was twice president of Peru. The general's second presidency (1876–1879) and his public career came to an abrupt end during the war with Chile under murky circumstances that would haunt his family for generations. In the twentieth century the general's sons—driven by the determination to vindicate the memory of their father—built an extensive economic empire and successfully pursued political power and position.

The Prados' economic profile differentiated them from the exporter majority of the oligarchy. Their interests were largely urban and financial. The family's powerful Banco Popular stood at the center of a sprawling network of family enterprises. Less dependent on large numbers of low-wage workers than the planter and miner oligarchs, they were less threatened by APRA and its associated unions. With income in *soles* rather than pounds and dollars, they had a different perspective on monetary matters.

The Prados were shrewd politicians. In a contested republic, they quickly grasped the possibilities of the trilateral system of post-1930 politics and manipulated it to their advantage. The family carefully cultivated military figures and APRA leaders, even when the party was banned. In 1939, Manuel Prado (youngest of the general's

179

sons) won the presidency with the backing of his predecessor, General Benavides, and some APRA support. Manuel later negotiated the *Convivencia* arrangement with APRA to achieve his return to the presidency in 1956.

The Prados' economic and political interests were increasingly intertwined. The Banco Popular became an important instrument for the pursuit of political power. At the same time, the Prado enterprises became increasingly dependent on government cooperation for their survival.

GENERAL MARIANO IGNACIO PRADO

In 1854, Mariano Ignacio Prado, an ambitious twenty-eight-year-old National Guard captain, arrived in Lima from his native Huánuco, in the central Sierra.[1] He promptly got himself imprisoned and deported to Chile for criticizing the government's handling of guano revenues. The regime was facing a rebellion over this very issue.

References to the Prados in a history of Huánuco indicate that they were members of the local political and social elite during the closing years of the colonial period and first decades of the Republican era. Several members of the family, including Mariano's father, Colonel Ignacio Prado, played leading political and military roles in the local independence movement. Colonel Prado was the first Republican mayor of Huánuco.[2]

Young Prado jumped off the ship that was carrying him to exile in Chile, near Arequipa in the far south. There he joined General Ramon Castilla's rebellion against the government. Having performed brilliantly in the triumphant campaign, he advanced to colonel and rewarded with a series of important political and military positions.

In 1864, Prado married Magdalena Ugarteche, daughter of a wealthy, aristocratic family of Arequipa, where he was serving as prefect (presidentially appointed governor). The following year, he staged a popular uprising from Arequipa against the government in Lima over the unpopular Vivanco-Pareja Treaty with Spain, widely regarded as a capitulation to Spanish aggression and as an affront to national honor. Prado's victory won him the presidency. His government allied with Chile and others against Spain and built up Peruvian defenses. When Peruvian forces managed to beat back a Spanish attack on the port of Callao in 1866, Prado became a national hero.

A memoir by Benjamin Vicuña Mackenna, a prominent Chilean who collaborated with Prado in this period, admiringly described him as a man (with the demeanor, the countenance, the heart . . . that we like to attribute to heroes. . . . Day and night you'd see him on horseback and he would say to us that his only relaxation was to be in the saddle. He has the qualities of a first rate soldier. [Commonly judged] audacious, . . . he prepares everything himself to the smallest details. . . . [H]e combines the inspiration of great deeds with a spirit of minute organization.) "Vicuña added that the people of Chile, whom [Prado] loves with his heart will always offer him shelter" (Vicuña Mackenna 1867: 59–60).

General Mariano Ignacio Prado, once a military hero and twice president of Peru, left his descendants a dark legacy.

Source: Public Domain.

Vicuña obviously knew something about the politics of the Spanish American republics. The year after his book was published, conservatives, angry over a new constitution, deposed Prado and forced him into exile in Chile. Prado apparently made good use of his time there. A biographical directory of foreigners in Chile notes that he had established himself in coal mining and "acquired a fortune that allowed him to travel to Europe" (Portocarrero 1995: 45).

With the emergence of the Civilista Party a few years later, Prado reappeared on the national scene. In 1872, he was promoted to general, and, two years later, he was elected to Congress, where he served as president of the Chamber of Deputies. His political rebirth was probably influenced by his ties to President Manuel Pardo, who had served in Prado's own cabinet in the 1860s. As his term in came to an end in 1876, Pardo perceived serious threats from the military to political stability, and it was probably for this reason that he favored Prado, a military man and still popular hero, as his successor. With Civilista support, Prado was elected to his second presidency that year.

THE WAR OF THE PACIFIC AND THE GENERAL'S DARK LEGACY

From the beginning, Prado faced severe political and economic problems. The government had been forced into bankruptcy before he took office. Relations between his administration and the Civilistas in Congress were bad. The Peruvian economy was faltering as guano income dwindled with the exhaustion of deposits, and Peru's bonds were worth a fraction of their face value in international markets. Many Peruvians looked to the valuable nitrate fields in the Atacama Desert on the south coast as an inviting new source of foreign income. But Peru was being drawn into a conflict with Chile, which was also interested in the area.

Prado understood that Peru, badly divided and poorly armed, was in no condition for war with a much stronger Chile. As he bluntly told the Bolivian foreign minister, "Peru has no navy, has no army, has no money: it has nothing for war" (Sater 2007: 36). Prado, moreover, liked Chile. He apparently retained some investments there from his time in exile. But popular passions, fed by the Lima press, favored war, as did the politicians, businessmen, and military officers who thought they had something to gain from the conflict. Prado gave in, according to an American observer, after "a furious mob appeared before the doors of the municipal palace and demanded his [the president's] intentions. Prado saw that he must renounce Chile or lose his life" (Sater 2007: 40).

Early in the war Prado led forces in the South himself but returned to Lima to face the worsening political situation. Peru's defeat, all but inevitable from the beginning, became a certainty after Peru suffered critical losses at sea, leaving the country unable defend its coasts or to supply its troops. In Lima, political rivals and angry street mobs blamed Prado. Nicolas Piérola, his chief political opponent, declined Prado's offer to join the government.

On December 18, 1879, Prado quietly departed on a trip to the United States and Europe with the stated intention of negotiating loans and arms purchases for his beleaguered country. Shortly after his departure, Piérola marched into Lima and seized power. In a subsequent decree the new president characterized Prado's departure as a "shameless desertion and flight" and stripped the general of his citizenship (Delgado 1952: 372–373). Although the resolution made no mention of this, Prado was later accused of having absconded with funds that had been raised through contributions in Lima to buy a badly needed naval vessel. Two years later, having had no greater political or military success than Prado, Piérola left the country himself, as the war dragged on.

Whatever Prado thought he was doing when he left Peru, there is little support for the most serious accusations against him. In particular the existing evidence and historiography strongly supports Prado's own claim that he did not steal funds designated for munitions.[3] The evidence did not, however, lay the charges to rest. The powerful political and economic position that the general's descendants established for themselves in Peru assured that they would not be forgotten.

The old accusations against the general resurfaced whenever family members were in the political spotlight. On several occasions when one of the general's sons was a presidential candidate, a pamphlet titled *Puede Ser un Prado Presidente del Perú?* (Can a Prado Be President of Peru?) circulated in Lima. The anonymously authored text asserted that General Prado was a traitor and a thief.[4] The circumstances surrounding the end of General Prado's public career would long haunt the family. Nearly a century after his mysterious departure from the country, one of the general's great-grandchildren would recall how a prep school teacher had harassed him with continual reminders of the black legend surrounding his famous ancestor. Judging from the currency of the tale in Lima in the 1970s, his experience must have replicated that of many of the general's descendants.

According to Lima journalist and political historian Chirinos Soto (1967: 70–71), it was a "well-known" fact in Peru that General Prado's sons the Prado Ugarteches aspired to the presidency in order to honor the memory of their father. In an interview, one of the general's descendants suggested that the accomplished Prado Ugarteches were driven forward by the "tragedy" of their father's life, which would have otherwise "poisoned" their own lives. A significant piece of confirming evidence for this point of view emerged when President Billinghurst was overthrown in 1914.

Jorge and Manuel Prado Ugarteche were the civilian leaders of the 1914 coup, in the course of which Jorge was sent into the presidential palace to speak for the rebels. In this interview, as Billinghurst recorded it,

> Young Prado, in a lengthy and pathetic discourse, expounded in synthesis, the following: That the rebels recognized my patriotism, integrity and capacity for government; that I had erred, however, in the direction that I had given to domestic policies (which, of course, didn't speak very well of my capacity for government), and, finally that the sons of ex-president Prado had to vindicate the memory of their father.

On this last point Billinghurst was particularly skeptical. In view of his "desertion" (as Billinghurst characterized it) and a series of lesser public sins, how could General Prado be vindicated by his sons? (Billinghurst 1915: 87).

THE PRADO UGARTECHES:
BUILDING THE FAMILY FORTUNE

General Prado's sons, the talented and ambitious Prado Ugarteches (born 1870–1889), were by all accounts among the most accomplished Peruvians of their generation (box 7.1). The eldest, Mariano, was a prime mover of the turn-of-the-century urban economy and the founder of a formidable economic empire that endured until 1970. Javier was among the most influential intellectuals of his generation, rector of the national university, and an important Civilista Party leader. Jorge and Manuel were also prominent political figures. Manuel, the youngest, would complete his second presidency in 1962, nearly a century after his father's first term in office.[5]

The black legend surrounding their father does not seem to have undermined the social standing of the Prado Ugarteches. Their position was bolstered by the high

---

Box 7.1. Generations of the Prados

I. General Mariano Ignacio Prado (1826–1901).
    Twice president of Peru. Left country during War of the Pacific.
II. The Prado Ugarteches (born 1870–1889)
    Sons of General Prado. Politically prominent from Civilista era to early 1960s.
      Mariano Ignacio Prado Ugarteche (1870–1946), leading entrepreneur and banker, **Javier Prado Ugarteche** (1871–1921), prominent intellectual and political figure, **Jorg Prado Ugarteche** (1887–1970), cabinet officer and presidential candidate in 1936, and **Manuel Prado Ugarteche** (1889–1967), president of Peru 1939 to 1945 and 1956 to 1962.
III. Prado Heudeberts and Peña Prados (born 1900–)
    Sons of Prado Ugarteches. Key figures were two cousins:
    Mariano Ignacio Prado Heudebert (1900–1974), politically powerful banker and **Juan Manuel Peña Prado** (1901–1985) (son of María Prado Ugarteche) executive in Prado enterprises, member of legislature in governments close to Prados.
IV. **Mariano Ignacio Prado Sosa** (ca. 1940–2009)
    Son of Mariano Ignacio Prado Heudebert and last family member to lead Banco Popular.

status of their mother's family, the Ugarteches of Arequipa (Paz Soldan 1921: 311). The brothers were accepted into the Club Nacional as young men. Mariano, the eldest of the brothers was elected president of the club on two occasions. He also served as president of the exclusive Jockey Club de Lima.

Mariano took primary responsibility for the family's economic activities. In the period from 1890 to 1915 he organized two groups of interrelated enterprises, one based in the industrial and public utility sectors, the other in the financial sector. The firms in the first group evolved successively out of functional linkages, beginning with the Santa Catalina woolen mill. To provide electricity to the mill, a power generating company was organized, which grew into Empresas Electricas Asociadas, the city's major utility. The electric company in turn spawned Ferrocarril Electrico (Electric Railway), a tram connecting Lima with its port of Callao.[6]

The lucrative Empresas Electricas was too big to be dominated by the Prados. Its directors included other important Lima capitalists, but the Prados were large stockholders and well represented on the board. Mariano managed the company until 1920. Thereafter, European capital entered the firm and the family withdrew. The Prados had likely sold their start-up stake for a healthy profit (Pacheco 1923: 355; *West Coast Leader*, February 7, 1935).

The financial group revolved around the Banco Popular, founded in 1899. Mariano presided over its board for many years. But he did not take over its direct management until the 1930s, when Popular became a family controlled firm. Initially a small, unimportant institution, it would become the country's second-largest bank. The Prados also participated in the creation of a series of insurance companies closely associated with the bank, which were ultimately joined together in the Prado-controlled firm, Popular y Porvenir.[7]

Finally, Mariano and the Banco Popular also played a key role in the founding of the Caja de Depositos y Consignaciones, a private company that gave the banks enormous power over state finances. The Caja, wholly owned by the Lima banks, collected taxes and channeled revenues to the government. Popular held 20 percent of the stock in this company that proved to be the most profitable enterprise in the financial sector (Bollinger 1971: 273; Yepes 1972: 204).

Where did the capital to fund Mariano's many enterprises come from? There were apparently significant family sources. The general was not a poor man. He lived well. He had married into the wealthy Ugarteche family and, during his years of exile in Chile following his first presidency, had prospered in coal mining (Portocarrero 1995: 45–46). According to family lore, the Prado Ugarteches received a significant inheritance, which presumably came from the general and from their mother's family.

The comfortable lifestyle of Mariano's brothers supports the notion of a Prado Ugarteche inheritance. They and their sister Maria were often among the "founding stockholders" of his ventures (Portocarrero 1995: 297–299), though their active participation was limited. Javier, Jorge, and Manuel devoted themselves largely to nonbusiness pursuits, most notably politics. Javier, who never married, was able to devote considerable time and money to his varied intellectual interests. For years he taught in the university (hardly a high paying job). He accumulated one of the best and largest libraries in Lima. He also put together an important natural science collection that forms the basis of Lima's Javier Prado Museum. The collection of his furniture in the National Museum of Art suggests that he did not live modestly.

Maria, under the forceful guidance of her mother, had married one of the wealthiest men in southern Peru, Manuel Peña Costas, heir to a large farm and mining fortune. Peña Costas was persuaded by his wife to sell his share of the family holdings and move to Lima where he could invest with his in-laws. According to one of their descendants, the couple spent two years in Paris with the general, living in ample quarters, before moving to Lima. Peña Costas was an active partner in the most important Prado enterprises, beginning with the textile mill and the power company. He died a relatively young man in 1917, leaving an estate that was managed by the Prados for sister Maria (Moreno Mendiguren 1956: 439). (Evidence from the 1960s analyzed later in this chapter shows that, by then, the Prado enterprises were controlled by descendants of Mariano and Maria Prado Ugarteche de Peña.)

In the early years, family money was not the only—probably not even the main— source of capital for Mariano's enterprises. Nonfamily members were key partners in both the industrial/utility and financial ventures. In various ways, Mariano was able to tap the new wealth then flowing from exports into the flourishing urban economy. Planters and miners were, for example, prominent on the board of the Banco Popular. In 1913 and 1921, the board included members of the Fernandini, Gildemeister, Mujica, Pardo, and de la Piedra families, but there were no Prado kin except Mariano himself, the chairman (Portocarrero 1995: 153).

The Prado Ugarteches in the Aristocratic Republic

Both Mariano and brother-in-law Peña Costas served in Congress during this period, but the real family politicians were Javier and the two younger brothers, Jorge and Manuel. The Prados would lurch back and forth between the two poles of Civilista politics: José Pardo and Agusto Leguía, but their unchanging, shared objective was a second-generation Prado presidency. The clan successively (and in birth order) promoted Javier, Jorge, and Manuel as presidential candidates.

By the beginning of the new century, Javier was a prominent Civilista leader. Along with José Pardo and the Miró Quesada brothers, he formed part of the young liberal wing of the party, which took over its central committee in 1904. Ironically, his brother Mariano was identified with the conservative wing, though there is no indication that ideological differences got in the way of their pursuit of the family's shared objectives. In Congress, Mariano was best remembered for his determined opposition to labor reform legislation, which, he asserted, would undermine the natural harmony between workers and employers (Levano 1967: 42–43; Portocarrero 1995: 61–65). In August 1908, Mariano spoke passionately against a workman's compensation bill (*ley de accidents*), starting from the premise that workman's compensation was a

> just, humane principle . . . which I accept and proclaim because I practice it. . . . . [H]onorable representatives, I have the honor of directing the noble labor of 1,800 workmen . . . With good conscience, I affirm . . . that the companies that I direct, that I have had the honor and fortune to found and develop . . . have established workman's compensation without there being a law that imposes it and they apply it, fulfilling their humane obligation to the victims of work more broadly and generously than any law ever required. . . . (Portocarrero 1995: 65)

Javier served in Pardo's government, elected in 1904, as minister of foreign relations. In 1906, however, he was forced to resign after his speech urging a more conciliatory attitude toward Chile was widely condemned. It is likely that the memory, still fresh, of General Prado's own misadventure in Peruvian–Chilean relations, had shaped the public reaction. The controversy apparently soured relations between Javier and Pardo and contributed to the Pardo's decision to favor Leguía instead of Javier as his successor.

Four years later, when Leguía as president faced an acute parliamentary crisis provoked by Pardo's allies, Javier came to his rescue, presiding over a "salvation cabinet," which rode out the tempest. However, in 1912, Javier was again passed over, when Leguía chose Antero Aspíllaga as his preferred presidential candidate. That year, with the party badly split between pro- and anti-Leguiista factions, all the Prados (including Peña Costas) lined up behind Leguía's candidate, Aspíllaga (Partido Civil 1911). But the election, decided in the Congress, resulted in the victory of protopopulist Billinghurst.

Two years later Jorge and Manuel Prado orchestrated the coup that removed Billinghurst from office. The brothers were subsequently honored at a banquet attended by the Civilista elite, where they were elaborately praised for having helped put an end to a lower-class threat to upper-class rule. At the time, Jorge wrote that he favored efforts to improve the lot of the masses but utterly rejected the notion of "popular sovereignty" which he equated with class hatred.

These events marked the beginning of an intimate association between the Prado clan and Colonel (later general) Oscar Benavides, the military leader of the coup and interim president. The Prados were his link to the Civilistas (Gerlach 1973: 50, 71, 75). Years later, he would help them achieve what they long desired: the presidency.

In the period following the ouster of Billinghurst, Javier led the anti-Leguía faction that called for new elections rather than the succession of the Vice-President Roberto Leguía (Gerlach 1973: 76). The anti-Leguía position prevailed, and in

1915 a convention of parties was convened to select a unity candidate. Prior to the convention Javier appeared to be the likely nominee. However, a military candidacy, that of General Pedro Muñiz, showed strength and Javier's candidacy abruptly deflated. At the convention, partisans of former president José Pardo persuaded Javier to withdraw. Pardo was nominated, and Javier received the rectorship of the national university as something of a consolation prize. Javier, it seemed, was again the victim of the family's black legend (Arenas 1941: 93–94; Sanchez 1969: I, 122–124).

Javier is reported to have been very bitter over the experience, and he subsequently led opposition within the party to President Pardo. In 1919 the Prados did not support Pardo's candidate, Antero Aspíllaga. Forgetting their earlier opposition to Leguía, they backed his candidacy in 1919 against Aspíllaga. After the election, Jorge and Manuel were among those who conspired with Leguía to overthrow Pardo before the end of his term to ensure Leguía's ascension and undermine Civilista resistance to the new regime.[8]

THE LEGUÍA YEARS

The 1919 coup resulted in the suppression of the Congress and the election of a new legislature, which was to frame a constitution for the new era. Javier, Jorge, and Manuel were all elected to this body. Javier, the family intellectual, was made chairman of the drafting committee, which produced a progressive document with ample guarantees of civil and social democracy. Approved by the full body, the 1920 Constitution was, as historian. Pike described it, "a model of the Peru that never was" (Pike 1967: 220). It presented a stark contrast with the regime's increasingly dictatorial policies.

Leguía was not willing to share power with the old Civilistas, and the Prados were no exception. Though they had supported him in 1919, they were treated no differently than the Aspíllagas, the Miró Quesadas, the Pardos, and other oligarchs who had opposed Leguía.

Jorge and General Benavides conspired against Leguía and were deported. They would continue their fruitless plotting from Ecuador. Manuel was also deported. Mariano was arrested in 1926 and held prisoner for a time on the Island of San Lorenzo. Javier, as rector of the national university, came into conflict with the Leguía government over questions of civil liberties and university autonomy. In 1921, he was arrested and locked up for eight hours with "drunks, thieves, etc.," after which he was released with the explanation that his detention had been a matter of mistaken identity—a surprising error given his prominence. That same year Javier died unexpectedly—by some accounts, a suicide, by others, the victim of his lover's husband. The poisoned political atmosphere in Lima inevitably encouraged dark speculation.[9]

At the time of Javier's death it was said that the family's financial situation was not good and had been damaged by the confrontation with Leguía. However, this was early in Leguía's long reign, and, in fact, the 1920s proved to be a prosperous period for the Prados. The rapid expansion of Lima under Leguía enabled them to earn healthy profits developing land they owned in the San Isidro and Miraflores districts of the city.

With Javier dead, Jorge and Manuel became the family's salient political figures and likely presidential candidates. They were General Prado's youngest sons, separated from Mariano and Javier by nearly two decades. While Javier had been active in politics through the Civilista years, their own participation had begun as the Aristocratic Republic was disintegrating. Their often conspiratorial political style emphasized close connections to the military. This was evident in the role Jorge and Manuel played in the overthrow of Billinghurst and in plots against Pardo and Leguía described above. There is no evidence of Javier's having been involved in these activities, although the overthrow of Billinghurst was apparently conducted with Javier's presidential candidacy in mind.

As young men both Jorge and Manuel had completed a reserve officer's course (apparently set up for sons of the upper class) at the national military school (Martínez 1935: 43). After his participation in the assault on the presidential palace in 1914, Manuel was promoted to the rank of lieutenant. (Jorge probably received similar treatment.)

THE TRANSFORMATION OF THE BANCO POPULAR

For all their ambition and ability, the Prado brothers could not have hoped to achieve much politically without the backing of the clan's economic power. In the 1930s the Prados would substantially strengthen their economic position. The most important change involved the rapid growth of the Banco Popular. The bank had been dwarfed by the country's larger financial institutions. In 1930, Lima's largest bank, the Banco del Peru y Londres, was forced into bankruptcy by the depression and the loss of the political support it had enjoyed from Leguía's regime.

While its competitors were suffering, Popular began its rise, which was particularly rapid after 1933, the year that Prado ally Benavides assumed the presidency after the assassination of Sánchez Cerro. That same year Mariano Prado, who had previously served only as chairman of the board, took direct control of the bank's operations. In the period from June 1933 to July 1934, the bank's net profits were nearly double the preceding twelve months (*Lima* 1935). By early 1935, Banco Popular had managed to cancel most of its debts and was planning a 50 percent increase in its capital (RAB 2–1–35). That same year the bank began to open branches in provincial cities. By the end of the decade Popular had twenty-two branches outside of Lima (Banco de Credito 1946–1968: 131–132).

As it grew, the bank's function was transformed. It became more directly identified with the Prado family and the enterprises they dominated. Banco Popular was also becoming an important instrument of political power. It is impossible to date this shift precisely but appears that foundations were being laid during these years. The assumption of direct control by Mariano Prado Ugarteche was a key step. In 1937, he made his eldest son Mariano Prado Heudebert chief operating officer, while he retained his position of board chairman. Gradually the presence of the Prados and their kin on the board and among the bank's executive personnel was expanded, though the board always included exporters, such as the Aspíllagas. The bank also became a holding company for Prado enterprises. For instance, in 1942 it was reported that a paper company (La Papelera Peruana) controlled by the Banco Popular had purchased a Lima newspaper, *La Cronica* from the planter Rafael Larco (*Peruvian Times*, August 1, 1942). *La Cronica* would be managed by members of the family and serve as their political organ.

The success of the Banco Popular came to be heavily dependent on the political finesse of the Prados and their close ties to a succession of national regimes. In the wake of Banco Popular's collapse in 1970, a Lima attorney long familiar with Peruvian banking commented, "The type of banking created by the Prados was a Creole type. Mariano [Prado Huedebert] was no banker, but he knew people—who to talk to, who to payoff."

If the bank gained from the political connections of the Prados, it also became a political force in its own right. The head of the bank, who was also the head of the family, became an pivotal figure in the national political system. As Popular grew into the country's second-largest bank, its actions became a matter of vital concern to national governments intent on maintaining national economic stability. Moreover, the Prados learned to use credit to build up a network of clients and allies. According to a number of well-informed political and military sources, the Prados had an extremely liberal loan policy toward military officers. Any officer could walk into the bank and get credit. If he was negligent about paying, there was no pressure from Banco Popular. Many officers had mortgages from the Prados. Since the bank was tied to an auto importer, it was easy for an officer to purchase and finance a car. Until the 1950s, salaries for even high-ranking officers were low and their standard of living modest, which made Popular's easy credit all the more attractive.

The Prados also used the bank to favor politicians and finance political campaigns. In the course of the trial that followed the revolutionary government's seizure of the Banco Popular, a number of instances came to light. For example, auditors of the bank's books found an irrecoverable $208,000[10] loan to Humberto Ponce Ratto, an Odriista congressman (*La Prensa*, March 8, 1973). A $37,100 loan made by the bank's Chiclayo branch to a man named Gerardo Reques, with no apparent resources, was probably use to finance Manuel Prado's presidential campaign on the north coast in 1956. The loan was later "pardoned" by the bank on the basis of the client's "economic insolvency" (*Expreso*, January 20, 1973).

THE PRADOS IN POLITICS, 1930–1945

In the 1930s, the Prados would renew their quest for the presidency, interrupted by Leguía's dictatorship. The key to their ultimate success was artful manipulation of the trilateral system, through relationships with the military and APRA.

Jorge Prado accompanied General Benavides back to Lima after the fall of Leguía in 1930 (Sanchez 1955: 330). During the long exile, the tie between Benavides and the Prado clan had been strengthened by the arranged marriage of one of the Peña Prados to Benavides' daughter Paquita (see figure 7.1). It was widely believed that the Prados had supported Benavides in exile, thereby sustaining the most prominent focus of resistance to Leguía, though the general's wife later denied this in an interview.

There is no indication of any connection of the Prados to the overthrow of Leguía or to Sanchez Cerro's government. But shortly after Benavides took power in 1933, he appointed Jorge Prado prime minister. Jorge presided over the "Peace and Conciliation" cabinet, which abandoned the repressive anti-Aprista policies pursued by Sanchez Cerro. As part of the new political program, Jorge visited APRA leader Haya de la Torre in prison and later arranged for his release. However, there was strong pressure against such policies from influential figures on the right, including the Miró Quesadas and the Aspíllagas. Jorge was forced to resign when he refused to endorse new press restrictions imposed after an Aprista organ had "insulted" the army (Gerlach 1973: 448–449). Benavides subsequently appointed him ambassador of Brazil. (Getting inconvenient friends out of town in this fashion was one of the frequently exercised prerogatives of Peruvian presidents.) But Jorge would return to Lima to compete in the 1936 presidential election as Benavides' official candidate.

The Prados were made for the politics of a contested republic. They were quick to recognize the benefits that could flow from the exploitation of APRA's mass following. Beginning in the early 1930s, they made repeated attempts to build an electoral strategy based on an understanding with the party. The "Peace and Conciliation" cabinet represented the first move in that direction. In 1935, as he prepared his presidential candidacy, Jorge approached the party through an intermediary about the possibilities of APRA support. They were not able to reach an understanding and APRA's (covert) backing in 1936 went to candidate Luís Eguriguren (Sanchez 1969: II, 547–549).

Jorge ran that year in a four-way race with Benavides' support. Among the agrarian oligarchs there was considerable resistance to Prado based on the not unreasonable fear that he would legalize APRA. The planter core of the oligarchy, led by Pedro Beltrán, backed anti-APRA conservative Manuel Vicente Villarán and financed the distribution of the anonymous pamphlet mentioned earlier, "Can a Prado Be President of Peru?"[11]

Beltrán and Manuel Mujica Gallo, member of a planter and mining family, were the pamphlet's presumed authors. The document's overarching theme is that General Prado had been a traitor in the war and the son of a traitor is not fit to be president.

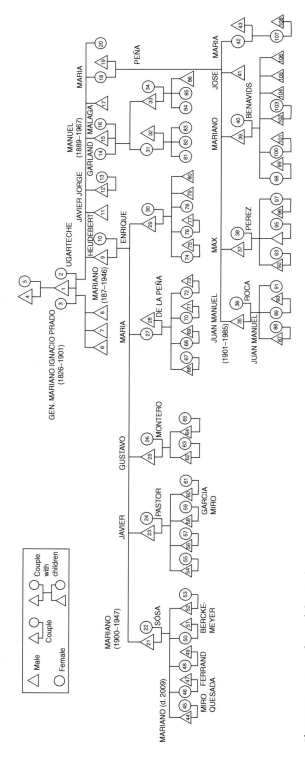

Figure 7.1. Genealogy of the Prados.

1. Mariano Ignacio Prado
2. Magdalena Ugarteche
3. María Avelina Gutierrez
4. Ignacio Prado
5. Francisca Ochoa
6. Leoncia Prado Gutierreza
7. Grocio Prado Gutierreza
8. Justo Prado Gutierreza
9. Mariano Prado Ugarteche
10. María Heudebert
11. Javier Prado Ugarteche
12. Jorge Prado Ugarteche
13. Grace Flinders
14. Enriqueta Garland
15. Manuel Prado Ugarteche
16. Clorinda Malaga Bravo
17. Maximiliano Prado Ugarteche
18. María Prado Ugarteche
19. Juan Peña Costas
20. Rosa Prado Ugarteche
21. Mariano Prado Heudebert
22. Mercedes Sosa Pardo de Zela
23. Javier Prado Heudebert
24. Augusta Pastor de la Torre
25. Gustavo Prado Heudebert
26. Ana Luisa Montero Muelle
27. María Prado Heudebert
28. José Miguel de la Peña Iglesias
29. Enrique Prado Heudebert
30. María Rey
31. Rosa Prado Garland
32. Hugo Parks Gallagher
33. Manuel Prado Garland
34. Natalia Kitchin
35. Juan Manuel Peña Prado
36. María Roca
37. Max Peña Prado
38. Estela Perez Castellanos
39. Mariano Peña Prado
40. Francisca Benavides
41. José Peña Prado
42. María Peña Prado
43. Jorge Arrospide de Loyola
44. Mariano Prado Sosa
45. Leonor Miró Quesada
46. Mercedes Prado Sosa
47. Javier Ferrand Cilloniz
48. María Prado Sosa
49. Aurelio Moreyra Garcia Sayan
50. Magdalena Prado Sosa
51. Oscar Berckemeyer Perez Hidalgo
52. Leoncio Prado Sosa
53. Sandra Rey
54. Javier Prado Pastor
55. Ursula Bustamante Olivares
56. Celso Prado Pastor

57. Rosario Orbegoso
58. Ignacio Prado Pastor
59. Cecilia Garcia Miró Elguera
60. Jorge Prado Pastor
61. Patricia Parro
62. Gustavo Prado Montero
63. Carmen Masias Marrou
64. Alfonso Prado Montero
65. Yolanda Ferrero Costa
66. José Mariano de la Peña Prado
67. Veronica Tschudi
68. Enriqueta Marta de la Peña Prado
69. Juan Pardo Aramburu
70. Rosarela de la Peña Prado
71. Juan Bautista Isola Cambana
72. María de la Peña Prado
73. Ernesto de Lozada
74. Rosario Prado Rey
75. Ismael Barrios Idiaquez
76. Inés Prado Rey
77. Francisco Giraldo Prato
78. Carmen María Prado Rey
79. Enrique Prado Rey
80. José Antonio Prado Rey
81. Mora Parks Prado82. Rosa Parks Prado
83. Enriqueta Parks Prado
84. Natalia Prado Kitchin

85. María Cristina Prado Kitchin
86. Miguel Prado Kitchin
87. Juan Manuel Peña Roca
88. Jean Henderson
89. María Rosa Peña Roca
90. Manuel Bartolome Ferreyros Balta
91. Rosa Peña Roca
92. Max Peña Perez
93. María Bonifaz
94. José Peña Perez
95. Monica de Cardenas Salazar
96. _____ Hartinger
97. Estela Peña Perez.
98. Francisca Peña Benavides
99. Francisco Vaso
100. Rosa Peña Benavides
101. Ricardo Gallagher Malaga
102. Mariano Peña Benavides
103. Pilar de la Jara
104. Oscar Peña Benavides
105. Alvaro Peña Benavides
106. Ignacio Peña Benavides
107. Malena Arrospide Peña
108. Jorge Bellido

Figure 7.1. (Continued)

General Prado is described as a coward, a deserter, and a thief, who absconded with "the enormous sum of 6 million soles," contributed by Peruvians for national defense. "That money," the document asserts, "is the origin . . . of the present fortune of the Prado family."

Some passages appear aimed at the military and its supporters, at a time when many depended on the army to resist APRA. "The elevation of a Prado to the Presidency," the pamphlet warns "would be the greatest insult to our armed forces." Prado was responsible, it claims, for the death of Admiral Miguel Grau, a national hero known to generations of Peruvian schoolkids, who died in an 1879 naval battle.[12]

The electoral process of 1936 was never completed. With Egriguren apparently winning, Benavides intervened to halt the counting of ballots and extend himself in power. (Benavides, suggests one well-informed observer, may have had this in mind from the beginning.) According to a source close to Prado's campaign this outcome was strongly resisted by Jorge's partisans. Finally, Mariano spoke with Benavides. He subsequently explained to Jorge that Egriguren had indeed won and that Benavides intended to stay in power for another three years, after which he would relinquish power to Manuel.

It is not clear why Manuel, two years younger than Jorge, was to be substituted for his brother. Perhaps Jorge, after his service in the "Peace" cabinet, was too closely identified with policies sympathetic to APRA. A close observer of the political scene in this period later described Jorge as a "bohemian" and someone who drank a lot. Years later a political associate of the Prados commented, "until the day of his death [Jorge] considered himself deeply offended, but I believe that his intense reaction was not seconded by the family." Whether or not such an agreement was actually reached by Benavides and the Prado clan, its "terms" are an accurate description of subsequent events. In 1939, Benevides brought Manuel into his cabinet and backed his successful presidential candidacy.

There are indications that Jorge had hoped to run again in 1939, but Mariano, the head of the family, was firmly behind Manuel, who became the Prados' candidate. Manuel sought support from the still-illegal APRA party. A pact was worked out by negotiators whereby the party would receive amnesty and legal status in exchange for votes, but the agreement produced sharp disagreements within the party and was finally repudiated. APRA leader Haya la Torre was particularly opposed to any agreement with someone he thought of as the son of the traitor of 1879. Having failed to sustain the agreement with the top leadership, the Prados began a well-financed campaign to win the support of a sector of the party. Pro-Prado APRA committees were set up and a rival version of the party organ was published. According to APRA leader Luís Alberto Sanchez, some Apristas "stained themselves with material bribes and low promises."[13]

Manuel's candidacy was carefully guided and supported by Benavides. Opposition to Prado was suppressed. For instance, *La Prensa*, the paper associated with the planters, which had been backing the rightest candidacy of José Quesada, was closed down by the government after it brought up the familiar accusations against General Prado and questioned the government's intention to conduct honest elections. The electoral process that finally brought one of the general's sons to power was commonly regarded as having been less than honest.[14]

Manuel Prado is remembered for his aristocratic bearing, courtly manners, and personal charm but also for the political agility that made him one of modern Peru's most effective politicians. He was shrewd, manipulative, and ideologically flexible. Once in office, he quickly won control of the Congress, which had been selected by Benavides and sent general himself out of the country to ambassadorial assignments in Madrid and Buenos Aires, just as Benavides had done with Jorge. He avoided conflict with the right by appointing a conservative upper-class cabinet. For the critical position of finance minister, he chose Juan Pardo Hareen,

Manuel Prado Ugarteche, among the shrewdest politicians of his era, was president of Peru from 1939 to 1945 and 1956 to 1962.

Source: Wikimedia Commons, Biblioteca Nactional del Peru.

member of an important planter family and son of President José Pardo, whom the Prados helped depose in 1919. While treatment of APRA was milder than it had been under the previous two regimes, the party was not legalized until shortly before the end of Manuel's term. Union activity was constrained through most of his presidency.[15]

When World War II broke out, Prado placed Peru on the side of the allies. There was some resistance to this from certain of his advisers and the considerable upper-class sector sympathetic to fascism (see, e.g., the discussion of the Miró Quesadas' attitudes in chapter 8), but fascist sentiment declined in the course of the war. Its leading Peruvian exponent José de la Riva Aguero died in 1944. The planters remained content during the war years because heavy international demand brought prosperity to the export economy.

As could be expected, Manuel carefully tended to relations with the military. He would appear in public in his reserve lieutenant's uniform to emphasize his sympathy for the armed forces. Prado strengthened his standing with the military through his government's successful prosecution of a war with Ecuador over border claims. Peru, still smarting over its ignominious experience in the War of the Pacific and a more recent defeat by Colombia, reacted to the victory with unbridled enthusiasm. Prado, suddenly a popular figure, was declared a national hero by the Congress. Manuel prudently responded with praise for the armed forces, but nothing could have been more satisfying for the son of General Mariano Ignacio Prado. He could at least hope that he had reduced the stigma attached to his family's history.[16]

As effective as he had proven politically as president, Manuel was not able to choose his own successor, as many presidents before him had done.[17] Toward the end of Prado's term, Benavides returned to the country intent on running himself. Prado joined the Miró Quesadas' *El Comercio* and some sectors of the military in rejecting Benavides' pretentions. Benavides relented, but in an unexpected move, he presided over the political marriage between reformist candidate José Luis Bustamante and APRA that produced the National Democratic Front government (1945–1948).

Manuel had himself urged Bustamante to run, presumably with his government's support. Bustamante refused. Manuel later suggested to Haya, who was still officially in hiding in Lima, that he abandon Bustamante and launch himself as a candidate; this would have required the preelection legalization of APRA by Manuel. Separately, Manuel's nephew Mariano Prado Heudebert (by then the effective leader of the Prado bank) had attempted to persuade APRA to support the candidacy of General Eloy Ureta, hero of the conflict with Ecuador. It is not clear whether Manuel and Mariano were coordinating their efforts. But the purpose of all this busy preelection maneuvering was apparently to install a new government, of whatever flavor, that would be obligated to the Prados.

In deference to the democratic spirit that spread across Latin America with the imminent defeat of the Nazis, Manuel legalized APRA, a few weeks before the election. Bustamante, with APRA support, won a strong, convincing victory.

FAMILY ORGANIZATION

The succession of Mariano Ignacio Prado Heudebert to the leadership of the Prado business empire created anomalous situation for the clan. The Prados were a descent group organized around patriarchal principles; authority was concentrated in successive eldest sons, all named Mariano Ignacio. The power of the Marianos extended beyond business to politics, as was evident in 1939, when Mariano Prado Ugarteche and Benavides agreed to make Manuel rather than brother Jorge the family's presidential candidate.

Since 1937, Prado Heudebert had been in charge of the bank, though his father, Manuel's oldest brother, had retained the position of chairman of the board of directors. With the death of his father in 1946, Prado Heudebert became the acknowledged head of the family empire and, as will be seen, one of the most powerful men in Peru. The anomaly, of course, was that his uncle Manuel, only a decade older, was a former president, and as it happened, future president of the republic. Who represented the family in politics? This was not a trivial question, since the business and political fortunes of the Prados were always intertwined.

A degree of tension between uncle and nephew was probably inevitable. Manuel was economically dependent on his nephew, as he repeatedly acknowledged. He maintained a distance between them by choosing his political assistants from the Peña Prado branch of the family rather than the Prado Heudeberts and by spending the years between his two presidencies in Paris. At times the two seemed to be at odds, but their mutual dependence generally compelled cooperation.

In economic matters, two branches of the family were preeminent: the Prado Heudeberts, descendants of Mariano Prado Ugarteche and the Peña Prados, descendants of sister Maria Prado Ugarteche (see figure 7.1).[18] These two lineages held the largest stakes and occupied the key positions in the family businesses, as can be seen in table 7.1, which shows positions held by family members, by lineage, in the mid-1960s. Mariano Prado Heudebert was clearly the central leader, but his cousin, Juan Manual Peña Prado, was also an important figure within the Prado empire. By the 1960s, Manuel Prado's only son had no connection to the Prado enterprises.[19] (The other Prado Ugarteche siblings left no heirs.)

THE PRADOS IN POLITICS, 1945–1962

The Bustamante government was the only administration in the period from 1933 to 1962 with which the Prados did not have close ties. How the Prado clan and its diverse enterprises got along with the new administration is unclear. However, in 1948, Mariano Prado Heudebert (who will hereafter be referred to as Mariano) made a substantial contribution to the "bolsa" that Pedro Beltrán and other oligarchs collected to finance Odría's coup.[20]

Table 7.1.   Positions Held by Members of the Prado Family in the Late 1960s, by Lineage

Lineages descending from General Mariano Ignacio Prado

Children / Grandchildren of the General	Great-grandchildren of the General
I. Mariano Prado Ugarteche	
A. Mariano Prado Heudebert	A1. Mariano Prado Sosa
Banco Popular (1)	Banco Popular (3)
Popular y Porvenir (1)	Popular y Porvenir (2)
Almacenes Santa Catalina (1)	Cementos Lima (5)
Cia. ABC (1)	Haras Michilin (4)
Cementos Lima (1)	Inversiones e Inmobiliaria La
Emp. Cinemagrafica Libertad (5)	Molina (1)
Fabrica Tecnicos Asociados (5)	Cia. Urbanizadora La Molina (5)
Inmobiliaria de Teatros y Cinemas (1)	Inversiones y Negocios
Tipografía Santa Rosa (1)	Inmobiliaria (1)
Refineria Conchan-California (1)	Cia Edificadora Condor (5)
Cia. Nacional de Inmuebles (1)	Cia. Inmobiliaria Nacional (5)
Financiera Peruana (5)	Cia Industrial de Alimentos (5)
Cia Edificadora Condor (1)	A2. Leoncia Prado Sosa
Cia. Inmobiliaria Manco Capac (1)	Cia. Urbanizadora La Molina (1)
La Papelera Peruana (1)	A3. Oscar Berckemeyer Perez H. (husband
Cia. Inmobiliaria Orrantia (1)	of Magdalena Prado Sosa)
Cia Inmobiliaria Nacional (1)	Banco Popular (5)
B. Javier Prado Heudebert	B1. Ignacio Prado Pastor
Banco Wiese (5)	Hormigon y Agregados (4)
Distribuidora de Autos (4)	Cia Inmobiliaria Orrantia (5)
Cia de Inversiones Lima (4)	B2. Jorge Prado Pastor
Cia Orrantia (4)	Transportes Granel (6)
Urbana Leuro (4)	
Urbana Magdalena (6)	
Constructora Portofino (6)	
Emp. Teatro Leuro, Miraflores (4)	
Soc. Agricola Orrantia (5)	
Teatro Colina (6)	
Distribuidora de Materiales (1)	
C. Gustavo Prado Heudebert	C1. Gustavo Prado Montero
Cronica y Variedades (1)	Crónica y Variedades (5)
Haras Los Laureles (4)	C2. Alfonso Prado Montero
La Papelera Peruana (4)	Agricola Santana (4)
Cia Nacional de Inmuebles (5)	Haras Santana (4)
D. María Prado Heudebert	D1. José Mariano de la Peña Prado
–	Banco Popular (7)
	Cia. Inmobiliaria Orrantia (5)

Table 7.1. (Continued)

II. María Prado Ugarteche

A. Juan Manuel Peña Prado
    Banco Popular (5)
    Popular y Porvenir (4)
    Exhibidora Cinematografica (5)
    La Positiva Seguros (5)
    Soc. Aurífera San Antonio de Poto (5)
    Urbanizadora del Norte (5)
    Urbanizadora Trujillo (5)

                                      A. Juan Manuel Peña Roca
                                               Aerolineas Peruanas (APSA) (5)
                                             Popular y Porvenir Seguros (7)

B. Max Peña Prado
    Cia. de Inversiones Inmobiliarias
    Pacifico (5)
    Cia. de Inversiones Salaverry (1)
    El Sol Seguros (5)

                                        B1. Max Peña Perez
                                               Cia de Inversiones Inmobiliarias
                                             Pacifico (5)
                                             Cia de Inversiones Salaverry (5)
                                             Fab. de Conservas Marfe (6)
                                             San Genaro (5)

                                        B2. José Peña Perez
                                               Cia. de Inversiones Inmobiliarias
                                             Pacifico (4)
                                           Cia. de Inversiones Salaverry (5)
                                             Fab. de Conservas Marfe (4)
                                         Absorvente Santa Ines (5)

C. Mariano Peña Prado
    Cia. de Almacenes Generales (4)
    Inmobiliaria Flamengo (6)

D. Jose Peña Prado
    Inmobiliaria e Inversiones San Pio (5)
    Soc. San Antonio de Poto (6)

III. Javier Prado Ugarteche

A. No descendants

IV. Jorge Prado Ugarteche

A. No descendants

V. Manuel Prado Ugarteche

A. Descendants held no positions by late
    1960s

Sources: Vernal 1968; *Oiga*, February 9 and 16, 1973.
Notes:
Code:
1 = *presidente* (chairman of board), 2 = *vice-presidente* (vice-chairman of board), 3 = *director ejecutivo* (executive director), 4 = *director-gerente* (manager/member of board), 5 = *gerente* (manager), 6 = *director* (member of board), 7 = *sub-gerente* (assistant manager)

The Prados were able to build a strong relationship with General Odría, and prospered during his presidency. A source close to the family recalls, "The Prados gave complete support to Odría. They financed him. Max Peña Prado was a close friend and family contact." A political associate of the Prados describes the period this way: "After a while, Beltrán fell out with Odría. While Manuel spent the Odria years in Paris, the clan remained close to this chief executive. Juan Manuel Peña Prado was president of the Chamber of Deputies and his brother Max had juicy public contracts. Those were the days of great prosperity (and extensive public building) brought by the Korean War."

The Prados were also in a position to profit from the enormous expansion of Peruvian metal mining under Odría. In 1953 the Marcona Mining Company was formed by two foreign mining companies with Prado participation (probably because of what the Prados had to offer politically). A state enterprise granted Marcona a lucrative iron concession (Malpica 1973: 183–198; Purser 1971: 176). The one limit on the Prado clan's influence on the regime was that Odría had even closer ties to Banco Popular's major competitor, the Banco de Credito, through friendships with Credito board chairman Enrique Ayulo Pardo and Vice-Chairman Hernando de Lavalle. Moreover, Ayulo Pardo's wife, the proud Cecilia Pardo de Ayulo, had successfully courted Odría's wife. As the 1956 election approached, Odría, facing resistance from both the planter oligarchs and the military to his continuance in office, chose Lavalle as his successor. This was interpreted as a tilt toward Credito over Popular but was accepted by the Prados led by Mariano. The clan apparently felt it could live comfortably with an Odría-sponsored Lavalle regime.[21]

Manuel's political associates were pressing him to return from Paris to run for the presidency again, even though he was approaching seventy and in uncertain health. (Manuel spent much of his life in Paris, where he would die in 1967.) The Prado clan, preferring to avoid a confrontation with Odría, was cool toward the sudden draft-Manuel campaign. "Mariano," reports a political ally of the ex-president, "did not want Manuel to expose the family in 1956." While Manuel's nonfamily supporters were beginning to promote his candidacy, *La Cronica*, the clan newspaper, was showing curiously little interest in the prospect. However, when Manuel finally decided to run, the family stood behind him.

Reenacting a by now familiar political dance, Pradistas had been in contact with certain APRA leaders, whose party had remained illegal under Odria. APRA's leader Haya had never been enthusiastic about Manuel or the Prados and was, coincidentally, an old friend of Lavalle. But a bigger threat to all concerned was the emergence of a third candidate, the charismatic young reformer Fernando Belaúnde. In the end, Manuel, always a shrewd player, collected the most important cards. Under the so-called Pact of Monterrico,[22] he was elected with support of both Odría and APRA.

The politics of the Convivencia period, treated in detail in chapter 5, will not be revisited here except to note that the special relationship between the Peruvian state and the Prado empire, described for the Odría years, was maintained under Manuel's new government. "The Convivencia," observed one of its staunchest enemies, "more than a political pact, is a joint stock company" (Miró Quesada Laos 1959: 217). Prado clan members and their business associates held many important public positions. The first and second vice presidents of the republic, Luis Gallo Porras and Carlos Moreyra y Paz Soldan, were both Banco Popular directors. Manuel Cisneros Sánchez, prime minister and later Finance Minister in Convivencia cabinets, was the brother of another member of the bank board. Juan Manuel Peña Prado, a key member of the family, who also held a position on the board, served in the Senate. More than ten attorneys and employees of Prado enterprises became senators and deputies. Many other Prado relatives and associates held important positions in government agencies.[23]

The Prados' various business interests did well under Manuel's government. In 1960, Marcona Mining Company, whose president by this time was Max Peña Prado, received further concessions from the government including the relaxation of requirements for the maintenance of mineral reserves that had been set up in the 1953 contract (Purser 1971: 156). The Caja de Depositos, the private tax farming agency owned by the banks, made Popular the government's main revenue-gathering agent. The Prados' control of cement production and distribution, based on political support and access to the best quarries, gave them enormous power over the entire construction industry. They were able to continue employing antiquated equipment and administrative methods while charging excessive prices (Bourricaud 1966: 23; Gall 1971: 296–297).

THE PRADO STYLE

From 1948 until the early 1960s the Prados were at their economic and political zenith. With Odría, and then Manuel himself in power, the Banco Popular and associated enterprises could be assured of accommodating treatment from national officials. Mariano was widely regarded as "the richest and most powerful man in Peru, envied, adulated, courted, insulted, feared and hated, as few people in the country" (*La Cronica*, November 2, 1974). Important men stood up when Mariano entered a room. His sumptuous office suite at the headquarters of the Banco Popular could just as easily have served a head of state, as the president of a bank. And, in fact, the stream of visitors was as likely to include politicians and military men, as business figures.

The Prados were, a society editor of the period observed, the "beautiful people" of that time. They set the social style that many hoped to imitate, with their enormous parties and formal weddings, yachts in the harbor at Ancón, black Cadillacs, fine horses at the raceway, and mansions full of colonial treasures and fine paintings (*La Cronica*, November 2, 1974). Decades before the notion of "home theater" gained currency, Mariano's mansion featured an auditorium where first run movies were shown. His beautiful daughters were trend setters in fashion.

However, there was a seamy underside to the Prado style. The Prados made many of their associates rich. But they also had their victims. It was said that "Mariano ate a man before breakfast each day." The Prados were slum lords. El Provenir, an enormous lower-class housing project begun under the protection of Manuel's first government, was seen as a means to exploit new migrants from the Sierra (*La Cronica*, November 2, 1974).

Mariano's son, known in Lima as "Marianito," was regarded as wild and arrogant, a womanizer, given to flashing large sums of money. In 1965, Marianito wrecklessly killed the daughter of a prominent attorney with his boat in the Ancón Harbor. A criminal case was brought against him, but dismissed. According to a Lima journalist, who covered judicial matters during the period, someone was bought off. The girl's father managed to bring a civil suit against Prado, which was settled for $111,000. After his marriage to a Miró Quesada, Marianito carried on an affair with the daughter of another prominent oligarchic family. When she became pregnant, the Prados paid someone to marry the woman and take her to Buenos Aires where she had the baby. Subsequently Marianito was caught alone by the girl's brothers and severely beaten.

It was widely believed that one cause of Marianito's wild ways was his desire to live down his father's public reputation as a "homosexual." Matters were not improved in 1965 when a Lima author who had somehow gained considerable first-hand knowledge of the Prados published a novel that depicted Mariano picking up boys on the street (Reynoso 1973).

Some of the conservative upper-class Limeños interviewed in the mid-1970s indicated that they placed the Prados somewhere beyond the limits of good society. It is by no means clear that they would have openly expressed this opinion before the fall of the Prado empire. If marrying well is an index of social standing, the Prados were at the top. Mariano's children were especially successful. One daughter married Aurelio Moreyra, son of a Banco Popular board member, from a wealthy and well-established family with colonial roots. Another married a Berckemeyer, son of one of the country's wealthiest families, represented in the Club Nacional since 1899. Marianito, after a highly publicized courtship, married a granddaughter of Luis Miró Quesada, patriarch of that powerful and prestigious clan.[24] The study of oligarchic marriages in chapter 9 reveals that the Prados were among the three families with the most links to the Inner Social Circle of Lima's most prestigious families. The other two were the Pardos and the Miró Quesadas.

POLITICAL AND FINANCIAL DECLINE, 1962–1970

In 1962 the Convivencia partners, with the additional support of Beltrán and other important oligarchic figures, backed APRA chief Haya de la Torre for the presidency. The Pradistas were predicting a fifty-year Convivencia (Payne 1968: 37). But it will be recalled that the armed forces intervened, in the wake of the election that had given Haya a narrow plurality, to prevent any such outcome. Ironically, Manuel's political career ended as it had begun in 1914, with a coup d'état—this time, with Prado on the receiving end. On July 18, a small contingent of well-armed soldiers, led by a Colonel Gonzalo Briceño, forced its way into the presidential palace and confronted Manuel in his office. Speaking for the armed forces, the colonel formally

"invited" Prado to come with them. Seated at his desk with his family and friends standing behind him, the chief of state declined their request. In a voice that at first trembled, but then firmed, he made a brief address, protesting the military's violation of the constitution. There were cheers and some angry shouts, followed by singing of the national anthem. At its conclusion, Prado put on his coat and hat, while the soldiers sent for his bags (Werlich 1978: 272).

These events represented turning point in the fortunes of the clan. The Prados had long been adept at using their carefully cultivated relations with the military to political advantage. But Manuel had been unable to prevent a military coup against his own government. The failure of the Convivencia continuity scheme would produce difficulties for the Prado business empire, which had become increasingly dependent on the family's political relationships.

The financial problems the Prados would experience in the mid-1960s, under Belaúnde, did not grow out of any particular animus the new government had for them. In fact, the Prados had amicable relations with Manual's successor, who was chary of confronting the financial and political power of the clan. No government was anxious to risk losing the support of the country's second-largest bank. Manuel's party retained control of a block of congressional seats and the clan still had friends among the military. Moreover, Belaúnde had actually received campaign funds from Mariano, who made a practice of covering his political bets by supporting multiple political contenders. Prado family members served in a number of minor appointive posts in the Belaúnde administration, and Mariano had easy access to the presidential palace. In an important gesture, Belaúnde invited Manuel, who had been living in Paris since 1962, to return to Lima for the celebration of the centennial of the May 2, 1866, victory over the Spanish at Callao. The "Dos de Mayo" was the battle that had established General Prado as a national hero and the inclusion of his son Manuel in the festivities was an implicit rehabilitation of the villain of 1879 (*Oiga*, April 29, 1966).

Despite this apparent congeniality, a number of important administrative decisions under Belaúnde went against the Prados. The Caja de Depositos, which had proven so profitable for Popular, was nationalized and became the Banco de la Nacion (Gall 1971: 296). The new entity became the official bank for government operations. This decision required the transfer of large government accounts. At the trial arising out of the collapse of the Banco Popular, the Prados' lawyers would argue that this decision had done considerable damage to the bank. When the cement cartel to which a Prado company belonged applied to Belaúnde's new government for a price increase, the request was turned down. A study on which the cabinet level decision was based showed that the financial difficulties of which the Prado firm complained were the result of its own inefficiencies and not uneconomic pricing. The Superintendency of Banks began to take note of a series of loans whose duration and size relative to the bank's total portfolio exceeded legal limits. Many of these credits had been extended to companies controlled by the Prados or their associates. In 1964 and again in 1967 the bank was officially warned that it must correct this situation. But only under the Velasco's military government did authorities take action against the bank.[25]

These administrative decisions and official warnings were not intended to damage the Banco Popular. They were simply an indication that the Prados no longer had the intimate connections to national power that they had enjoyed with every administration since 1933, with the exception of Bustamante's. A Belaúnde cabinet minister who participated in the cement decision later commented, "The genius of Mariano was managing the state. He was not a great capitalist—that's not classical capitalism. We were never against the Prados, but they lost control of the state." The Prados' great strength had become their greatest weakness.

In the 1960s certain Prado enterprises ran into increasing economic difficulties. The cement and textile companies, operating with antiquated equipment, were struggling (*La Cronica*, January 20, March 6, 14, 1973). The real estate companies were selling off their assets (which probably represented the remainder of a land inheritance the Prados had been slowly dissipating since the 1920s), while running up huge debts through financial manipulations involving the bank (*Oiga,* February 16, 1973).

While the political situation remained cloudy and serious economic difficulties developed, Mariano's health was declining. Under these conditions the clan decided in 1965 to transfer primary responsibility for the conduct of the bank and associated enterprises to his wayward son, Marianito Prado Sosa, who was already serving on the Popular board. Marianito, who was scarcely thirty at the time, was given the newly invented title of "Executive Director," while his father continued officially as president and chairman of the board.

The precise division of authority between father and son was a matter of contention at the Banco Popular trial, though testimony demonstrated that Marianito had considerable power in the affairs of the bank and Prado group enterprises from 1965 to 1970.[26] Interviews with two individuals close to the family made clear that a decision had been made, with the support of Mariano's children, who were important stockholders, to give Marianito substantial authority. He was expected to make drastic changes calculated to salvage the clan's financial situation. Marianito brought to the bank a group of aggressive financial advisers, referred to during the trial as the "New Wave," who were to help him to design a rescue operation. The key member of this new group was an American, John Kuesell, who was tried and convicted with the Prados.

After 1965, a series of drastic measures were taken that were intended to disguise the bank's troubles and allow the Prados to recoup their financial situation. As revealed in the course of the trial, these included the falsification of profit and loss statements, the evasion of taxes, and the maintenance of inadequate reserves. At the same time, the bank was extending loans to Prado firms, far in excess of their financial worth or earning capacity. Often these loans were made to finance the purchase of equally marginal Prado group enterprises. The final resting place of this money was mysterious. Nearly 75 percent of the total sum loaned to these firms was deemed irrecoverable. Banco Popular was also guaranteeing bonds issued by Prado companies with no real capacity to service them.[27]

The Prados helped finance the 1968 military coup that ousted Belaúnde a few months before the end of his term. By then they would probably have given aid to any conspiracy likely to be successful, in the hope of buying friendly relations with a new government and support for their failing empire. However, the Prados had particular reasons to expect good treatment from the revolutionary military government. Their ties to President Juan Velasco went back some years. When Manuel was still in office, Mariano had intervened on Velasco's behalf to save his career from a hostile minister of war. (A story, perhaps apocryphal, which later circulated in Prado circles, has it that Mariano was warned about Velasco at the time, "Don't do it. He is a raven who will pluck out your eyes.") Some members of the Prado family had maintained personal ties to Velasco. Max Peña Prado, for instance, had been an usher at his wedding.

For at least a year after the coup, the Prados were on excellent terms with the new regime. Their paper, *La Crónica*, gave the government strong support in 1968 and 1969. Although the clan had some misgivings about the direction the generals were taking, the Prados were confident of their direct ties with Velasco. They were also encouraged by the fact that General José Benavides, Mariano Peña Prado's conservative brother-in-law, was a member of Velasco's cabinet.

During this period, the Prados prepared their ultimate salvage operation, a merger between the Banco Popular and Lima's Banco Continental, controlled by the Chase Manhattan Bank of New York. A preliminary agreement that had been worked out between the parties had some striking features. The Chase group would manage the new institution. Stock shares to be received by the Prado group would be held in escrow until Popular's financial situation could be properly assessed, at which time they would be liable to adjustment. Continental's stockholders were subject to no such provision. The Prados had presumably been more candid with their future partners than they had with public officials about the bank's condition. The agreement required the Prados to obtain a new line of credit from the central bank amounting to approximately $26 million, much of which would go toward the refloating of Prado group enterprises obligated to the bank. The Prados were also to secure the cooperation of the Peruvian government in such areas as the reduction of Popular's work force and relaxation of stringent new banking laws regulating the participation of foreign capital. The merger seemed predicated on the Prados' weakened political muscle (Dominguez 1970; *La Cronica*, April 18, 1973).

Why would the three parties—the Prados, Chase, and the military government—want such an agreement? For the Prados, the merger seemed to represent one last chance to salvage their economic situation. For Chase, the combination with Peru's second-largest bank (and the only bank with branches throughout the country) offered the opportunity to become the giant of Peruvian banking. Under new banking laws, Continental, as a foreign-controlled bank, could not open additional branches or increase its deposits. The merger offered a way around both provisions. The Prados must have assumed, along with Chase, that the Peruvian government was not willing to allow a major bank to fail, so it would be willing to go along with the agreement.

This was their principal miscalculation. The government was, in fact, unwilling to have the bank fail. But it was equally unwilling to have a key financial institution fall under foreign control. On June 12, 1970, as the Popular board met with Chase representatives at the bank's headquarters in Lima to sign the agreement, Mariano and his son were called to a meeting with the president of the central bank and the Superintendent of Banks at the latter's offices. The Peruvian officials, aware of Mariano's failing health, had a cardiologist on hand, in case he was unable to sustain the shock. The Prados were informed that, on the basis of a cabinet level decision, the government was nationalizing the bank. Within minutes the government's representatives took possession of Popular's headquarters.

In the coming months as the new managers of Banco Popular began to unravel its tangled affairs, they discovered what was probably suspected well in advance: The bank's liabilities grossly outweighed its true assets. It was revealed that over $56 million out of $60.3 million in Popular's loan portfolio had been extended to seventy persons and legal entities that were tied to the administration of the bank. Some $44.3 million of this amount was deemed irrecoverable (*Oiga*, February 9, 1973). Much of it represented money of depositors and other creditors that the government was obligated to make up if the bank was to avoid failure.

It is likely that the Prados moved large sums abroad in the late 1960s. Some of the elaborate financial machinations of which they were later convicted point in that direction. For instance, the bank loaned $180,800 to the Tradex Corporation, registered in Panama, capitalized at fifty dollars, and formed by a lawyer and his secretary. The money, regarded by the court as irrecoverable, was used to purchase shares in Popular y Porvenir, the Prado insurance company (*La Cronica*, February 7, 1973; Rivero Velez 1973). The Prados may have also used a branch of the Banco Popular in Bolivia to transfer money out of the country.

In 1973 Mariano and his son were put on trial along with several top employees. The charges ranged from fraudulent credit policies and illegal manipulation of Prado group stocks and bonds to falsification of accounts and direct misappropriation of deposited funds. By the time those charges were brought, Marianito had fled the country and Mariano was in a police hospital slowly dying. He finally expired on

November 1, 1974. The other defendants appeared in court without their former employers. Both Prados were represented by attorneys. After a trial that lasted six months, the two Prados were condemned to ten years prison and the payment of $210,000 each in fines. They were, in addition, obligated for $31.9 million they were judged to have defrauded the bank, but which the Peruvian state had little hope of recovering. Their employees received lesser sentences (*La Cronica, El Comercio,* June 27, 1973).

The Prado Empire: Patrimonialism in the Private Sector

In the late 1960s, the Prado empire, revolving around the Banco Popular, consisted of some thirty-three companies in finance, real estate, textiles, construction, and other fields. The clan controlled a newspaper (*La Cronica*), an auto dealer, and an airline. These were formally separate corporate entities, but they were connected by a web of interlocking boards and executive positions. Key family members occupied multiple positions across sectors and companies. The family's close associates, employees, and clients strengthened the web with additional links.[28]

The structure of the Prado empire enabled the financial manipulations revealed at the trial and facilitated a style of administration that we can compare to what Max Weber called "patrimonialism" in the control of the state. The essential characteristics of patrimonialism are the centralization of authority in the person of the patrimonial ruler and the lack of distinction between the state and the ruler's own household. State officials are relatives or personal retainers of the ruler. The treasury and property of the state are indistinguishable from the ruler's own. The division of labor within the state is not clear cut, since responsibilities are distributed on a case by case basis by the patrimonial ruler (Weber 1947: 341–359).

Mariano Prado Heudebert's administration of the clan's economic empire was very like the manner in which Weber's patrimonial ruler runs the state. This was particularly evident at the Banco Popular. An American consulting firm retained in the late 1960s to carry out an administrative reorganization withdrew after considerable effort, stating flatly "No reorganization of the Banco Popular del Peru is possible. There exists a paternalistic familistic system which has left the bank in a state of chaos and places all kinds of obstacles in the path of reorganization" (*La Cronica,* April 18, 1973).

The consultants highlighted the extreme centralization of authority in Mariano himself. The constitution of the bank granted Prado Heudebert (and in the bank's last years, his son) virtually unlimited powers to obligate the bank. At the same time, other Popular executives had limited powers (*La Cronica,* April 24 and 25, 1973). The board had formal power over Mariano. However, one of the bank's top nonfamily executives, who was responsible for preparing minutes of the meetings of the board, testified, "decisions were not made nor was there even deliberation (at board meetings)." The minutes containing the principal decisions were prepared prior to the meetings and only modified to include less important details (*El Comercio,*

April 7, 1973). The testimony of the directors confirmed this version of their meetings. Several were explicit in indicating that Prado ran the bank according to his
own desires.[29]

The directors' testimony might be seen as an effort to deny their own legal
responsibility. However, a lawyer close to the government's case and a high official
of the bank's new administration both agreed that that management of the bank had
indeed been highly centralized and personalistic.

Just as the patrimonial ruler does not distinguish between the state's treasury and
his own property, Mariano and his son treated the funds available to them (which
represented the bank's capital, earnings, depositor's money, and the credits extended
by the central bank) as if they were their own. In the case of the bank's capital and
income, this was more or less the case since the bank was approximately 90 percent
owned by the Prados.[30] However, by the late 1960s both earnings and capital were
imaginary. The Prados were dipping into deposits and utilizing semipublic credit
when they extended millions of dollars in unsecured loans to their own companies.
These operations, which were the primary cause of the bank's financial collapse,
came in response to the precarious state of the Prado empire at the time; but the
trial brought out many less extravagant examples of patrimonial administration of
capital that suggest an institutionalized pattern. An audit showed that between 1967
and 1969 the bank paid out large sums to certain family members for supposed
"representation expenses." These payments particularly went to older members of the
family, including Manuel Prado Ugarteche ($12,000), Manuel's first wife, Enriqueta
Garland ($2,000), and Jorge Prado Ugarteche ($20,000). The same audit showed
a pattern of unjustified payment of overdrafts and cancellation of debts on behalf
of kin and associates of the clan. An overdraft, on the account of Eugenio Isola, a
director of the bank, was so large ($182,000) that it evoked a warning from the
Superintendent of Banks.[31]

The staffing of the bank also reflected the patrimonial style. A knowledgeable,
well-connected Peruvian informant observed,

> Mariano disliked professionals, who might question his decisions. He would prefer to en-
> gage for key positions in his enterprise either ex-lovers (homosexuals) and protégés—who
> would be grateful and would not dare to speak up because they feared expulsion from the
> Prado empire (they suffered from a kind of circus freak complex) or outright gangsters
> who were tough enough to command admiration, but were also disciplined and discrete
> in the style of the mafia. Managerial capabilities were conspicuously absent.[32]

This patrimonial mode of administration assumes profit through political power
rather than economic efficiency. Mariano's unrestrained power at the bank freed
him to use its assets politically, as he did with liberal credit for military officers, the
irrecoverable loan destined for Manuel's political campaign, and the contribution to
the "bolsa" for Odría's 1948 coup. Political power and free access to credit, in turn,
sustained the inefficient enterprises of the Prado empire. The vulnerability of this
patrimonial style is obvious. When political power wanes, so do monopoly profits,

and economic erosion further undermines political power, setting off a downward spiral.

Using examples obviously drawn from observation of the Prados, Bourricaud (1966) presents this politicized, patrimonial business style as the defining characteristic of the oligarchy. But his brilliantly drawn ideal type of the oligarch rests on this extreme case. In varying degrees, all oligarchic clans shared the Prados' leadership style and pursuit of economic advantage from political power. But many were unwilling to assume the risk that came with overdependence on politics. And the exporter core of the oligarchy, like the Aspíllagas at Cayaltí, was ultimately subject to the discipline of international markets they could not control politically. What they needed from politics was control over labor which they sought collectively.

Ironically, the Prados themselves did not initially take this path. Mariano Prado Ugarteche was a successful, pioneering entrepreneur, who invested in new sectors of the turn-of-the-century economy, with capital from family and nonfamily sources. The Prado Ugarteche brothers sought political office to vindicate their father, the general, and out of personal ambition. They were not indifferent to the private economic advantage to be derived from political power, but it was not the primary driver of their quest for the presidency. Mariano Prado Heudebert and his generation—at a greater distance from the tragedy of 1879—seem to have had different objectives. The clan's initial resistance to Manuel's second presidential bid in 1956 reflects this generational divergence. From Prado Heudebert's perspective, the glory of high office was less desirable than the practical advantages of discreet power.

NOTES

1. Prado left behind in Huánuco three sons. Ironically, one of them, Leoncio Prado, died a well-remembered heroic death fighting in the war that discredited his father. Prado apparently recognized these sons, though he never married their mother, María Avelina Gutiérrez, a woman of humble origin (Portocarrero 1995: 40–41).

2. On General Prado and the origins of the Prado family see Portocarrero 1995: chapter 2; Tauro 1966; San Cristoval 1966; Delgado 1952; Guimet 1955; Varallanos 1959; Lavalle 1893; Osores 1878.

3. See Quimper 1881: 66–67; Ahumada 1885: II, 265–273; III, 385; Paz Soldan 1884: 354–357; Castro 1880: I, 16–24; Paz Soldan 1943: 70–75; Delgado 1952; Vargas 1971: 286–287; Dulanto 1947: 230–231; Basadre 1971: 28–29. The unanimity of these authors is all the more striking, because some are quite hostile politically to Prado and most are critical of his decision to take on the arms buying mission himself. In 1884 a government commission was set up to investigate the handling of 400,000 pounds sterling, which had been collected for arms purchases. The tone of the commission's report (*El Pais*, November 21, 25 and December 12, 1884) is quite unfriendly to Prado, but its conclusion was simply that he had illegally drawn 3,000 pounds from the treasury on the "pretext" of needing expense money for an arms buying mission. On the other hand, vast sums of money turned over to other individuals and official and commercial entities (including 56,000 pounds to Grace Company) remained unaccounted for.

4. The pamphlet circulated during the 1936, 1939, and 1956 elections. It reproduces a series of historical documents, which, even if accepted as a full and accurate portrayal of events, contain nothing whatever which ties Prado himself to the missing funds.

5. A fifth brother, Max, an engineer died in an accident in 1903. For biographies of Mariano, Javier, and Manuel, see Tauro 1966: 580–581 and Portocarrero 1995: chapter 2. On Mariano see Ramirez 1962, *La Cronica*, March 26, 1946, and San Cristoval 1966: 99–101. On Jorge, Paz Soldan 1921: 313–314, Prado 1936, and *Lima* 1935. On Manuel, *La Prensa*, August 15, 1967. On Javier, Sanchez 1973; on his intellectual contribution, Pike 1967: 161–162 and Salazar Bondy 1965: 40–71.

6. On these ventures see Yepes 1972; *West Coast Leader*, May 27, 1927; Empresas Eléctricas Asociadas 1966; "Mariano Prado Ugarteche," *La Cronica*, March 27, 1946.

7. On Popular's early history Basadre 1964: VII, 3191; Yepes 1972: 165; Laos 1927: 396. Regarding the insurance companies, *Lima* 1935: chapter 13; Laos 1927: 396; *La Popular* 1904; *El Financista*, December 10, 1912.

8. Chirinos 1962: 134; Miró Quesada Laos 1961: 447; Gerlach 1973: 124.

9. Gerlach 1973: 177, 193; Belaunde 1967: II, 602–603; Miró Quesada Laos1961: 449; Sanchez 1973.

10. At 1968 exchange rates. The date of the 8 million sol loan is not indicated.

11. "Puede Ser un Prado President del Peru." Over the years various editions of this pamphlet appeared. The version consulted for this chapter does not indicate author[s], publisher, or place of publication but, from internal evidence, was obviously published in 1936. See also Miró Quesada Laos1961: 480; Gerlach 1973: 463; Sanchez 1969: II, 549; and Portocarrero 1995: 31–20.

12. Ironically, the candidates for first and second vice-president on Jorge's ticket in 1936 were Miguel Grau and Amadeo Pierola. The first was apparently related to the admiral, and the second was the son of caudillo who assumed power after General Prado's departure in 1879 and stripped him of his citizenship. Perhaps these candidacies were Prado's answer to the "Puede un Prado" pamphlet.

13. Sanchez 1955: 366–367 and 1969: II, 565; North 1973: 128.

14. RAB 9–11–39; Pike 1967: 276; Gerlach 1973: 497; North 1973: 128; Miró Quesada Laos 1961: 480; Villanueva 1962: 98.

15. Pike 1967: 276–279; Klaren 2000: 281–285; Werlich 1978: 221–234; Payne 1965: 46–48, 54; Chirinos 1962: 60.

16. Moreno 1956: 472; Sanchez 1969: II, 1084; Gerlach 1973: 503.

17. Gerlach 1973: 507–509; Sanchez 1955: 395; Sanchez 1969: II, 742.

18. The superior economic position of these lineages presumably reflects the bigger stake of Mariano Prado Ugarteche in the family's turn-of-the-century enterprises and the Peña inheritance.

19. Manuel Prado Garland held a relatively minor position at the Banco Popular in the mid-1950s, but left the bank in 1957 (Banco Popular 1954–1969; *La Cronica* April 27, 1957). In 1946, he owned 6 percent of BP shares, the only member of his branch with shares. The BP document, which is the source of this information, suggests that Mariano Prado Ugarteche's lineage held one third or more of the shares at the time. The Peña Prados and Jorge Prado also owned shares, but it is impossible to determine the size of their holdings from the document (Portocarrero 1995: 150–151).

20. This statement is based on interviews with two sources close to the Prados and a third with a national security official of the Bustamante government who was aware of the growing

conspiracy at the time. The Prados were not among the chief civilian organizers of the coup who were mainly planters.

21. Sanchez 1969: II, 1060–1084; Miró Quesada Laos 1959: 177–214; Chirinos 1962: 111–126; Payne 1968: 25–31; Pike 1967: 295.

22. For details see chapter 5.

23. Dominguez 1970: 5–6. Some minor factual errors in this text that may be due to mistranslation have been corrected here.

24. Their marriage was supposed to have established peace between their families, which had long been bitter enemies. See chapter 8.

25. *La Prensa*, September 7, 1973; *La Cronica*, January 5, 1973; *Expreso*, April 7, 1973.

26. Rivero Velez et al. 1973, the decision handed down by the Special Tribunal that heard the Prado case contains a detailed summary of evidence presented at the trial including considerable information on financial and administrative aspects of the Banco Popular and associated enterprises in the 1960s. Much of the same information is available in the Lima dailies especially *La Cronica* for the trial period December 1972–June 1973.

27. Rivero Velez et al. 1973; *Oiga*, February 16, 1973.

28. Table 7.1 and Gilbert 1982: 191, Cuadro 4–3.

29. *La Cronica*, April 25, 1974; *Expreso*, April 17, 1974; *La Prensa*, May 3, 1974; *La Cronica*, April 30, 1974; *La Prensa*, April 19, 1974.

30. No precise information on the distribution of B.P. stock is available. This figure is an estimate by a knowledgeable post-Prado executive of the bank.

31. *Expreso*, February 12, 1973; Rivero Velez et al. 1973; *La Cronica*, April 3, 1973.

32. From an interview conducted by William F. Whyte. Quoted here with his permission.

8

The Miró Quesadas:
Aristocratic Reformers

A. There is a difference between the reformers and the resentful ones.
Q. And who are the resentful ones?
A. They are those who have no name. Social reform must be made with a sense
of nobility. And that is what they lack.

—Interview with Luís Miró Quesada

The Miró Quesadas were the owners of *El Comercio*, for many decades the country's most influential newspaper. Their control of this potent political instrument, substantial wealth, and a firmly established position in elite society all placed them among the oligarchs. Yet they differed from the other families in important ways, and their distinctness explains some ironic twists in the family's history and influence in national affairs.

They were a family of intellectuals, with worthy accomplishments in areas as diverse as mathematics and colonial history (Tauro 1966). They did not have any significant economic interest other than the newspaper. And while newspaper ownership was typical of the most powerful oligarchic families, exclusive dedication to publishing was not.

The family's outlook was characterized by strongly held aristocratic values, an especially patriarchal form of family organization, and a strong sense of their own right to rule—all of which are essential to understanding their history. Yet, these profoundly conservative "un-modern" men gave crucial support (which they would later regret) to the modernizers in Peruvian politics.

ORIGIN[1]

José Antonio Miró Quesada was the first of his family to work at *El Comercio*. His parents Tomás Miró and Joséfa Quesada had come to Peru from Panama in 1846

213

Box 8.1.   Generations of the Miró Quesadas

I.   **José Antonio Miró Quesada** (1845–1930)
     First MQ family director of *El Comercio*
II. Miró Quesada de la Guerras (born 1875–)
     Sons of José Antonio. Prominent in Civilista-era politics and influential
     until end of Old Regime as owners of *El Comercio*.
       Antonio MQ de la Guerra (1875–1935), succeeded father as director
     of *El Comercio*.
       Aurelio MQ de la Guerra (1877–1950) and
       Luís MQ de la Guerra (1880–1976) succeeded their brother Antonio
     as co-directors of *El Comercio*, but Luís was dominant family figure.
III. Sons of the Miró Quesada de la Guerras (born early 20th century)
     Cousins with key positions at *El Comercio*.
       Luís García Miró, **Aurelio MQ Sosa** (1907–1998), **Alejandro MQ
     Garland** (1915–2011), and **Francisco MQ Cantuarias** (1918–), who
     served in Belaunde cabinet in 1960s.

---

with several children. They settled in Lima's port, Callao, where Tomás dedicated himself to the import trade during the bonanza years of guano. The family's economic situation was not particularly good when they arrived and not much better when Tomás died in 1883. Shortly before his death he compiled some notes on the family's genealogy for his heirs, not out of pride, he insisted, but because it is a "satisfactory thing to have knowledge of one's progenitors" (Miró Quesada Sosa 1945: 174). Tomás' father and grandfather were Spanish military officers, who served in Spanish America. In their native Valencia, the family's estate had been modest at best, but family lore preserved stories of past glories and aristocratic descent.

THE RISE OF THE MIRÓ QUESADAS

José Antonio started at *El Comercio* as its Callao correspondent. By 1876 he was "co-director," and in 1898 on the death of his partner, Luís Carranza, he became sole director. (In Peruvian journalism, the "director" has traditionally combined the functions of editor-in-chief and publisher.) The following year he bought out Carranza's heirs. As late as 1893, José Antonio's son Antonio was the only other Miró Quesada employed by the newspaper (*El Comercio* 1894: 28–30), but with the purchase of Carranza's share, *El Comercio* became a family enterprise with broad family participation. And for the Miró Quesadas and those who observed them, the paper would become the focus of the family's identity.

Home of El Comercio, *Peru's most influential newspaper since the mid-nineteenth century. Here decorated for national independence day.*

Source: Wikimedia Commons.

José Antonio's children, the Miró Quesada de la Guerras, inherited a secure social position, which was consolidated by their own energetic careers. They adopted the compound paternal surname, "Miró Quesada," a gesture with aristocratic overtones which demonstrated their sense that an important family tradition was being launched in Peru. José Antonio's position at *El Comercio* gave him access to elite social and political circles. As co-director, he was already a member of the exclusive Club Nacional, and of the informal inner circle of Civilista leadership, "The Twenty-Four Friends," that regularly met there.

The Miró Quesada de la Guerras all married into socially prominent families. The paper apparently gave them a comfortable economic base. All had considerable time to devote to some combination of politics, diplomacy, intellectual pursuits, and travel. There is no indication that any of them was ever economically dependent on employment outside the paper. They became leading figures in the Civilista Party. Both Antonio Miró Quesada de la Guerrra and his brother Luís held congressional seats through much of the Aristocratic Republic. Antonio was at different times presiding officer of the Senate and the Chamber of Deputies. The brothers formed part of the reformist liberal wing of the party.[2]

Luís took a particular interest in labor questions and played an important role in obtaining passage of the workman's compensation law in 1911. Between 1900 and 1908, he published a series of studies of "the social question" which showed serious concern for the conditions of the working class. He called for passage of protective legislation to regulate the employment of women and children, provide for worker health and safety, limit the length of the working day, and establish retirement benefits. These pieces were written before labor conflicts had become a serious problem in Peru, but Miró Quesada showed considerable awareness of contemporary proletarian movements in Europe (Miró Quesada 1965). In these early writings, Luís warned his own class of the need to provide legislative remedy for social injustices before class conflict became a disruptive force in Peru. Though he showed sympathy with worker demands in some early strikes, Luís clearly regarded strikes and the militant worker organizations that promoted them a social threat. His solution was government arbitration of worker demands. These paternalistic views were reflected in *El Comercio*.

Antonio, the eldest son, became director of *El Comercio* when his father retired in 1905. At the same time, he served in the Congress and held a university chair (as did Luís). Such linking of institutional positions by oligarchic figures was particularly common under the Aristocratic Republic. *El Comercio* was viewed as a semi-official Civilista organ, and its offices were an important gathering place for the party elite (Miró Quesada Laos 1957: 190).

UNDER LEGUÍA

The Miró Quesadas participated conspicuously in congressional resistance to Leguía's rising ambitions. In 1912, their paper supported Billinghurst over the Leguiista candidate, Antero Aspíllaga. Leguía's triumph in 1919 was a hard political blow to them as it was for most of the Civilistas (Stein 1980: 33). *El Comercio*, because of its close identification with Civilism, was one of Leguía's special targets. A few months after he took power, Lima mobs with the apparent encouragement of the government attacked the offices of *El Comercio*, and its competitor *La Prensa*. At *El Comercio*, family members armed themselves to drive off the attackers. The defense was successful, but the same mob managed to burn down Antonio's home.

At various points during Leguía's eleven years in power, members of the family were jailed or deported. Antonio spent much of the period in exile, and the paper was run by a nonfamily managing editor.[3] Leguía did not, however, seize *El Comercio* as he had *La Prensa*. When such action was suggested to him, Leguía reportedly replied that it was unnecessary "because just the idea that they might be shut down is enough to scare them to death" (Capuñay 1951: 188). In fact, *El Comercio* seldom criticized Leguía after his first couple of years in office.[4] But whatever the Miró Quesadas lost politically during the period, they seem to have gained economically.

The transformation of *La Prensa* into a government organ effectively removed *El Comercio*'s chief competitor for readers and advertisers. Its position in Lima would remain unchallenged until Pedro Beltrán revived *La Prensa* in the 1950s.

With Leguía's demise, the Miró Quesadas regained the political influence that they had lost in the 1920s. Although family members would never again hold elective office, as they had during the Aristocratic Republic, and rarely held appointive office, they remained a potent force in Peruvian politics.

THE REACTIONARY YEARS

From 1930 to 1956, the Miró Quesadas passed through the most reactionary phase in their history. The family and the paper were unreservedly and relentlessly anti-Aprista. They were among the early supporters of Sánchez Cerro and the harsh solutions he represented to the political and economic crisis of the period. (If they were not co-conspirators with him against Leguía in 1930, they had certainly been in contact with him prior to the coup and aware of his intentions). *El Comercio* argued that since Leguía had done away with the civilian parties, Sánchez Cerro and the army were the country's best hope. Luís served in Sánchez Cerro's inaugural cabinet, and the paper gave the regime strong support for its anti-APRA, anti-union, and generally anti-civil libertarian positions. The controversial Emergency Law, chief legal instrument of government repression, found ready support on the pages of *El Comercio*.[5]

Such positions marked a striking departure from the more liberal political spirit which had animated the Miró Quesadas and their paper in the early Civilista years. Just the backing of a military regime represented a significant break with the past. In the early years of the century, *El Comercio* had praised the military for having learned to stay out of politics The paper now editorialized that Sánchez Cerro and the army represented Peru's best hope.[6]

The shift appears to have grown out of a strong sense of threats to the established social order, epitomized by the Russian Revolution and embodied in the growth of leftist movements in Peru after 1915. This attitude was reflected in *El Comercio*'s support in 1927 for Leguía's fierce campaign against labor and radical organizations. Several days of articles on the subject warned of "the horrors of Communism," "red terrorism," "World Bolshevism," and those who would "poison the hearts of the working class . . . against those who give them work" (*El Comercio*, June 9–12, 1927).

The Miró Quesadas could greet Hitler's rise to power in Germany in the early 1930s with enthusiasm. (At the time, many upper-class Latin Americans were attracted to fascism.) Though they would later support the allies in World War II, *El Comercio* initially applauded Hitler's "appeal to the civic conscience of the German people" and interpreted Nazism as a strong blow against Communism. Throughout the decade of the 1930s, the paper failed to condemn, and at times even seemed to approve of Hitler's invasions and his treatment of the Jews.[7]

The determined backing which *El Comercio* and its owners gave Sánchez Cerro, their initial enthusiasm for Hitler, and their persistent attacks on APRA reflected a consistent ideological perspective during this period. For the Miró Quesadas, APRA represented a Marxist threat to the nation. Like Communism, APRA was an alien, subversive force. At the same time that *El Comercio* supported Sánchez Cerro's most repressive measures, the paper was editorializing that the abrogation of civil liberties by regimes in "certain European countries" was justified by the international and internal threats to stability (Miró Quesada 1953: I, 109, 303–305, 383–386).

THE CRIME

On May 15, 1935, Antonio Miró Quesada and his wife, Maria Laos, were assassinated as they approached the Club Nacional on Lima's Plaza San Martin. The assassin was a nineteen-year-old Aprista, Carlos Steer, who shot Maria as she came to her husband's aid and then attempted to kill himself. Steer claimed to have acted on his own, a point that would be debated endlessly by APRA's friends and enemies.[8] Whatever the truth, it is clear that Steer was reacting to the strident anti-aprismo of the Miró Quesadas and their newspaper.

The event, known within the family as "The Crime," would shape the political emotions of Miró Quesadas living and unborn in 1935 for decades to come. It froze the Miró Quesada and their paper in an unyielding anti-APRA position, even as the party and the national political system evolved. For decades the anniversary of the assassination was marked with a front-page picture of Antonio and his wife and a bitter editorial condemning the party. The event and *El Comercio*'s constant reminders of it did much to reinforce anti-APRA sentiment in Peru.

El Comercio helped bring to power the right-wing military regimes which were analyzed in chapter 5. But the best predictor of the attitude that *El Comercio* would take toward any government, at any moment, was that government's attitude toward the APRA. Though all of the military regimes took repressive measures against APRA, any show of leniency toward the party evoked a strong reaction from *El Comercio*. Thus, Benavides' refusal to order the execution of Antonio's young assassin turned the Miró Quesadas against him. *El Comercio*'s hostility toward Bustamante's National Democratic Front government and its early support of Odría's anti-Aprista regime were predictable. But Odría lost *El Comercio* when he yielded to international pressure and allowed Haya de la Torre to end several years of diplomatic refuge in the Colombian embassy and leave the country.

THE 1936 ELECTIONS

In the days leading up to the October 1936 presidential election, *El Comercio*'s coverage of the campaign was meager and uninformative. Readers might have inferred the family's political mood from *El Comercio*'s extensive daily coverage of the Spanish Civil War, which was notably sympathetic to General Franco's right-wing Nationalist forces. But they would not have found any clear indication of the owners' preference among the four, ideologically diverse candidates for the presidency of Peru.

This uncharacteristic reticence probably reflected the ideological diversity within the family that periodically led to conflicts. Two of the candidates in 1936—Luís Eguiguren, who was drawing unofficial Aprista support, and Jorge Prado, who had favored a conciliatory policy toward APRA as Benavides' prime minister—were presumably unacceptable to all the Miró Quesadas. The other two candidates were anti-APRA. Luís Flores, a former interior minister, led an openly fascist party, whose black-shirted militants attacked Apristas and other leftists. Manuel Villarán, a more traditional Peruvian conservative and former Civilista, was supported by the planter core of the oligarchy. Flores would have appealed to those Miró Quesadas—especially, Carlos Miró Quesada Laos, son of the assassinated Antonio—who especially admired the contemporary fascist regimes of Europe. Villarán presumably attracted others in the family who wanted a milder right-wing alternative. Family members argued over how the paper should treat fascism. *El Comercio* would not publish some of Carlos' more extreme pro-fascist pieces.

REORGANIZING THE FAMILY

Family discord over politics during this period came in the wake of a succession crisis precipitated by Antonio's assassination. Antonio, as the eldest son of founder José Antonio, had taken over the paper three decades earlier. With Antonio's death, the family passed the directorship to the founder's oldest surviving son, Aurelio (see box 8.1 and figure 8.1). Brother Luís, who was in Europe at the time, serving in a diplomatic post, immediately resigned his position and rushed back to Lima to argue that no decision should have been made in his absence and to demand the director-ship for himself. Luís was the fourth of José Antonio's five sons. He had been, like Antonio, a prominent political figure in the Aristocratic Republic. Luís never fully accepted Antonio's authority at the paper and had frequently challenged him on editorial matters (Pardo Castro 1961: 20–21).

The succession dispute was mediated by Oscar, the youngest brother, and it was agreed that Luís and Aurelio would be co-directors. But Aurelio never had Luís' keen grasp of national politics and could not match the force of his character, so Luís came to dominate editorially well before Aurelio's death in 1950. His power over editorial decisions (and, in effect, political decisions) made him powerful not only within the family but also in the national political arena where he was regarded as the personal embodiment of the power of *El Comercio*.

Although Luís was never inclined to relinquish authority, younger members of the family would assume increasing responsibility for the daily operations of the paper

Luís Miró Quesada led El Comercio *and became one of the most powerful men in mid-twentieth-century Peru.*

Source: Luis Miró Quesada: Ofrenda Jubilar. 1953.

in the 1950s and 1960s. By this time Luís was in his seventies and eighties. The new generation would bring new political perspectives to the paper and push Luís' own thinking to the left.

The elevation of this third generation of Miró Quesadas, José Antonio's grandsons, to positions of responsibility at *El Comercio* inevitably raised the question of succession to Luís. For a number of years, Aurelio Miró Quesada Sosa, Alejandro Miró Quesada Garland, Francisco Miró Quesada Cantuarias, and Luís García Miró rotated daily editorial responsibility. Each of these cousins represented a separate lineage within the descent group. But none of Antonio's sons participated in the cousins' rotation, and Carlos, a talented journalist, was largely eased out of the paper (Pardo Castro 1961: 31).

Later an arrangement was worked out under which cousins Alejandro and Aurelio became co-directors, with Luís above them in the newly created position of general director. Francisco edited the Sunday cultural supplement. Luís García Miró, an engineer, moved to the business/industrial side of the newspaper, following his older brother, Pedro Garcia Miró, and their father, Pedro Garcia Irygoyen, husband of José Antonio's only daughter.[9]

By the early 1970s, a triumvirate of Luís, Alejandro, and Aurelio formed the central power clique at the newspaper. Luís, remarkably strong and lucid in his early nineties, was still the dominant figure. His son, Alejandro, was the heir apparent. This central clique was advised by certain nonfamily figures. The best known of these was Alfonso Baella Tuesta, a lawyer and the political editor of *El Comercio*. Baella Tuesta reportedly also served as political factotum—perhaps even *consigliere*—for the Miró Quesadas, who liked to handle political matters through intermediaries. It was obvious that Baella Tuesta, who addressed family members with the familiar *tu* and moved freely in and out of Luís' home, was close to the central clique. His influence on decision making was reportedly greater than that of many family members.

The distribution of positions and stock in *El Comercio* among the Miró Quesada lineages is shown in table 8.1. The information is from late 1972. By this time there were five surviving lineages, and it appears that the stock once held by Miguel Miró Quesada de la Guerra, who died in 1948 without descendants, had gone to Luís. (Miguel and Luís had married sisters). Members of all surviving lineages held jobs at the paper, but Antonio's descendants were relegated to one inconsequential post, with no editorial responsibility.[10]

THE TRANSFORMATION OF *EL COMERCIO*

In the late 1950s, the Miró Quesadas found themselves in political isolation. Their efforts to secure the election of an anti-APRA candidate in 1956 had failed.[11] Prado's Convivencia arrangement with APRA put the family's worst enemies close to power, while providing evidence of the party's growing reconciliation with the rest of the oligarchy. An Aprista president was becoming a real possibility. During this same period, Pedro Beltrán (who served for a time as Prado's prime minister) was transforming the long-moribund Lima daily *La Prensa* into a dynamic, modern newspaper, capable of challenging the Miró Quesadas both politically and commercially.

The differences between the revitalized *La Prensa* and *El Comercio* were vast.[12] The Miró Quesadas practiced a very old-fashioned brand of journalism. In the early 1950s, *El Comercio*'s layout was rigid and graceless. Headlines were long and uninspired. This was particularly so for political articles, whose titles were dictated by Luís himself. (When editors complained that one of Luís' political headlines would not fit properly in the available space, he would respond bluntly, "Make it fit.") Articles were rambling, with lengthy paragraphs that often read like the weekly minutes of some civic organization.

Pedro Beltrán, educated in England and married to an American, was a great admirer of Anglo-Saxon organization, technology, and cultural models. (The Miró Quesadas, in contrast, were attached to French, culture.) When he took over *La*

Table 8.1. Positions and Stockholdings in *El Comercio* by Lineage[a]

Lineage (Children of José Antonio MQ in Birth Order)/ Name	Position	Percentage of Stock	
I. Joséfa MQ de la Guerra			
Pedro García Miró	Director-manager/ member board	4.2	
José Antonio García Miró	Legal advisor/manager board	4.2	
Luís García Miró	Assistant manager (technical)	4.2	
Manuel García MQ	Photography section	1.0	
Delfina García MQ de Llona	–	1.0	
José Antonio García MQ	–	1.0	
Amilia García MQ		1.0	
Total stock			16.6
II. Antonio MQ de la Guerra			
Enrique MQ Laos	Assistant manager (distribution)/member board	2.1	
Delfina MQ Laos de García Miró	–	2.1	
Amalia MQ Laos de Chopitea	–	2.1	
Matilde MQ Laos de Mansano	–	2.1	
María Cornejo Viuda de MQ Laos	–	1.9	
María Dudek Viuda de MQ Laos	–	1.8	
Estate of Manuel MQ Laos	–	2.1	
Estate of Carlos MQ Laos	–	2.1	
Delfina MQ de Wiese	–	0.1	
María Luísa MQ Dudek	–	0.2	
María Ofelia MQ Cornejo	–	0.1	
Total stock			16.7
III. Aurelio MQ de la Guerra			
Aurelio MQ Sosa	Director/member board	4.2	
José Antonio MQ Sosa	Editor	4.2	
Estate of Beatriz MQ Sosa de Mackhenie	–	4.2	
Pepita MQ Sosa de Rapuzzi	–	4.2	
Total stock			16.8
IV. Luís MQ de la Guerra			
Luís MQ de la Guerra	General Director	13.3	
Alejandro MQ Garland	Director	5.4	
Luís MQ Garland	Sunday director	5.4	
Enriqueta MQ Garland de Graña	–	5.4	

Table 8.1.   (Continued)

Lineage (Children of José Antonio MQ in Birth Order)/ Name	Position	Percentage of Stock	
Elvira MQ Garland	–	5.4	
Luís MQ Valega	Credit and collections section	0.1	
Total stock			35.0
V. Oscar MQ de la Guerra			
Oscar MQ de la Guerra	Chairman board/ scientific editor	13.3	
Francisco MQ Cantuarias	Sunday director	1.8	
Total stock		15.1	
VI. Miguel MQ de la Guerra			
No descendants		0.0	
			100%

ª *Source: El Comercio,* September 19, 1972. This table does not include one board position and a corresponding small block of stock held in common by *El Comercio's* employees under the "Industrial community" arrangement imposed on all large enterprises by the present government.

Prensa in 1947, Beltrán visited major dailies in the United States and returned to introduce modern journalistic techniques to Peru. Under Beltrán, *La Prensa* featured captivating headlines, terse prose, and a more attractive makeup. *La Prensa* learned to get the news out faster than *El Comercio*. Even the business side of *La Prensa* ran more efficiently than the equivalent operation at *El Comercio*, which had faced no serious competition since the early 1920s.

El Comercio was forced to modernize in response to *La Prensa's* challenge. Nonetheless, Beltrán made serious inroads into the Miró Quesadas' advertising and readership. By 1968, *La Prensa* had 40 percent of the advertising market, against *El Comercio's* 32 percent. *La Prensa's* circulation of 135,000 exceeded *El Comercio's* 106,400 (Gargurevich 1972: 59, 139).

What *La Prensa* never achieved, never could achieve, was the sense of solid tradition and integrity that surrounded the Miró Quesadas and their paper. There was no way to duplicate the age of *El Comercio* (founded in 1839) or the enormous social prestige of the Miró Quesada name. And the very stodginess of the paper, its sober, solemn, conservative atmosphere, only reinforced its special position. The lesson was nowhere so evident as on the social page. If "sociales" in *La Prensa* had a tabloid flavor and found space for the nouveaux riches, *El Comercio's* counterpart was a veritable social register and recognized as such. Thus, the Miró Quesadas were powerful arbitrators of Lima society, even if sociales in *El Comercio* was tedious reading.

El Comercio had made the Miró Quesadas rich and powerful, but in the late 1950s they were far from invulnerable. That was demonstrated by the response to *El Comercio's* nationalistic editorial campaign against the American-owned International Petroleum Company. The company's friends inside and outside of the Prado government began to mobilize diverse pressures against *El Comercio* and the Miró Quesadas. The government suddenly decided to examine *El Comercio*'s tax situation and discovered that its owners were in arrears. Advertisers were placed under strong pressure to withhold business from *El Comercio*, from a radio station owned by the paper, and from a television channel the Miró Quesadas were setting up in a partnership with NBC. They were even subject to social pressure for the paper's stand against the American company. It was charged in some upper-class social circles (and implied in the columns of *La Prensa*) that the Miró Quesadas were becoming "communists." Political observers in Lima were convinced that Beltrán, whose paper supported the IPC, was orchestrating the anti-Miró Quesada campaign.

While the clan was too proud to yield to these concerted pressures and abandon its editorial position, the attack subjected them to serious financial losses. *El Comercio* was forced to give up its interest in the radio station (although Alejandro Miró Quesada, Luís' son, retained a significant share on his own), and abandon what had been a potentially very lucrative venture in television (Zimmerman 1968: 168–169).

El Comercio's IPC stand was not surprising. The Miró Quesadas were consistent nationalists, especially in regard to matters concerning the control of mineral resources.[13] But the IPC editorial campaign which *El Comercio* launched in the 1950s also reflected a major ideological shift at the paper, abandoning the reactionary stance of the 1930s. In its criticism of Prado's government and in a battle of editorials waged with *La Prensa*, *El Comercio* defined a new political position in opposition to Beltrán's laissez faire liberalism and the APRA-oligarchy Convivencia.[14] The Miró Quesadas known in Lima for their aristocratic values and right-wing politics began to call for the economic and social modernization of Peru.

El Comercio's editorials now called attention to problems such as malnutrition, poor housing, and low levels of education, which reflected the backward state of the national economy. No one doubted the need for economic development, but the Miró Quesadas distinguished themselves from Beltrán by calling for state involvement in the economy to promote growth, placing greater emphasis on *national* control of the economy, and noting the need for *redistribution* along with growth.

El Comercio favored a strong, activist state that would promote progressive capitalist development. In repeated editorials it called for a national economic plan, outlining national needs and prescribing concrete programs to meet them. The emphasis was on development of the internal market through a process of import-substitution industrialization, an idea which was, by then, national policy in much of Latin America. *El Comercio* explicitly challenged the interests of the exporter majority of the oligarchy by calling (rather inelegantly) for "a substantial modification of the predominantly exporter economic regime, which each year must pay more for imported goods and resign itself to receiving less for each ton it exported" (August 20, 1960).

An important element in *El Comercio*'s program was agrarian reform, to modernize the country's agriculture, counter social injustice, and reduce rural social tensions. Redistribution in the countryside was seen as the key to an expansion of the internal market, providing a consumer basis for industrialization (Editorials, March 6 and August 4, 1959).

THE ROOTS OF ARISTOCRATIC REFORMISM:
ENEMIES AND ALLIES

How had this ideological transformation of the Miró Quesadas and their newspaper come about? Certainly there was little in the political positions which the family had maintained since 1930 which would lead anyone to expect it. Interviews with family members and a number of close family associates suggest that the Miró Quesadas were responding to new political and business pressures in the 1950s but were also influenced by deep-rooted family values. The Convivencia left the Miró Quesadas as odd men out. The family felt a need to define a new political position for themselves and, implicitly, to seek new political allies. At the same time, the Miró Quesadas were concerned with the future stability of Peruvian society. If a radical upheaval like the Cuban Revolution were to be avoided in Peru, the country would have to embark on a program of reform (Editorial, January 4, 1961). As a key family member explained it, the editorial demand for "social justice" grew out of a "sense of realism" about existing conditions.

The Miró Quesadas were also responding to the challenge from Beltrán and *La Prensa*. Since the 1930s, the two papers had conducted periodic editorial battles over monetary policy, with *La Prensa* defending the interests of its planter owners and *El Comercio* defending the commercial and industrial sectors dependent on imports. The Miró Quesadas themselves were importers, having no significant economic interest outside the paper, which required imported newsprint, ink, and machinery. But once Beltrán took over *La Prensa* the conflict between the two papers moved to a new level. *El Comercio* was faced with serious commercial competition for the first time in several decades. Intellectually, Beltrán's well-argued editorials also presented a challenge.

The editorial battle over the IPC's claims was intense. It engaged the immense family pride of the Miró Quesadas and particularly that of the family patriarch Luís. *La Prensa* impugned Miró Quesadas' patriotism and suggested they were becoming Communists. At one point *La Prensa* questioned actions taken forty years previously by Antonio on the claims later involved in the IPC matter. Antonio's sons, Carlos and Joaquin, were so outraged by the insult to their assassinated father's memory that they challenged Beltrán to a duel. Beltrán rejected their offer with great fanfare.[15]

It was under these conditions that the family's more reform-oriented members began to gain increased influence in family councils. Notable among them was Francisco Miró Quesada Canturarias, the philosopher and university professor who would become an important leader of Belaúnde's Acción Popular Party. In a process which a family member later described as "taking advantage of the psychology of Luis" and the family leaders closest to him, the family's reformers used Beltrán's contumelies to argue for a broadening of *El Comercio*'s political response. "Every time Luís got mad at Beltrán, *El Comercio* moved further to the left," recalled one of them. The ideological transformation of the newspaper was by no means a smooth process. In fact, there were many heated arguments over the publication of particular articles.

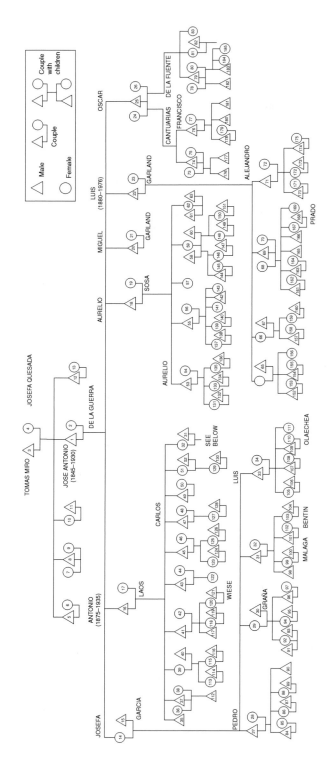

Figure 8.1. Genealogy of the Miró Quesadas.

1. José Antonio Miró Quesada de la Guerra
2. Matilde de la Guerra
3. Tomás Miró
4. Josefa Quesada
5. Tomás Miró Quesada
6. María Chenet
7. Rosaura Colmenares
8. Joaquín Miró Quesada
9. Teresa Ingunsa
10. Josefa Miró Quesada
11. Juan Vallarino.
12. Gregorio Miró Quesada
13. Manuela Carassa
14. Josefa Miró Quesada de la Guerra
15. Pedro García Yrigoyen
16. Antonio Miró Quesada de la Guerra
17. María Laos
18. Aurelio Miró Quesada de la Guerra
19. Rosa Sosa
20. Miguel Miró Quesada de la Guerra
21. María Garland
22. Luis Miró Quesada de la Guerra
23. Elvira Garland
24. Josefina Cantuarias
25. Oscar Miró Quesada de la Guerra
26. Rita de la Fuente
27. Pedro García Miró
28. Talía Elguera
29. Josefina García Miró
30. Carlos Graña Elizalde
31. José Antonio García Miró
32. Delfina Miró Quesada Laos
33. Luis García Miró
34. Licia Elguera
35. José Antonio Miró Quesada
36. Enriqueta Pardo
37. Manuel Miró Quesada Laos
38. Rosa Larco de la Fuente
39. Amalia Miró Quesada Laos
40. José Ignacio Chopitea
41. Joaquín Miró Quesada Laos
42. María Cornejo Parro
43. Hernán Miró Quesada Laos
44. Marishka Dudek
45. Enrique Miró Quesada Laos
46. Carmen Inés Arias

47. Carlos Miró Quesada Laos
48. Rosa Moreyra Paz Soldán
49. Raúl Miró Quesada Laos
50. Reneé Tenaud
51. María Matilde Miró Quesada Laos
52. Alberto Marsano Campodónico
53. Aurelio Miró Quesada Sosa
54. Elizabeth Martens von Ohlendoff
55. José Antonio Miró Quesada Sosa
56. Isabel Ferreyros Pérez Velasco
57. Rosa Miró Quesada Sosa
58. Mario Matta Echaurren
59. Josefa Miró Quesada Sosa
60. Luis Papuzzi de Albertis
61. José del Campo Freudt
62. Beatriz Miró Quesada Sosa
63. Carlos Mackehenie de la Fuente
64. Elvira Miró Quesada Garland
65. Bernardo Roca Rey
66. Enriqueta Miró Quesada Garland
67. Alejandro Graña Garland
68. Leonor Valega Sayán
69. Luis Miró Quesada Garland
70. Alicia Hudtwalcker
71. Alejandro Miró Quesada Garland
72. Adriana Cisneros Ferreyros
73. Jean Salevo
74. Oscar Miró Quesada Cantuarias
75. Eva Mack
76. Francisco Miró Quesada Cantuarias
77. Doris Rada Jordán
78. Alicia Vegas
79. Alfonso Miró Quesada de la Fuente
80. Susana Koecklin
81. Marta Miró Quesada de la Fuente
82. Konrad Meier
83. Victoria Miró Quesada de la Fuente
84. Pedro García Miró Elguera
85. Suzanne George
86. Telia García Miró Elguera
87. Hernando de Lavalle
88. Cecelia García Miró Elguera
90. Miguel García Miró Elguera
91. José de la Riva Agüero
92. Josefa Graña García Miró
93. Roberto Rizzo

94. Malena Graña García Miró
95. John Cannock Espejo
96. Carlos Graña García Miró
97. Diana Pardo Alvarez Calderón
98. José Antonio García Miró Quesada
99. Delfina García Miró Quesada
100. Pablo Llona Málaga
101. Manuel García Miró Quesada
102. María Amalia Bentín
103. Amalia García Miró Quesada
104. Federico Palacios Sosa
105. Licia García Miró Elguera
106. José Carrillo Ramos
107. Luis García Miró Elguera
108. Eleana Peschiera
109. Carlos García Miró Elguera
110. Augusto Olaechea Aljobín
111. Magdalena García Miró Elguera
112. Manuel Miró Quesada Larco
113. Amalia Chopitea Miró Quesada
114. Francisco Palacio Moreyra
115. Rosa Chopitea Miró Quesada
116. Alejandro Tudela Garland
117. Joaquín Miró Quesada Cornejo
118. María Miró Quesada Cornejo
119. Jorge de Orbegoso González
120. Delfina Miró Quesada Cornejo
121. Guillermo Wiese de Osma
122. Marysienka Miró Quesada Dudek
123. María del Carmen Miró Quesada Arias
124. Peter Cannock Espejo
125. Cecilia Miró Quesada
126. Dionisio Peláez
127. María Miró Quesada Moreyra PS
128. Enrique Graces Sinz
129. Matilde Marsano Miró Quesada
130. Juan Plenge Washburn
131. Elizabeth Miró Quesada Martens
132. Martín Yrigoyen
133. Beatriz Miró Quesada Martens
134. Jaime Mujica Diez Canseco
135. Milagros Miró Quesada Martens
136. Emilio Rodríguez Carrain
137. Isabel Miró Quesada Ferreyros
138. Michael Sydney
139. Carmen Miró Quesada Ferreyros

140. Octavio de la Romaña
141. Inés Miró Quesada Ferreyros
142. Jose Antonio Miró Quesada Ferreyros
143. Silvia Miró Quesada Ferreyros
144. Mario Matta Miró Quesada
145. María Isabel Hormazábal
146. Josefa Matta Miró Quesada
147. Victor Coll
148. Ana María Rapuzzi Miró Quesada
149. Jaime de Orbegoso
150. Rapuzzi Miró Quesada
151. Alberto Céspedes
152. Bernardo Roca Miró Quesada
153. Cristina Deatchi
154. Alvero Roca Miró Quesada
155. Susana Arias Colfer
156. Elvira Aldonza Roca Miró Quesada
157. José Alejandro Graña Miró Quesada
158. Teresa Cánepa Yori
159. Enriqueta Graña Miró Quesada
160. Luis Brañein Aguapara
161. Miguel Miró Quesada Valega
162. Valery Scott
163. Luis Miró Quesada Valega
164. Rosemarie Elejalde
165. Juan José Miró Quesada Valega
166. Rafael Miró Quesada Valega
167. Lenor Miró Quesada Valega
168. Mariano Prado Sosa
169. María Soledad Miró Quesada Valega
170. Alejandro Miró Quesada Cisneros
171. Cecilia Quintero
172. María del Pilar Miró Quesada Cisneros
173. Carlos Benavides
174. Gabriel Miró Quesada Cisneros
175. Sussy Bohanovich
176. Oscar Miró Quesada Salevo
177. Ronald Miró Quesada Salevo
178. Francisco Miró Quesada Rada
179. Ana María Wesphalen
180. Eduardo Miró Quesada Rada
181. Diego Miró Quesada Rada
182. Racso Miró Quesada Vega
183. Alfonso Miró Quesada Koechlin
184. Ursula Miró Quesada Koechlin
185. Analise Miró Quesada Koechlin

Figure 8.1. (Continued)

There were limits beyond which the family's fundamentally conservative leadership could not be pushed. *El Comercio* did not, for instance, give up the basic anti-union bias which had been evident even in Luís' writings on labor reform at the beginning of the century. The attitude was apparent both in *El Comercio*'s editorial columns and its attitude toward its own employees.[16] (Beltrán had accepted and come to terms with an APRA-dominated union at *La Prensa* in the 1950s, but the owners of *El Comercio* would still be resisting unionization in the 1970s.) The reformers never came anywhere near getting everything they wanted, but the changed political atmosphere of the editorial page and the Sunday magazine, which was their particular redoubt, reflected their efforts.

The Miró Quesadas' new politics implied new political allies. But in the first electoral test of that proposition in 1962, *El Comercio* was ambivalent. Of the three presidential candidates—APRA's Haya de la Torre, former president Odria, and Belaúnde—the paper supported two: Odría, whose exporter-dominated regime had embodied virtually everything they were fighting in Beltrán, and Belaúnde, the reformer whose ideas seemed more in tune with *El Comercio*'s new line. Apparently, the Miró Quesadas were willing to accept anyone before Haya; their feelings about APRA transcended all ideological questions. But the refusal to choose between Odría and Belaúnde reflected continuing division in the family. The García Miró branch of the family (figure 8.1) had close ties to Odría, and in fact one of its younger members ran for Congress on Odría's ticket. Aurelio Miró Quesada Sosa and reformers such as Francisco favored Belaúnde. The patriarch, who was not known for reticence about his political opinions, had no preference.

El Comercio responded to Haya's slim plurality in the balloting that year with a vociferous campaign to have the elections annulled (Miró Quesada Cáceres 1974). A tense, uncertain political atmosphere prevailed for several weeks after the balloting. Some forty-eight hours before the 1962 military coup, Luís flew back to Lima from Europe and consulted privately with military leaders. Exactly what passed between them or what effect it had on the military's thinking cannot be known. But the members of the new junta could hardly have been surprised at *El Comercio*'s enthused response to their takeover.

Odría's failed attempt to arrange an alliance with APRA on the eve of the coup put an end to the Miró Quesadas' political schizophrenia. There could be no question of supporting a man who would make a deal with the APRA devil. The family's reformers took advantage of the new situation. In the 1963 election *El Comercio* exclusively supported Belaúnde, now the only trustworthy anti-Aprista presidential candidate.

The paper supported President Belaúnde as he struggled with the obstructionist Odriísta-Aprista Coalition in Congress. With most of the oligarchy now supporting the Coalition—in effect, a broadened Convivencia—the Miró Quesadas were more isolated than ever. In 1964, APRA used its position in Congress to force the censure and removal of Belaúnde's education minister, Francisco Miró Quesada Cantuarias, after the raucous session described in chapter 1.

THE ROOTS OF ARISTOCRATIC REFORMISM:
FAMILY VALUES

Beyond contempt for APRA and the Convivencia, the ideological transformation of *El Comercio* was rooted in a set of values that family members themselves describe *aristocratizantes* (aristocratic). Notable among them were family loyalty, personal *dignidad*, patriotism, and social hierarchy. Loyalty to family (i.e., the extended patriarchal family) is clearly the most closely held of these values. "What a man most values," Luís said shortly before his ninety-fifth birthday, "is his family name." The last editorial the Miró Quesadas published in *El Comercio* before it was seized by the military government on July 26, 1974, argued that "loyalty to family" was the foundation of society. As a member of another oligarchic family observed in an interview, if you offended one of the Miró Quesadas, you offended them all. "There is a definite line with them and when you cross it, you feel it." Loyalty to family long held the Miró Quesadas together. Ironically, there would be moments in the Miró Quesadas' confrontation with the military when suspicion of *disloyalty* fomented severe tensions among family members.

The traditional Latin American concept of *dignidad de la persona* is the basis of another Miró Quesada value. According to anthropologist John Gillin, writing in the 1950s, dignidad refers to "the inner integrity or worth which every person is supposed to have originally and which he is supposed to guard jealously. . . . [A] person who submits abjectly and without emotion to slurs upon it is usually regarded as much 'lower' than one who merely breaks the laws established by society. Thus, words or actions that are interpreted as *insults* to the individual's soul are highly explosive. . .. " (Gillin 1965: 508). A family member who listed defense of dignidad among the central values with which the Miró Quesadas had been raised defined it as "the determination not to allow oneself to be dominated by anyone." Members of the clan, he emphasized, are ready "to draw the sword. . . . This we all have."

Family members linked the concept of dignidad to family loyalty. For instance, in 1902 Luís, his younger brother Oscar, and two companions were involved in a violent incident growing out of articles in an anti-establishment publication which were considered insulting to the Miró Quesadas. *La Idea Libre* had printed an article stating that the first Miró Quesada in Peru had supported themselves collecting human excrement, in the years before Lima had modern sanitation (a job, at the time generally assigned to Lima's Chinese). In order to prevent publication of another such article by the journal, Luís led the group to a direct confrontation with its editor in which a close friend of the family was killed.[17]

Another value shared by the Miró Quesadas is "love of the fatherland" (as one of them phrased it). The humiliating defeat of Peru in the 1879 conflict with Chile (during which Luís himself was born) left an indelible impression on family thinking. It led the clan to insist on the need for military strength and to resist any suggestion that Peru should compromise any dispute with its neighbors or with foreign companies, like the IPC.[18] Beltrán's suggestions that Antonio had somehow been unpatriotic with regard to IPC mineral claims was intolerable in a way that other insults he had thrown at *El Comercio* and its owners were not.

Finally, the Miró Quesadas valued social hierarchy and shared a sense of their right to a leading position in society. Though they were, at various points in their history, strong backers of social reform, they never accepted egalitarianism as a reform goal. In the 1950s and 1960s, they were aristocratic reformers, who believed that change must come from above. In a 1974 interview Luís made a distinction between "reformers" and "*resentidos*" (literally "the resentful ones").[19] "The resentful ones are those who want to do away with society." And who are the resentful ones? "They are those who have no name." Presumably, no family name, no social position. "Social reform," he continued, "must be made with a sense of nobility. And that is what they lack." Such comments are not particularly surprising from a man who was born to privilege two decades before the end of the nineteenth century. Another key family member, many years Luís' junior, repelled by the Velasco government's populist appeals, commented, "Demagoguery it seems to me, is in *very poor taste*." A third member of the clan revealed a related sentiment in this observation about what he described as the central problem of politics: "It is impossible to govern with the masses. Every government must neutralize them."

Seen in the context of Peruvian political history since 1930, such attitudes imply a contempt for APRA's middle-class leaders, based on their use of the lower-classes to force their way into the Peruvian political system. For the Miró Quesadas, a middle-class, provincial, mestizo APRA leader burning with hatred of the white metropolitan elite would have been the archetypical resentido. The Miró Quesadas exposed their conception of how Peru should be ruled in 1956 when, with the help of in-law Augusto Wiese, they organized a convention of notables, heavily weighted with oligarchic figures, but excluding the one party with a mass following, to nominate a consensus presidential candidate. The gathering, an archaic gesture reminiscent of the 1915 convention which placed Civilista José Pardo in the presidency, failed miserably.[20]

Were these same values held by other oligarchic clans? Probably, yes, by many, but in varying degrees. Beltrán was said to regard the more aristocratic notions of the Miró Quesadas as ludicrous, but Beltrán was more Anglo-Saxonized than most upper-class Peruvians. The Prados were closer to the Miró Quesada pattern. Among the Aspíllagas, these values seem to have weakened over time. Certainly, notions of family loyalty, dignidad, and hierarchy/right-to rule were common among the oligarchs at mid-twentieth century. But these ideals were seldom so intensely held, so defining for the family, as they were for the Miró Quesadas.

THE MIRÓ QUESADAS AND THE REVOLUTION OF THE ARMED FORCES

Whether the Miró Quesadas wanted the October 3, 1968, coup that ended the Old Regime is unclear, but they helped bring it about. *El Comercio* had maintained the life of the IPC question and was critical of the Belaunde administration's settlement with the company. For that reason alone a bitter oligarch interviewed several years after the coup blamed the Miró Quesadas for the revolutionary military government that he despised.

The Miró Quesadas had tutored the armed forces for the role they would take on after 1968. *El Comercio* had continuously directed the attention of the military to the problem of petroleum. For instance, in 1959 it praised the incorporation of the military into a national petroleum council, saying that oil was "a strategic element which ought to be protected" (November 9, 1959). More broadly, the paper had connected national defense with the problems of underdevelopment. "[W]ithin the modern concept the country is stronger the further it is from underdevelopment. And for that reason when the armed forces contribute to improve the standard of living of the population it is strengthening . . . the defense of Peru" (April 4, 1962). Moreover, the paper had praised the development studies being carried on at CAEM (May 10, 1959). In 1959, Luís' son, Alejandro Miró Quesada, lectured there on the need for national planning (Villanueva 1972: 93).

Whatever influence *El Comercio* had on the military's reorientation must have been amplified by the Miró Quesadas' long-standing support of the armed forces and personal ties to military officers. General Valasco, for example, was on friendly terms with certain family members well before the coup that made him president. José Antonio had had close friendships with military officers. Of course, the family descend from a line with a strong military tradition. Through most of the twentieth century there have been high-ranking officers from these Miró Quesada collateral lines, with whom the newspaper family maintained ties. Two of these military Miró Quesadas served in Velasco's government.

El Comercio's influence among the officer corps was enhanced by its consistent defense of the interests of the armed forces. The paper always supported military expenditures and glorified the national role of the military.[21] At the same time, the Miró Quesadas appealed to and cultivated the military's historic anti-APRA sentiments.

For months after the military takeover in October 1968, *El Comercio* defended the new regime and its modernization program. The following May, the paper editorialized, "Those who govern us today have assumed the responsibility of guiding a process of national transformation. Many reforms are necessary to elevate the standard of living of each Peruvian. . . . Some . . . will frighten those who still affect ancient privileges. But they must be undertaken. The revolutionary government has given its word and will receive the support of the country. . . ." (May 11, 1969). The editorial makes an implicit distinction between the Miró Quesadas themselves and the privileged class—a distinction, which, it turned out, meant little to the new government.

By mid-1970, it was apparent from *El Comercio*'s editorials that the family leadership had recognized that the government's intentions were far more radical than anything they had anticipated or could accept. While there were those in the family who, having moved leftward in the course of the 1960s, were sympathetic to the government and privately maintained contacts with officials, they were unable to prevail on Luís. The paper began to criticize the regime's policies.

The break became definitive with an editorial which Luís regarded, at the time he penned it, as the last of his life. He was on his way to the United States for an operation he could not expect to survive at the age of ninety. The editorial may well have been directed as much at his own family as it was at the government and the readers of *El Comercio*. Titled "Where Is the Government Leading the Country?" the editorial reaffirmed the paper's commitment to democratic change, but severely criticized recent government actions which, Luís argued, compromised judicial integrity and freedom of the press. Peru had reached a point at which "fundamental values of Western, 'Christian Civilization'" were at stake. Those fundamental values ranged from democracy to "the necessity of private property under law" (*El Comercio* 1970: 71–74).

In the course of 1970 and for the remainder of the time *El Comercio* remained under the control of the Miró Quesadas, the paper's readers would hear a great deal about both civil liberties and private property.[22] The latter notion was not one which had received frequent attention in the paper since the early 1950s. Concern with the rights of private property was more likely to emanate from Beltrán's *La Prensa*. The aristocratic modernizers who owned *El Comercio* had been forced to recognize that they too were part of a propertied class threatened by revolution.

The defection of the Miró Quesadas was not received well by the government and its closest supporters. The enormous prestige of the family and the paper they controlled, their influence among the military, and the credentials they had established for themselves in recent years as supporters of democratic modernization all contributed to the impact of the position they were taking. Beginning in 1970, *El Comercio* and the Miró Quesadas were the target of attacks from government organs (especially the daily *Expreso*) and from certain high-ranking government officials.

By 1973, bitter charges and countercharges were being traded on an almost daily basis between *El Comercio* and its new enemies. It became apparent that there was conflict at the top of the military government over the treatment of the paper, which, in turn, reflected a profound division over the direction of the revolution itself. For the more radically inclined, discrediting the paper and its owners became an urgent matter in the internal debate.

LABOR AND LOYALTY AT *EL COMERCIO*

El Comercio's opponents chose to attack the Miró Quesadas at the one point where they were weakest: labor relations.[23] The Miró Quesadas dealt with their employees in a traditional manner that was appropriate to their aristocratic values. They expected loyalty and obedience from those who served them. For those who committed no serious transgression on either ground, there was very little chance of ever being dismissed. Salaries were low, though a small group of employees on all levels who were close to the family were compensated handsomely and treated kindly. When salaries were being negotiated in 1971, the Miró Quesadas proposed "loyalty" as one criterion (*Expreso*, June 6, 1971).

As one of Lima's best known journalists later commented, "*El Comercio* languished in a paternalist limbo." The atmosphere surrounding the key family figures, including Luís, his son Alejandro, and nephew Aurelio, was one of "total reverence." They isolated themselves from most of their employees. A former member of the news staff described the difficulties of obtaining an interview with Alejandro in the following terms: "You had to get past a porter. Just about impossible. If he opened the door for you, you had to confront a secretary and to get past her—well, perhaps if the place was burning down or something." A reporter who had worked for the Miró Quesadas later commented that it was easier to get an interview with the president of the republic than with Luís Miró Quesada.

A distant relative of the family who worked at the paper recalled a daily ritual that epitomized the gulf separating the Miró Quesadas from their workers. Luís would arrive at the paper at five in the afternoon and take tea. For the event, a liveried butler with white gloves would depart from the cafeteria and transit the entire length of the building carrying an enormous silver tea service. "He would walk past all those poorly paid employees, proud because he was one of the few who got past that door into the realm of Don Luís."

Unionization, as far as the Miró Quesadas were concerned, was unthinkable. Until the Velasco government came into power there had never been a union at *El Comercio* and any employee who participated in union organizing was quickly dismissed. Moreover, according to Gargurevich (1972: 18), *El Comercio* had never lost a case before the Labor Ministry authorities. This in itself was an indication of the immense power of the Miró Quesadas and their paper.[24]

The labor situation at *La Prensa* was very different. There had been a union (APRA dominated) since Beltrán's early years at the paper, and salaries were higher than those at *El Comercio*. Beltrán made himself accessible to those who worked for him and mixed easily with them on informal occasions. *La Prensa* proved impervious to the sort of labor problems that were foisted on *El Comercio* under the military government. One of the Miró Quesadas later suggested that the bourgeois Beltrán had an important advantage over the Miró Quesadas with their aristocratic notions: "All he was interested in was profit."

Before *El Comercio*'s labor difficulties began, the family received explicit warnings. Their enemies in the regime wanted the paper's editorial line to swing back to the government and they wanted Francisco, who was regarded as sympathetic to the government, to displace the ancient Luís as director. They also wanted Aurelio and Alejandro removed from their positions. "The military said, 'If you don't accept this, we are going to do away with *El Comercio*.'" This was hardly the best approach to take with the Miró Quesadas. It somehow assumed that Luís was a general who could be relieved of his command when necessary, rather than a prince who held his position as a birthright. Above all, it underestimated the boundless pride of the Miró Quesadas. They could never think of acceding to such pressure.

When their labor problems began, family leaders were shocked to learn how vulnerable they were. Perhaps their isolation from the great majority of their employees led them to overestimate the loyalty of those who were outside the charmed circle of favor-ites.[25] Between early 1971 and July 1974, *El Comercio* passed through a series of strikes and assorted work stoppages. On several occasions the paper was off the newsstands for a week or more. In 1973 a strike closed the paper for a full month, during which the workers were in full control of the plant for at least five days. In the course of these conflicts the Miró Quesadas were forced to accept a union for the first time, required to reestablish the afternoon tabloid, *El Comercio Grafico,* which had been discontinued because it was proving unprofitable, and compelled to accept large wage increases.

Statements by certain government officials and labor leaders (some of whom would occupy important positions at the paper after it was seized by the government in 1974) left little doubt that political considerations were at least as important as labor issues in these events.[26]

The 1973 strike proved very damaging to the family itself. Where Beltrán's attacks had drawn the family together, the revolutionary government's campaign against the Miró Quesadas pulled it apart. Many family members believed that Francisco, who was by then regarded in some family quarters as a left-wing "extremist," was conspir-ing with the government to force himself into Luís' place. The accusation, apparently unfounded, was vehemently denied by Francisco. Relations between his branch of the family and the rest of the clan were not improved when Francisco's eldest son Paco, who was working as an editor, announced that he was joining the strike then in progress and marched into the plant to the cheers of the occupying employees. In the family code, this betrayal was the worst conceivable sin. Although Francisco subsequently required his son to leave the paper, the damage was done. Ironically, Paco, who had exercised his family right as an eldest son to gain the position, could not be fired under existing law.

In mid-1974, a contentious debate over press freedom erupted in Lima. Members of the military cabinet publicly disagreed, a very rare event. A related controversy surrounded a solidarity luncheon of leading Peruvian and foreign journalists, at which the best known of the diners was Luís Miró Quesada. Not long after the lun-cheon, the navy reportedly attempted a coup, and Admiral Luís Vargas Caballero, who had been *El Comercio*'s staunchest defender in the government, was forced out of the cabinet. These events were prologue to the expropriation on July 27, 1974, of the Lima dailies, including *El Comercio.* It was the government's stated intention to remove the newspapers from the control of families or narrow interest groups, and turn them into organs of expression for the major sectors of the revolution. *El Comercio* was designated to serve the nation's peasants. In retrospect, it was apparent that the expropriations and the related 1974 press law grew out of the defection of the Miró Quesadas (DESCO 1974).

ECONOMIC BASE AND POLITICAL POWER

The Miró Quesadas differed from other oligarchic clans in their economic base and the character of the political power they exercised. Family members repeatedly asserted that *El Comercio*'s editorial integrity was guaranteed by the fact that they had no economic interest outside the newspaper. The claim to exclusive dependence on the paper is substantially correct, excepting the broadcasting ventures of the 1950s. Their economic situation did allow them a degree of independence not shared by their chief competitor, *La Prensa,* which for decades was closely tied to major land-owning interests. But *El Comercio* was itself an economic interest to be defended. It is not surprising that *El Comercio,* employer of a large un-unionized work force, was strongly anti-union, or that the defender of import interests in a long series of monetary policy controversies was dependent on imported newsprint, ink, and machinery, or, finally, that the paper, a lucrative private enterprise, resisted a military government that seemed bent on destroying private enterprise.

At times the patriotism, family pride, and integrity of the Miró Quesadas led them into positions which hurt them economically. But it would be a stretch to claim that they were indifferent to their own interests or somehow above social class. The Miró Quesadas had extensive ties to other oligarchic families and to the exclusive Inner Social Circle of upper-class society, as the analysis in the next chapter will show.

El Comercio allowed the descendants of José Antonio to maintain a sumptuous lifestyle. Luís in his nineties, seated in his palatial residence, commented, "I have sought to live in the best possible fashion. I am obligated to do so." He was ranked #186 among the top 500 taxpayers in the country in 1970. Five other members of the family were on the list (*El Comercio,* April 26, 1972).

Despite their affluence, the Miró Quesadas had none of the money-based political power that was characteristic of the oligarchy. Their economic "empire" consisted largely of the newspaper. Above all, they had none of the control over capital that made the Prados and the major sugar growers so powerful. The power of the Miró Quesadas rested on their editorial control of *El Comercio,* the country's most influen-tial newspaper. When *El Comercio* opined, its opinion needed to be taken seriously. If *El Comercio* thought a person or an issue was noteworthy, they were. Two very important groups were thought to be especially attentive to *El Comercio*: the middle class and the officer corps.

The influence of *El Comercio* emerged repeatedly in interviews and informal conver-sations with educated Peruvians. An agrarian reform official in the Velasco government admitted begrudgingly, "I always read *El Comercio*. It was independent, not like *La Prensa*. You could trust it more than the others, anyway, because it wasn't tied to the interests." "They talk of the seriousness of *El Comercio,*" said a retired university presi-dent. "Its opinion always carried weight." Another kind of influence was suggested by a journalist who noted, "People had great fear of an attack in *El Comercio*."

El Comercio's most determined efforts to influence national politics came in regard to APRA. The Miró Quesadas used the paper to construct barriers to the party's access to legitimate power. *El Comercio* insisted that APRA was akin to Communism, that it was anti-Catholic (not that the Miró Quesadas were especially religious themselves), anti-patriotic, anti-military, and guilty of creating assassins. Annually, *El Comercio* rehearsed the gruesome details of the murder of Antonio and his wife in 1935 by a young Aprista and of the execution of military prisoners by Aprista fighters in the 1932

Trujillo uprising. The latter was a particularly important occasion, because it enabled the paper to appeal directly to anti-APRA sentiments among the military.

El Comercio's anti-APRA crusade extended beyond the explicitly political realm. Apristas, especially the more prominent members of the party, became non-persons as far as *El Comercio* was concerned. Their names were not allowed to appear in the paper, even on the social page. This denial seemed to de-legitimate their very existence. An Aprista congressman tacitly conceded the effectiveness of this tactic when he complained on the floor of the lower house that the Miró Quesadas were "attempting to govern the country" from the social page of their newspaper (*La Tribuna*, April 28, 1968).

The Miró Quesadas conducted editorial campaigns against governments that incorporated Apristas or proved in any way sympathetic to APRA. In 1945, *El Comercio* helped block General Benavides' return to the presidency. The paper's attacks on Bustamante's National Front government, elected that year with APRA support, helped strip away the cloak of legitimacy that a duly elected government could claim, and encouraged the military intervention of 1948. The paper's most telling success against the party came in the wake of the 1962 elections when its strident editorial campaign encouraged the military to prevent Haya from claiming the presidency when it was finally within his grasp (Miró Quesada Cáceres 1974).

The Miró Quesadas' direct participation in politics after the Aristocratic Republic was limited. Luís served briefly in Sánchez Cerro's first cabinet and Francisco served in Belaúnde's until he was forced out by the APRA-Convivencia opposition. The Miró Quesadas seem also to have been involved, from time to time, in conspiratorial politics. In a 1974 interview, Luís said that he had "conspired" against Leguia with Sánchez Cerro, but did not know in advance of plans for his 1930 Arequipa revolt. The Miró Quesadas did have advance knowledge of General Odria's plans in 1948. Luís, as noted above, seems to have personally encouraged the 1962 military intervention.

Perhaps the Miró Quesadas did not have the financial strength to back a coup or a political campaign. But the threat of unfriendly coverage or hostile editorials had to be taken seriously by other political actors. An illustration of the latter possibility can be drawn from the Prado's first administration. The president reportedly called Luís "urgently" to consult about certain concessions Peru was about to make under pressure from the United States in negotiations with Ecuador. Prado saw no alternatives. "We must do it," he contended. "Then I will write in opposition," responded Luís. Further discussion followed among those present and it was decided to resist concessions (*Oiga*, December 4, 1970).

In Lima, close observers of the clan stressed Luís' near omniscience about political developments. He was frequently consulted by political and military leaders and was described as an adroit player in behind-the-scenes political maneuvering, often dealing through intermediaries like his trusted political editor Baella Tuesta. In the final analysis, though, the exact nature of the Miró Quesadas' closed-door involvement in politics is less important than the power of the paper itself. Whatever persuasiveness they could have had in private depended on that.

NOTES

1. For the early histories of the Miró and Quesada families and the origins and evolution of the surname Miró, see Miró Quesada Sosa 1945: 9–21. On the early history of *El Comercio* and the career of José Antonio see Miró Quesada Sosa 1945; Delgado 1937; *El Comercio* 1894; and centennial edition of May 4, 1939.

2. Miró Quesada Sosa 1945; Tauro 1966; Basadre 1968: XI & XII; Delgado 1937.

3. Basadre 1964: VIII, 3951; Miró Quesada Sosa 1945: 299–300; Pike 1967: 225; Pardo Castro 1961.

4. Capuñay 1951: 188; Pike 1967: 225; Basadre 1968: XV, 146. The family has attempted to deny this (Miró Quesada 1953: I, 261–263) but in general prefers not to dwell on the period.

5. See, for example, several relevant articles in *El Comercio*, January 9, 1932.

6. Delgado 1937: II, 154–155; *El Comercio,* January 22, 1931, cited in Gerlach 1973: 374.

7. See *El Comercio*, January 11 and 12, 1932; January 31, 1933; September 10–16, 1935; November 5–19, 1938; and Miró Quesada 1953: I, 109 & II, 337.

8. See Sánchez 1955: 347–348; Miró Quesada Laos 1959: 137–139; Gerlach 1973: 460–462; and Gargurevich 1972: 14.

9. The descendants through this maternal line adopted the compound surname Garcia Miro to preserve their identity as members of the clan, while distinguishing their own lineage.

10. The son employed at the paper was a member of the paper's board, but the board here, as at other oligarchic enterprises seems to have been a body of no consequence.

11. See Miró Quesada Laos 1959: 190–210; Gargurevich 1972: 16; and *La Prensa*, January 14, 1956.

12. This discussion is based on interviews with a number of Lima journalists and members of the Miró Quesada family and Gargurevich 1972: 147–151.

13. Miró Quesada 1953: I, 11–12, 25–28; Delgado 1937: I, 162–164.

14. Roberto Miró Quesada Cáceres has written a perceptive study (1974) of this ideological conflict on which I have drawn for the present discussion. I am also indebted to him for allowing me to use his notes on *El Comercio* editorials from 1956 to 1962.

15. *El Comercio,* January 27,1960; *La Prensa*, January 20, 1960.

16. See editorials on July 10, 1957, January 1, 1959, August 21, 1968 and Pardo Castro 1961; Gargurevich 1972: 17–18.

17. *Unidad*, August 16, 1973; *Oiga*, December 4, 1970; Gargurevich 1972: 15.

18. Miró Quesada Cáceres 1974; *Oiga*, December 4, 1970; *El Comercio* editorial, July 16, 1974.

19. The latter term was in common usage among upper-class Limeños at the time.

20. *La Prensa*, January 4, 1956; *Unidad*, August 16, 1973, and interviews. Among those invited were J.V. Nicolini, J. de la Piedra, Carlos Moreyra (along with other representatives of Prado's personalist party), Manuel Mujica Gallo, and Pedro Rossello (a close political associate of Beltrán's). Representatives of a series of insignificant minor "parties" were also invited.

21. Editorials November 24, 1956, August 5, 1960, May 18, 1968.

22. Editorials May 8, 1970, August 20, 1970, June 24, 1970.

23. The following account is based on interviews with a number of employees and ex-employees of *El Comercio* (some of whom later worked for *La Prensa*), and with several family members. It is confirmed by Gargurevich 1972: 17–23.

24. Two family members who read this passage noted that the family's resistance to unionization was less about economic issues than concern about APRA's influence in a union, which could be turned against the family and compromise the paper's editorial independence.

25. This account of *El Comercio*'s labor problems is based on extensive clippings in the *La Prensa* Archive during this era, which included articles from *El Comercio, Prensa, Expreso, Oiga,* and other Lima publications. These published materials were supplemented with interviews.

26. *Oiga,* August 17, 1973 and *Extra,* August 2, 1973.

III

CONCLUSIONS

9

Class, Clan, and Cohesion

The domination of an organized minority, obeying a single impulse, over the unorganized majority is inevitable.

—Gaetano Mosca

The preceding chapters describe three oligarchic clans exercising power in changing ways, to varied ends. Their histories illuminate the question of elite cohesion. At certain critical junctures these three families joined with their peers to defend broad class interests that seem to be at risk. The removals of unfriendly governments in 1914 (Billinghurst) and 1948 (Bustamante) are prime example. At other times—most decisively in the last years of the Aristocratic Republic—these families were caught up in intra-elite conflict that weakened oligarchic power. This chapter examines the question of elite cohesion, starting from the perspectives of the Aspíllagas, the Prados, and the Miró Quesadas.

ASPÍLLAGAS

The Aspíllagas were not an especially memorable or colorful clan (in contrast to the Prados and Miró Quesadas). Peruvian history would not have taken a different path had they never existed. But the Aspíllagas are significant because they were representative of the planter core of the oligarchy—the largest, most cohesive, best organized, and most powerful sector of the oligarchy.

The Aspíllaga correspondence, supplemented with interviews, opens a window on planter politics. Two facets stand out: the intensity of collaboration among the planters and the diverse means that the planters employed to gain their political ends. The shared political activity of the planters was not episodic, but more or less continuous. They were in regular contact, conferring quietly, organizing, and plotting. They worked with local and national authorities to suppress labor activity, backed the army's war against APRA with plantation resources, turned *La Prensa* into a powerful voice for exporter interests, promoted press campaigns through the National Agrarian Society, lobbied governments for favorable policies, financed national political campaigns, and organized the overthrow of governments. (The planters, in particular, were responsible for the 1948 coup.) They had potent political resources at their disposal, but ultimately, what made the planters so powerful was cohesion—their capacity, based on shared interests to act collectively.

PRADOS

The drivers of the Prados' political behavior were more idiosyncratic than collective. In this they obviously differed from the Aspíllagas. The second-generation Prado Urgarteche brothers were talented and ambitious but, above all, determined to vindicate the memory of their father by claiming the presidency. The family put forward three brothers, successively and in birth order, as presidential candidates, until the third, Manual Prado Ugarteche, won the presidency in 1939. The power of this family did not depend on ties to other oligarchic clans, though they sometimes collaborated with them. The keys to their political success were the cultivation of close ties to the military and their recognition, early on, that an understanding with APRA was the only way to win power electorally.

Over time, the family's political objectives appeared to shift. The general's vindication seemed less important. Perhaps it had been achieved with Manuel's first presidency. Perhaps it mattered less to the third generation of Prados. The practical importance of power grew relative to its symbolic value as the clan's business interests became increasingly dependent on their political influence. The clan initially resisted Manuel's second presidential bid in 1956, apparently convinced that seeking high office risked dangerous exposure and that holding office was not as important as sustaining less visible forms of power.

The Prados' courtship of APRA earned them the political hostility of the planter core until the late 1950s and that of the Miró Quesadas until the end of the Old Regime. There were reasons, which will be explored below, that urban sector oligarchs, like the Prados, might be more open to APRA than the rural export sector oligarchs were. It could be argued that the Prados' politics were shaped by shared sectoral interests. But the history of the family suggests that it sought power for reasons closer to home.

MIRÓ QUESADAS

The Miró Quesadas were notable for their relentless hostility to APRA and for the trajectory of their politics, which shifted from the moderate labor reformism in the early twentieth century, to an ultra-right wing stance in the 1930s, and, finally, to promotion of a broad program of national modernization in the late 1950s and the 1960s.

During Peru's oligarchic republic, the Miró Quesadas, like the Aspíllagas and the Prados, had been part of the inner circle of Civilista Party. During the contested republic, their combative anti-Aprismo (evident early on, but intensified by the assassination of Antonio Miró Quesada in 1935) united them with the exporter majority of the oligarchy in the politics of the 1930s, 1940s, and early 1950s. But it left the Miró Quesadas out of steep with their peers, as APRA and the oligarchy drew together. In their last political incarnation under the Old Regime, the Miró Quesadas appear, like the Prados, idiosyncratic—driven more by family passions than by class or sectoral interests. None of this would have mattered much were it not for the extraordinary power of their newspaper.

ELITE COHESION AND THE POLITICS OF THE CONTESTED REPUBLIC

Historian Geoffrey Bertram (1991) has interpreted Peruvian politics of the years 1930 to 1960 in terms of a struggle between two factions of the oligarchy: a "right-wing" exporter faction he identifies with the planters, their political leader Pedro Beltrán, and the Miró Quesadas, opposed by an "urban-mercantile" faction he identifies with the Prados. He points to two issues dividing these factions. The first involved monetary policy and exchange rates. As Bertram explains, "Bankers and importers opposed devaluation [of the Peruvian *sol*] and profited from exchange crises; exporters pressed for early devaluation when export markets fell" (401). Each of five monetary crises between 1931 and 1967 was resolved in favor of the exporters. The exchange rate was a recurrent, acrimonious but transitory issue.

A more contentious, more fundamental question revolved around APRA and the labor organizations associated with it. For many years, the exporter-oligarchs, dependent on large numbers of low-wage workers, supported a repressive hard line against the party and labor. According to Bertram, accommodating labor was easier for the urban oligarchs because they could pass their labor costs along to consumers. That was harder for the exporters to do in international markets. The urban elite was thus more open to an understanding with APRA.

Evidence of conflict among the oligarchs is not hard to find. Consider the anonymous circulation of the pamphlet, "Can a Prado Be President of Peru?" rehearsing the family's black legend for voters when the Prado brothers sought the presidency in the 1930s. The planter core of the oligarchy, troubled by the Prados' pro-APRA politics, was behind this gesture. Another example, years later, was the malicious treatment of the Miró Quesadas by their peers when *El Comercio* began promoting a national program of social and economic reform, which threatened the interests of the elite.

The aborted 1936 presidential election has been cited, by Bertram and other historians, as evidence that the oligarchy couldn't rule because the oligarchs were divided. There were four candidates that year, with varying degrees of elite support. The three families related to the contest in different ways. The Prados backed one of their own, Jorge Prado Ugarteche, who was also President Benavides' chosen candidate. The Aspíllagas joined other planters in supporting Manuel Vicente Villarán. The Miró Quesadas seem to have divided among themselves over both national and family issues; *El Comercio* did not endorse anyone in 1936.[1]

Jorge Prado was a member of a powerful oligarchic clan, but he did not have notable oligarchic support outside his own family.[2] There is no indication of oligarchic backing for the other two candidates: Peruvian fascist leader Luís Flores with his black-shirted street fighters or Luís Eguiguren, a moderate, who drew unofficial support from banned APRA.

If the oligarchy had a candidate in 1936, it was Villarán. A distinguished lawyer and scholar who had served in Civilista governments and had been president of the Club Nacional, he was well prepared for the role. His candidacy was organized by Pedro Beltrán, political leader of the planters. According to Gustavo Aspíllaga, writing several months before the election, Villarán "[is] a great man who we are helping in every way. . . . Villarán has with him all the productive forces of the country; that ought to be enough to get him elected," added Aspíllaga hopefully, "but one sees some queer things in politics nowadays" (GAA 6–18–36).[3] Villarán was supported by members of the Mujica, Lavalle, Ayulo, Olaechea clans, in addition to Beltrán, the Aspíllagas, and other planters.[4] This incomplete list is notable for the inclusion of both rural exporters and urban banking families.

The ballot counting, halted by Benavides when the results became obvious, showed Villarán dead last, with a tiny proportion of the popular vote and Eguiguren, with APRA's help, in the lead.[5] If the oligarchs could no longer win elections, it wasn't because they were divided—most lined up behind one candidate—but because they lacked popular support in an era of mass politics, support that only APRA could provide.

The diverse oligarchic support for Villarán in 1936 undercuts the idea of opposed rural/urban oligarchic factions. Bertram himself concedes that the line between the two was sometimes blurry. Peru was so export dependent that the fortunes of bankers, merchants, and newspaper publishers could not be separated from the health of the export economy. As it happens, the great majority of the oligarchs were exporters. Among the twenty-nine families of the oligarchy on the list presented in chapter 1 (table 1.1), twenty-two were exporters, including fifteen planters.[6] The planter core was, as the experience of the Aspíllagas shows, cohesive, well organized, and active. The other significant exporter group, the miners, maintained a lower profile, but followed the planters' lead in politics.

The seven non-exporter families had largely urban interests. They seem to have shared similar views of monetary questions and some were, as Bertram argues, more open to APRA than their rural peers. But it is difficult to think of them as a coherent faction, regularly cooperating in defense of mutual interests, like the exporters. The Miró Quesadas consistently defended urban monetary views in their newspaper, but they were, for more than two decades, on the side of the rural oligarchs with regard to APRA and related presidential politics. In the political maneuvering preceding the 1956 presidential election, Manuel Prado found himself competing for APRA support with Hernando de Lavalle, member of another banking family. Here were two men vying for a big prize and, at the same time, two banks and their associated families fighting over the advantages that would come with the presidency. If there was an urban oligarchic sector, it was not very cohesive.

The notion of a factionalized oligarchy owes something to the outsized influence and high profiles of the Prados and Miró Quesadas. They were bound to be noticed: Only one oligarchic family produced a president during the contested republic, and only one controlled a daily mouthpiece that shaped the national agenda. Both were compelled by family tragedy. The Prados sought historic vindication and, increasingly, protection for their empire, rather than some definable sectoral interest. The Miró Quesadas were arguably motivated by class concerns—as were their oligarchic peers—in their initial vociferous opposition to APRA. But, after 1935, they were driven less by class or sectoral interests than by memory of "the Crime" and a passion for reform rooted in their own aristocratic values. While they called for development of the urban domestic economy, there is no evidence of collaboration between the family and the urban entrepreneurs, oligarchic or otherwise, that their program assumed. In truth, they had no allies.

Rather than thinking of the oligarchy as split into two factions, we should conceive of it as a generally united circle of exporters comprising the majority, led by their planter core, and surrounded by a smaller, less coherent outer circle of urban oligarchs.

COHESION AND ELITE SOCIETY

Over the long history of the Peruvian oligarchy, divergent interests, idiosyncratic concerns, and personal ambitions sometimes divided the oligarchs, but elite society drew them together. The key to the cohesive power of elite society was the dense web of kinship created by decades of endogamous marriages. In the course of three or four generations, affinal (marriage) ties were established among all but a few of the Oligarchic 29 (table 9.1). Seventy-six percent of the families (including the Aspíllagas, Prados, and Miró Quesadas) had at least two links to other oligarchic clans. Three elaborately connected families—the Miró Quesadas, the Prados, and the Pardos—had eight or more links to other clans.[7] However, the oligarchy's social world was not defined by the oligarchic elite itself but, more broadly, by the upper class. There was considerable overlap between the oligarchy and what can be called the Inner Social Circle, the prestigious families at the very center of Lima society.

The membership of the Inner Social Circle was determined with the help of four expert judges: two members of socially prominent Lima families, a society page editor, and another close observer of Lima society. They were asked in the mid-1970s to select the families who, during the previous three decades, were most likely to be invited to exclusive social gatherings; whose own invitations were most valued; and whose children were considered the most socially prestigious marriage prospects. The resulting list of eighty-eight families included twenty of the Oligarchic 29, among them the Aspíllagas, Prados, and Miró Quesadas. There was a high level of affinal connection between the Circle and the oligarchy. A study of 203 oligarchic marriages (all recorded marriages of members of the oligarchy who were about twenty-five to fifty years of age at the time) found that the great majority of oligarchic clans were linked to the Inner Social Circle by at least 25 percent of their marriages (table 9.2).[8] Even among the nine oligarchic families who did not appear on the "society" panel list, six had at least 50% of their marriages to members of the Inner Social Circle.[9] Taken together, these data demonstrate a close identification between the oligarchy and the Inner Social Circle.

The Peruvian oligarchy's social standing and affinal exclusivity can be better appreciated by considering its location within the larger social elite, conceived as a

Table 9.1. Affinal Links among the Oligarchic 29

Number of Families	Links/Family	Cumulative Percentage of Families
1	16	3
1	10	7
1	8	10
4	4	24
7	3	48
8	2	76
2	1	83
5	0	100
N = 29		

Table 9.2. Affinal Links between the Oligarchic 29 and the Inner Social Circle

Number of Families	Percentage of Marriages of Individual Oligarchic Families with All Families of the Top Social Circle	Cumulative Percentage of Families
3	75–100	11
7	50–74	37
10	25–49	74
3	1–24	85
4	0	100.0
TOTAL=27		

NA=2
NA. No marriages in generation studied or data not available.

series of concentric circles. At its core was the Inner Social Circle with fewer than 100 families, surrounded by a wider circle of the 500 families represented in the 1960 member list of the Club Nacional. As noted earlier, two-thirds of the Oligarchic 29 were included in the Inner Social Circle, and all but one were represented in the Club National.[10] The outermost circle encompassed the roughly 3,000 families represented in the 1955 edition of the *Libro de Oro*, a listing of socially "known families," similar to the American *Social Register*. The *Libro de Oro* included many families who would be classified as upper-middle class in economic terms, but who subscribed to values and maintained elements of a lifestyle considered appropriate in upper-class Lima. In particular, they sent their children to elite private schools.

As emphasized in chapter 1, the oligarchs in Peru, as elsewhere in Latin America, were immersed in an intimate social world defined by elite schools, clubs, favored neighborhoods, and summer resorts, but, above all, by marriage and kinship. The exclusivity of this social setting defined them as members of an elect minority, superior to and apart from the vast majority. It also drew them together and acted as a mechanism of social control in politics and business. The oligarchs were sometimes at odds, but the social cost of offending your friends, your kin, your in-laws, your clubmates, and, by extension, people who were important to them dampened the potential for conflict. The enormous social pressure imposed by members of the upper class on the Miró Quesadas in the 1950s and 1960s reminded others of the cost of perceived disloyalty in the upper-class social world.

CONFLICT AND COHESION

Conflict among the oligarchs, a key factor in the disintegration of the oligarchic republics, was less critical to the demise of the contested republics, as the analysis at the end of chapter 3 demonstrated.[11] In the Peruvian case, the countervailing forces bolstering elite cohesion included the social glue of elite society, the shared interests of the exporter majority, and the political leadership of the planter core.

NOTES

1. See discussions of this election and sources cited in chapters 5–8.

2. An exception was Rafael Larco Herrera, a planter who was a vice presidential candidate on Jorge's ticket that year. He was apparently a Pradista, who later was elected first vice president under Manuel Prado in 1939 and was for years associated with the Prados' paper *La Cronica*.

3. Gustavo wrote in English to a British business associate.

4. Members of most of these families were candidates for Congress on Villarán's list, according to a campaign ad in *El Comercio*, October 2, 1936. The planter backing for his candidacy, led by Belrán, is mentioned in most accounts of the campaign and is obvious in the Aspíllaga correspondence. As noted in an earlier chapter Beltrán and Manuel Mujica Gallo

were behind the "Can a Prado?" pamphlet that circulated in 1936 (Miró Quesada Laos 1961: 480; Portocarrero 1995: 31–32).

5. Tuesta Soldevilla 1998; Werlich 1978: 210.

6. I am assuming here that my list is reasonably representative and I believe it is. Readers can judge for themselves by reading the text associated with table 1.1 and Appendix A.

7. For the purposes of this analysis, the oligarchic family was defined as encompassing the lineage descending, typically through three generations, from the founder to those who reached marriage age in the 1950s and 1960s. The primary source of genealogical data was successive editions of Lima's social register, the *Libro de Oro*. The published sources cited in connection with table 1.1 were also consulted. Information from these sources was supplemented with interviews.

8. It is notable that the first two judges, who were consulted independently, named each other and that there was considerable overlap between their lists. The combined list of eighty-eight families they produced was presented to the two secondary judges, who were separately asked to evaluate it and eliminate families they felt did not belong. Both found the list accurate; only two names were eliminated. All the remaining families were approved by at least three judges. Aside from the opinions of the judges, this analysis relies on the definition of family and data sources cited in the proceeding footnote.

9. Perhaps the six were on the margins of the Inner Social Circle or the list, heavily dependent on the recall ability of the first two judges, was not quite exhaustive.

10. The single exception was Luis Banchero, whose fortune was both enormous and recent.

11. See especially table 3.3.

10

The Sources of Oligarchic Power

> They conquer by gold and not by steel.
>
> —Vilfredo Pareto

> [We] need to be in a position to speak loudly and call things by their name.
>
> —Pedro Beltrán

In 1919, the oligarchy lost and never regained the ability to directly and openly govern the country. Beginning in 1930, the oligarchs faced a well-organized threat from below. Yet they generally managed, through the years of the contested republic, to bend governments to their will. The one government that was wholly beyond their grasp (Bustamante 1945–1948) was deposed in an oligarchy-organized military coup. Their continuing influence reflected the relative weakness of their opponents, the support—at least until the early 1960s—of the military, and political arrangements that permitted them to stymie reform. At a deeper level, their success during these decades reflected the advantage derived from power resources they had long possessed. These are the subject of this chapter.

MONEY, PRESTIGE, AND THE HABITS OF POWER

The power of the oligarchs flowed from many sources. The most obvious one was money. In *Oligarchy*, Winter (2011) singles out concentrated wealth as the defining feature of oligarchic politics. Especially in the form of "cash money," it is an extraordinarily "versatile and potent" political resource. It extends the reach of those who possess it well beyond the limits of their own talents and energy. It can buy armed defenders; the services of lawyers and other trained professionals; and the cooperation of politicians, soldiers, police, and judges. It can be used to purchase legislative action, buy elections, and call mobs into the street to destabilize governments.

The Peruvian oligarchs and their peers in the other four countries had large sums of money at their command when others had very little, and they were not reluctant to use it for political purposes. Preceding chapters have shown the Aspíllagas covering expenses for the removal of political undesirables from Lambayeque, the Prados offering credit on generous terms to military officers, Beltran and the Gildemeisters buying and transforming *La Prensa* into an influential political organ, and the larger oligarchic tribe contributing to a "bolsa" to finance the 1948 coup. In Chile's oligarchic republic, the votes of so-called free electors were purchased by wealthy candidates, who might spend the equivalent of $100,000 to buy a Senate seat. In Rio de Janeiro, during the same period, representatives of the dominant state oligarchies consolidated their national power by bribing members of Congress and buying friendly coverage in the national press.

A more subtle source of power was the oligarchy's position at the center of upper-class society. The Peruvian oligarchs inhabited an intimate social world that strengthened elite cohesion and contributed to oligarchic power in other ways. Many outsiders were awed by the aurora of social exclusivity that surrounded the oligarchs and all the more likely to follow their lead in matters from lifestyle to politics. Rising middle-class professionals, politicians, and soldiers were drawn to them. A notable example was Colonel, soon-to-be-president, Sánchez Cerro, a dark-skinned soldier of relatively modest provincial origins. He was apparently attracted to Lima "society," became a member of the Club National, and was, as one of the Aspíllagas noted, "gracious to those who have helped him so much" (LAA 9–3–32).

Their social world also gave the oligarchs a distinctive capacity for what Imaz (1964), writing on Argentina, termed "horizontal mobility"—that is, an ability of members of the elite to move among institutions, to link them, because they have dense networks of valuable social ties (which today might be termed "social capital"). For the individual, this capacity was an important resource, which provided advantages over less-connected others. It also served the class as a whole in significant ways. For instance, in the last years of his reformist administration, President Fernando Belaúnde increasingly depended on certain conservative upper-class advisors. He felt compelled to do so because they had personal links to the banking and business world whose support his financially troubled government needed.

Mosca (1939) points to another source of the resilience of oligarchy, which he compares to the force of "inertia" in physics. It might be called the habits of power. The oligarchs were powerful because they had long been powerful. They had grown up with power, were knowledgeable in the ways of power, and felt entitled to exercise it. Many others deferred to them, likewise out of habit, often in the hope that there might be some profit in it, but also out of fear of the oligarchs.

STRATEGIC RESOURCES

Beyond wealth, prestige, and habit, the Peruvian oligarchs were empowered by the resources they controlled in three strategic sectors: export enterprises, banks, and newspapers. Oligarchic fortunes, including those of the Prados, the Aspíllagas, and the Miró Quesadas, were typically identified with one of these sectors, though many had investments in more than one. The accounts of the oligarchic republics in chapter 2 show that the oligarchies of Mexico, Brazil, Argentina, and Chile were also closely associated with export activities and banking (see table 2.1). The examples of two powerful conservative dailies, *La Prensa* in Buenos Aires and *El Mercurio* in Santiago, both owned by prominent oligarchic families, suggest that newspaper ownership was also strategic oligarchic resource in these countries.

The strategic political significance of these three sectors is suggested by the actions taken by Velasco's revolutionary government. Its most sweeping and publicized moves were a major land reform, which was inaugurated with the sudden seizure of the sugar plantations in 1969; a series of measures which established government control of mining; government takeover of several banks and the establishment of mechanisms to tighten control of the financial sector; and, finally, the nationalization of the major Lima newspapers. The regime seemed determined to obliterate the power of those whom Velasco described as "the beneficiaries of the *status quo* . . . the irreducible adversaries of our movement . . . the oligarchy" (Velasco 1973: 65).

As table 10.1 indicates, the oligarchic clans were very likely to have stakes in these three sectors, frequently in combination, in sharp contrast to other wealthy families,

Table 10.1. **Strategic Resources of the Oligarchic 29 and Top Taxpayers[a]**

	Oligarchic families (N = 29) percent	Top taxpayer families (N = 297) percent
A. Own export enterprise (land/mines)[b]	82.8	8.1
B. Represented on board of commercial bank	75.8	10.1
C. Newspaper publisher or stockholder	34.5	1.7
Families with all 3 of A, B, and C (as above)	27.6	0.0
Families with 2 of A, B, and C	37.9	2.7
Families with 1 of A, B, and C	31.0	14.5
Families with none of A, B, and C	3.4	82.8
	100%	100%

[a] *Sources:* Top taxpayers, *El Comercio*, April 25, 1972; bank boards, Vernal 1968; land and mines, Malpica 1973; and newspapers, Espinosa Uriarte and Osorio 1971.
[b] Land: own over 500 hectares (1,250 acres) of coastal land. Mining: sole owners of one or more metal mining firms with over 500 total employees or at least $1 million aggregate gross output in 1965 or listed by Malpica among principal stockholders of firms with over 1,000 employees or at least $2 million output. In only three cases were holdings in foreign firms the principal basis of classification as mine owners (Benavides, Prado, and Beltrán). In the first two cases, at least, Malpica makes clear that their respective interests in these firms were quite substantial. On Beltrán, Malpica is less explicit.

whose holdings in these sectors were relatively meager. The table compares the Oligarchy 29 clans with non-oligarchic families who were represented on an official list of the country's 500 biggest taxpayers in 1970.[1]

EXPORTS

Nearly all the Oligarchy 29 had an ownership stake in the export economy in the late 1960s. Export agriculture (mainly sugar and cotton) was always the quintessential oligarchic enterprise. Ten of the nineteen coastal landholdings in excess of 5,000 hectares (12,500 acres) were owned by oligarchic families. Virtually all of the major sugar plantations—the source of most of the largest Peruvian fortunes—were oligarchy-owned. (The enormous holdings of the Grace Corporation constituted the most notable exception [Malpica 1973].)

A few oligarchic fortunes were based on metal mining (e.g., Fernandini, Malaga, Rizo Patron), and many families had substantial mining investments. The oligarchy had played the leading role in the revival of Peruvian mining after the War of the Pacific. But early in the twentieth century, control of large-scale Peruvian mining passed into foreign hands. By the 1960s three American companies accounted for 75 percent of total output in this sector (Purser 1971: 111). Most of the remainder of the sector was in the hands of medium-scale producers, some of whom were dependent on the major firms. These independents were usually closely held companies controlled by one or more oligarchic clans (Malpica 1973).

The fishmeal industry, until it was nationalized by the Velasco government, was creating a whole new sector of the oligarchy. Given the industry's export orientation, the political interests of its owners were inevitably aligned with those of the established oligarchy. In 1967, for instance, fishmeal exporters cooperated with agricultural interests to force a devaluation on the Belaúnde government.

In contrast to the oligarchy's traditional orientation toward primary exports, the oligarchs had very limited involvement in manufacturing, even after a spurt of industrial growth in the 1950s and 1960s. In 1968, sixteen of the twenty-nine oligarchic clans had investment in industry. But their holdings in individual firms were typically modest, with average nominal values a little over $100,000 (in current U.S. dollars) and total industrial portfolios worth approximately $265,000, small amounts relative to the value of their export properties. These investments were often in foreign controlled firms, and rarely in companies whose largest stockholder was from one of the twenty-nine families. Only a few oligarchic clans, such as the Berckemeyers and the Rizo Patrons, were significantly committed to manufacturing.[2]

The significance of the oligarchy's close identification with export activities has been stressed repeatedly in the preceding chapters. It was through the production of guano, sugar, cotton, and metals for export that the oligarchs were able to accumulate the capital that allowed them to expand their influence into other sectors of the economy, especially the critical financial sector. In an economy heavily dependent on exports, those who controlled incoming foreign exchange were in a powerful position. In a country where the stability of national regimes has often fluctuated with the exchange rate, governments have found themselves in the position of appealing to major exporters for support of the national currency.[3]

The oligarchy's export orientation was reflected in the maintenance of a political economy bound to the interests of exporters. This pattern could not have been sustained for decades without the oligarchy's determined political backing. During the 1930s and 1940s, oligarchy-backed regimes in Peru resisted pressure to seize the opportunity presented by the depression and the war to reorient economic policy toward import-substitution industrialization, as was done by several other Latin American countries and urged in APRA's early platforms.

BANKS

Banks, of course, are of strategic importance to any economy, and those who control them are likely to be powerful. Prior to Velasco's revolution, Peruvian bankers were in an especially powerful position, since regulation of the banks by national authorities was weak and the sort of formal, institutionalized capital market which would limit the power of individual banks did not exist. Discussing the oligarchy Bourricaud comments:

> What characterizes business in Peru is that the saver, the banker and the investor are one in the same person. . . . A Peruvian banker, investing his own money in a concern whose registered capital is in his hands and which is managed by his son, cousin, son-in-law or father-in-law, will not apply the same criteria of rationality as an American banker who collects liquid assets on the capital market to invest them in joint-stock organizations under non-shareholding managers. (1970: 45)

Bourricaud fails to note, in this context, that the funds which a commercial bank can make available in the form of credit are not limited to what its owners can provide, but include a proportion of the bank's deposits from other savers and money which is loaned to the bank by the central bank. Those who control banks are not simply playing with their own money. But, as the Banco Popular case made clear, Bourricaud's general point is quite relevant. Loans which the Prados made to their own enterprises and to those of friends and associates, such as the Aspíllagas at Cayaltí, were obviously extended on highly particularistic criteria. A smaller Lima bank, the Banco Union, got into serious economic trouble for exactly the same reasons and was liquidated in 1967 (*Oiga*, February 21 and 28, 1969).

Banco Popular and Banco Union appear to have been extreme cases. But what they suggest in an extravagant form was to a lesser degree characteristic of the entire financial system. A foreign consulting firm found, for example, that the Peruvian textile industry, was indebted far beyond its financial capacity, but was still receiving new credits in the 1960s, apparently extended on the basis of personal ties (Werner

Consulting 1969: 302 and report summary). A report on Peruvian industrialization prospects commented: "The weakness of the capital market is partly due to the fact that industry in Peru has generally been financed by individuals, families, or small groups, usually in association with banking institutions which are frequently controlled by the same interests" (Little 1960: 26). It appears that such practices were common in Latin American banking generally and constituted a serious obstacle to economic development (Glade 1969: 466–467).

The power of Peruvian commercial banks was enhanced by their relative freedom from government control, another aspect of the laissez faire political economy supported by the oligarchy. Both the Banco Popular and Banco Union cases demonstrated that bank misconduct had to go to rather extreme lengths before national banking authorities would intervene. Illegal practices aside, Peruvian banking laws, in effect, placed the entire financial system under the power of the commercial banks.

In 1931 and again in 1949, basic laws regulating the central bank were promulgated. Both were formulated with the help of special American missions invited by the Peruvian government, and both severely restricted the role of central banking authorities. In 1949, shortly after the coup which brought Odría to power, the Klein Mission was contracted by two oligarchic figures, Pedro Beltrán, then president of the central bank, and Fernando Berckemeyer, the Peruvian ambassador in Washington. There is evidence that the Americans were carefully guided to their conclusions by the oligarchs, who had gained influence under the recently installed military dictatorship (Julius Klein prefaced his preliminary report with the following observation: "In its preparatory studies . . . this mission has bound itself to the declaration of President Odría that the goal of the government's policy is to orient the country toward a free economy, which will best serve the interests of the Peruvian people)."[4]

The central bank law provided for a board of directors dominated by representatives of the banks and other organizations heavily influenced by the oligarchy, such as the National Agrarian Society (Tamagna 1963: 225–222, Cuadro II). The central bank was not allowed to become an instrument for the promotion of economic growth through planned allocation of capital among sectors of the economy as was done in some other Latin American countries. An attempt to change this feature in 1961 was beaten back in the Convivencia Congress (Aguirre 1962: 51–52). Even after changes were made in the structure of the central bank's board early in Belaúnde's administration, the government's control of the institution was so tenuous that on the eve of the 1967 devaluation the commercial banks had vital information from the central bank on the foreign exchange situation which was unavailable to the treasury minister.

The semi-public development banks, which had ostensibly been set up to provide low interest credit to small- and medium-sized farmers, miners, and industrialists, were also controlled by the commercial banks through representatives on the boards of these banks. According to a Lima lawyer well acquainted with local banking practices, such banks would demand impossible guarantees from potential borrowers who were not well connected, thus forcing them to resort to high interest loans from the commercial banks. At the same time, the director of a commercial bank could obtain a long-term, low-interest loan from one of the development banks with the help of his own bank's representative on the development bank's board.

Another crucial element of the power of the commercial banks, to which reference has been made in previous chapters, was their ownership of the Caja de Depositos, the national tax-collecting agent (Aguirre 1962: 51). Through the Caja, the banks were paid for collecting taxes. But the benefits which accrued to them did not end there. The money which the Caja collected was not channeled continuously to the government, but transferred at three-month intervals. In the interim, the money collected was deposited in the commercial banks. If the government needed funds during this period, it might apply to the central bank (also controlled by the commercial banks) for a monetary emission, but was likely to be turned down on the grounds that such action would be inflationary. Thus, the government was likely to be forced to apply to the banks for a short-term loan guaranteed by the Caja funds. The government, in effect, was borrowing its own money. (Belaúnde's government finally nationalized the Caja. It became the government-controlled Banco de la Nation.)

The capacity to squeeze government finances using the Caja placed the banks in a very powerful position. Here was not only a vehicle for profit, but an important political weapon as well. The same private financial institutions which controlled the flow of capital into the private sector also had substantial control over the government's revenues. In 1948, according to the Lima attorney referred to earlier, the oligarchy's position in the financial sector enabled it to "destabilize" the Bustamante government prior to its overthrow. Using the central bank, the Caja, and the commercial banks, "the oligarchy turned off the faucet," with devastating results.

A final element in the power of the banks under the Old Regime in Peru was their control of foreign currency exchange. The government had little power over exchange transactions. Moreover, the open economy tradition did not give the government the power to regulate imports in a way that would influence exchange rates. If foreign exchange crises were perilous for Peruvian governments, they were golden opportunities for the banks and the enterprises associated with them. Their direct access to central bank information on the exchange situation placed them in a position to engage in profitable currency speculation, as they did in 1967. Of course, this only aggravated the government's difficulties. On the other hand, a decision by the larger banks to support the local currency could have a significant stabilizing influence. At the time of the 1968 coup, Peru's two largest banks, Credito and Popular, controlled 45 percent and 10 percent, respectively, of the nation's foreign exchange holdings. At the request of the new regime, they restricted the outflow of dollars, stabilizing the Peruvian sol.

Credito and Popular quite reasonably expected favorable treatment from the new government, for themselves and for banking generally. They might well have acted differently if they had had any idea of the degree to which the new government would reverse the traditional situation and strengthen state regulation of the financial sector. Soon after taking power, the military government nationalized the central bank, removing all private sector representatives from its board. The government tightened its control of over credit and foreign exchange transactions. Determined to reduce foreign participation in Peruvian banking, the government vetoed the Prados' plan to merge their bank with a local Chase Manhattan affiliate and took over the Banco Popular.

NEWSPAPERS

Under the Old Regime the major Lima dailies were almost always controlled by oligarchic interests.[5] In 1968 the capital had five newspapers of national significance. *El Comercio* was owned and run by the Miró Quesadas, as it had been since the late nineteenth century. *La Prensa* was firmly under the control of Pedro Beltrán, political leader of the exporters. The paper had been founded in 1903 by Pedro de Osma (certainly among the oligarchs of that day, though the Osma family was much less important by the mid-twentieth century). It was seized by Leguía and became a regime organ in the 1920s. In the 1930s, *La Prensa* was acquired by a group from the National Agrarian Society, among whom Ramon Aspíllaga Anderson figured prominently, and, from that time on, it was the principal journalistic spokesman for export interests generally and the coastal planters in particular. From the late 1940s, the paper was directed by Beltrán.[6]

La Cronica had also been a Leguiísta paper. After Leguía's overthrow it was purchased by Rafael Larco, a major sugar planter who became first vice president (1939–1945) under Manuel Prado. In 1942, Larco sold it to the Prados who would control the paper until it was taken over by the government in 1970 along with other firms tied to the Banco Popular.

By 1968, the two remaining papers, *Correo* and *Expreso*, were controlled by figures we might describe as new men of power. *Correo* was the flagship of a national chain of papers started by fishmeal magnate Luis Banchero. *Expreso* had belonged to planter Manuel Mujica, who had used it to support Belaúnde's election. In 1965, it was acquired by Manuel Ullao, member of a prestigious Lima family, who had returned to Peru after earning a considerable fortune abroad. He soon became a high-profile national political figure, the dynamic head of one of Belaúnde's cabinets, and a presidential prospect for the 1969 election (Jaquette 1971: 175–198).

The Miró Quesadas, Beltráns, Prados, Mujicas, and Banchero were all counted among the Oligarchy 29. Thus, as late as 1965, all five major dailies were, as defined here, under oligarchic control. Four still were in 1968.

WE NEED A VOICE

The critical importance of the press to the oligarchs is evident in a 1945 exchange of letters between Pedro Beltrán, then Peruvian ambassador in Washington, and his friends, Juan and Augusto Gildemeister, Peru's wealthiest sugar planters. Their letters, written in English, use lightly coded language to discuss sensitive matters: Pedro is "Peter," the Miró Quesadas' newspaper *El Comercio* is "the trade" and the competing *La Prensa* is "the press." Beltrán, writing in the wake of Bustamante's election with APRA support, is surprisingly optimistic. He tells the Gildemeisters that he is "very pleased that a free election has taken place and that the majority is going to prevail. This is a tremendous improvement . . . the only way to have political stability. But he is also worried that Bustamante is politically naive, ignorant of economic matters and likely to fall into unorthodox policies. [We] need to be in a position to speak loudly and call things by their name," in order to influence policy without destabilizing the government. "[T]his can only be done by means of a newspaper widely read, that really carries weight with public opinion. [T]he trade is the only one in that position." Beltran proposes that they (presumably, the Gildemeisters and other planters) buy *El Comercio*, which, he concedes, would be an expensive proposition. "[I]t would be easier to buy the press, [but] you will never wield as much power."

A few days later, a skeptical Augusto replies. "My dear Peter, thanks very much for your sermon. . . . [I] can only hope that you are right being so pleased with the free election." Yes, they and their friends, do need a voice. But, no, they cannot buy the *El Comercio*. The owners (unnamed) would never be willing to sell it to them. They are, instead, looking into buying *La Prensa*, a much weaker, planter-oriented paper, which they might revitalize. Gildemeister further notes that he doesn't necessarily need to "wield more power," as Beltran suggests, but only "to defend myself." Beltran soon responds, "Now if you think you that you can defend yourself by being weak, I am damned if I know how. . . . I see that it is the underdog that is trampled upon and if you want to defend yourself you ought to be as powerful as possible." Beltran would assume control of *La Prensa*, apparently with the backing of the Gildemeisters, sometime after the January 1947 assassination of publisher Francisco Graña.

Beltrán and Gildemeister felt that they needed a newspaper in order, variously, to influence policy, defend interests, or wield power. Years later, Luís Banchero's decision to enter newspaper publishing was widely interpreted as evidence that he—a man of modest origins and outsized ambitious—intended to exercise the political influence which his fortune permitted and the protection of his extensive interests required. "You are a lot more convincing," observed one of his associates in an interview, "when you have a newspaper behind you." The oligarchy's enemies apparently held a similar view of the power of press ownership, which they expressed with violent physical attacks on the major newspapers during periods of political tension and the assassinations of the publishers of *El Comercio* (1935) and *La Prensa* (1947). Toward the end of Odria's reign in 1956, when the dictator's oligarchic support was melting away, his police invaded *La Prensa* and carted off forty employees, including Pedro Beltrán. Velasco went further, with the expropriation of the major dailies in 1974.

From the perspective of a world saturated with television and Internet media, it is difficult to appreciate the power that Peruvians, as late as the 1960s, attributed to their daily newspapers. For the oligarchy, the uses of the press were both short-term tactical and long-term strategic. In moments of crisis, the oligarchic press helped to de-stablize hostile regimes and to shore up friendly ones. Prime examples are the roles played by *La Prensa* and *El Comercio* in undermining Bustmante's government and supporting Odría's coup in 1948 and by *El Comercio* in depriving Haya of his electoral victory in 1962.

Strategically, the press was a vehicle for the propagation of a conception of Peruvian society and politics which legitimized the privileges of the oligarchy and de-legitimized the efforts of its critics and political enemies. Over decades, the hostile treatment of APRA in *El Comercio* undermined the party's middle-class support outside its traditional geographic bastions and reinforced anti-APRA sentiments among the military, despite the Aprista sympathies of some officers. Analysts of Peruvian politics in the last decades of the Old Regime stress the importance of Beltrán's defense through *La Prensa* of the country's laissez faire political economy and his dismissal of developmentalist and socialist alternatives as dangerously impractical. In the late 1950s, *La Prensa* attacked the economic policies of Manuel Prado's government, until Prado gave in and appointed Beltrán premier and finance minister.[7] Even in the Belaúnde years, high government officials concerned with economic matters were little inclined to question the basic tenets of the laissez faire model.[8] Only after 1968, under a transformed military, trained at CAEM and tutored by *El Comercio*, did the country move away from the creole liberalism which had been its default economic philosophy for many decades.

If some military and middle-class readers of the oligarchic press remained skeptical or ambivalent concerning its content, the character of the Peruvian press minimized their exposure to alternative versions of Peruvian realities. Not only did the oligarchy dominate the major dailies, but the right-wing governments supported by the oligarchs regularly suppressed such anti-establishment publications as appeared. The career of *La Tribuna*, the Aprista organ, is indicative. The paper was closed down on thirteen separate occasions and was in fact illegal during most of the period 1931–1956 (Gargurevich 1972: 44–47; Miró Quesada Laos 1957: 239).

Even in periods of relative press freedom, financial restraints tended to restrict the alternative press. The economics of newspaper publishing dictated the sale of at least half a paper's space to advertisers or support in the form of substantial subsidies (which *La Prensa* apparently received from planters in the 1930s and 1940s) to sustain a newspaper. Under the Old Regime, advertising revenues, which tended to come from a very small number of big advertisers, went overwhelmingly to the major, oligarchy-controlled papers. Big subsidies were not available to anti-establishment publications for obvious reasons (Espinosa Uriarte and Osorio 1971; Gargurevich 1972: 50–63).

Of course, there were differences among the major papers, especially in the last decade or so of the Old Regime. *El Comercio* and *La Prensa* were, for a time, at odds as the former passed through its most liberal phase. In the 1960s *Correo* and *Expreso*, controlled by men new to the political scene, presented fresh outlooks. But if there was debate, the range of that debate was constricted, and certainly never faithfully expressed the diversity of national political opinion. If *El Comercio* and *La Prensa* came to argue for different patterns of capitalist development, where was the daily partisan of socialist development? If *La Prensa* spoke for planter interests, *La Cronica* for the bankers, and *Correo* for the fishing industry, which paper represented industrial workers, or the peasants or, for that matter, Sierra landlords? (The Velasco press reform was putatively designed to give voices to some of these voiceless, but, especially after the first year, the reformed papers spoke for the government [Gilbert 1979].)

RESOURCES AND LINKAGES

The oligarchs did not just own land and mines, banks, and newspapers, but they, almost uniquely, held them in combination, as can be seen in table 10.1 All but one of the Oligarchy 29 clans were connected to at least one of the three strategic sectors, most to two or three sectors. The single exception was the Chopitea family, owners of one of the country's largest sugar plantations who came on hard times in the late 1930s and were compelled to sell their land to the Gildemeisters. Among the non-oligarchic rich, participation in any of these sectors was rare. Rarer still among them were families whose holdings linked sectors.

In the 1950s and 1960s, Luis Banchero, who might be described as a "new oligarch," followed the path that the Aspíllagas and others had taken, over a half-century earlier, assuming the classic oligarchic profile. Having accumulated a considerable fortune exporting fishmeal (Abramovitch 1973), Banchero took a seat on a bank board (Banco de Credito) and launched a chain of newspapers. An astute observer of Peruvian politics during this period describes Banchero as a powerful figure, who "controlled ministers" and was able to gain important advantages for himself and his industry. Another observer remarked that the military feared Banchero, because he had enough money to finance a coup. (One facet of elite status apparently eluded Banchero: acceptance by upper-class society. He had applied for admittance to the Club Nacional and had been turned down in 1960. His application was premature, according to a club member who thought he would have been accepted if he had waited and re-applied.)[9]

The established oligarchic clans, like this new oligarch, were powerful because they controlled and linked potent resources, which they could mobilize, acting alone or collectively, to achieve objectives, from shaping narrow policy decisions (the price of cement) to the removal of an inconvenient president (the 1948 coup).

LESSONS FROM THE PERUVIAN CASE STUDY

What does the case study of the Peruvian oligarchy in chapters 4 through the current chapter contribute to our understanding of other Latin American oligarchies?

It provides more detailed and systematic evidence of tendencies that were suggested for all five countries in the early chapters of the book. The analysis of strategic resources reveals the characteristic and distinctive connection of the oligarchs with exports, finance, and the press. The discussion shows, with concrete examples, how these resources contributed to the power of the oligarchy. The analyses of marriage patterns and of the overlap between the oligarchy and upper-class society in Peru are consistent with evidence in part I for the other countries, gleaned from secondary sources. With the example of Peru, it is easy to imagine how upper-class society functioned, across the region, as a basis of elite cohesion and social control under the Old Regime. At the same time we learn that the forces undermining elite cohesion may include personal ambitions and the idiosyncratic concerns of individual oligarchic clans.

The Peruvian study illuminates aspects of oligarchic political life which would otherwise be invisible, from the financing of military coups to the less dramatic, everyday exercise of power (the use of local authorities to control plantation labor, the easy loans to military officers, etc.). The details may differ from country to country, but we are reminded that, especially in contested republics, oligarchic power is often exercised out of public view.

NOTES

1. The Oligarchy 29 are listed in table 1.1. After members of the oligarchic families were removed from the top taxpayer list, the remaining individuals were grouped into the 297 non-oligarchic families represented in the table. Time and available data did not permit construction of 297 additional genealogies. These "families" were delineated by surnames. This technique implies a definition broader in scope than that used for the Oligarchy 29, since kin more distant than second cousins and even non-kin might be included. On the other hand, individuals related through a maternal link would not be included, thus narrowing the scope. Experience with the oligarchic families suggests that the effects of either of these potential errors would be trivial in connection with the tax list and other sources employed for tables 9.1 and 9.2.

2. Calculated from stockholding data in Instituto National de Planificación 1973a–e.

3. On political stability and the exchange rate, see Jaquette 1971: 183–185. On at least one occasion the Aspíllagas were contacted by the Minister of Finance and asked to support the national currency (RAB 6–29–39). The refusal of exporters to cooperate with the government in 1967 forced a politically damaging large devaluation on the Belaúnde government.

4. Romero 1994: II, 225–227; *Oiga*, April 28, 1969 and March 28, 1969; CDA, "Correspondencia Gildemeister-Allen."

5. This section draws on Gargurevich 1972; Miró Quesada Laos 1957; Espinosa Uriarte and Osorio 1971; *La Prensa*, September 23, 1973, Gilbert 1979, and interviews.

6. Beltran took over the paper after the murder of publisher (and cotton planter) Francisco Graña in 1947. But it is not exactly clear who the owners were. *La Prensa* had long served the planters. The Aspíllagas had an ownership stake for decades and sometimes held a board position. The exchange of letters discussed in the chapter shows that Beltran and the

Gildemeisters, also sugar planters, had considered buying the paper in 1945. One of Beltran's top editors in the postwar period told me Beltran had total control of the paper; he suspects that the Gildemeisters gave him their shares.

7. Prado was the ultimate winner in this contest. Beltrán took the blame for presiding over a very unpopular austerity program. When the economy later improved due to rising demand for Peru's exports, Prado was the hero.

8. Jaquette 1971: 64–68; Bourricaud 1970: 197–202; Astiz 1969: 65–70.

9. Banchero was murdered in 1972, at age forty-two. His gardener's son was convicted of the crime but without a clear motive, and he was later pardoned. The military government nationalized his companies.

11

The End of the Old Regime:
Peru in Comparative Perspective

Forget Cayaltí. That page has turned. Enjoy yourself.

—Ramón Aspíllaga to his brother, 1973

I have faith that El Comercio will return to us.

—Luís Miró Quesada, 1974

I want to die like a Christian. . . . What I most regret
is the injustice and the absence of my friends.

—Mariano Prado, 1974

One day in late 1974, Mariano Prado expired quietly in his bed at the Police Hospital in Lima. Among those who came to the Virgin de Pilar Church that evening to offer condolences to the family was a frail Luís Miró Quesada. Two years later Luís was dead at the age of ninety-five. Other representative men of the Old Regime were gone by the end of the decade, among them Ramón Aspíllaga Anderson, planter-politician Pedro Beltrán, general and president Manuel Odría, and APRA leader Victor Raúl Haya de la Torre. These men had no successors. The Old Regime perished with them. Velasco's revolution had seen to that.

Some of the oligarchs managed to preserve at least part of their family fortunes, and some continued to appear on lists of the top taxpayers, but, by the time Velasco stepped down in 1975, their numbers were fewer and their collective rank was lower.[1] The Prados' Banco Popular and the Aspíllagas' Hacienda Cayaltí were bankrupt when seized by the government and would not be restored to the families. As patriarch Luís had anticipated, *El Comercio* was returned to the Miró Quesadas, a few years after his death. They would build a new media empire around it, but they would not recover the enormous political power they had exercised in the middle decades of the twentieth century. In 1980, the country returned to civilian rule under a new constitution that granted the vote to illiterates, empowering the poorest Peruvians and the people of the Sierra. Democratically elected governments of varied complexions followed, none of them linked to the oligarchy, a connection had been the norm for most of preceding century.

The question to be asked in the wake of the Peruvian revolution was not why the Old Regime had finally succumbed, but how it endured so long. The oligarchs remained a force in Peru well after oligarchic power had faded as a consequential factor in the politics of most Latin American nations. Why was Peru different?

The Peruvian oligarchy was, in many ways, a conventional example of the species. The oligarchic families were a mix of late-colonial and nineteenth-century arrivals to Peru. They accumulated fortunes in last decades of the nineteenth century and early years of the twentieth—most in export activities, some in finance. They established an intimate world of overlapping social ties and elite institutions. Throughout their lives, they were surrounded by friends, kin, and associates—people comfortably like themselves. Others recognized them and judged them as members of a particular oligarchic clan.

In the late nineteenth century, they created an oligarchic republic that served their interests. Its leading figures were, appropriately, planters. After a generation, it was toppled by one of their own—a man who rode to power with the changes that oligarchic development had set in motion. Under Leguía, the Peruvian oligarchs endured an eleven-year dictatorship that marginalized them politically, but protected their fortunes and held at bay the political forces that threatened them. At the end of this period, they regained some of the power they had lost. The eleven years had been a respite from politics. Now they had to confront new political actors representing long excluded sectors of Peruvian society. They were compelled to exercise power indirectly, discreetly, in a contested republic. But they retained potent unofficial sources of power, as we saw in the previous chapter.

In all these ways, the Peruvian oligarchy was typical or at least not terribly atypical. It was their long endurance within a contested republic that set the Peruvian oligarchs apart. The era of contested oligarchic power in Peru stretched over a longer period and ended at a later date than it did in the four other countries (see table 3.2). In Brazil, the contested republic ended not long after it began in 1930, with São Paulo's military defeat in 1932, followed by the declaration of the Estado Novo in 1937. The contested period in Mexico, prolonged by the stalemate among revolutionary factions, ended with the election of Cárdenas in 1934. The closest case to Peru is that of Chile, where oligarchic power persisted until the passage of an electoral reform law in 1958, well before the military revolution in Peru.

In the long run, the Old Regime across Latin America was doomed by elite disunity and by the export-driven process of modernization promoted by the oligarchs. The oligarchies were divided by varied sectoral, regional, political, and personal differences. Export development created societies that were more urban, literate, and integrated, with expanding middle and working classes and professionalized militaries. The process exacerbated divisions among the oligarchs, opened alluring political opportunities for ambitious men among them, and created social bases for organized challenges to oligarchic power from labor organizations and anti-establishment political parties.

The Peruvian oligarchy was, of course, not immune to these perils, but possessed countervailing advantages that slowed their effects. Two were negative. The Peruvian oligarchs did not confront the explosive land issue that drove the Mexican Revolution to its radical climax because export agriculture in Peru developed on the thinly populated coast, separated from the Indian population and the communal landholdings of the Sierra.[2] Nor did the Peruvian oligarchs face an urban working class of sufficient magnitude and militancy to support a Peruvian Perón.[3]

Beyond these negative advantages the Peruvian oligarchy owed its endurance to four factors:

1. *Geographic centralization* bolstered elite cohesion among the Peruvian oligarchs. Oligarchic economic, political, and social life was concentrated in Lima and on the Peruvian coast north and south of the capital. In Lima oligarchic clans maintained family residences and business headquarters. There members of the elite encountered each other frequently, in varied settings, as friends, kin, partners, and allies. The Chilean oligarchy, concentrated in Santiago and the central valley, came closest to the Peruvian case. In contrast, Brazil and Mexico, large, decentralized countries with widely separated, economically differentiated state oligarchies, provided only limited bases for cohesion. The São Paulo oligarchs, for example, had surprisingly few ties to their peers in other states. The Argentine oligarchy had the advantage of geographic concentration (in Buenos Aires and on the pampas), but had been forced to share power with the elites of the interior provinces.

2. *The planter core,* the largest, most engaged and most powerful sector of the Peruvian oligarchy, was united by well-defined interests and the habits of a long history of formal and informal collaboration. Though the planters rarely held public office after 1920, they remained politically active. The Chilean oligarchs were similarly bound and empowered by their stake in central valley land. Well after the custom had largely been abandoned elsewhere, upper-class Chilean men were expected to serve in political office. Their landholdings and the associated hacienda system of labor sustained their political power.

3. *Military support.* Among the five national elites considered here, the Peruvian oligarchy stands apart in its long dependence on conservative military regimes. The overthrow of Billinghurst in 1914, toward the end of the oligarchic republic, signaled what was to come. Right-wing military governments were created with oligarchic encouragement and ruled with oligarchic advice. During Peru's contested republic, they suppressed APRA, protected oligarchic interests, and preserved the bases of oligarchic power, such as the oligarchs' control of the financial system. The closest parallel to these Peruvian regimes was military backing for the Argentine Concordancia of the 1930s. In Chile and Brazil, in

contrast, the officer corps, especially younger officers, played a more progressive role, supporting political change at critical moments in the 1920s and 1930s. It was not until the 1950s that the Peruvian military began to develop an independent conception of its national role and not until the early 1960s, that this new conception made itself felt.

4. *The Convivencia and the Living Museum.* The extended survival of oligarchic power in Peru owed much to the Convivencia. The arrangement was an instance of Anderson's "living museum" of Latin American politics. In the living museum, new political actors, having demonstrated both their disruptive capacity and their willingness to play by rules of the game that preserve all players, are admitted to the legitimate political arena, where they must coexist with archaic political life forms. A proto-convivencia emerged in the 1930s, promoted by the Prados, who quickly perceived the value to themselves of an alliance with APRA. Manuel Prado won a second presidency in 1956 with open APRA support by committing to the party's legalization. In the 1960s, a broader oligarchy-APRA Convivencia failed to secure the presidency for Haya de la Torre but won control of Congress and was able to thwart Belaúnde's reformist program. Plans for a new convivencia government died with the Old Regime, when the tanks rolled out in October 1968. Chile, during this same period, evolved its own form of living museum politics, based on an implicit understanding between the landed oligarchy and urban reformist and leftist forces. This political and social arrangement preserved the hacienda system and the veto power of the oligarchy in exchange for concessions to the working and middle classes.

These four factors were together responsible for the longevity of the Peruvian oligarchy relative to its peers elsewhere in Latin America. The geographic concentration of oligarchic life provided a strong basis for the development of the planter core, which, in turn, played a central role in the installation and shaping of right-wing military governments. The life of the Old Regime in Peru was extended beyond any reasonable expectation when the planter core joined the Convivencia. The intervention of a transformed military was finally required to end to its long history.

NOTES

1. Gilbert 1980: 26–27. The figures this article presents in Table 2 refer to the relative standing of oligarchs and other high-income individuals on lists of top taxpayers for 1970 and 1975.

2. The peasant movements that developed in the Sierra toward the end of the Old Regime did not involve the oligarchy directly, though they did weigh in the military's decision to assume power in 1968.

3. For national comparisons of rural and labor issues see tables 2.1 and 3.1 and related text.

Appendix: Selecting the Oligarchic 29

The "Oligarchy 29" list of families in table 1.1 was constructed by a reputational method. As noted in chapter 1, the families were selected by a panel of seven highly qualified Peruvian judges, including members of two of the families listed and others who were associates and other close observers of the oligarchs. Given the difficulty of approaching these men on a potentially sensitive matter, an informal procedure was employed. In the course of interviews on related topics, the informants were asked to list those whom they felt comprised "the oligarchy." No names were suggested to them, nor was any definition provided. The judges were asked to limit themselves to families that had been important sometime during the period 1930–1968. *After* a list of names was elicited, each informant was asked how he would define the oligarchy. Although there was some minor variation in understanding of the term, all definitions given centered on the notion of a group of families that built substantial political power on a base of economic power.

Individual judges suggested varying numbers of families. In total, fifty-three different families were named (table A.1). Almost all were well known to me after a year of fieldwork, and the list included virtually all the contemporary families who appeared economically important. There was a high degree of consensus about the three families (Aspíllagas, Prados, and Miró Quesadas) which are the subjects of separate chapters in this book: each was named by at least five of the seven judges.

The Oligarchic 29 list consists (with one exception) of all families named by two or more judges. The exception is D'Onofrio, a wealthy industrial family that was eliminated from the list although named by two judges. This family had apparently never been politically active and did not share any of the economic or social characteristics, such as export investments or membership in the Club Nacional, that were common to the others.

The advantage of this method is that it avoids suggesting to respondents answers the researcher expects. The disadvantage is that it depends on respondents' recall—which might, for example, be less reliable for families that had lost the wealth and power they had held ten or fifteen years earlier. The D'Onofrio dilemma could have been avoided and the general reliability of the final list improved by taking the additional step of resubmitting the initial, composite list to at least some of the original judges or to several new judges to get a better read of the consensus concerning these families. Resubmission would have supported a higher bar (agreement of three or more judges) for inclusion on the final list. This was the procedure employed to determine the Top Social Circle.

Table A.1. Families Named by Judges

Family	Number of Judges Listing	Family	Number of Judges Listing
Alba	1	Lanatta	1
Alvarez Calderón	1	Larco	3
Aspíllaga	5	Lavalle	2
Ayulo	5	Madueño	1
Banchero	3	Malaga	2
Barreda	2	Martinto	1
Bellido	1	Miró Quesada	5
Beltrán	6	Moreyra	1
Benavides	2	Mujica	3
Bentín	2	Nicolini	1
Berckemeyer	2	Olaechea	3
Boza	1	Orbegoso	2
Brescia	3	Osma	1
Carrillo	3	Pardo	7
Cilloniz	1	Picasso	4
Chopitea	2	Piedra	7
D'Onofrio	2	Prado	6
Duran	1	Raffo	1
Ferreyros	1	Ramos	2
Fernandini	4	Reiser	1
Ferrand	2	Riva Agüero	1
Gallo	1	Rizo Patrón	2
Ganoza	1	Romero	1
Gildemeister	7	Thorndike	1
Graña	2	Ugarteche	1
Isola	1	Wiese	4
Izaga	1		

Bibliography and Archival Sources

I. ARGENTINA

Alexander, Robert J. 2003. *A History of Organized Labor in Argentina.* Westport, CT: Praeger.

Alonso, Paula. 2010. *Jardines Secretos, Legitimaciones Públicas.* Buenos Aires: edhasa.

Bethell, Leslie, ed. 1993. *Argentina since Independence.* Cambridge: Cambridge University Press.

Botana, Natalio R. 1994. *El Orden Conservador: La Política Argentina entre 1880 y 1916.* Nueva edición Buenos Aires: Editorial Sudamericana.

Brown, Jonathan C. 2010. *A Brief History of Argentina.* 2nd ed. New York: Facts on File.

Bryce, James. 1916. *South America: Observations and Impressions.* New York: Macmillan.

Cortés Conde, Roberto. 1993. The Growth of the Argentine Economy, c. 1870–1914. In *Argentina since Independence*, ed. Bethell.

Deutsch, Sandra McGee. 1993. The Right under Radicalism, 1916–1930. In *The Argentine Right: Its History and Intellectual Origins, 1910 to the Present*, ed. Sandra McGee Deutsch and Ronald H. Dolkart. Wilmington, DE: Scholarly Resources, Inc.

Díaz Alejandro, Carlos Federico. 1970. *Essays on the Economic History of the Argentine Republic.* New Haven, CT: Yale University Press.

Dolkart, Ronald H. 1993. The Right in the Década Infame, 1930–1943. In *The Argentine Right: Its History and Intellectual Origins, 1910 to the Present*, ed. Sandra McGee Deutsch and Ronald H. Dolkart. Wilmington, DE: Scholarly Resources, Inc.

Edsall, Thomas More. 1999. *Elites, Oligarchs, and Aristocrats: The Jockey Club of Buenos Aires and the Argentine Upper Class, 1920–1940.* Doctoral dissertation, Tulane University.

Falcoff, Mark and Byron Crites. 2008. Argentina in the Twentieth Century. In *Encyclopedia of Latin American History and Culture*, ed. Jay Kinsbruner and Erick D. Langer. 2nd ed. New York: Charles Scribner's Sons.

Falcoff, Mark and Ronald H. Dolkart. 1975. Political Developments. In *Prologue to Perón: Argentina in Depression and War, 1930–1943*, ed. Mark Falcoff and Ronald H. Dolkart. Berkeley: University of California Press.

Gallo, Ezequiel. 1993. Society and Politics, 1880–1916. In *Argentina since Independence*, ed. Bethell.

Gibson, Edward L. 1996. *Class and Conservative Parties: Argentina in Comparative Perspective.* Baltimore: Johns Hopkins University Press.

Goodwin, Paul B. and Vicente Palermo. 2008. Irigoyen, Hipólito (1852–1933). In *Encyclopedia of Latin American History and Culture*, ed. Jay Kinsbruner and Erick D. Langer, ed, 2nd ed. New York: Charles Scribner's Sons.

Hora, Roy. 2001a. *The Landowners of the Argentine Pampas: A Social and Political History, 1860–1945.* Oxford: Clarendon.

———. 2001b. Landowning Bourgeoisie or Business Bourgeoisie? On the Peculiarities of the Argentine Economic Elite, 1880–1945. *Journal of Latin American Studies* 34: 587–623.

———. 2003. The Making and Evolution of the Buenos Aires Economic Elite in the Nineteenth Century: The Example of the Senillosas. *Hispanic American Historical Review* 83: 452–486.

———. 2014. The Impact of the Depression on Argentine Society. In *The Great Depression in Latin America*, ed. Paulo Drinot and Alan Knight. Durham, NC: Duke University Press.

———. n.d. *La trayectoria económica de al familia Anchorena* (1800–1945). Unpublished manuscript.

Horowitz, Joel. 1999. Populism and Its Legacies in Argentina. In *Populism in Latin America*, ed. Michael Conniff Tuscaloosa: University of Alabama Press.

———. 2008. *Argentina's Radical Party and Popular Mobilization, 1916–1930.* University Park: The Pennsylvania State University Press.

Imaz, José Luís de. 1964. *Los Que Mandan.* Buenos Aires: Eudeba.

Losada, Leandro. 2007. ¿Oligarquía o elites? Estructura y Composición de las Clases Altas de la Ciudad de Buenos Aires entre 1880 y 1930. *Hispanic American Historical Review* 87: 43–75.

———. 2008. *La Alta Sociedad en la Buenos Aires de la Belle Epoque: Sociabilidad, Estilos de Vida e Identidades.* Buenos Aires: Siglo XXI Editora Iberoamericana.

Lynch, John. 1993. From Independence to National Organization. In *Argentina since Independence*, ed. Bethell.

McGann, Thomas Francis. 1957. *Argentina, the United States, and the Inter-American System, 1880–1914.* Cambridge, MA: Harvard University Press.

Piccirilli, Ricardo, Francisco L. Romay, and Leoncio Gianello, eds. 1953–1954. *Diccionario Histórico Argentino.* Buenos Aires: Ediciones Historicas Argentinas.

Potash, Robert. 1969. *The Army and Politics in Argentina, 1928–1943: Yrigoyen to Peón.* Stanford: Stanford University Press.

Remmer, Karen L. 1984. *Party Competition in Argentina and Chile: Political Recruitment and Public Policy, 1890–1930.* Lincoln: University of Nebraska Press.

Richmond, Douglas W. 1989. *Carlos Pellegrini and the Crisis of the Argentine Elites, 1880–1916.* New York: Praeger.

Rock, David. 1975a. *Politics in Argentina, 1890–1930: The Rise and Fall of Radicalism.* Cambridge: Cambridge University Press.

———, ed. 1975b. *Argentina in the Twentieth Century.* Pittsburgh: University of Pittsburgh Press.

———. 1993a. Argentina in 1914: The Pampas, the Interior, Buenos Aires. In *Argentina since Independence,* ed. Bethell.

———. 1993b. From the First World War to 1930. In *Argentina since Independence,* ed, Bethell.

———. 2002. *State Building and Political Movements in Argentina, 1860–1916.* Stanford, CA: Stanford University Press.

———. 2005. Argentina: A Hundred and Fifty Years of Democratic Praxis. *Latin American Research Review* 40: 221–234.

Romero, Luis Alberto. 1994. *Argentina in the Twentieth Century.* University Park: The Pennsylvania State University Press.

Scobie, James R. 1964. *Argentina: A City and a Nation.* New York: Oxford University Press.

———. 1974. *Buenos Aires: Plaza to Suburb, 1870–1910.* New York: Oxford University Press.

Smith, Peter H. 1974. *Argentina and the Failure of Democracy: Conflict among Political Elites, 1904–1955.* Madison: University of Wisconsin Press.

———. 1978. The Breakdown of Democracy in Argentina, 1916–1930. In *The Breakdown of Democratic Regimes: Latin America,* ed. Juan J. Linz and Alfred Stepan. Baltimore: The Johns Hopkins University Press.

Solberg, Carl. 1985. Land Tenure and Settlement Patterns in the Canadian Prairies and the Argentine Pampas. In *Argentina, Australia and Canada: Studies in Comparative Development, 1870–1965,* ed. D. C. M. Platt and Guido di Tella. New York: St. Martin's.

Strickon, Arnold. 1965. Class and Kinship in Argentina. In *Contemporary Cultures and Societies of Latin America: A Reader in the Social Anthropology of Middle and South America and the Caribbean,* ed. Dwight B. Heath and Richard N. Adams. New York: Random House.

II. BRAZIL

Bethell, Leslie, ed. 1989. *Brazil: Empire and Republic, 1822–1930.* Cambridge: Cambridge University Press.

———. 2008. Politics in Brazil under Vargas, 1930–1945. In *The Cambridge History of Latin America.* Vol. IX, *Brazil since 1930,* ed. Leslie Bethell. New York: Cambridge University Press.

Bresser Pereira, Luiz Carlos. 2009. From the Patrimonial State to the Managerial State. In. Sachs et al. eds.

Burns, E. Bradford. 1980. *A History of Brazil.* 2nd ed. New York: Columbia University Press.

———. 1993. *A History of Brazil.* 3rd ed. New York: Columbia University Press.

Conniff, Michael L. 1999. Brazil's Populist Republic and Beyond. In *Populism in Latin America,* M. L. Conniff. Tuscaloosa: University of Alabama Press.

———. 2008. Tentismo. In *Encyclopedia of Latin American History and Culture,* ed. Jay Kinsbruner and Erick D. Langer. 2nd ed. New York: Charles Scribner's Sons.

Dean, Warren. 1969. *The Industrialization of São Paulo.* Austin: University of Texas Press.

———. 1989. Economy. In *Brazil: Empire and Republic,* ed. Bethell.

Fausto, Boris. 1989. Society and Politics. In *Brazil: Empire and Republic,* ed. Bethell.

———. 1999. *A Concise History of Brazil.* Translated by Arthur Brakel. Cambridge: Cambridge University Press.

Font, Mauricio A. 2010. *Coffee and Transformation in São Paulo, Brazil.* Lanham, MD: Rowman and Littlefield Publishers, Inc.

Freyre, Gilberto. 1922. Social Life in Brazil in the Middle of the Nineteenth Century. *Hispanic American Historical Review* 5: 599–627.

Hagopian, Frances. 1996. *Traditional Politics and Regime Change in Brazil.* Cambridge: Cambridge University Press.

Levi, Darrell E. 1987. *The Prados of São Paulo Brazil: An Elite Family and Social Change, 1840–1930.* Athens: The University of Georgia Press.

Levine, Robert M. 1978. *Pernambuco in the Brazilian Federation, 1889–1937.* Stanford, CA: Stanford University Press.

———. 1998. *Father of the Poor: Vargas and His Era.* New York: Cambridge University Press.

Lewin, Linda. 2003. *Surprise Heirs, Volume 1: Illegitimacy, Patrimonial Rights, and Legal Nationalism in Luso-Brazilian Inheritance, 1750–1821.* Stanford, CA: Stanford University Press.

———. 2009. Some Historical Implications of Kinship Organization for Family-Based Politics in the Brazilian Northeast. *Comparative Studies in Society and History* 21: 262–292.

Love, Joseph. 1980. *São Paulo in the Brazilian Federation, 1889–1937.* Stanford, CA: Stanford University Press.

Love, Joseph L. and Bert J. Barickman. 1986. Rulers and Owners: A Brazilian Case Study in Comparative Perspective. *Hispanic American Historical Review* 66: 743–765.

Needell, Jeffrey D. 1987. *A Tropical Belle Epoque: Elite Culture and Society in Turn-of-the-Century Rio de Janiero.* New York: Cambridge University Press.

Pinheiro, Paulo Sérgio. 2009. Political Transition and the (Un)rule of Law in the Republic. In Sachs et al. eds.

Poppino, Rollie. 2008. Getúlio Vargas Dornelles. In *Encyclopedia of Latin American History and Culture*, ed. Jay Kinsbruner and Erick D. Langer. 2nd ed. New York: Charles Scribner's Sons.

Sachs, Ignacy, et al., eds. 2009. *Brazil: A Century of Change.* Chapel Hill: University of North Carolina Press.

Skidmore, Thomas E. 2007. *Politics in Brazil, 1930–1964: An Experiment in Democracy.* 40th Anniversary Edition. New York: Oxford University Press.

———. 2010. *Brazil: Five Centuries of Change.* 2nd ed. New York: Oxford University Press.

Topik, Steven. 1987. *The Political Economy of the Brazilian State, 1889–1930.* Austin: University of Texas Press.

Viotti da Costa, Emília. 1989. 1870–1889. In *Brazil: Empire and Republic*, ed. Bethell.

Wirth, John. 1977. *Minas Gerais in the Brazilian Federation, 1889 – 1937.* Stanford: Stanford University Press.

Wolfe, Joel 2014. Change with Continuity: Brazil from 1930 to 1945. In *The Great Depression in Latin America, ed.* Paulo Drinot and Alan Knight, eds. Durham, NC: Duke University Press.

Woodard, James P. 2006. "All for São Paulo, All for Brazil": Vargas, the *Paulistas*, and the Historiography of Twentieth-Century Brazil. In *Vargas and Brazil: New Perspectives*, ed. J. R. Hentschke. New York: Palgrave Macmillan.

Young, Jordan M. 1967. *The Brazilian Revolution of 1930 and the Aftermath.* New Brunswick, NJ: Rutgers University Press.

———. 2008. Brazil: The Revolution of 1930. In *Encyclopedia of Latin American History and Culture*, ed. Jay Kinsbruner and Erick D. Langer. 2nd ed. New York: Charles Scribner's Sons.

III. CHILE

Angell, Alan. 1993. Chile since 1958. In *Chile since Independence*, ed. Bethell.

Balmaceda Valdes, Eduardo. 1932. *De Mi Tierra y De Francia*. Santiago, Chile: Ediciones Ercilla—Contemporáneos.

Barros Lezaeta, Luis and Ximena Vergara. 1978. *El Modo de ser Aristocraìtico: El Caso de la Oligarquìa Chilena Hacia 1900*. Santiago: Ediciones Aconcagua.

Bauer, Arnold J. 1975. *Chilean Rural Society from the Spanish Conquest to 1930*. Cambridge: Cambridge University Press.

Bethell, Leslie, ed. 1993. *Chile since Independence*. Cambridge: Cambridge University Press.

Blakemore, Harold. 1993. From the War of the Pacific to 1930. In *Chile since Independence* ed. Bethell.

Cavarozzi, Marcelo. 1977. *La Etapa Oligárquica de Dominación Burguesa en Chile*. (Documento CEDES/G.E.CLACSO/N°7). Buenos Aires: Consejo Latinamerico de Ciencias Sociales.

Collier, Simon. 1993. From Independence to the War of the Pacific. In *Chile since Independence*, ed. Bethell.

Collier, Simon and William F. Sater. 2004. *A History of Chile, 1808–2002*. 2nd ed. Cambridge: Cambridge University Press.

DeShazo, Pater. 1983. *Urban Workers and Labor Unions in Chile: 1902–1927*. Madison: University of Wisconsin Press.

Drake, Paul. 1993. Chile, 1930–1958. In *Chile since Independence*, ed. Bethell.

Fernández Darraz, Enrique. 2003. *Estado y Sociedad en Chile, 1891–1931: El Estado Excluyente, la Lógica Estatal Oligárquica y la Formación de la Sociedad*. Santiago: LOM Ediciones.

Lagos, Ricardo 1965. *La concentración del poder económico*. Santiago: Editorial del Pacific.

Loveman, Brian. 1988. *Chile: The Legacy of Hispanic Capitalism*. 2nd ed. New York: Oxford University Press.

Marcella, Gabriel. 1973. *The Structure of Politics in Nineteenth-Century Spanish America: The Chilean Oligarchy, 1833–1891*. Master's thesis, Notre Dame University.

Pike, Fredrick B. 1963. Aspects of Class Relations in Chile, 1850–1960. *The Hispanic American Historical Review* 43: 14–33

Portales, Felipe. 2004. *Los Mitos de la Democracia Chilena: Tomo I, Desde la Conquista a 1925*. Santiago: Catalonia.

Remmer, Karen L. 1984. *Party Competition in Argentina and Chile: Political Recruitment and Public Policy, 1980–1930*. Lincoln: University of Nebraska Press.

Sater, William. 2008. Chile, Parliamentary Regime. In *Encyclopedia of Latin American History and Culture*, ed. Kinsbruner and Langer. 2nd ed. Vol. 2. Detroit: Charles Scribner's Sons.

Subercaseaux Browne, Julio. 1976. *Reminiscencias*. Santiago: Editorial Nascimento.

Vergara, Angela. 2014. Chilean Workers and the Great Depression, 1930–1938. In *The Great Depression in Latin America*, ed. Drinot and Knight.

Vial Correa, Gonzalo. 1981. *Historia de Chile (1891–1973)*. *3v.* Santiago: Ed. Santillana del Pacifico.

Villalobos, Sergio. 1987. *Origen y Ascenso de la Burguesía Chilena*. Santiago: Editorial Universitaria.

Zeitlin, Maurice and Richard Ratcliff. 1988. *Landlords & Capitalists: The Dominant Class in Chile*. Princeton, NJ: Princeton University Press.

IV. MEXICO

Benjamin, Thomas and William McNellie, eds. 1984. *Other Mexicos: Essays on Regional Mexican History, 1876–1911*. Albuquerque, NM: University of New Mexico Press.

Benjamin, Thomas and Mark Wasserman, eds. 1990. *The Provinces of the Revolution*. Albuquerque, NM: University of New Mexico Press.

Bethell, Leslie, ed. 1991. *Mexico since Independence*. Cambridge: Cambridge University Press.

Buffington, Robert and William French. 2000. The Culture of Modernity. In *The Oxford History of Mexico*, ed. Meyer and Beezley.

Camp, Roderic A. 1989. *Entrepreneurs and Politics in Twentieth Century Mexico*. New York: Oxford University Press.

Coatsworth, John. 1974. Railroads, Landholding, and Agrarian Protest in Early Porfiriato. *The Hispanic American Historical Review* 54: 48–71.

González, Luis. 2000. El Liberalismo Triunfante. In *Historia General de México*. Versión 2000. Mexico City: El Colegio de México.

Guerra, François-Xavier. 1988. *México: Del Antiguo Régimen a la Revolución*. 2 vols. México: Fondo de Cultura Económica.

Haber, Stephen, Armando Razo, and Noel Maurer. 2003. *The Politics of Property Rights: Political Instability, Credible Commitments, and Economic Growth in Mexico, 1876–1929*. Cambridge: Cambridge University Press.

Hamilton, Nora. 1982. *The Limits of State Autonomy: Post-Revolutionary Mexico*. Princeton, NJ: Princeton University Press.

Hansen, Roger D. 1971. *The Politics of Mexican Development*. Baltimore: Johns Hopkins Press.

Hart, John Mason. 1987. *Revolutionary Mexico: The Coming and Process of the Mexican Revolution*. Berkeley: University of California Press.

Iturriaga, José. 1951. *La Estructure Social y Cultural de México*. Mexico City: Fundo de Cultura Económico.

Joseph, Gilbert M. and Jurgen Buchenau. 2013. *Mexico's Once and Future Revolution*. Durham, NC: Duke University Press.

Joseph, Gilbert M. and Allen Wells. 1986. Summer of Discontent: Economic Rivalry among Elite Factions during the Late Porfiriato in Yucatán. *Journal of Latin American Studies* 18: 255–282.

Kandell, Jonathan. 1988. *La Capital: The Biography of Mexico City*. New York: Random House.

Katz, Friedrich. 1981. *The Secret War in Mexico: Europe, the United States and the Mexican Revolution*. Chicago: University of Chicago Press.

———. 1991. The Liberal Republic and Porfiriato, 1867–1910. In *Mexico since Independence*, ed. Bethell.

Knight, Alan. 1986. *The Mexican Revolution*. 2 vol. Cambridge: Cambridge University Press.

———. 1991. The Rise and Fall of Cardenismo, c. 1930–c. 1946. In *Mexico since Independence*, ed. Bethell.

Krauze, Enrique. 1998. *Mexico: Biography of Power: A History of Modern Mexico, 1810–1996*. New York: HarperPerennial.

LaFrance, David. 1984. Breakdown of the Old Order. In *Other Mexicos*, ed. Benjamin and McNellie.

Langton, William. 1984. Coahuila: Centralization against State Autonomy. In *Other Mexicos*, ed. Benjamin and McNellie.

Lomnitz, Larissa Adler and Marisol Perez-Lizaur. 1987. *A Mexican Elite Family, 1920–1980: Kinship, Class, and Culture*. Princeton, NJ: Princeton University Press.

Meyer, Jean. 1991. Revolution and Reconstruction in the 1920s. In *Mexico since Independence*, ed. Bethell.

Meyer, Michael C. and William H. Beezley, eds. 2000. *The Oxford History of Mexico*. New York: Oxford University Press.

Moreno-Brid, Juan Carlos and James Ros. 2009. *Development and Growth in the Mexican Economy: A Historical Perspective*. New York: Oxford University Press.

Negretto, Gabriel L. and José Antonio Aguilar-Rivera. 2000. Rethinking the Legacy of the Liberal State in Latin America: The Cases of Argentina (1853–1916) and Mexico (1857–1910). *Journal of Latin American Studies* 32: 361–397.

Newell, Roberto and Luis Rubio. 1984. *Mexico's Dilemma: The Political Origins of Economic Crisis*. Boulder, CO: Westview.

Nutini, Hugo G. 1995. *The Wages of Conquest: The Mexican Aristocracy in the Context of Western Aristocracies*. Ann Arbor: University of Michigan Press.

Rath, Thomas. 2013. *Myths of Demilitarization in Postrevolutionary Mexico*. Chapel Hill: University of North Carolina Hill.

Saragoza, Alex. 1988. *The Monterrey Elite and the Mexican State, 1988–1940*. Austin: University of Texas Press.

Smith, Peter H. 1979. *Labyrinths of Power: Political Recruitment in Twentieth-Century Mexico*. Princeton, NJ: Princeton University Press.

Tutino, John. 1990. Regions, Classes, and the New National State. In *The Provinces of the Revolution*, ed. Benjamin and Wasserman.

Wasserman, Mark. 1984. *Capitalists, Caciques, and Revolution: The Native Elite and Foreign Enterprise in Chihuahua, Mexico, 1854–1911*. Chapel Hill: University of North Carolina Press.

———. 1995. *Persistent Oligarchs: Elites and Politics in Chihuahua, Mexico, 1910–1940*. Durham, NC: Duke University Press.

Wells, Allen. 1982. Family Elites in a Boom-and-Bust Economy: The Molinas and Peóns of Porfirian Yucatán. *Hispanic American Historical Review* 62: 224–253.

———. 1992. All in the Family: Railroads and Henequen Monoculture in Porfirian Yucatan. *Hispanic American Historical Review* 72: 159–209.

V. PERU AND GENERAL WORKS

Abramovitch, Jaysuno. 1973. *La Industria Pesquera en el Perú: Génesis, Apogeo y Crisis*. Lima: Centro de Investigaciones Económicas y Sociales de la Universidad Nacional Villarreal.

Adler, Mortimer, et al. 1952. The Great Ideas: Syntopicon of Great Books of the Western World. Vol II Chicago: Encyclopedia Britannica.

Aguirre Gamio, Hernando. 1962. *Liquidación Histórica del Apra y del Colonialismo Neoliberal*. Lima: Eds. Diba.

Ahumada Moreno, Pascual. 1885. *Guerra del Pacifico: Recopilación Completa de Todos los Documentos Oficiales, Correspondencia I Demas Publicaciones*. Valparaiso: Americana.

Alba, Victor. 1968. *Politics and the Labor Movement in Latin America*. Stanford, CA: Stanford University Press.

Albert, Bill. 1976. *An Essay on the Peruvian Sugar Industry, 1880–1922, and The Letters of Ronald Gordon, Administrator of the British Sugar Company in the Canete Valley, 1914–1919*. Norwich, UK: School of Social Studies, University of East Anglia.

———. 1985. External Forces and the Transformation of Peruvian Coastal Agriculture, 1880–1930. In *Latin America, Economic Imperialism and the State: The Political Economy of the External Connection from Independence to the Present*, ed. Christopher Abel and Colin Lewis. London: Athlone Press.

Alberti, Giorgio. 1976. Peasant Movements in the Yanamarco Valley. In ed. Chaplin.

Alexander, Robert. 1962. *Labor relations in Argentina, Brazil, and Chile.* New York: McGraw-Hill.

———. 1973. *Aprismo: The Ideas and Doctrines of Victor Raul Haya de la Torre.* Kent, OH: Kent State University Press.

Almandoz, Artturo. 2010. *Planning Latin America's Capital Cities 1850–1950.* New York: Routledge.

Alzamora, Issac and M. F. Arrospide. 1890. *Defensa de los Herederos de Ramon A. Aspíllaga . . ..* Lima: Imp. de Juan Francisco Solis.

Anderson, Charles. 1967. *Politics and Economic Change in Latin America.* New York: Van Nostrand.

American Factors, Ltd. 1965. Hacienda Cayaltí. (Unpublished Report) Honolulu.

Arenas, German. 1941. *Algo de Una Vida.* Lima: Sanmartin.

Astiz, Carlos. 1969. *Pressure Groups and Power Elites in Peruvian Politics.* Ithaca, NY: Cornell University Press.

Ballantyne, Janet C. 1976. *The Political Economy of Peruvian Gran Mineria.* Latin American Studies Program Dissertation Series, Cornell University, Ithaca.

Balmori, Diana, et al., eds. 1984. *Notable Family Networks in Latin America.* Chicago: University of Chicago Press.

Baltzell, E. Digby. 1958. *Philadelphia Gentleman: The Making of a National Upper Class.* Glencoe: The Free Press.

Banco Central de Reserva del Perú. n.d. *Cuentas Nacionales 1960–1969.* Lima.

Banco de Credito. 1946–1968. *Vadamencum del Inversionista.* Lima: Banco de Credito.

Banco Popular. 1954–1969. *Memorias.* Lima: Banco Popular.

Barreda y Laos, Felipe. 1954. *Manuel Pardo Ribadeneyra: Regente de la Audiencia del Cuzco.* Lima.

Barreto, C. A. and G. de la Fuente 1928. *Diccionario Biográfico de Figuras Contemporáneas.* Lima: Lit. T. Scheuch.

Basadre, Jorge. 1931. *Perú: Problema y Posibilidad.* Lima: Liberia Francesa Científica.

———. 1964. *Historia de la Republica del Perú*, 10 V. Lima: Ediciones Historia.

———. 1968. *Historia de la Republica del Perú*, 16 V. Lima: Editorial Universitaria.

———. 1971. *Introducción a las Bases Documentales Para la Historia de la Republica del Perú, con Algunas Reflexiones.* Lima: Ediciones P.L. Villanueva.

Bejar, Hector. 1970. *Perú 1965.* New York: Monthly Review Press.

Belaunde, V. A. 1967. *Trayectoria y Destino: Memorias*, 2 V. Lima: Ediciones De Ediventas.

Bergquist, Charles. 1986. *Labor in Latin America: Comparative Essays on Chile, Argentina, Venezuela, and Colombia.* Stanford: Stanford University Press.

Boletín de la Sociedad Nacional Minera.

Bertram, I. Geoffrey. 1974a. Development Problems in an Export Economy: A Study of Domestic Capitalists, Foreign Firms, and Government in Perú: 1919–1930. Ph.D. Thesis, Oxford University, Oxford.

———. 1974b. Metal Mining in Perú since the Depression. Unpublished Paper.

———. 1991. Peru, 1930–1960. In *The Cambridge History of Latin America* , ed. Leslie Bethell. Vol VIII. Cambridge: Cambridge University Press.

Bethell, Leslie, ed. 1986. *The Cambridge History of Latin America. Vol IV 1870–1930.* Cambridge: Cambridge University Press.

Billinghurst, Guillermo. 1915. *El Presidente Billinghurst a la Nación*. Santiago: Imprenta Diener. *Boletin de la Sociedad Nacional Minera.*

Bollinger, William. 1971. The Rise of United States Influence in the Perúvian Economy. M.A. Thesis, University of California, Los Angeles.

Bonilla, Heraclio. 1974. *Guano y Burguesía en el Perú*. Lima: Instituto de Estudios Peruanos.

Bottomore, Tom. 1966. *Elites in Modern Society*. New York. Pantheon Book.

Bourricaud, Francois. 1966. Structure and Functions of the Peruvian Oligarchy. *Studies in Comparative International Development* 2: 17–36.

———. 1969a. Notas Acerca de la Oligarquía Peruana. In *La Oligarquía en el Perú*, ed. Matos Mar.

———. 1969b. La Clase Dirigente Peruana: Oligarcas e Industriales. In *La Oligarquía en el Perú*, ed. Matos Mar.

———. 1970. *Power and Society in Contemporary Perú*. New York. Praeger Publishers.

Bourricaud, Francois, et al. 1972. *La Oligarquía en el Perú*. Buenos Aires: Amorrortu Editores.

Bulmer-Thomas, Victor. 2003. The Economic History of Latin America since Independence. 2nd ed. Cambridge: Cambridge University Press.

Burga, Manuel and Alberto Flores Galindo. 1984. *Apogeo y Crisis de la Republica Aristocratica*. Lima: Ediciones Rikchay Perú.

Bustamante y Rivero, Jose. 1949. *Tres Anos de Lucha Por la Democracia en el Perú*. Buenos Aires.

Camprubi Alcazar, Carlos. 1966. Un Cubana Al Servicio del Perú: Jose Payan. *Revista Histórica* 29: 5–78.

Capuñay, Manuel A. 1951. *Leguía, Vida y Obra del Constructor del Gran Perú*. Lima.

Castro, N. 1880. *Opusculo Sobre La Guerra y Dictadura*. Lima: Imp. del Universo.

Cevallos, Maria Antonieta. 1972. Sindicalismo Azucarero Durante el Periodo 1956–1962. *Cuadernos de Taller de Investigacion Rural*, No. 12, Programa Academico de Ciencias Sociales, Universidad Catolica, Lima.

Chaplin, David, ed. 1976. *Peruvian Nationalism*. New Brunswick, NJ: Transaction Books.

Chirinos Soto, Enrique. 1962. *El Perú Frente a Junio de 1962*. Lima: Ediciones de Sol.

———. 1967 *Actores en el Drama del Perú y del Mundo*. Lima.

Clawson, David 2012. Latin America and the Caribbean: Lands and Peoples. New York: Oxford University Press. *El Comercio (Lima)*

Club Nacional. 1896–1960. *Memorias*. Lima.

Collier, David. 1976. The Politics of Squatter Settlement Formation in Perú. In ed. Chaplin.

Collier, Ruth Berins and David Collier. 1991. *Shaping the Political Arena: Critical Junctures, the Labor Movement, and Regime Dynamics in Latin America*. Princeton, NJ: Princeton University Press.

Doughty, Paul 1976. Social Growth and Urban Policy in Lima. In Chaplin, ed. .

El Comercio. 1894. *Al Señor J. Antonio Miró Quesada*. Lima: *El Comercio*.

———. 1919. *Almanaque de El Comercio*. Lima: El Comercio.

———. 1970. *Luís Miró Quesada*. Lima: El Comercio.

Comisión Creada para la Resolución Suprema No. 400. 1968. Informe Sobre la Sequia en el Norte del Pais.

Contreras, Carlos and Marina Zuloaga. 2014. *Historia Minima del Perú*. Mexico DF: Colegio de Mexico.

Correo (Lima). 1970–1975.

Cossio del Pomar, Felipe. 1961, 1969. *Victor Raul, Biografia de Haya de la Torre*, 2 Vols. México: Ed. Cultura.

Cotler, Julio. 1970a. The Mechanics of Internal Domination and Social Change in Perú. In *Masses in Latin America*, ed. Irving L. Horowitz. New York: Oxford University Press.

———. 1970b. Political Crisis and Military Populism in Perú. *Studies in Comparative International Development* 6 (5): 95–113.

———. 1970c. Traditional Haciendas and Communities in a Context of Political Mobilization in Perú. In *Agrarian Problems and Peasant Movements in Latin America*, ed. Rodolfo Stagehagen. New York: Anchor Books.

La Crónica (Lima). 1940–1975.

Cultura Peruana. 1960. Cayaltí, Centro Azucarcro, Cumple Un Siglo, May 21.

Dagicour, Ombeline. n.d. Political Invention in the Andes: The Peruvian Case. An Essay on President Augusto B. Leguía's Strategies and Practices of Power during the Oncenio (1919–1930). Unpublished paper.

Dahl, Robert 1958. A Critique of the Ruling Elite Model. *The American Political Science Review* 52: 463–469.

Drake, Paul W. 2009. *Between Tyranny and Anarchy: A History of Democracy in Latin America, 1800–2006*. Stanford, CA: Stanford University Press.

Delgado, Luís Humberto. 1937. *Historia de Antonio Miró Quesada. 1875–1935*. 2v. Lima: Ariel.

———. 1952. *Mariano Ignacio Prado: Caudillo y Prócer del Perú*. Lima: Ariel.

DESCO. 1974. *Perú: 1968–1973, Cronología Política*, 2 Vols. Lima: Industrial Grafica.

Descola, Jean. 1968. *Daily Life in Colonial Perú, 1710–1820*. New York: Macmillan and Company.

Dominguez, Carlos. 1970. Fall of the Prado Empire Discussed. La Libertad (San Jose) October 10. Translated. Joint Publications Research Service (International Development), 9, Reel No. 148, Trans. No. 428, 96–104.

Drinot, Paulo and Alan Knight, eds. 2014. *The Great Depression in Latin America*. Durham, NC: Duke University Press

Dulanto Pinillos, Jorge. 1947. *Nicolas de Piérola*. Lima: Cía. de Impresiones Publicidad.

Echegaray Corea, Ismael R. 1965. *La Camera de Diputados y Las Constituyentes del Perú, 1822–1965*. Lima: Imprenta del Ministerio de Hacienda y Comercio.

Einaudi, Luigi. 1969. *The Peruvian Military: A Summary Political Analysis*. Memo Rm- 6048-Rc. Santa Monica, CA: The Rand Corporation.

———. 1976. Revolution from Within? Military Rule in Perú since 1968. In Chaplin, ed.

Empresas Eléctricas Asociadas. 1966. *60 Años de Empresas Eléctricas Asociadas*. Lima: Empresas Eléctricas Asociadas.

Escuelas Americas. 1943. *Diccionario Biográfico del Perú. . . .* Lima.

Espinosa Uriarte, H. and Jorge Osorio. 1971. El Poder Económico en el Sector de Medios de Comunicación de Masas. In *Dependencia Económica: Caso Peruano*, ed. Espinosa, et al. Lima: Centro de Investigaciones Económicas y Sociales de la Universidad National Villarreal.

Espinoza, Enrique L. 1905. Informe Sobre el Departamento de Lambayeque. *Boletín del Ministerio de Fomento*: 51–55.

Expreso (Lima). 1964–1975.

Gall, Norman. 1971. The Master Is Dead. *Dissent*, June.

Gargurevich, Juan. 1972. *Mito y Verdad de los Diarios de Lima*. Lima: Editorial Grafica Labor.

Garland, Alejandro. 1895. La Industria Azucarera en el Perú. Typescript, U.S.D.A. Library, Washington, D.C.

———. 1908. *Peru in 1906 and After*. Secvond Editionl Lima: La Industria Printing Office.

Gerlach, Allen. 1973. Civil-Military Relations in Perú: 1914–1945. Ph.D. Thesis, University of New Mexico, Albuquerque.

Gilbert, Dennis. 1977. *The Oligarchy and the Old Regime in Perú*. Latin American Program Dissertation Series, Cornell University, Ithaca.

———. 1979. Society, Politics, and the Press: An Interpretation of the Peruvian Press Reform of 1974. *Journal of Interamerican Studies and World Affairs* 21(3): 369–393.

———. 1980. The End of the Peruvian Revolution. *Studies in Comparative International Development*, Febrero.

———. 1981. Cognatic Descent Groups in Upper-Class Lima (Peru). *American Ethnologist* 8: 739–757.

———. 1982. *La Oligarquía Peruana: Historia de tres Familias*. Lima: Editorial Horizonte.

Gillin, John. 1965. Ethos Components in Modern Latin American Culture. In *Contemporary Cultures and Societies of Latin America*, ed. Dwight B. Heath and Richard Adams. New York: Random House.

Glade, William P. 1969. *The Latin American Economies: A Study of Their Institutional Evolution*. New York: Van Nostrand.

Gonzales, Michael J. 1978. Cayaltí: The Formation of a Rural Proletariat on a Peruvian Sugar Plantation 1875–1933. Doctoral Dissertation. University of California, Berkeley.

———. 1985. *Plantation Agriculture and Social Control in Northern Peru, 1875–1933*. Austin: University of Texas Press.

———. 1991. Planters and Politics in Peru, 1895–1919. *Journal of Latin American Studies* 23: 515–541.

González, Luis 2000. El Liberalismo Triumfante. In *Historia General de Mexico*. Mexico City: Colegio de Mexico

Goodwin, Richard N. 1969. Letter from Perú, *New Yorker*, May 17.

Granick, David. 1964. *The European Executive*. Garden City, KS: Doubleday and Company.

Guimet J., Armando. 1955. *Prado Versus Piérola en 1873: Una Polémica Histórica*. 3rd ed. Lima.

Hall, Michael and Hobart Spalding, Jr. 1986. The Urban Working Class and Early Latin American Labour Movements, 1880–1930. In *The Cambridge History of Latin America*, vol. IV, ed. Leslie Bethell. Cambridge: Cambridge University Press.

Haya de la Torre, Victor Raúl. 1976. *Obras Completas*. 7t. Lima: Mejia Beca.

Hilliker, Grant. 1971. *The Politics of Reform in Perú*. Baltimore: Johns Hopkins Press.

Horton, Douglas E. 1973. Haciendas and Cooperatives: A Preliminary Study of Latifundist Agriculture and Agrarian Reform in Northern Perú. Research Paper, No. 53, Land Tenure Center, University of Wisconsin, Madison.

Huertas Vallejos, Lorenzo. 1974. *Capital Burocrático y Lucha de Clases en el Sector Agrario (Lambayeque, Perú 1920–50)*. Seminario de Historia Rural Andina, Universidad de San Marcos, Lima.

Hunt, Shane. 1973. Growth and Guano in Nineteenth Century Perú. Discussion Paper No. 34, Woodrow Wilson School, Princeton University, Princeton.

Instituto Nacional de Planificación (INP). 1973a. Estructura de la Propiedad e Industrias Textiles. Lima.

———. 1973b. Estructura de la Propiedad e Industrias Metal Mechanics. Lima.

———. 1973c. Estuctura de la Propiedad e Industrias de Caucho, Archilla. Lima.

———. 1973d. Estructura de la Propiedad e Industrias Diversas. Lima.

———. 1973e. Estructura de la Propiedad e Industrias Alemanticias. Lima.

Jaquette, Jane S. 1971. *The Politics of Development in Perú*. Latin American Studies Program, Dissertation Series, Cornell University, Ithaca.

Johnson, John J. 1958. *Political Change in Latin America: The Emergence of the Middle Sectors*. Stanford, CA: Stanford University Press.

————. 1964. *The Military and Society in Latin America*. Stanford, CA: Stanford University Press.

Karno, Howard L. 1970. Augusto B. Leguía: The Oligarchy and the Modernization of Perú, 1870–1930. Ph.D. Thesis, University of California, Los Angeles..

Kenashiro, Luisa and Jorge Rueda. 1972. Clases Sociales y Dominación en Loreto (Trujillo: La Libertad). B.A. Thesis, Universidad de San Marcos, Lima.

Kilty, Daniel. 1967. *Planning for Development in Perú*. New York: Praeger Publishers.

Kinsbruner, Jay and Erick D. Langer, eds. 2008. *Encyclopedia of Latin American History and Culture*. 2nd ed. New York: Charles Scribner's Sons.

Klaren, Peter F. 1976. *La Formación de las Haciendas Azucareras y los Origines del Apra*. 2d. Edicion. Lima: Instituto de Estudios Peruanos.

Kuzcynski, Pedro Pablo 1977   Peruvian Democracy under Economic Stress: An Account of the Belaúnde Administration.   Princeton: Princeton University Press.

————. 1986. The Origins of Modern Peru, 1880–1930. In *The Cambridge History of Latin America*, vol. V., ed. Leslie Bethell. Cambridge: Cambridge University Press.

————. 2000. *Peru: Society and Nationhood in the Andes*. New York: Oxford University Press.

————. Forthcoming. *Historical Dictionary of Peru*. Scarecrow Press.

Laos, Cipriano. 1927. *Lima: Cuidad de los Virreyes*. Lima: Editorial Perú.

Larson, Magali Sarfatti and A. E. Bergman. 1969. *Social Stratification in Perú*. Institute of International Studies, University of California, Berkeley.

Lasarte, Ferreyros, Luís. 1938. *Familias Establecidas en el Perú Durante la Conquista y el Virreyanto*. Lima: Imprenta Torres Aguire.

————. 1993. *Apuntes sobre cien Familias establecidas en el Peru*. Lima: Rider Ediciones Nacionales.

Lavalle, J. A. de. 1893. *Galería de Retratos de Los Gobernantes del Perú Independiente (1821–71)*. Lima: Liberia Clásica y Científica.

Lévano, César. 1967. *La Verdadera Historia de la Jornada de las Ocho Horas en el Perú*. Lima: publisher unknown.

Levin, J. M. 1960. *The Export Economies: Their Pattern of Development in Historical Perspective*. Cambridge: Harvard University Press.

Libro de Oro. 1914–1969. Lima.

Lima en el IV Centenario de Su Fundación: Monografía de Departamento de Lima. 1935. Lima: Minerva.

Little, Arthur D., Inc. 1960. *A Program for the Industrial and Regional Development of Perú*. Cambridge: Arthur D. Little, Inc.

Macera, Pablo, ed. 1973. Cayalti, 1875–1920. *Organizacion del trabajo en una Plantacion Azucarera*. Seminario de Historia Andina.

Maiguasha, Juan. 1967. A Reinterpretation of the Guano Age 1840–1880. Ph.D. Thesis. Oxford University, Oxford.

Malpica, Carlos. 1973. *Los Dueños del Perú*. 5th ed. Lima: Ediciones Persa.

Martin, José Carlos. 1948. *José Pardo y Barreda*. Lima: Cia de Impresiones y Publicidad.

————. 1949. *Historia de la Facultad de Ciencias Politicas y Administratives: 1875–1920*. Lima.

Masterson, Daniel. 1991, *Militarismo and Politics in Latin Amierica: Peru from Sanchez Cerro to Sendero Luminoso.* Westport, CT: Greenwood.

Martínez, Pedro Pablo. 1935. *Haciendo Historia.* Lima: publisher unknown.

Martínez de la Torre, Richardo. 1949. *Apuntes Para Una Historia Marxista del Perú* 4 V, Lima: Empresas Editora Peruana.

Mathews, William. 1968. The Imperialism of Free Trade: Perú, 1820–1870. *The Economic History Review* 21: 562–579.

———. 1970. Perú and the British Guano Market 1840–1870. *Economic History Review* 33: 112–128.

———. 1972. Foreign Contractors and the Peruvian Government at the Onset of the Guano Trade. *Hispanic American Historical Review* 52: 598–620.

Matos Mar, José, ed. 1969. *La Oligarquía en el Perú.* Buenos Aires: Amorrortu Editores.

Maushammer, Robert. 1970. Investor Groups, Informal Finance, and the Economic Development of Perú. Ph.D. Thesis, University of Wisconsin, Madison.

McAlister, Lyle, Anthony Maingot, and Robert Potash. 1970. *The Military in Latin American Sociopolitical Evolution: Four Case Studies.* Washington: Center for Research in Social Systems

McArver, Charles. 1974. The Cerro de Pasco Tunnel Controversy. Unpublished Manuscript.

Mendiburu, Manuel de. 1931. *Diccionario Historico Biográfico del Peru.* 11v. Lima: Enrique Palacios.

Miller, Rory. 1982. The Coastal Elite and Peruvian Politics, 1895–1919. *Journal of Latin American Studies* 14: 97–120.

Miranda Romero, Ricardo 1959. Vda de Piedra e Hijos y entidades afiliades. In *La Monografia General del Departmento de Lambayeque.* No publisher.

Miró Quesada, Luis. 1953. *Ofrenda Jubilar del Personal de El Comercio . . .* . Lima: El Comercio.

———. 1965. *Albores de la Reforma Social en el Perú.* Lima: Talis. Grafs. P.L. Villanueva.

Miró Quesada Cáceres, Roberto. 1974. Contradicciones al Interior de la Burguesía Peruana a Través del Análisis de los Diarios "El Comercio" y "La Prensa," 1956–1962. B.A. Thesis, Universidad Católica, Lima.

Miró Quesada Laos, Carlos. 1940. *Lo Que He Visto en Europe.* Lima: Imprenta Torres.

———. 1947. *Sánchez Cerro y Su Tiempo.* Buenos Aires: El Ateneo.

———. 1957. *Historia del Periodismo Peruano.* Lima: Librería International del Perú.

———. 1959. *Radiografia de la Política Peruana.* Lima: Ediciones Paginas Peruanas.

———. 1961. *Autopsia de los Partidos Políticos.* Lima: Ediciones Paginas Peruanas.

Miró Quesada Sosa, Aurelio. 1945. *Don José Antonio Miró Quesada (1845–1920).* Lima: Torres Aguirre, S.A.

Montagne Markholz, Ernesto. 1962. *Memorias.* Lima: unknown publisher.

Moreno Mendiguren, Alfredo. 1956. *Reporterio de Noticias Breves Sobre Personages Peruanos.* Madrid: Sanchez Ocana.

Mosca, Gaetano. 1939. *The Ruling Class.* New York & London: McGraw Hill Book Company.

North, Liisa. 1966. *Civil-Military Relations in Argentina, Chile, and Peru.* Berkeley: Institute of International Studies, University of California.

———. 1973. The Origins and Development of the Peruvian Aprista Party. Ph.D. Thesis, University of California, Berkeley.

Odria, Manuel. 1950. *Discurso y Programa Leído Ante el Congreso . . . Lima, 28 de Julio de 1950.* Lima: Dirección General de Informaciones.

Oiga (Lima). 1963–1975.

de Oliveira, Orlandina and Gryan Roberts 1998. *Urban Social Structures in Latin America, 1930–1990. Latin America Economy and Society since 1930*, ed. *Leslie Nethell*. New York: Cambridge University Press.

Osma, Felipe de. 1963. *Reseña Histórica del Club Nacional*. Lima: Club Nacional.

Osores, Ricardo. 1878. *Biografía de S.E. General Mariano Ignacio Prado*. Lima: P. Lira.

Pacheco, Artemio. 1923. *Cabezas Dirigentes del Alto Comercio del Perú*. Lima: Camera de Comercio.

Palma, Ricardo. 1953. *Tradiciones Peruanas*. Madrid: Aguilar.

Palmer, David Scott. 1973. *Revolution from Above: Military Government and Popular Participation in Perú, 1968–1972*. Latin American Studies Program Dissertation Series, Cornell University, Ithaca.

Pardo Castro, Jose. 1961. *Amos y Siervos en El Comercio*. Lima: Periodistas Unidas.

Pareto, Vilfredo. 1935. *The Mind and Society*. New York: Harcourt Brace.

Parker, David S. 1998. *The Idea of the Middle Class: White Collar Workers and Peruvian Society*. University Park , PA: Penn State University Press.

Parker, William Belmont. 1919. *Peruvians of To-Day*. Lima: Southwell Press.

Partido Civil. 1911. *Proclamación del Señor Aspíllaga, Candidato a la Presidencia de la Republica*. Lima: Tip. de El Lucero.

Payne, Arnold. 1968. *The Peruvian Coup d'Etat of 1962*. Washington: Institute for the Comparative Study of Political Systems.

Payne, James L. 1965. *Labor and Politics in Perú: The System of Political Bargaining*. New Haven, CT: Yale University Press.

Paz Soldan, Juan. 1921. *Diccionario de Peruanos Contemporáneos*. Lima: Imp. Gil.

Paz Soldan, Luís Felipe. 1943. *Paginas Históricas de la Guerra del Pacifico*. Lima: Imprent Americana.

Paz Soldan, Mariano Felipe. 1884. *Narracion Historica de la Guerra de Chile Contra el Perúy Bolivia*. Buenos Aires: Imp. y Lib. de Mayo.

El Peruano (Lima). 1866.

Peruvian Times (Lima). 1940–1975.

Pereyra, Omar 2015. *Contemporary Middle Class in Latin America: A Study of San Felipe*. Langham: Lexington Books.

Pike, Frederick. 1967. *A Modern History of Perú*. New York: Praeger.

———. 1986. *The Politics of the Miraculous in Peru: Haya de la Torre and the Spiritualist. Tradition*. Lincoln: University of Nebraska Press.

Pinelo, Adalberto Jose. 1972. The Nationalization of the International Petroleum Company in Perú: The Multinational Corporation as an Actor in Latin American Politics. Ph.D. Thesis, University of Massachusetts, Amherst.

Plaza, Orlando. 1971. Historia del Sindicato de Cayaltí. B.A. Thesis, Universidad Católica, Lima.

Portocarrero Suárez, Felipe. 1995. *El Imperio Prado: 1890–1970*. Lima: Universidad del Pacifico, Centro de Investigacion (CIUP).

Powell, Sandra. 1976. Political Participation in the Barriadas. In ed. Chaplin.

Prado, Jorge. 1936. *Ideales Democraticos*. Lima: Editorial Huascar.

———. n.d. *Artículos Políticos*. Lima: Imp. E. Moreno.

La Prensa (Lima). 1945–1975.

Puede Ser Un Prado Presidente del Perú? [n.d., but 1936 according to internal evidence].

Purser, W.F.C. 1971. *Metal Mining in Perú: Past and Present*. New York: Praeger.

Quijano, Anibal. 1968. Tendencies in Peruvian Development and Class Structure. In *Latin America: Reform or Revolution*, ed. Jamis Petras and Maurice Zeitlin. New York: Fawcett Publications.

———. 1971. *Nationalism and Capitalism in Perú*. New York: Monthly Review Press.

Quimper, Jose Maria. 1881. *Manifesto del Ex-Ministro de Hacienda y Comercio, J.M. Quimper a la Nacion*. Lima: Imp. de F. Masias y H.

Quiroz, Alfonso W. 1988. Financial Leadership and the Formation of Peruvian Elite Groups, 1884–1930. *Journal of Latin American Studies* 20: 49–81.

———. 1993 *Domestic and Foreign Finance in Modern Peru, 1850–1950*. Pittsburgh: University of Pittsburgh Press.

———. 2008. *Leguía, Augusto Bernardino (1863–1932)*. In *Encyclopedia of Latin American History and Culture*, ed. Kinsbruner and Langer.

Ramirez y Berrios, Guillermo. 1962. *Mariano Prado y Ugarteche*. Lima: Instituto de Altos Estudios Juridicos.

Revisita Historica (Lima) 1956–1957.

Reynoso, Oswaldo. 1973. *En Octubre No Hay Milagros*. 3rd ed. Lima: Ediciones Kantus.

Rivero Velez, Antonio, *et al.* 1973. Vista la Causa . . . en Audiencia Publica. No. 557–571, *Tribunal Correccional Especial*, Lima, June 26.

Rodriguez Pastor, Humberto. 1969. *Caquí: Estudio de Una Hacienda Costeña. Serie: Estudios del Valle Chancay*, No. 9. Lima: Instituto de Estudios Peruanos.

Romero, Emilio. 1949. *Historia Económica del Perú*. Buenos Aires: Sudamérica.

Rouquiè, Alain. 1982. *The Military and the State in Latin America*. Berkeley: University of California.

———. 1998. The Military in Latin American Politics since 1930. In *Latin American Politics and Society since 1930*, ed. Leslie Bethell. New York: Cambridge University Press.

Roxbourgh, Ian. 1998. Urban Labor Movements in Latin America since 1930. In *Latin American Politics and Society since 1930*, ed. Leslie Bethel. New York: Cambridge University Press

Sacchetti, Alfredo. 1904. *Inmigrantes Para el Perú*. Turin, Italy: Tip Salesiana.

Salazar Bondy, Augusto. 1965. *Historia de las Ideas en el Perú*. 2 V. Lima: Francisco Moncloa Editores.

San Cristoval, Evaristo. 1966. *General Mariano. Ignacio Prado: Su Vida y Su Obra*. Lima: Imprenta Gil.

Sanchez, Luís Alberto. 1955. *Haya de la Torre y el Apra*. Santiago: Ed. del Pacifico.

———. 1969. *Testimonio Personal: Memorias de Un Peruano del Siglo XX*. 3 V. Lima: Ed. Villasan.

———. 1973. Javier Prado, Hombre de Diversas Horas. *Siete Dias*, September 21.

Sater, William F. 2007. *Andean Tragedy: Fighting the War in the Pacific, 1879–1884*. Lincoln and London: University of Nebraska Press.

Scobie, James 1986. The Growth of Latin American Cities, 1870-1930. In Leslie Bethell, ed. *The Cambridge History of Latin America*. Vol IV. Cambridge: Cambridge University Press.

Senado. 1961. *Comisiones Directivas, y Señores Senadores, 1829–1960*. Lima.

Skidmore, Thomas E. and Peter H. Smith. 2001. *Modern Latin America*. 5th ed. New York: Oxford University Press.

Smith, Peter. 2012. *Democracy in Latin America: Political Change in Comparative Perspective*. 2nd ed. New York: Oxford University Press.

Spalding, Hobart and Byron Crites. 2008. Labor Movements. In *Encyclopedia of Latin American History and Culture*, ed. Kinsbruner and Langer.

Stein, Steve. 1980. *Populism in Peru: The Emergence of the Masses and the Politics of Social Control.* Madison: University of Wisconsin Press.

Stewart, Watt. 1951. *Chinese Bondage in Perú: A History of the Chinese Coolie in Perú, 1849–1874.* Durham, NC: Duke University Press.

Sulmont, Denis. 1972. Dinámica Actual del Movimiento Obrero Peruano. Taller de Estudios Urbano-Industriales, Universidad Católica, Lima.

———. 1974. El Desarrollo de la Clase Obrero en el Perú. *Series: Publicaciones Previas* No.1, Centro de Investigaciones Sociales, Económicas, Políticas y Antropológicas, Universidad Católica, Lima.

Tamagna, Frank. 1963. *La Banca Central en América Latina.* Mexico: Centro de Estudios Monetarios Latinoamericanos.

Tauro, Alberto. 1966. *Diccionario Enciclopédico del Perú.* 3 V. Lima: Editorial Mejia Baca.

Thorndike, Guillermo 1973. *El Caso Banchero.* Barcelona: Barrel Edifice.

Thorp, Rosemary. 1967. Inflation and Orthodox Economic Policy in Perú, *Bulletin of Oxford University Institute of Economics and Statistics,* 29: 185–210.

Thorp, Rosemary 1986. Latin America and the International Economy." Leslie Bethell, ed,. The Cambridge History of Latin America: 1870 to 1930. Vol. IV. New York: Cambridge University Press.

———. 1998. *Progress, Poverty and Exclusion: An Economic History of Latin America in the 20th Century.* Washington, DC: The Inter-American Development Bank.

Thorp, R. and Bertram, Geoffrey. 1976. Industrialisation in an Open Economy: The Case of Peru 1890–1940. In *Social and Economic Change in Modern Peru,* ed. R. Miller, C.T. Smith, and J. Fisher (University of Liverpool: Centre for Latin American Studies, Monograph Series No. 6).

———. 1978. *Peru 1890–1977: Growth and Policy in an Open Economy.* New York: Columbia University Press.

La Tribuna (Lima). 1956–1968.

Tuesta Soldevilla, Fernando 1998. Las Anuladas Elecciones de 1936. *El Peruana.* May 15. (blog. pucp.edu.pe).

United Nations Department of Economic and Social Affairs. 1969. *Growth of the World's Urban and Rural Population, 1920–2000.* ST/SOA/Series A/44. New York: United Nations.

U.S. Bureau of the Census. 1975. *Historical Statistics of the United States: Colonial Times to 1970.* Part 1.

U.S. Senate. Committee on Intergovernmental Operations. 1974. *Disclosure of Corporate Ownership.* December 27, 1973.

U.S. Tariff Commission. 1940. *Foreign Trade of Latin America.*

Varallanos, José. 1959. *Historia de Huánuco.* Buenos Aires: Imprenta Lopez.

Vargas Ugarte, Ruben. 1971. *Historia General del Perú.* 10 Vols. Lim: Editorial Carlos Milla Batres.

Vda [Viuda]. de la Piedra, e Hijos S.A. n.d. *50 Años V.P.H.* Lima: Imp. Rimac.

Velasco Alvarado, Juan. 1973. *La Revolución Peruana.* Buenos Aires: Editorial Universitaria de Buenos Aires.

———. 1974. *Plan Inca: o, Plan de gobierno revolucionario de la Fuerza Armada del Perú.* Lima: C. L. Cabrera V.

Velez Picasso, José. n.d. *Ricardo Bentín, 1853–1953.* Lima: Torres Aguirre.

Vernal Consultores, S. A. 1968. *Directorio de Gerente.* 3rd ed. Lima.

Vicuña Mackenna, Benjamin 1867. *Diez Meses de Misión a los Estados Unidos.* Santiago: Imp de la Libertad.

Villanueva, Víctor. 1962. *El Militarismo en el Perú.* Lima: Empresa Grafica T. Scheuch.
———. 1963. *Un Ano Bajo el Sable.* Lima: Empresa Grafica T. Scheuch.
———. 1969. *Nueva Mentalidad Militar en el Perú?* Lima: Editorial Replanteo.
———. 1972. *El Caem y la Revolución de la Fuerza Armada.* Lima: Instituto de Estudios Peruanos.
———. 1973a. *Ejercito Peruana: Del Caudillaje Anárquico Al Militarismo.* Lima: Juan Mejia Baca.
———. 1973b. *La Sublevación Aprista del 48: Tragedia de Un Pueblo y Un Partido.* Lima: Editorial Milia Batres.
Waley, Daniel. 1969. *The Italian City Republics.* New York: McGraw-Hill Book Company.
Weber, Max. 1947. *The Theory of Social and Economic Organization.* New York: Oxford University Press.
Werlich, David. 1978. *Peru: A Short History.* Carbondale, IL: Southern Illinois University Press.
Werner Consulting. 1969. Estudio de la Industria Textil Peruana Nov.
West Coast Leader (Lima). 1912–1940.
Wilkie, James 1974. Statistical abstract of Latin America. Supplement series 3. Los Angeles: UCLA Latin America Center Publications.
Wilkie, James, ed. 2002. *Statistical Abstract of Latin America.* Vol. 38. Los Angeles: UCLA Latin America Center Publications.
Winters, Jeffrey. 2011. *Oligarchy.* Cambridge: Cambridge University Press.
Yepes del Castillo, Ernesto. 1972. *Perú 1820–1920: Un Siglo de Desarrollo Capitalista.* Lima: Instituto de Estudios Peruanos.
Zimmerman, Augusto. 1968. *La Historia Secreta de Petróleo.* Lima: Ed. Grafica Labor.

VI. ARCHIVAL SOURCES

Biblioteca Nacional (Lima). Oficina de investigaciones

Escobar y Bedoya, Expediente sobre la averiguación practicada por la Comisión China, asesorada por funcionaries del Gobierno respecto a la situación de sus connacionales que prestan sus servicies en las haciendas. 9 de mayo de 1887.

Centro de Documentación Agraria, (Lima) (CDA)

Correspondence

Cited by writers' initials and date:

AAB = Antero Aspíllaga Barrera
AG = Augusto Gildemeister
GAA= Gustavo Aspíllaga Anderson
IAA = Ismael Aspíllaga Anderson
JG = Juan Guildemeister
LAA Luis Aspíllaga Anderson
NSS = N. Silva Salgado
PB = Pedro Beltrán

RAA Ramon Aspíllaga Anderson
RAB Ramon Aspíllaga Barrera
RN = Ricardo Neumann

Kendall. Lima-Londres, diciembre de 1911 a abril de 1914.
Kendall. Lima-Londres. febrero de 1915 a setiembre de 1916.
Cartas Administrativas. Lima-Cayaltí, noviembre de 1919 a noviembre de 1920.
Cartas Reservadas. Lima-Cayaltí, diciembre de 1922 a diciembre de 1923.
Cartas Reservadas. Cayaltí-Lima, setiembre a diciembre de 1923.
Cartas Reservadas. Lima-Cayaltí, mayo de 1925 a febrero de 1926.
Cartas Reservadas. Lima-Cayaltí, 1926.
Cartas Reservadas. Lima-Cayaltí. abril de 1927 a abril de 1929.
Kendall. Lima-Londres. agosto de 1928 a enero de 1931.
Cartas Particulares. Lima-Cayaltí, 1930–1932.
Cartas Particulares. Lima-Cayaltí, marzo de 1930 a febrero de 1933.
Cartas Reservadas. Cayaltí-Lima, julio a diciembre de 1930.
Cartas Particulares. Cayaltí-Lima, enero a diciembre de 1931.
Cartas de Gustavo Aspíllaga, 1932–1936.
Cartas Particulares. Cayaltí-Lima, enero a diciembre de 1932.
Cartas Reservadas. Cayaltí-Lima, enero de 1933 a diciembre de 1934.
Cartas Reservadas. Lima-Cayaltí, 1934–1936.
Cartas Reservadas. Lima-Cayaltí, mayo de 1934 a abril de 1936.
Cartas Reservadas. Lima-Cayaltí, mayo de 1935 a abril de 1936.
Cartas Reservadas. Cayaltí-Lima, noviembre de 1935 a diciembre de 1936.
Cartas Reservadas. Lima-Cayaltí, abril de 1936 a febrero de 1939.
Cartas Reservadas. Cayaltí.-Lima, enero de 1937 a diciembre de 1938.
Cartas Reservadas. Lima-Cayaltí febrero de 1939 a junio de 1941.
Cartas Reservadas. Lima-Cayaltí. julio de 1941 a diciembre de 1944.
Caras Reserva as. Lima-Cayaltí, enero de 1946 a diciembre de 1948.
Cartas Administrativas. Lima-Cayaltí-Lima. febrero de 1949 a mayo de 1953.
Cartas Administrativas. Lima-Cayaltí-Lima. 1953–1957.
Cartas Oficiales. Lima-Cayaltí-Lima. 1958–1959.
Correspondencia Gildemeister-Beltrán.

Other Documents

Aspíllaga historia familiar: Recortes de periodicos, 1910–1944.
Banco del Perú y Londres, Señor Ramón Aspíllaga, Relación de los valores, 31 de diciembre
    de 1927.
Balances 1962–1967.
Finanzas del Señor Ramón Aspíllaga, enero a junio de 1928.
Hermanos Gildemeister: Division de Bienes, 1941–1945.
Plan de Financiación Señor Rafael Gonzales Cardenas, 1967–1969.
Proyecto de Constitución de la Sociedad Anónima denominada Negociaciones Agricolas
    Cayaltí. y Palto. Anexo No.1, 20 de diciembre de 1926.
Cia. Aurifera Beditani

Bill Albert Private Collection

Henry Kendall & Sons, correspondencia sobre American Factors 1965. Londres, julio a octubre de 1966.

Private Archive (Lima)

Cartas del Señor Ramón Aspíllaga Ferrebú, febrero 6, 1871.
Patente de Navegación, 13 de octubre de 1852.

Library of Felix Denegri Luna (Lima)

Manuel Argumaniz Muñoz, Memorias. Manuscrito, s.f.

Index